Mughal Warfare

Mughal Warfare offers a much-needed new survey of the military history of Mughal India during the age of imperial splendour from 1500 to 1700. Jos Gommans looks at warfare as an integrated aspect of pre-colonial Indian society.

Based on a vast range of primary sources from Europe and India, this thorough study explores the wider geo-political, cultural and institutional context of the Mughal military. Gommans also details practical and technological aspects of combat, such as gunpowder technologies and the animals used in battle. His comparative analysis throws new light on much-contested theories of gunpowder empires and the spread of the military revolution.

As the first original analysis of Mughal warfare for almost a century, this will make essential reading for military specialists, students of military history and general Asian history.

Jos Gommans teaches Indian history at the Kern Institute of Leiden University in the Netherlands. His previous publications include *The Rise of the Indo-Afghan Empire, 1710–1780* (1995) as well as numerous articles on the medieval and early modern history of South Asia.

Warfare and History
General Editor
Jeremy Black
Professor of History, University of Exeter

Air Power in the Age of Total War
John Buckley

The Armies of the Caliphs: Military and Society in the Early Islamic State
Hugh Kennedy

The Balkan Wars, 1912–1913: Prelude to the First World War
Richard C. Hall

English Warfare, 1511–1642
Mark Charles Fissel

European and Native American Warfare, 1675–1815
Armstrong Starkey

European Warfare, 1660–1815
Jeremy Black

The First Punic War
J. F. Lazenby

Frontiersmen: Warfare in Africa Since 1950
Anthony Clayton

German Armies: War and German Politics, 1648–1806
Peter H. Wilson

The Great War 1914–1918
Spencer C. Tucker

Israel's Wars, 1947–1993
Ahron Bregman

The Korean War: No Victors, no Vanquished
Stanley Sandler

Medieval Chinese Warfare, 300–900
Susan Rose

Modern Chinese Warfare, 1795–1989
Bruce A. Elleman

Modern Insurgencies and Counter-insurgencies: Guerrillas and their Opponents since 1750
Ian F. W. Beckett

Naval Warfare, 1815–1914
Lawrence Sondhaus

Ottoman Warfare, 1500–1700
Rhoads Murphey

Seapower and Naval Warfare, 1650–1830
Richard Harding

The Soviet Military Experience
Roger R. Reese

Vietnam
Spencer C. Tucker

The War for Independence and the Transformation of American Society
Harry M. Ward

War and the State in Early Modern Europe: Spain, the Dutch Republic and Sweden as Fiscal-military States, 1500–1660
Jan Glete

Warfare and Society in Europe, 1792–1914
Geoffrey Wawro

Warfare at Sea, 1500–1650
Jan Glete

Warfare in Atlantic Africa, 1500–1800: Maritime Conflicts and the Transformation of Europe
John K. Thornton

Warfare, State and Society in the Byzantine World, 565–1204
John Haldon

War in the Early Modern World, 1450–1815
Jeremy Black

Wars of Imperial Conquest in Africa, 1830–1914
Bruce Vandervort

Western Warfare in the Age of the Crusades, 1000–1300
John France

The Irish and British Wars, 1637–1654: Triumph, Tragedy, and Failure
James Scott Wheeler

European Warfare, 1494–1660
Jeremy Black

War and Society in Imperial Rome, 31 BC–AD 284
Brian Campbell

Mughal Warfare: Indian Frontiers and High Roads to Empire, 1500–1700
Jos Gommans

Mughal Warfare

Indian Frontiers and High Roads to Empire, 1500–1700

Jos Gommans

London and New York

First published 2002
by Routledge
11 New Fetter Lane, London EC4P 4EE

Simultaneously published in the USA and Canada
by Routledge
29 West 35th Street, New York, NY 10001

Routledge is an imprint of the Taylor & Francis Group

Typeset in Bembo by
Florence Production Ltd, Stoodleigh, Devon
Printed and bound in Great Britain by
TJ International Ltd, Padstow, Cornwall

British Library Cataloguing in Publication Data
A catalogue record for this book is available from the British Library

Library of Congress Cataloging in Publication Data
A catalog record for this book has been applied for

ISBN 0–415–23988–5 (hbk)
ISBN 0–415–23989–3 (pbk)

سفر کن سفر کن سفر کن سفر
سفر کن که بسیار یابي ظفر

***

March, march, march away.
March for you'll be victorious.

Abul Fazl
(*AN*, III, p. 1061 [Persian text, III, p. 712])

Contents

Illustrations

Plates and Figures

Maps

Tables

Abbreviations

AA Abul Fazl Allami, *The A-in-i Akbari*, translated by H. Blochmann and H.S. Jarrett, 2nd revised edition by D.C. Phillott and J. Sarkar, 3 vols (New Delhi, reprint, 1989; first published 1927–49). Persian text edited by H. Blochmann, 2 vols (Calcutta: Bibliotheca Indica 58, 1872–7).

AAl Hamid al-Din Khan Bahadur, *Anecdotes of Aurangzib* [*Ahkam-i Alamgiri*], translated by J. Sarkar (Calcutta, 4th edition, 1963).

AN Abul Fazl Allami, *The Akbarnama of Abul Fazl*, translated by H. Beveridge, 3 vols (Delhi, reprint, 1989–3; first published 1902–21). Persian text edited by Maulawi Abdul Rahim, 3 vols (Calcutta: Bibliotheca Indica 79, 1875–86).

Ap Ramachandrapant Amatya, 'The Ajnapatra or Royal Edict', translated by S.V. Puntambekar, *Journal of Indian History*, 1–2 (1928).

ARA Algemeen Rijksarchief, The Hague.

BG Mirza Nathan, *Baharistan-i-Ghaybi. A History of the Mughal Wars in Assam, Cooch Behar, Bengal, Bihar and Orissa During the Reigns of Jahangir and Shah Jahan by Mirza Nathan*, translated by M.I. Borah, 2 vols (Gauhati, 1936).

BL British Library, London.

BN Babur, *The Baburnama. Memoirs of Babur, Prince and Emperor*, translated by W.M. Thackston (New York and Oxford, 1996).

BN(B) Babur, *Babur-Nama*, translated by A.S. Beveridge (Delhi, reprint, 1989; first published 1921).

EI *Encyclopaedia of Islam* (Leiden, 1954–).

EIC English East India Company.

EIr *Encyclopaedia Iranica* (London and New York, 1985–).

FN Sa'adat Yar Khan Rangin, *Faras-nama*, translated by D.C. Phillott (London, 1911).

GI Firishta, *History of the Rise of the Mahomedan Power in India* [*Gulshan-i Ibrahimi*], translated by J. Briggs, 4 vols (Delhi, reprint, 1981; first published in 1829).

HA Munshi Udairaj alias Taliyar Khan, *The Military Despatches of a Seventeenth Century Indian General* [*Haft Anjuman*], translated by J.N. Sarkar (Calcutta, 1969).

KA Kautiliya, *The Kautiliya Arthasastra: A Critical Edition with a Glossary*, edited and translated by R.P. Kangle, 3 vols (Delhi, 1988; first published 1960).

KF Amir Khusrau, *The Campaigns of Ala'ud-din Khilji Being the Khaza'inul Futuh (Treasures of Victory) of Hazrat Amir Khusrau of Delhi,* translated by M. Habib (Madras, 1931).

MA Saqi Musta'id Khan, *Maasir-i-Alamgiri: A History of the Emperor Aurangzib-Alamgir,* translated by J. Sarkar (Delhi, reprint, 1986; first published 1947).

Md Ibn Khaldun, *The Muqaddimah: An Introduction to History*, translated by F. Rosenthal and N.J. Dawood (London, 1987; first published 1967).

MI *Encyclopaedic Dictionary of Medieval India: Mirat-ul-Istilah*, translated by Tasneem Ahmad (Delhi, 1993).

MJ Muhammad Baqir Najm-i Sani, *Advice on the Art of Governance: Mau'izah-i Jahangiri of Muhammad Baqir Najm-i Sani: An Indo-Islamic Mirror for Princes*, edited and translated by S.S. Alvi (Albany, NY, 1989).

ML Khafi Khan, *Khafi Khan's History of Alamgir* [*Muntakhab al-Lubab*], part. translated by S. Moinul Haq (Karachi, 1975). Persian text edited by Kabir al-Din Ahmad and T.W. Haig, 3 vols (Calcutta: Bibliotheca Indica 60, 1869–1925).

MM Sidi Ali Reis, *The Travels and Adventures of the Turkish Admiral Sidi Ali Reis* [*Mir'at al-Mamalik*], translated by A. Vambery (London, 1899).

MN (Baba Shah Musafir), *Sufis and Soldiers in Awrangzeb's Deccan: Malfuzat-i Naqshbandiyya*, translated by S. Digby (Oxford, 2001).

MS Sikandar b. Muhammad Manjhu, *The Local Muhammadan Dynasties: Gujarat* [*Mir'at-i Sikandiri*], partly translated by Sir E.C. Bayley and Nagendra Singh (Delhi, reprint, 1970; first published 1886). Persian text edited by S.C. Misra and M.L. Rahman (Baroda, 1961).

MT Bada'uni, *Muntakhabu-t-Tawarikh*, translated by G.S.A. Ranking, W.H. Low and Sir Wolseley Haig, 3 vols (Delhi, reprint 1986; first published 1898–1924). Persian text edited by Maulawi Ahmad Ali, 3 vols (Calcutta: Bibliotheca Indica 51, 1868–9).

MU Nawab Samsam al-Daula Shah Nawaz Khan and his son Abdul Hayy, *The Maathir-al-Umara*, translated by H. Beveridge and Baini Prashad, 2 vols in 4 parts (Delhi, reprint, 1979; first published 1911–64). Persian text edited by Maulawi Abdul Rahim and Mirza Ashraf Ali, 3 vols (Calcutta: Bibliotheca Indica 112, 1888–91).

OIOC Oriental and India Office Collections.

PN Abdul Hamid Lahauri, *Padshahnama*, edited by Maulawis Kabir al-Din Ahmad and Abdul Rahim, 2 vols (Calcutta: Bibliotheca Indica 56, 1866–72).

QN Kai Ka'us Ibn Iskandar, *The Mirror for Princes, the Qabus Nama by Kai Ka'us Ibn Iskandar Prince of Gurgan*, translated by R. Levy (London, 1951).

RA *Ruka'at-i-Alamgiri or Letters of Aurangzebe*, translated by J.H. Bilimoria (London & Bombay, 1908).

SJN Inayat Khan, *The Shah Jahan Nama of Inayat Khan*, translated by W.E. Begley and Z.A. Desai (Delhi, 1990).

TA Muhammad Arif Qandhari, *Tarikh-i-Akbari*, translated by Tasneem Ahmad (Delhi, 1993).

TB Ibn Battuta, *The Travels of Ibn Battuta A.D. 1325–1354*, translated by H.A.R. Gibb and C.F. Beckingham, 4 vols (Cambridge and London: Hakluyt Society, 1958–94).

TD Bhimsen, *Sir Jadunath Sarkar Birth Centenary Commemoration Volume: English Translation of Tarikh-i-Dilkasha*, translated by J. Sarkar and V.G. Khobrekar (Bombay, 1972).

TFS Barani, 'Tarikh-i Firoz Shahi', translated by H. Elliot, in H.M. Elliot and J. Dowson, *The History of India as Told by its Own Historians, III* (Delhi, reprint, 1990; first published 1867–77), pp. 93–268.

TJ Jahangir, *The Tuzuk-i-Jahangiri or Memoirs of Jahangir*, translated by A. Rogers and H. Beveridge (Delhi, reprint, 1978; first published 1909–14).

TM (Amir Muhammad Sami Ganj Ali Khan) *Tadhkirat al-Muluk: A Manual of Safavid Administration*, translated and edited by V. Minorsky (Cambridge, 1980).

TN Minhaj al-Din, *Tabakat-i Nasiri*: A General History of the *Muhammadan Dynasties of Asia, Including Hindustan*, translated by H.G. Raverty, 2 vols (New Delhi reprint, 1970; first published Calcutta, 1881).

TR Mirza Muhammad Haidar Dughlat, *The Tarikh-i-Rashidi*, translated by E. Denison Ross (Delhi, reprint, 1986; first published 1895).

TSA Abdulla Khan, *Tarjumah-i Salawtar-i Asban: Die Pferdeheilkunde des Abdullah Khan Emir am Hofe des Großmoguls*, translated by S. Oloff (from the English by J. Earles) (Munich, 1981).

TSS Abbas Khan Sarwani, *Tarikh-i-Ser Sahi*, translated by B.P. Ambashthya (Patna, 1974).

VOC Verenigde Oostindische Compagnie (Dutch East India Company).

WM Shaikh Rizqulla Mushtaqi, *Waqi'at-e-Mushtaqui*, translated by I.H. Siddiqui (Delhi, 1993).

Note on transliteration

To accommodate the general reader this book dispenses with diacritical marks in transcribing the original Arabic and, in occasional cases, Devanagiri scripts. The same goes for references to titles of translated works that have otherwise retained their original spelling. Foreign terms not in common English use have been italicised when used for the first time. The Perso-Arabic *ain* (ع) and *hamza* (ء) have been indicated by a simple apostrophe (') when necessary for pronunciation, in particular when used between two vowels. Plurals have been indicated by adding the letter *s* with the exception of the more common *ulama* instead of *alims*. Otherwise, to facilitate the identification of personal names and technical terms, I have adopted the rules of the *Encyclopaedia of Islam*, albeit slightly adjusted to common Indo-Persian usage following F. Steingass, *Persian-English Dictionary* (London, 1977; 1st ed. 1892), thus *dj* (ج) becoming *j*; *dh* (ذ) becoming *z*; *d* (ض) becoming *z*; *k* (ق) becoming *q*. For the combination of two related words I have used the Persian *izafa -i,* and the Arabic *al-*, with the exception of the more common combinations in personal names like Abul, Abdul, Abdulla and Zulfiqar. The *ha-yi hawwaz* (ه) has only been transcribed in the combination with the vowel *i, o* or *u*, (hence *sih, karoh, tawajjuh*, but *khana*).

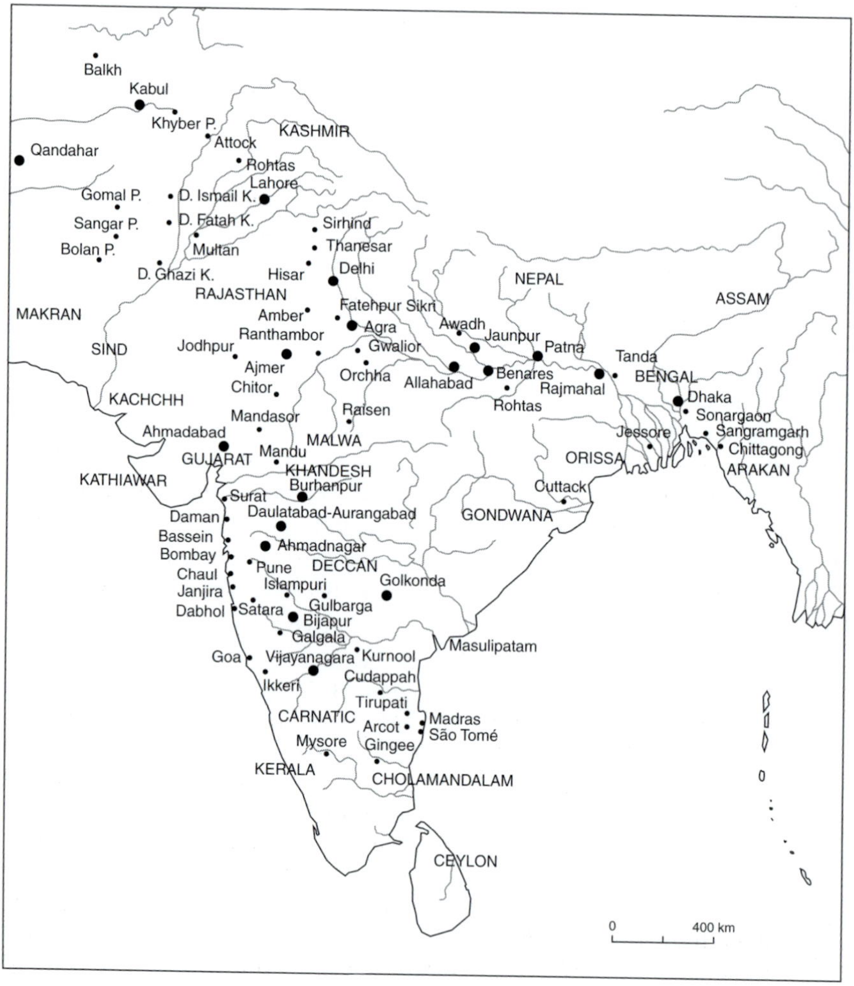

Map 1.1 Mughal India: human topography

Introduction

> I always enjoy conversing about the Moguls. It is the chief pleasure I know. You see, those first six Emperors were all most wonderful men, and as soon as one of them is mentioned, no matter which, I forget everything else in the world except the other five.
>
> (Dr Aziz in E.M. Forster's *A Passage to India*)

In many ways the history of Mughal warfare has been and still is extremely unfashionable. No books have been written on the subject since Horn's and Irvine's path-breaking, but also highly descriptive, monographs published about one century ago.[1] This does not mean that, since then, there have appeared no other publications dealing with various aspects relating to Mughal warfare. Here, the solid work of various scholars of the Aligarh Muslim University and the almost classical studies of the late Jadunath Sarkar come to mind. While the Aligarh historians have focused on the *mansabdari* organisation of the Mughal Empire and, more recently, on the introduction and use of gunpowder technology, Sarkar concentrated on the tactics of battles and sieges as well as on the personalities of colourful emperors and generals. Beyond the sub-continent, studies by Richards, Kolff, Gordon and Streusand relate to military issues, but only the latter two scholars approach their subject as traditional military historians analysing Mughal battles and sieges, their tactics and weaponry. For most other historians working on Mughal history, warfare is seen as an integrated part of Mughal society at large and is treated as such. As I have written elsewhere, these historians tend to regard wars as something beyond the guts and glory of the purely military and as closely related to the socio-economic and cultural conditions of the Indian sub-continent as a whole.[2]

What should readers expect of this study? In a way it offers just a survey of the various, scattered contributions of the past. I have dispensed with investigating new material such as unpublished Indo-Persian chronicles or the extensive documentation still available in European archives. This is something still to be done by a more patient and more skilful scholar. For the present purpose I decided to content myself by rereading the still enormous quantity of better-known, published chronicles and travel accounts, but now specifically from the point of view of the military historian. Thus, although this volume pays tribute to the manifold Mughal historians of the past, it also aims to present the military historian and South Asianist alike with a fresh, integrated analysis that, for the first time since Horn and Irvine, treats the subject of Mughal warfare as a whole. Hence, the overall result of this book should be seen as not more and not less than a reappraisal, a new hypothesis based on old, mostly primary material, which, hopefully, will stimulate the scholarly debate that has been missing so far, as well as result in new historical research that will also open up unexplored sources.

Another limitation of the book is the restricted period that it investigates. Since it concentrates on the traditional period of the so-called Great-Mughals, that is, the period of imperial splendour from about 1500 to 1700, it will not investigate the important eighteenth-century changes on the sub-continent, although there is some space dedicated to the equally important Indian antecedents of Mughal warfare, as well as to the contemporary developments in West and Central Asia. I have preferred to focus on the sixteenth and seventeenth centuries because, in terms of military development, this period can be treated as a whole. Although various changes took place, it is in this period that one can really speak of *Mughal* warfare, i.e. the wars waged by Mughal emperors in command of Mughal armies. Although in theory Mughal rule held on until the Mutiny of 1857, in practical terms the Mughal army of the eighteenth century metamorphosed relatively quickly into the regional armies of the various Mughal successor-states. As regional variation became increasingly important, this would not only require separate studies involving the incorporation of regional elements and regional sources, but would also go much beyond the scope of actual Mughal warfare. This is not to deny my overall contention that the timespan from Babur to Aurangzeb should be considered a sensible historical unit that represents the culmination point of a long-term military development that started with the coming of the Mongols and Turks and ended with the eighteenth-century process of regional centralisation.

As this book builds on the contributions of South Asianists in the past, it can only adopt their point of view by looking at Mughal warfare as an integrated aspect of Mughal, or rather Indian, society as a whole. The first three chapters, especially, are meant to describe the wider geo-political, as well as cultural and institutional, context of the Mughal military. Here, the South Asianist should feel perfectly at home, although he or she will take issue with many of the new, at times rather speculative, interpretations involving such complicated concepts as the military labour market or the mansabdari system. The extent of analysis is also justified by the awareness that one of the prime functions of Mughal warfare was to bridge the various *inner* frontiers of empire. But as important as the ongoing military campaigns of the Mughals were, the socio-economic and cultural aspects of warfare were crucial in connecting the numerous regions and peoples of the empire to each other. Thanks to the Dutch Indologist-cum-historian Johan Huizinga, we should be aware that pre-modern warfare often had a certain element of game in it, which, through its competitiveness and playfulness, as well as through its shared rules and conventions, brought together various parts of society.[3] As such, the first three chapters focus on the societal rules of the 'game' that is known as Mughal warfare.

In the last three chapters, it is hoped that the military historian will feel rewarded for his or her patience and will feel more comfortable with the more conventional military subjects, such as weaponry and tactics, campaigns and battles. Apart from gunpowder weaponry, much space is reserved for the main instruments of Mughal locomotion: in particular, horses and elephants, and, to a lesser extent, dromedaries and bullocks. In the last chapter, three specific Mughal operations are dealt with in more chronological detail aimed at illustrating the operational and logistical challenges facing the Mughal army when marching along the farthest bounds of the imperial road system. Actually, it is this system of high roads, connecting the outer and inner frontiers of empire, that forms the basis of Mughal state formation. Finally, the Conclusion and epilogue will briefly reformulate those arguments that have an immediate bearing on the developments of the eighteenth century, culminating in colonial conquest.

Readers should be warned that this book is written neither by a soldier nor even by a military historian. Actually, my military experience is limited to a few weeks of compulsory military service, after which I was happy to be discharged because of 'bad eyesight'. Therefore, I am most grateful to those real military specialists who helped me to come to grips with the complexities of military technology, in particular Jan Piet Puype and J. Lenseling, both of the Army Museum in Delft. In various other ways I am indebted to Herman Tieken, Ishtiyaq Ahmad Zilli, Sanjay Subrahmanyam, Rudy Matthee, Dirk Kolff, Pauline Scheurleer, Ikuko Wada, Jacques Leider, Janet Kamphorst, Freek Plasmeijer and Michiel de Jong. The same goes for the Foundation for the Advancement of Tropical Reseach (WOTRO), since it financed part of my fieldwork in India. Jan Heesterman, Gijs Kruijtzer and my wife Marianne went through the entire manuscript and, each in their own way, were indispensable in bringing the book to its conclusion. Of course, none of those listed above can be blamed for any mistakes that might appear.

The central argument of the book is in many ways reminiscent of that of the fourteenth-century Arabic historian Ibn Khaldun, who also analysed the process of state formation on the basis of the dynamic interaction between sedentary and nomadic peoples. This does not mean, though, that I would agree with him on each and every point, the more so because seventeenth-century India is different from the fourteenth-century Middle East, and also because history turned out to be more dynamic and less cyclical than imagined by Ibn Khaldun. This being said, without him this book would have looked entirely different and it seems appropriate to conclude this introduction with his words, by wishing that 'admission saves from censure' and that 'the kindness of colleagues is hoped for'.[4]

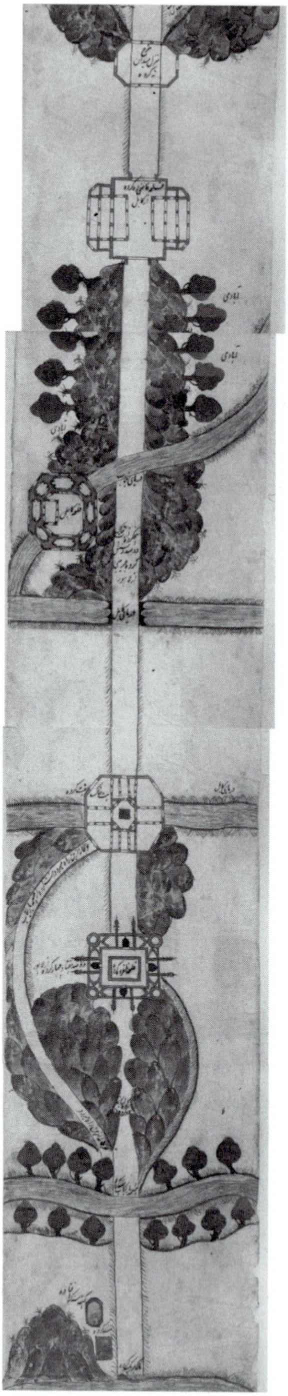

Plate 1 Section from a Mughal scroll route map from Delhi to Qandahar, *c.* 1775. At the top it shows the high road, the rivers (Nilab and Kabul) and the hills around Kabul fort, the latter being 206 *jaribi karoh* (*c.* 525 km) from Lahore. To the bottom, the high road continues, after crossing the Kabul river a second time, through the Lataband mountains, up towards Qila Zafar. The side-road on the left probably indicates a road that is less steep and thus more convenient for transporting heavy cannon. The size of the map is 2,000 × 25 cm, its length illustrating the linear perspective of the Mughal rulers (see also J.B. Harley and D. Woodward (eds) (1992), pp. 424–5, and S. Gole, (1989), pp. 94–104).

Source: *BL:OIOC,* Pers. Ms. I.O. 4725

CHAPTER ONE

The Indian frontier[1]

> India abounds with forests and extensive wildernesses, full of all sorts of trees; so much so, that these wastes seem to offer inducements, both to rajas and subjects, to revolt from the government. The agricultural population, and the abundance of cattle, in this country, exceed that of all others; but its depopulation and desolation are sudden and rapid beyond conception.
>
> (Firishta)[2]

The history of warfare cannot do without geography. Therefore, this chapter pays tribute to the geographic dimension of history as suggested by those almost forgotten early geographers like Alexander von Humboldt and Carl Ritter. Decades before the emergence of the famous French *Annales* school, they aimed to investigate the ways in which the physical environment affected human societies. In our case, we will examine to what extent the military campaigns of the Mughal emperors were ruled by the long-term geo-political imperatives of the Indian sub-continent. First, we will find that India's well-known monsoon winds created, in fact, two entirely different ecological zones: open drylands in the west, and dense humid forests and marshes in the east. As a result, India emerges as an extensive transitionary area between the so-called Arid Zone dominating West and Central Asia, and Monsoon Asia covering East and Southeast Asia.[3] Here, it will be highlighted that these zones were governed by entirely different conditions for agricultural and pastoral production that determined the availability of military recruits and of crucial instruments of war, such as elephants and warhorses as well as of food and fodder. Despite the image of a civilisation despising violence and reserving it for certain martial castes, during Mughal times India experienced a remarkably high degree of military participation from almost all sections of its population. Indeed, the social distinctions appeared to be less important than the ecological circumstances that gave India's drylands, both in terms of man- and horsepower, by far the largest military potential. On the other hand, Indian armies also needed the rich supplies of India's agrarian centres, either in its more humid parts or well watered by its various river valleys. Hence, the Mughal Empire tended to gravitate towards an ever-open inner frontier between settled agriculture and arid marchland, whereas the dense and humid forests and marshes of northern and eastern India were clearly part of its more natural, outer frontier.

Further elaborating on the frontier theme, the second section will stress the pattern of India's network of long-distance routes. As in the case of the Roman Empire, in principle these Indian *limites* were unbounded and, as such, dictated the direction of unrestricted expansion.[4] Indeed, as a kind of saddle state, the survival of the Mughals hinged on the combined control of both the areal inner frontiers and the linear limites of empire. Interestingly, both converged most ideally in those areas that, throughout India's history, developed as more or less perennial nuclear zones or bases of political power; in other words, those regions that combined a rich agrarian base with extensive pasturage and important long-distance commercial connections.[5]

Monsoon and Arid India[6]

In broad ecological terms, the monsoon winds give some kind of uniformity to India as a whole. But, even in ecological terms, this apparent uniformity again turns out to be no more than another version of India's well-known unity in diversity motto. In its most general terms, the monsoon winds deliver a climate in which a cool, dry season of northerly winds, i.e. the northeast monsoon from December to February, gives way to a hot, dry season from March to early June, followed by a hot, wet season of southwesterly winds, i.e. the southwest monsoon from July to September, then a return to the dry, cool season of the winter months. As early as June the monsoon has an effect at the southwest coast, thanks to the high Western Ghats. Somewhat later, in July, the monsoon hits Bengal, after which it gradually spreads towards the northwest with rainfall decreasing and becoming less reliable. India's double agricultural season neatly follows this annual rhythm of the monsoon. Especially, the so-called *kharif* harvests profit from the monsoon torrents. Here, sowing begins after the first onset of rain, while harvesting takes place in about September or October. In some cases, the harvests occur much later, depending on the crops and the long-term availability of water through irrigation. The winter, or *rabi*, crops need less water but cannot stand the heat of summer. They are sown soon after the rains – that is, almost simultaneous with the kharif harvest – and are usually taken in during spring. In the drier regions, rabi crops are important in areas under irrigation or with some precipitation during winter, such as along the southeast coast following the northeast monsoon or, to a lesser extent, in the Punjab as a result of the depression rains during the winter months.

Despite these unifying characteristics of the monsoon, in practical terms it is more fitting to emphasise an east–west dichotomy in India's monsoon climate, in which the eastern parts are more humid with higher and more reliable agricultural yields, primarily through transplanting cuttings and seedlings of rice, whereas the western parts are more arid with lower and less certain harvests, mainly through direct seeding of millet and wheat, and mostly depending on irrigation by rivers, canals, tanks or wells. In the latter case, an exception should be made for the very humid southwest coast of Malabar and the Konkan as well as for the marshy Terai of the Himalayan foothills. The critical difference between the two zones is the supply of water. This depends on both the amount of rainfall and its distribution throughout the year, all in combination with factors that determine the length of the growing period of plants, such as soil storage and evaporation. Geographers generally refer to India's drylands as having a growing period of less than 180 days that corresponds roughly, of course hinging on the regional circumstances, with 1,000 mm of annual rainfall.[7]

As mentioned already in the Introduction, these drylands are part of that much wider, frequently broken, ecological continuum of the Arid Zone – sometimes called Saharasia – that includes all the drier zones of Eurasia, stretching from the Atlantic coast of northern Africa to the eastern and southern extremes of the Indian sub-continent.

To be somewhat more specific, in India it extends from the very dry tracts of Sind and Rajasthan, branching off in eastern and southern

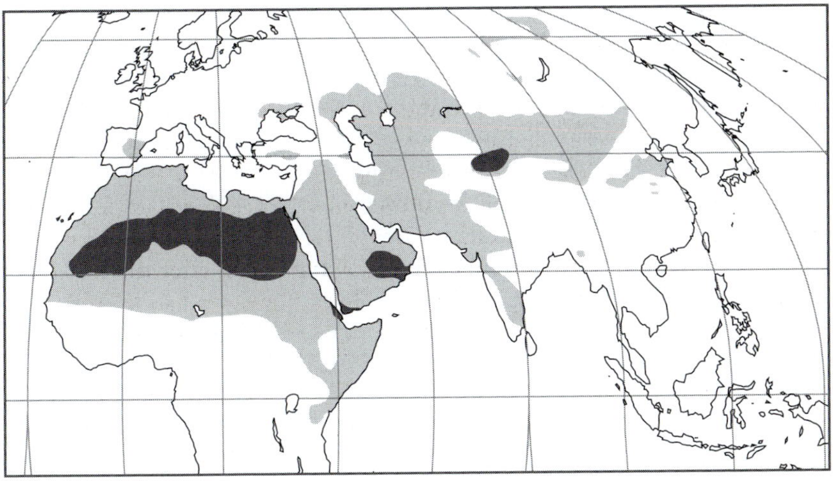

Map 1.2 Saharasia

directions. Going eastward, while embracing the large medieval capitals of Lahore, Delhi and Agra, it follows the courses of the Yamuna and Ganges rivers and, subsequently, narrows down along the southern banks of the Ganges until it reaches, at the head of the Ganges delta, the fertile and more humid paddy tracts of eastern Bengal. Going southward, it stretches from the extremely arid Thar Desert across the Aravalli Mountains into Malwa. Behind the dry lee side of the Western Ghats, it continues towards the dry western Deccan plateau. The eastern slopes of the mountains or Mavals still receive substantial amounts of rainfall and, as such, serve as a transitional zone between the humid littoral – its 4,500 mm permitting intensive rice cultivation – and the dry interior of the *desh* – its less than 500 mm making this the natural habitat of pastoral groups. The high aridity of this area continues in a southeastern direction into the Raichur doab between the rivers Tungabhadra and Krishna and extends towards the so-called Rayalaseema, literally 'the frontier of the kingdom', around Kurnool and Cudappah in the south. This became a hotly contested border region between the prevalent powers in the Deccan to its north and the Carnatic to its south. South and east of the Rayalaseema, rainfall increases again, partly profiting from the northeast monsoon, but usually stays well under 1,000 mm. In the southwest, the Mysore Plateau, with rainfall of between 600 and 900 mm, still belongs to the Arid Zone and, from there, several dry outliers reach the extreme southern end of the sub-continent. In the southeast, the Arid Zone descends the relatively gentle slopes of the Eastern Ghats towards the more humid Coromandel Coast. Although rainfall is far from excessive, its numerous wide river deltas have made this one other core area of intensive rice cultivation. As such, the Arid Zone serves well as a kind of central dry axis connecting the three ancient centres of sedentary civilisation emerging along the Indus valley in the west, along the Ganges and Yamuna valleys in the north, and along the river valleys of southeastern Cholamandalam.

Although in terms of rainfall these ancient centres of civilisation are part of the Arid Zone, India's life-giving rivers have made these alluvial lowlands fertile and well irrigated. Hence, the Arid Zone consists of major, for the most part alluvial, agricultural areas intersected with arid marchlands where agriculture is far less stable.

In most of the Arid Zone, millet and wheat dominate the production throughout the agrarian year. Compared with rice, these require less intensive labour but, at the same time, produce lesser and more unreliable harvests. Although India distinguishes between at least two agricultural seasons, most areas concentrate on one harvest only, while in the other season fields are left fallow for longer periods. More complex forms of rotation are also common, as well as the risk-avoiding custom of sowing two different crops simultaneously in the same field, such as wheat with cotton. Not surprisingly, the drier parts of the Arid Zone are often equated

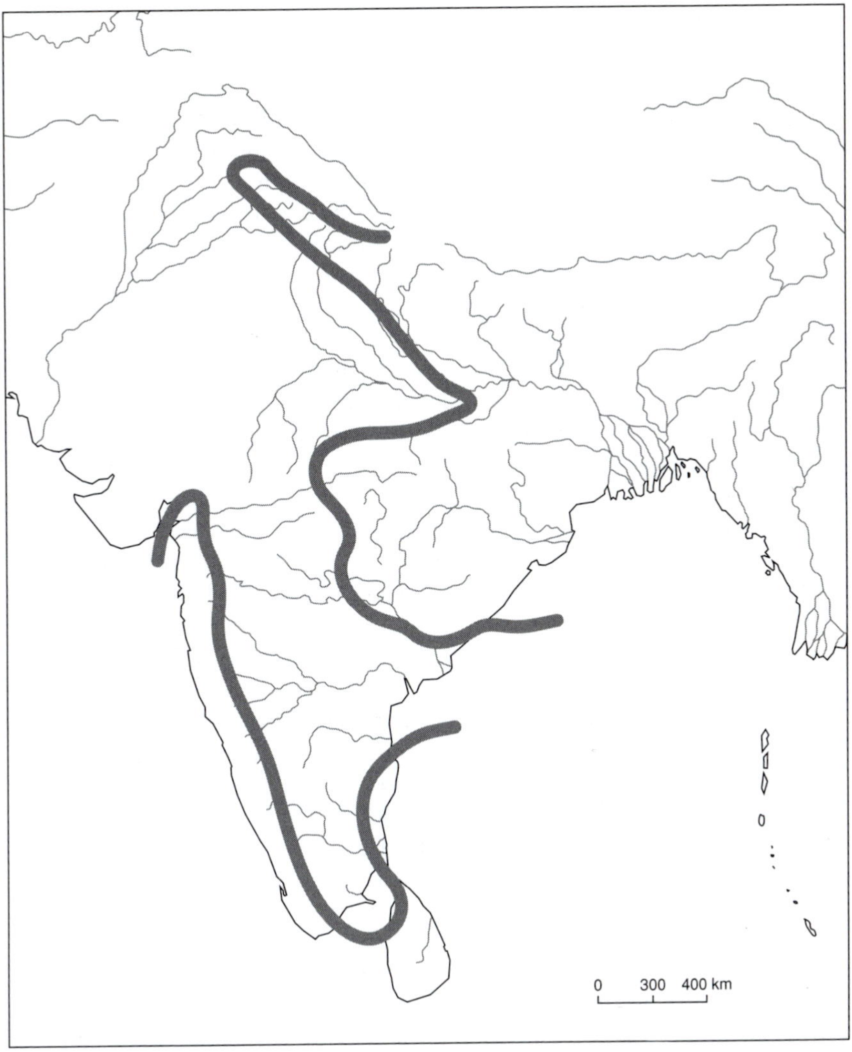

Map 1.3 Arid India

with a famine tract, in which the inhabitants always had to resort to wide-ranging survival strategies in case of failing monsoons. In some areas, they sought additional livelihoods like cattle tending, spinning or weaving, or peddling. But, as pointed out by Dirk Kolff, many of these peasants looked for temporary employment at the mostly booming military labour market of Hindustan.[8] Many peasants offered their services at the end of the agrarian season in October, either after kharif harvesting or rabi sowing. Indeed, the existence of a most extensive military labour market supplying tens of thousands of armed peasant-soldiers each year is one of the most salient features of military life in northern India and should be closely linked to the specific conditions of India's drylands. Hence, October not only marked the start of the peasant's off season but also the beginning of the war season – setting out for campaigns of plunder and conquest. In classical Indian texts it finds expression, for example, in the timing of the ancient horse sacrifice, when the sacrificer-king sent out a whole army to follow and protect the horse that, later, on its return from the campaign, would be immolated. Its armed retinue was licensed to plunder those who would oppose the horse's triumphant progress. Later on, we find similar examples of this kind of military parody, such as in the annual nine-day Dashahara or Mahanavami festival, in which the king's military potential was displayed and reviewed in exuberant processions. Indeed, after the retreat of the monsoon, as roads became more accessible and pastures were at their most luxurious, raiding always provided a tempting option to tide over the long agrarian off season.[9]

All this does not mean, however, that all arid regions were equally sensitive to such risk-avoiding considerations. On the fertile black soils of the northern Deccan, for example, cotton was cultivated and processed, which required an almost year round labour input. Besides, apart from plundering or more regular military labour, there could be many other alternatives for employment during the off season, such as trading or, as we shall see, cattle-tending. But, more generally speaking, with the combination of unreliable harvest and a long off season, the peasant population of the Arid Zone appears to have been more liable to the attractions of military service than that of Monsoon Asia. In areas with heavy rainfall, such as Bengal or Kerala, but also in those areas that were more permanently irrigated, it was easily possible to alternate kharif and rabi crops on the same fields every other year. In some areas, which were dominated by paddy cultivation, there were even three annual crops that kept peasants busy all year round, producing heavy yields per acre. Of course, all this does not imply that the paddy fields of eastern India did not produce military labour. The crucial point is that the organisation of military labour tended to be different in both zones. In the drylands, military labour tended to be part-time, seasonal and thus less specialised. The arid tracts were the ideal recruiting ground for irregulars, as easily gathered as dissolved at the end of the campaign. By contrast, in areas in which peasants did not have a long off season, military labour tended to be full-time and more professionalised. Such more regular armies required, however, long-term financial investments. This appears to have been exactly the policy of the East India Company, which recruited its well-drilled infantry sepoys mainly from the fertile eastern tracts of Hindustan. The same goes, probably, for the reputedly well-trained infantry units of the Nayars in Kerala or the Ahoms in Assam. By contrast, the Mughals took the bulk of their army from those more arid parts that Stewart Gordon recently designated as India's three major military recruitment zones: the Rajput zone in the northwest, the Maratha zone in the eastern Deccan and the Nayaka zone in the southern Carnatic.[10]

Not surprisingly, perhaps, the basic physiological divide between Arid and Monsoon Asia can also be traced in the old Sanskrit texts dealing with Ayurvedic medicine. As analysed by Francis Zimmermann, these highly idealised and normative treatises also draw a clear-cut distinction between the marshy *anupa* lands of the east and the dry *jangala* lands of the west. Anupa represents all the places where water abounds, not just marshes, but also rain forests and liana forests and mangroves, with all kinds of unhealthy connotations of fevers and parasites. The opposite is the jangala – clearly distinct from the present-day meaning of the word – defined by the scarcity of water, and mostly consisting of wild, open savannahs. In modern-day medicine, its Ayurvedic divide reappears in the distinction between the eastern areas where malaria is endemic and those western areas where it is epidemic. What is most interesting to the military historian, however, is that these idealised texts seem to confirm the ecological division of military labour. For example, they distinguish between two different types of human species: the eastern ones being fat, rotund and susceptible to disorders of the phlegm, the western ones being thin, dry and of a bilious temperament. One also finds other instances in which the vegetarian India is contrasted with the warlike regions of the north and northwest, with their eaters of meat and drinkers of alcohol.[11] Chris Bayly gives other examples of this traditional strand of anthropogeography that links climates and products of places to certain characteristics of its inhabitants. Hence, the martial Marathas become depicted as dry and hot because their diet consists of pulses, oils and chillies.[12] In a way these associations seem not that much different from the later, racist descriptions of British surveyors selecting the so-called martial tribes of India. Far from being natural phenomena, however, these normative portrayals partly appear to reflect real ecological and agricultural circumstances of the Arid Zone, which made military employment a viable and – as we shall see in the next chapter – attractive option in the survival strategy of both peasants and landlords.

The distinction between Arid and Monsoon India based on the agricultural regime corresponds neatly with that of pastoral production: pigs, buffaloes and ducks in the east; horses, camels, cows, sheep and goats in the west.[13] In the east, there is almost no room for extensive nomadic pastoralism since the jungles contain dense tropical rainforests or swamps, whereas the arable land consists of permanently worked paddy fields. Although there exist a few transhumant pastoralists tending larger herds of buffaloes or bullocks, the range of their movements is confined to a relatively limited area, as, for example, those transhumant herding communities travelling up and down the Himalayas. Most of the inhabitants of the monsoon forests combine some form of shifting cultivation with hunting or gathering. In military terms, they are not in a position to prevail over the peasants of the more settled society. Not surprisingly, the forest tribes often served as slaves, either used in the local households or exchanged in the long-distance trade. Apart from the famous Himalayan slave trade, the market in eunuchs from Assam and Bengal provides a well-known example. We should not forget, though, that these same forests contained one of the most important instruments of war in India: the elephant. To the forest dwellers the animal hardly rendered any military might since elephants were fit for neither breeding nor tending by pastoralists. In fact, at the age that they became useful for military or other purposes, they were caught by large-scale hunting expeditions. For the Mughals, this royal prerogative was the main attraction that drew them towards the unhealthy, malaria-infested forest fringes of the Himalayas, Assam, Bengal and Orissa.

The wild jungles of the drylands stand in sharp contrast to this. These jungles mostly consisted of open savannahs providing extensive pasture for large herds of camels, horses, bullocks, goats or sheep. Apart from sheer space, its nutritious natural grasses and fodder crops made the Arid Zone more suitable for stock-breeding. Apart from its grasses and forest scrub, cottonseed or the stalk and leaf of dry millet, two of the major dry crops, served as excellent supplementary fodder. In Chapter 4 I will point out the link between arid grasses and the breeding quality of warhorses. Although the best warhorses came from West and Central Asia, India's drylands could produce excellent horses, in particular when provided with streams as well as with good long-distance connections to the major breeding centres of the northwest. Hence, the dry valleys of the Sutlej and Bhima rivers grew into healthy breeding grounds for horses. For the present argument, it will suffice to conclude that, for the supply of their warhorses, the Mughals crucially depended on the pastoral economy of the Arid Zone. In addition, the same dry marches not only produced horses but also excellent breeds of dromedaries, which, like horses and elephants, were used as military instruments but which, more significantly, also served extremely well as beasts of burden. Because the radius of action of the dromedary was limited to India's sandy drylands, the bullock served better to supply armies in the more humid and marshy parts of the sub-continent. Although excellent breeds of the latter were bred all over India, the large herds of thousands of bullocks supplying the marshy army en route across the country clearly operated best on the open pastures of the Punjab, the Deccan and the Carnatic. Indeed, more generally speaking, an enormous Mughal army, consisting of thousands of mounted warriors supplied by at least an equal number of dromedaries and bullocks, needed wide, open space. Obviously, moving such an army was a tremendous logistical challenge, the more so when it had to pass through extensive agricultural fields. Of course, since it could not do without the supplies and other riches of the settled society, it always tried to keep as near as possible to the agrarian bases but, at the same time, it also had to keep the latter at a certain distance in order to avoid the ruining of fields or the splitting up of troops. As we have stressed already, the locomotive power of the army reached its maximum when marching at the very frontier between the settled society that provided supplies and the arid marchlands that provided pastures and moving space. In this respect, the Mughal army stands somewhere between the sedentary armies of Monsoon Asia and Europe and the nomadic armies of West and Central Asia; its magnitude hinging on India's tremendous agrarian potential, its mobility on India's extensive marchlands.

Of course, although the rigid dichotomy may be helpful for the analysis of Mughal geo-politics in general, we should be aware that the distinction between dry and humid regions is much more complicated, since large parts of the Arid Zone are naturally irrigated by India's many life-giving rivers. Indeed, these produced the ancient centres of Indian civilisation, along the Indus in the east, along the Ganges and Yamuna in the centre, and along the Vaigai, Kaveri, Ponnaiyar and Palar in the southeast. These fertile alluvial valleys and deltas represent the major agricultural areas of the sub-continent, linking up well with the fields of intensive rice cultivation in, for example, Bengal and Assam. Hence, in our definition, those parts that are naturally or artificially irrigated by rivers, lakes, canals, tanks or wells are, properly speaking, not part of the Arid Zone, although these areas are intersected with arid jungles everywhere. Nonetheless, from the historical point of view, the distinction between arid and humid areas remains vital as it reflects two different kinds of frontiers: the first a more open, inner frontier with dry, savannah-like marchland intersected by cultivated zones, the latter a more closed, outer frontier of impenetrable forest or swamp. For the large mounted armies of the Mughals, while crossing the latter was impossible, passing through the first was imperative.

Frontiers and limites

Obviously, the idea of the frontier as a straight line on a map is entirely modern. As we have hinted at already, the frontiers of the Mughal Empire were never lines but always zones. This is shown, for example, in the Persian word for frontier, *marz*, which, like the German *Mark*, denotes an areal space. It may be inhabited by *marzanishan* or ruled by a *marzban* or lord marcher, also translated as 'guardian of the frontier'. We also find marzban in the more general meaning of 'chief', as identical with the most autonomous connotation of the term *zamindar* or landlord.[14] Apart from being areal in nature, this frontier also implies a zone of transition, for example between two different ecological or administrative regions. In both latter cases, the frontier has a natural tendency, not to separate but to unite and integrate. In the words of the sinologist Owen Lattimore, the frontier itself is an area inviting entrance. The more the central administration invests in the area, for example for defence or control, the more its liability to become top-heavy, to break away and to start a new centre of its own. This paradox of centripetal policies having centrifugal effects is a rather common phenomenon in world history, as may be witnessed, for example, in the eleventh- and twelfth-century emergence of vigorous new states along the traditional frontiers of settled empires, such as those of the Khitan and Jürchen in China and the Seljuks in Iran.[15]

Looking at India's own history one may observe a similar process. From about 1000 AD, the interior of the sub-continent began to operate as a kind of dry central axis connecting the rich permanent centres of Madhyadesha and Cholamandalam more closely with the Arid Zone of the Middle East and Central Asia. Hence, at the former fringes of settled society, new conquest states emerged that fully exploited India's extensive drylands both for agrarian expansion and the breeding and keeping of warhorses and other cattle. Hence, there emerged several saddle states straddling the frontiers between arable and jungle: Ghaznavids and Ghurids between Kabul and Delhi, the Yadavas in the Deccan and the Hoysalas in the Carnatic. In their wake, we soon see the rise of new well-mounted or well-fortified warrior groups such as the Rajputs in the north, the Marathas in the west, and the Nayakas in the south. They provided the new military elite of these states and of the successor sultanates in Delhi, Gulbarga and Vijayanagara. It was the major achievement of the Mughals that they not only managed to bring all three sultanates under one imperial umbrella, but also managed to tie them more closely than ever to the traditional sedentary cores along the river valleys and the coast. But again, the highpoint of imperial centralisation under emperor Aurangzeb coincided with the start of the imperial downfall. Hence, the eighteenth-century decline of the empire also implied the regional centralisation at its former fringes and, for example, triggered off the foreign invasions of the Afghans from the northwest and the British from the northeast.

The integrating and connecting capacity of the frontier may remind us of its Roman counterpart, the *limes*, which literally signifies a road, a meaning which indeed aptly describes the working of the Roman frontier: not a defensive, dividing line keeping people out, but lines of communication penetrating deeply into areas beyond direct imperial control. It is my contention that this concept, of lateral lines of communication radiating outwards, is also relevant for understanding the process of imperial expansion under the Mughals.[16] Especially during the early stages of expansion, state building under the Mughals often came down to road building. Like the marchlands of the arid interior, the imperial highways served to connect the administrative and commercial centres with each other as well as with their agrarian hinterlands. In other words, they provided the nexus which could convert the agrarian produce into cash revenue. Hence, successful imperial rule not only involved the control of India's various inner frontiers but also of its major routes of communication. Although specific sub-routes were always shifting, from its earliest history the basic pattern of India's limites remained more or less the same. Let us attempt to pin it down on the map.

According to various early Indian texts, more or less confirmed by the contemporary accounts of Chinese pilgrims, the sub-continent consisted of five regions: Madhyadesha or the Middle Country, Uttarapatha or Northern India, Pracya or Eastern India, Dakshinapatha or Southern India and Aparanta or Western India. Here we have the usual number of five relating to the four wind directions emanating from a centre. Interestingly, two of these Sanskrit names literally refer to the meaning of road or *patha*, hence Uttarapatha becomes northern road and Dakshinapatha becomes southern road. Both remained India's main long-distance arteries, at least until the coming of the railways, the first being perhaps better known as the Grand Trunk Road connecting the Ganges–Yamuna river system through the Punjab to Central and Western Asia. The Dakshinapatha is the southeastern road connecting Madhyadesha, through Malwa and the Deccan plateau, to the Carnatic towards the Bay of Bengal.

Both highways very neatly follow the eastern and southern Indian extensions of the Arid Zone. In fact, the Buddhist texts were perfectly content with this, even more simple, tri-partite division of India: the two highways with Madhyadesha at their T-junction. In all these accounts the latter area is considered the most important.[17] The symbolic western and eastern limits of this country, which was also called the domain of the early Aryans, or Aryavarta, occur where the Sarasvati is lost in the sands of the Hisar region, and where it is supposed to reappear at the confluence of the Ganges and Yamuna. But from this traditional location it gradually expanded eastward, again not along a continuous front, but along the great river plains, radiating out from a series of nuclei of Aryan civilisation, gradually assimilating the non-Aryan tribes into the caste system or else pushing them back into the margins of the arable lands, into inhospitable zones of marchland or dense rain forests that were part of the eastern direction, or Pracya, comprising Bengal and including the whole of the Gangetic Delta together with Sambalpur, Orissa and Ganjam. Under the Mughals this eastward expansion of the frontier was vigorously carried on into the eastern jungles of Bengal. Hence, we have an ever-expanding centre with long-distance connections to the north, south and east. What remains to be explained is the western connection with Aparanta. This probably reflects the important linkage of Madhyadesha, either through the Indus river or overland, with the ports along the northwestern coast in Sind, Gujarat and the Konkan. It was important, because it crossed that other crucial

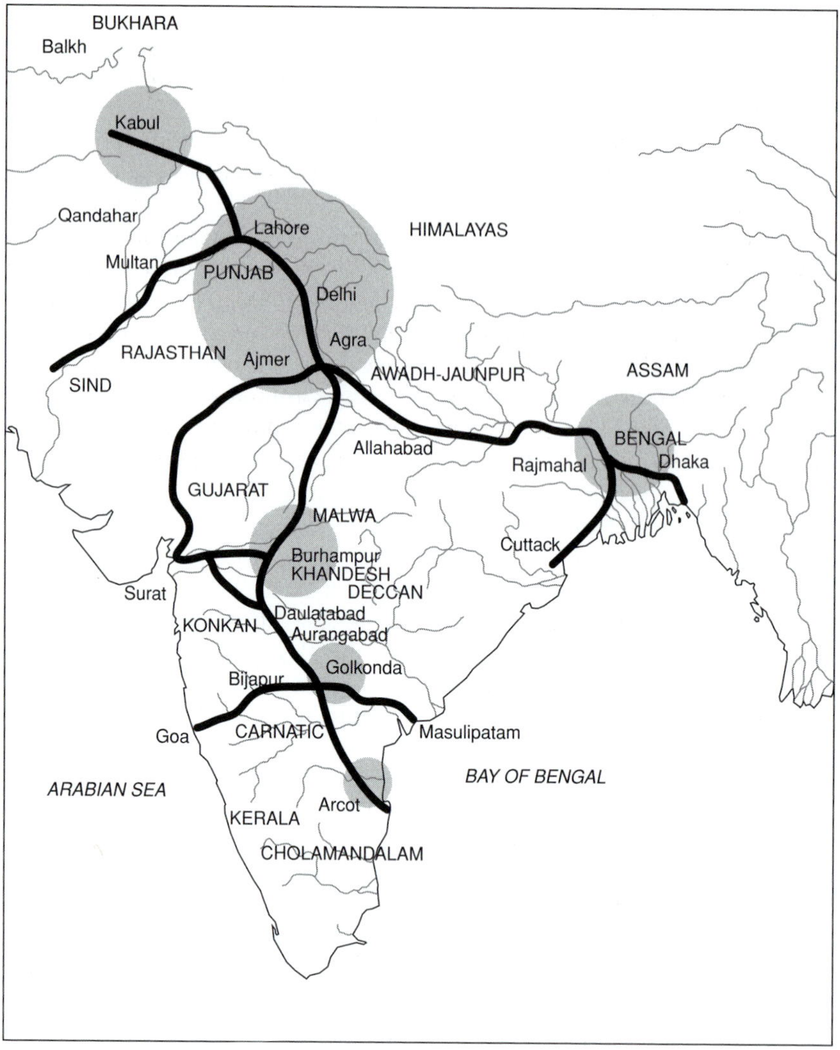

Map 1.4 Mughal India: high roads and nuclear zones of power

frontier of empire, the one between coast and interior. Like its arid counterpart, the coastal frontier gave the interior access to the major markets for its produce, in the case of India mostly in exchange for bullion and, at a later stage in history, horses.

As mentioned already, despite the continuous shifting of rivers and routes, the basic pattern of India's limites remained unchanged and, as such, greatly determined the overall direction of state formation in northern and central India. In his pioneering study of India's road systems, Jean Deloche detected a Z-pattern consisting of a northern link between Bengal and Kabul, branching off in the middle towards Gujarat, crossing the Deccan plateau in southeasterly direction towards the east coast somewhere between Masulipatam and Madras, then again going westwards through the Palghat gap across the Western Ghats towards Travancore.[18] Deloche offers a more detailed, empirical elaboration of the more abstract Sanskrit divisions. Both patterns point out, however, the structural importance of the northern and southern routes criss-crossing India's extensive eastern drylands as well as the significance of the various roads towards the coast. Besides, from Deloche's Z-pattern the Dakshinapatha not only stands for a north–south relation, but also for an east–west connection between the Arabian Sea and the Bay of Bengal. As we will see in more detail below, these east–west roads emerged as lifelines for the various political capitals situated in the drier parts of the Deccan interior. Hence, along the Dakshinapatha we come across a whole range of road junctions connecting port with capital,

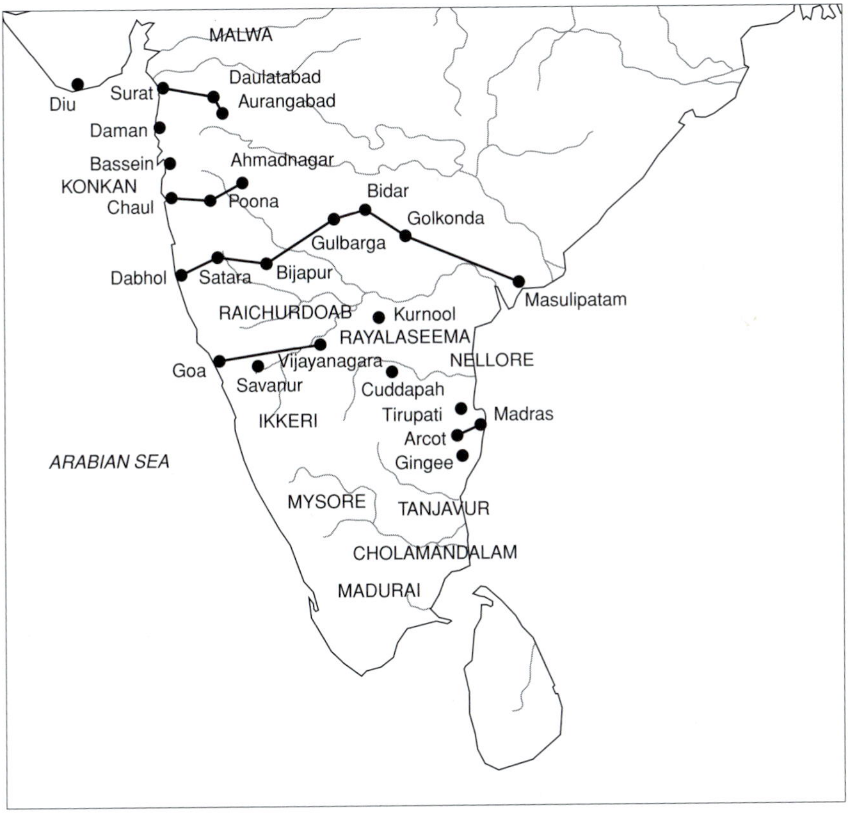

Map 1.5 Mughal South India: side roads of the Dakshinapatha

such as Chaul–Ahmadnagar, Dabhol–Bijapur, Masulipatam–Golkonda and Goa–Vijayanagara.

More generally speaking, the southeastern direction of the Dakshinapatha is clearly the result of the need to connect the dry Carnatic with the rich agrarian heartlands of Cholamandalam.

How do these lateral limites and areal frontiers exactly relate to the imperial policy of the Mughals? To what extent do they reflect the administrative division of the empire? First of all, the concept of the limites fits in rather well with the lack of interest of the Mughals in the external boundaries of their power. The official Mughal ideology, as expressed in imperial panegyrics and various court-sponsored miniatures, was one of an empire without limits, but with lines fanning out from the imperial centre in all directions towards an endless horizon. In this respect, the names and titles of the Mughal emperors may be illustrative enough: Jahangir, Shah Jahan or Shah Alam, the first meaning the world-conqueror, the latter two, the king of the world. The courtier Muhammad Baqir dedicated his 'mirror for princes' to Jahangir, in verse:

> The ruler of the countries of the world,
> Because of his justice and banner of power,
> Bestows crowns upon the rulers ascending the throne;
> Under his sovereignty are the East and West.
> The Turks and Dailamites are his slaves
> Caesar is among his warders;
> All of his ancestors with fortunate dispositions
> The masters of the crown and throne since Adam.[19]

This originally Persian claim of universal *padishahi* or *shahanshahi* over 'the seven climes' finds its Islamic counterpart in the almost equally universal Caliphate. Numerous references in the Mughal sources suggest that the Mughal emperor himself should be considered the new Caliph ruling from Delhi, the *dar al-khilafat*, the House of the Caliphate. From this perspective, regional military operations are presented as the initial stages of world conquest; the campaign into Assam aimed at the conquest of China, the campaign against Balkh aimed at the pacification of Turan.[20] Interestingly, the common Mughal word for 'abroad', mostly but not always referring to the northwest, was *wilayat*, which means province, the whole outside world, in fact, becoming an outer province of the Mughals; hence, we find the combination *mamlakat-o-wilayat*, which may be translated as the inner and outer provinces of empire.[21] This endless, cosmological perspective also may explain the poor state of cartography in Mughal India. Indeed, conspicuously missing from virtually all Mughal maps are territorial limitations. Most of the maps that have been discovered are extremely rough and appear to focus on the lateral lines of roads and rivers (see Plate 1).[22]

Of course, all this imperial rhetoric does not mean that there were no political limits to Mughal rule. First of all, Mughal claims of global sovereignty were met by the equally ambitious claims of other rulers, most emphatically those of the Safavid emperors of Iran, who on their part viewed Hindustan as part of their eastern provinces. The sultanates of the Deccan also, time and again, turned openly towards Shi'ism and acknowledged Safavid suzerainty. Hence, both in the northwestern direction of Qandahar and in the southern direction of Bijapur and Golkonda, the Mughals were constantly reminded of the fact that their realm was limited. But even within the inner range of their universal kingdom, the Mughals had to divide space into two broad administrative divisions: first, the organised territory of *ra'iyati* paying revenue under imperial regulation, or *zabt*, and, second, the tribal areas, or so-called *mawas*, which were kept beyond imperial regulation and at best had an incidental, tributary relationship with the Mughal court.[23] This dual division even turns up in that showpiece of imperial centralisation, Abul Fazl's *A'in-i Akbari*, which reflects Akbar's attempt to produce an immense cadastral survey of his empire.[24] Clearly, like other grand projects of imperial cadastration, all the facts and figures of the *A'in* have a strongly utopian character, used in a period of expanding power and imperial foundation as the dream of a distant administration for organised control. As such, it was an ideological attempt to bring order upon the land at a time of particularly fluid frontiers. Hence, between the lines of more or less factual information, we find a tremendous amount of imperial wishful thinking, which shows itself most emphatically in the opening lines of the provincial survey of Bengal:

> Since the conceptions of sovereign rule embrace the universe, I propose to begin with Bengal which is at one extremity of Hindustan and to proceed to Zabulistan and I hope that Turan and Iran and other countries may be added to the count.[25]

Although part of the imperial propaganda, this does not mean that these surveys were altogether useless for the more practical needs of imperial administration. In fact, they were a means of organising internal control. As may be witnessed in Habib's unsurpassed *Mughal Atlas*, although districts had no clear-cut boundaries, they were described by the listing of villages belonging to them.[26] Indeed, within the boundless realm of the Mughals there were provinces and districts that were under direct imperial control and in which it was possible to make regular calculations of the actual revenue to be collected by the government officials. At the time of Akbar, these administrative areas were mostly located immediately around the core provinces of Lahore, Delhi, Agra, Awadh and Allahabad. But beyond these regulated areas there were regions that paid revenue by custom or by rough estimation only, both often the result of negotiations between the local landholders and tax-gatherers. According to Abul Fazl, in some areas, such as Bengal, harvests were so abundant that measurement was not insisted upon.

Obviously such regions with high natural levels of population, production, trade and revenue were at the focus of imperial expansion. At the same time, though, the very riches of these areas made the long-term control of them extremely precarious. Now the military factor starts to play a crucial role. Although the excessive food production of these areas alleviated the logistical problem of supplying the huge Mughal armies, the bulk of these armies consisted of thousands of warhorses accompanied by an even larger number of bullocks and camels. One can imagine how landlords and peasants may have feared for their precious harvests at the approach of such capacious armies. But this was also the serious concern of the Mughals themselves, eager to facilitate the supply of their army and the collection of the revenue. Hence, what was needed was extensive, nearby grazing grounds offering space and pasturage to the army. This was exactly what was provided by India's Arid Zone: well-watered, rich riverine tracts intersected by extensive zones of dry, open marchland. Imperial control gravitated towards the frontier between the arable lands, whether under zabt or the mawas, and whether or not under tribute. In addition, the financial and commercial resources of the major trade routes provided the means to regulate the collection of supplies and revenue. In other words, the control of the imperial highways obviated the need for the army of plundering fields and cities. As a consequence, the process of state formation in India involved the command over both the inner frontier and the limites. In more practical terms, for the Mughals this imperative came down to the control of five or six nuclear zones of power which epitomised this combination of agrarian surplus, extensive marchland and long-distance trade routes (see Map 1.4, p. 18). In a way, these zones neatly followed the traditional tracts of the two major Indian limites: the Uttarapatha from Kabul in the northwest via Delhi–Agra to Rajmahal in the east; and the Dakshinapatha from the crossroads of Agra–Delhi in the north to Malwa in the south. Expanding southwards, there was the extensive dry Deccan plateau interspersed with various oasis-like centres, mostly artificially irrigated by tanks, wells and, sometimes subterranean, canals. Although the Deccan provided extensive pastures for horses and cattle, local food production levels were less reliable. As a result, the bulk of the trade gravitated towards the richer agrarian resources and ports along the coast. The Maratha cities and hill forts on the slopes of the Western Ghats, strategically situated at the elevated interface of humid littoral and dry interior, benefited most from these vital east–west connections. Hence, as it has turned out, the fruitless fight to capture these hill forts. More to the southeast, the areas around Golkonda and Arcot were important in this respect and consequently provided the two final stepping stones of Mughal expansion in the south.

Nuclear zones of power[27]

The Mughals began their Indian empire from Kabul. For Babur and his Mughals, India was their second-best choice, since they were repeatedly driven from their Central Asian homeland of Ferghana by their more powerful rivals, the Uzbeks. As a kind of nostalgia for the innocent days of their youth, for at least one-and-a-half centuries, even after they were well established in their far more sumptuous Indian capitals, the Mughals kept longing for their rugged 'paradise lost' in Samarkand. Although Kabul was conquered by Babur in 1504, it was only from 1516 that the Mughals started their raids into Hindustan. In 1522 they conquered Qandahar and four years later they decided to stay in India after they had defeated the Lodi-Afghans at the famous first battle of Panipat in 1526. After another Indo-Afghan dynasty had ousted Babur's son and successor Humayun from India in 1540, the latter – after a short humiliating asylum at the Safavid court in Iran – managed to settle himself in Kabul again. Here Babur's history repeated itself. After ruling this place for several years with Iranian support, Humayun regained his father's Indian empire after beating the Sur-Afghans near Sirhind in 1555.

Kabul was the major passageway from Turan to India. But compared with the other major cities in the area, especially Herat and Qandahar, it could be considered the most northwestern part of the Indian sub-continent. For example, it was one of the last northwestern areas to experience the effects of the Indian monsoon climate, while the Kabul river ran into the Indus. More importantly, compared to its northern and western connections, Kabul was within easy distance of Hindustan thanks to the Khyber Pass, which had a low altitude, was gradual in ascent and was well watered. In spite of its all-time fame, though, it was especially under emperor Akbar that this pass became the most important highway to India, as it was made accessible to wheeled vehicles.[28] Equally important were Akbar's successful campaigns to make the Khyber more secure against the attacks of the Afghan tribes surrounding the pass, for which purpose he shifted the capital from Fatehpur Sikri to Lahore in the period 1585 to 1598. From Kabul the passes through the Hindu Kush to the north and west were far more difficult to cross and only traversable during a few months after April when there was little snow and the streams were low.[29] Hence, any army coming from the Indian plains had a natural logistical advantage compared to potential Turanian or Iranian adversaries. Nonetheless, even Indian armies were faced by tremendous logistical problems. One mid-eighteenth-century source considered the Kabul area a land of snow:

> Men and cattle from India are not able to withstand the icy cold winds of that area. That is why it is difficult for the people of India to capture and occupy the Muslim countries of that area.[30]

Looking at Qandahar, this important commercial city was far less within the easy reach of Indian armies. First of all, the southern passes across the Sulaiman hills of the Bolan, Sangar and Gomal posed tremendous problems. Although the Bolan Pass was not steep and, for example, served as a route for the Mughal artillery under Dara Shukoh in 1653, during the winter all these passes were avoided because of the extreme cold. During spring torrents could obliterate armies that tried to traverse the narrow passes too early in the season. During midsummer, searing heat and lack of water made travel virtually impossible. Even during the autumn there could be major logistical problems because the pastoralists of the region would travel eastward making it impossible to hire camels for the westward trip. For the huge Mughal armies there was the additional problem of extensive deserts along the southern route to Qandahar, which necessitated transporting supplies over long distances. Hence, as proved by the three Mughal campaigns between 1649 and 1653, any siege of Qandahar launched from India was predestined to fail, since it had to be rounded off in a few months during the summer.

Although being more closely tied to Hindustan, Kabul stood very much at the interface between India and Central Asia. Still taking in India's monsoon climate, it also experienced the northern Parwan winds from Central Asia. According to Babur, Kabul's moderate climate was even better than the already excellent weather conditions in other metropolitan capitals, such as Tabriz and Samarkand. Indeed, Kabul was neither Turan nor Hind but combined the characteristics of both:

> Nearby are regions with both warm and cold climates. Within a day's ride from Kabul it is possible to reach a place where snow never falls. But within two hours one can go where the snow never melts – except in the rare summer so severe that all snow disappears. Both tropical and cold-weather fruits are abundant in Kabul's dependencies, and they are nearby.[31]

These extreme differences within a relatively short distance were also noticed when Babur entered nearby Nangarhar from Kabul on his way to Hindustan:

> When we reached Nangarhar, a new world came into view – different plants, different trees, different animals and birds, different tribes and people, different manners and customs. It was astonishing, truly astonishing.[32]

Although Babur thought of Kabul as being in the midst of cultivated lands, he was, at the same time, boasting about its excellent meadows that agreed so well with horses.[33] Indeed, from the military point of view, it was the supply of strong warhorses which made the control of Kabul so crucial to the Mughals. For about two months during the summer, Kabul's northern pastures near Parwan served to fatten these horses on their long way from Turkistan to Hindustan.[34] But apart from the supply of horses, Kabul served as the hub of India's trade with Central Asia and, to a lesser extent, with Iran as well. It was not only a commercial but also a financial centre where one could cash Indian bills of exchange. As a result, the agrarian, pastoral and commercial capacities of the Kabul area time and again made it a springboard for the building of Indian empires.[35]

Although Babur and Humayun made their fortunes from Kabul, it was to be the latter's son Akbar who would strike firm roots in India by further expanding its limits deeper into the sub-continent. During his reign, Akbar shifted the capital from Agra (1556–71) to the new palace of Fatehpur Sikri (1571–85), to Lahore (1585–98), and back to Agra (1598–1605). Apart from these more or less fixed capitals, Akbar continuously moved his military camp from one place to the other, but mostly kept within the strategic triangle Agra–Ajmer–Lahore depending on the focus of expansion: Agra looking east towards Bihar and Bengal, Ajmer looking west towards Gujarat, and Lahore looking north towards Kabul. In the centre of this triangle there was Delhi, which was destined to become the centre of the empire from Shah Jahan's time onwards. As we have seen already, this area more or less overlapped with the ancient centre of Madhyadesha, which stood at the crossroads of the Uttara- and Dakshinapatha. Part of its traditional importance grew out of its rich agrarian fields along the Ganges and Yamuna rivers. Immediately to its west, though, began extensive wilderness. This dry area at the south of the Siwalik mountains and connecting the Indus and Ganges–Yamuna river systems, is still called Jangal Desh or Jungle Country, and although it was less conducive for settled agriculture, it was important as a grazing area for pastoral breeders as well as for invading armies from the northeast. For example, the so-called Lakhi Jungle near the Sutlej river developed as one of the best horse-breeding grounds in India thanks to the repeated addition of Turkish horses taken from the invading armies.[36]

Not surprisingly, these marchlands at the gate of the sedentary riches of the Ganges–Yamuna doab became the site par excellence for India's most decisive battles, from the imaginative Kurukshetra of the *Mahabharata* to the well-attested battles of Tarain and Panipat, which marked the Muslim invasions of northern India. This area also served as the last extensive grazing station for cavalry armies heading east. After having crossed the Yamuna the military logistics became entirely different – less focused on grazing, and more on supplies coming from the rivers. This also suggests that the area was a major zone of transshipment linking the overland traffic of camels and bullocks to conveyance by riverboats. Indeed, the northern rivers considerably eased the rapid transportation of bulk goods, with relatively low costs, in both directions and during all seasons. As far as Bengal, this brought a great deal of economic and cultural coherence to the river valleys and tied them more closely to the capital in Agra. As we have seen already, Lahore was an important strategic centre for the Khyber Pass, as well as being easily connected with some well-cultivated areas of the Punjab and with the Indian Ocean through the Indus river. Lahore, however, was far less well situated for taking care of the affairs of Gujarat and Bengal, both conquered in the early 1570s. As we have seen, for the latter Agra was the most suitable, whereas for the former Ajmer was the site to be, especially as long as the Mughals did not fully control Khandesh in southern Malwa, that other gateway to the eastern ports, which was only taken in 1601. Hence, from 1576 to 1580 we see Akbar almost annually heading for Ajmer to do pilgrimage at the shrine of the Chishti saint Mu'in al-Din. This worked particularly well as long as the saint's death-anniversary (*urs*) in the Islamic month of Rajab coincided with the arrival of the camel caravans from Surat and Ahmadabad in September. But in 1580 Akbar himself had to admit that 'these good old customs (of pilgrimage) were not religious exercises except under certain conditions, and . . . royal expeditions were not meritorious if undertaken without consideration of the public weal'.[37] At that time his attention was fully drawn towards quenching a revolt of Turkish and Afghan amirs in Bengal. As we have seen, some years later he even shifted the whole capital to Lahore in order to pacify the northwestern Khyber and the southern Indus route.

For our purpose, it is most noteworthy that the whole area between Lahore, Agra and Ajmer was of prime importance for the empire since it gave relatively easy access to all parts of northern and central India. Closely related to this, at the watershed of the fertile and highly productive Indus and Ganges river systems, the area contained extensive pastures that could sustain armies with large numbers of warhorses, camels and bullocks. In addition, Lahore, Delhi and Agra were all huge commercial entrepots along the Grand Trunk Road, all in close contact with the major ports of the Arabian Sea. Hence, the first thing Akbar attempted to do, after he had conquered this area in about 1558, was to run to the coasts in order to literally cash in on his conquests.[38] First, after the campaign into Malwa (1560–1) and the famous sieges of Chitor (1567–8) and Ranthambor (1569; see Plate 5) he almost smoothly took Gujarat in 1572–3. Akbar's second target was Bengal.

Between Agra and Bengal was the richest and most settled agrarian area of Hindustan. Of course, to control this area was of crucial importance to the Mughals. Although, through its rivers, naturally tied to the Delhi–Agra region, at times of political weakness in the latter area, the former tended to become autonomous, as in the case of the fifteenth-century sultanate of Jaunpur or the eighteenth-century Mughal successor-state of Awadh, following the sack of Delhi by Timur and Nadir Shah respectively.

Sher Shah Sur, the main rival of Babur and Humayun, also came from the same area in between the Ganges and Gogra rivers. But at times when power was well established around the western capitals, it appears that the better supply of mounted warriors as well as warhorses gave a natural military preponderance to the northwest. It was only in the most humid eastern parts of Hindustan that warhorses lost their ascendancy to other forms of warfare, mostly based on riverboats and infantry. Because as the climate of Bengal was very injurious to horses, Akbar had even doubled the allowances of the nobles stationed in Bengal.[39] Indeed, the humid conditions of Bengal, in combination with its extensive network of waterways hindering the movement of cavalry, contributed to Bengal's relatively independent position throughout its history. The Mughals considered it an area of almost permanent sedition, a *bulghakkhana*, or a 'house of strife', as they called it.[40] For the mounted archers of the west, the natural location at which to halt was at the head of the Bengal delta which was one of the driest parts of Bengal. Some geographers describe it as an arid tropical steppe full of grass and bush; in more historical terms, it was the most eastern part of the Arid Zone, the last natural campsite for the mounted armies of the northwest.[41]

Situated near the Padma river, this area was situated at the head of the western delta and, as such, was by far the best place to control the riverine traffic. At this stage even river boats had to adjust to different circumstances, the boats of the mid-Gangetic region being more flat and spherical to avoid sandbanks, whereas the boats of the delta were more slender to give them stability in rapid streams.[42] All in all, this area north and south of the Padma river served as a dual funnel zone with, on the eastern side, converging river traffic, and on the other side converging caravan routes. Hence, almost all medieval capitals were located in this area, such as Nudiya under the Senas, Lakhnauti under the Delhi Sultanate, Pandua under the Ilyas dynasty, Gaur under the Husain-shahis and Tanda under the Afghans.

The Mughals seized Tanda from the Afghans in 1574. Two years later, after their defeat at Rajmahal, the latter retreated into the dense forests of Bhati or the eastern part of Bengal, which was unfamiliar ground for the Mughal cavalry. In the early 1590s the Mughals under Man Singh took Orissa, which remained, however, too remote for close Mughal control. Having lost their stick, the Mughals had to try their luck by carrot alone. Although they built their own capital in Rajmahal, again in the western part of the Delta, it took them more than three decades before they could annex the eastern Delta as well, this time with the help of a huge flotilla of war boats. In the end, the Mughals succeeded partly because the main river courses had gradually shifted eastward, which enabled them to remove their capital from Rajmahal to Dhaka in 1610.[43] This eastward movement of Bengal's rivers also linked the Ganges to the Brahmaputra and thus opened up a new limites towards the north into Assam. But even after that date, the Rajmahal area remained of importance as a resting place for cavalry armies from the west and as an area giving access, albeit with increasing difficulty because of the silting process, to the major Bengali seaports along the Hugli river. What is most important from the military point of view, Rajmahal served as a natural terminus for Mughal armies heading east. Beyond, military logistics and technology became entirely different.

Tracing our steps back to the Delhi–Agra region, going south along the junction of the Dakshinapatha, the next strategic terminal offering a combination of high food production, excellent pasturage and a flowering commercial market was the larger Malwa region, i.e. including Khandesh to its south. Being more or less identified with the Vindhya and Satpura Ranges, this area is often considered the almost perennial borderland between north and south India. Parallel to the mountains run, in a westward direction, the Narmada and Tapti rivers. Like all the southern rivers of the sub-continent, although these are not navigable, they provide rich alluvial soil and opportunities for irrigation.[44] Hence, situated in the midst of the extremely dry or less fertile surroundings of Rajasthan and the western Deccan plateau, the Malwa–Khandesh region served as the essential springboard for further military operations towards the south, the more so because the hills provided it with excellent opportunities for fortified defence and storage. During the early fifteenth century the area gained independence under the Khaljis who came into prominence as so-called 'wardens of the marches', protecting the long-distance trade routes towards the south.[45] Perhaps even more important than the southern connection, though, was Malwa's hold over the rich coastal provinces of Gujarat and the northern Konkan. During Mughal times, there was an intensive overland trade between Surat on the coast and Burhanpur, the trade centre situated at the homonymous north–south gap of the Satpura Range. Especially during the dry seasons, this route was preferred to the desert route via Ajmer, since it could be traversed by ox-carts which were more efficient than either camels or bullocks.

In a similar way to Rajmahal and the Bengali ports, through Ajmer, and especially through Burhanpur, it was easily possible to control the ports of the northwestern coast. As a result, the Mughals gave Gujarat a relatively free rein, the more so because the province itself was hardly suitable for large-scale cavalry armies. Of course, in its drier western parts, in Kachchh and Kathiawar, it possessed one of India's best breeding areas for horses, but these were situated off the major highways connecting the coast with the interior. By contrast, Malwa and Khandesh provided more than enough space for advancing armies from the north; its driest western parts, the so-called Nimar area, was even famous for its excellent breeding ground for black cattle.[46] The logistical problems facing the Mughal army at the frontier of Malwa and Gujarat are well attested by emperor Jahangir's description of the changing countryside. Entering Gujarat near Dohad, leaving the extensive jungles of Malwa behind, he exclaimed:

> it was from this stage that all things appeared different. The open plains and soils are of a different kind; the people are different and the language of another description. The jungle that appeared on the road has fruit-bearing trees, such as the mango and khirni and tamarind, and the method of guarding the cultivated field is with hedges of zaqqum. The cultivators separate their fields with cactus and leave a narrow road between them for coming and going.[47]

Not surprisingly, a few instants later, Jahangir dismounted from his horse to step into a cart. Here one may conclude that the Mughals ruled Gujarat from the trade routes and marchlands of the interior, partly from Rajasthan but mainly from Malwa. Although Akbar conquered Malwa as early as 1561, it was only forty years later that he definitively annexed Khandesh, including Burhanpur and its fort Asirgarh. Thanks to the supplies and transport facilities of Malwa and, not least, the financial facilities of the Burhanpur–Surat axis, Akbar successors could start to think about heading deeper south.

South of Malwa we find the nuclear zones of state formation at the interior edges of the Eastern and Western Ghats. From about 600 metres in the north, the Western Ghats rise towards 2,500 metres in the south; the slopes of the Eastern Ghats are less high and more gradual. For the tremendous Mughal armies of the north, the Deccan tableland was difficult to cross, not because of the lack of pasturage, but mainly because of the lack of local supplies. The Deccan rivers seem to drain the country rather than to water it as they flow rapidly in deep rocky valleys. Only nearer to the coast have dams been thrown across them and their waters used for irrigation. Many of the political centres of the interior are at some distance from the rivers bringing the water by underground channels.[48] The driest parts of the Deccan were situated in the west, where the Western Ghats created an extensive shadow-zone of very low rainfall. Although not conducive to intensive cultivation, it contained excellent pasturage for horses and cattle, the pastoralists of the region often taking their cattle up and down the slopes of the Western Ghats.[49] For example, during the Bahmani sultanate, the Bhima valley served as a rallying point for the sultan's armies en route to do battle with the armies of Vijayanagara, and as a resting point for the Islamic armies returning from wars in the south.[50] Later it became the foremost breeding place for Maratha warhorses, as well as the permanent camping ground for the imperial Mughal army during the later 1690s. Before turning towards Islampuri along the Bhima in 1695, the army had stayed for five years at Galgala along the Krishna river, an area also well known for its pastoralist characteristics. Although there appears to have been plenty of pasturage in this area, food supplies had to come from the coastal regions in the west or from Malwa in the far north. As a result, the capitals of the interior were closely connected through the Ghats to the coastal ports of the Konkan such as Daman, Bassein, Chaul, Dabhol and Goa. Hence, both in terms of trade and pastoralism, the passes and meadows of the Western Ghats served as crucial lifelines for the oasis-like capitals of the interior, such as Ahmadnagar, Daulatabad, Bijapur and Gulbarga.[51] From their various hill forts, the Marathas benefited most from these important east–west connections between coast and interior. Perhaps the Maratha capitals represent the best Deccan examples of state formation taking place at the frontier of fields and marchlands. Take, for example, this description of Satara by T. Ogilvy:

> The entire territory of Satara is divided into two distinct and very dissimilar parts, by a chain of hills branching off from the north to south for fifty or sixty miles nearly to the banks of Krishna near Walwa. The district lying to the west . . . is well peopled with industrious agriculturalists, is well cultivated, and productive, and is rendered fertile and salubrious by seasonable showers. The division of the territory to the east of that chain of hills is, though still intersected by spurs, more flat and barren, and it is ill cultivated by a thin unsettled, and in some degree predatory population. The fall of rain is scanty and precarious, and the climate is hot and insalubrious. These districts yield, however, excellent pastures, which have encouraged the breeding of horses, celebrated among the Marathas, and they maintain numerous flocks and herds.[52]

More generally speaking, however, the western Deccan did not possess natural centres of political power to be compared with the Malwa or the Delhi–Agra region in the north. Its nuclear political zones shifted along the Western Ghats and the elongated dryland to its east. The vital east–west connections created commercial and pastoralist crossroads, which the Mughals, like any political power of the interior, needed to control. It was at these east–west connections that the Marathas emerged as the prime rival of Mughal power in the region.

Summing up, from Malwa we find various western stepping stones towards the south, the east being almost impenetrable because of the extensive, dense tropical forests of Gondwana. From north to south the major examples were Daulatabad–Aurangabad, Ahmadnagar and Bijapur, as well as the old capitals of Gulbarga and Vijayanagara. Going southwards, the open Deccan plateau widened towards the east, giving access to Golkonda, situated at the edge of the Deccan plateau and to the strip of coastal lowland of the Northern Circars.[53] In fact, the more southeastward, the more the conditions for agriculture improved as a result of the rainfall produced during the northeast monsoon. Along the northern Coromandel Coast, the double delta of the Godavari and Krishna rivers became an inter-regional food supplier, also providing alternative supply lines for the more western centres mentioned before. It appears that, towards the end of the sixteenth century, when maritime links between the southeastern coast and the western Indian Ocean were limited, overland links from Golkonda and Masulipatam to west-coast outlets such as Goa, Dabhol and Surat assumed an increased importance.[54] To Deccan's south, we find the extremely fertile settlements of Cholamandalam, which, in addition to its many rivers, received by far the largest amount of rainfall. Hence, it should far from surprise us that military expansion from the Deccan tended to go towards the southeast. The bulky armies, however, had to keep more or less close to the more spacious wastes of the interior. Golkonda, for example, was not situated in the fertile coastal region itself but at its western fringe on the first rise of the Eastern Ghats. With extensive wastes to its south, it partly matches the other, more fragile, capitals of the Deccan. More to the south, the Mughal headquarters became situated near Arcot, which, according to some local source, derived from the Tamil *ar*, for river, and *katu*, for forest. During the southern Mughal campaign of the 1690s, the Mughal commander Zulfiqar Khan

> chose the bank of a river and the skirt of a forest [*daman-i sahrai*][55] as the camping ground for the army of Islam, and for raising the standards of the victorious forces. Twelve long years of continuous habitation replaced the tents by thatched houses which, in the course of time, changed into tiled ones; when it became the capital it gradually developed into a big town and became famous on the lips of one and all.[56]

In a way, here we again come across the usual process by which natural encampments of armies evolve into settled administrative centres. Indeed, Arcot was well situated in the midst of the fertile Coromandel Coast, with all its lucrative maritime connections of the Bay of Bengal, and with the two main interior routes, one from Golkonda in the north, the other from Bijapur in the northwest. The latter diverged in about this area, most conspicuously visible at the important religious and commercial centre of Tirupati, which attracted pilgrims and traders from all over India. For cavalry armies, the route to Arcot was not an easy one, since the woods became denser towards the southeast. At the time the Mughals entered the region in the early 1690s, the area south of Cudappah to Kanchi comprised thick and thorny jungle, through which only the coming and going of the imperial army had formed a track where horsemen could pass with difficulty, and elephants and camels only with great hardship.[57] After this time, it appears that this region was opened further, partly thanks to the intensified exploitation of the diamond mines near Ramallakota. Along this southeastern road, in Kurnool and Cudappah, Afghan horse-traders and military entrepreneurs carved out their own principalities. Tirupati itself became one of the last southeastern outposts of the overland horse trade with Central Asia.[58] In addition, all these pilgrims, horse-dealers and other merchants from the north brought silver into the city, which not only made it a centre for money changing and other financial transactions, but also linked it more closely to the northwest.[59] Above all, this area of the Rayalaseema and its neighbouring Nellore district possessed large numbers of excellent bullocks that provided the logistical basis for Mughal as well as later British expansion.[60] Hence, Golkonda and the larger Arcot area – be it in Arcot itself or in other places like Vellore, Gingee or Madras – should be considered as more structural nuclei of political power than the more fragile capitals in the rain shadow-zone of the Western Ghats. As mentioned already, these were the two final stepping stones of Mughal expansion along the Dakshinapatha. To the south of Arcot were the states of Tanjavur and Madurai, commanding the paddy fields of the most southern and most humid heartland of Tamil Nadu, which, like large parts of eastern Bengal, remained beyond the logistical reach of the Mughal army. West of Arcot was the most southern extension of the Deccan plateau, which was dominated by the two Vijayanagara successor states of Mysore and Ikkeri. Being less accessible because of the high mountainous bend of the Bubabudan Hills and Bangalore, but also being less lucrative in strategic and economic terms, it remained outside the predominant southeastern thrust of Mughal expansion.

Now looking at the history of events, after the taking of Khandesh by Akbar in 1601, the Mughals launched several seasonal raids into the Deccan. More permanent Mughal expansion required the taking of several well-fortified strongholds surrounded by difficult and often uncultivated terrain that made the siege of such places an enormous logistical challenge. This either required the taking of the shortest supply lines across the Western Ghats or provision by long-distance grain-carriers from Malwa and Berar. This explains why the Mughals made their first major inroads as late as the 1630s, during the reign of Akbar's grandson Shah Jahan. After more or less protracted sieges, the forts of Dharur (1631), Daulatabad (1633), Udgir (1636) and Ausa (1636) were taken, Ahmadnagar was annexed, and Bijapur and Golkonda were made tributary (see Map 6.3, p. 188). Hereafter, the same forts served as forward grain warehouses supplying the army en route to the south. According to one Mughal source, this Mughal success in the Deccan was entirely the result of a strategic alliance between the Mughal commander Mahabat Khan and the Banjara hauliers of the north.

> It is said that during the thirty or forty years many governors came to the Deccan and returned as they experienced serious difficulties

> at Balaghat, and owing to the scarcity of corn even though there was no fighting. No one had been able to find a solution for this problem. The first arrangement that Mahabat Khan made during his tenure of the government (of the Deccan) was that he conciliated the Banjaras of India by presents of elephants, horses and robes of honour, and won them over so completely that there was one head of the Banjaras at Agra and Gujarat and the other in Balaghat. He ordered that whether corn was cheap or dear, they would supply it at the rate of ten seers to the rupee.[61]

Also of importance was the annexation of Baglana in 1637, the small Rajput kingdom sitting astride the direct route from Surat to Daulatabad and Golkonda, leaving Burhanpur to its north. Not far from Daulatabad, at the fresh crossroads of the southern and eastern highways, Aurangzeb, as viceroy of the Deccan, founded the new provincial capital of Aurangabad. The Deccan campaigns against Bijapur and Golkonda under emperor Aurangzeb again illustrated the problem of moving supplies over long distances, which necessitated the flanking operations against the Maratha forts commanding the east–west passes across the Ghats. Although having some success during the 1660s, the Marathas retained their de facto autonomy. Nevertheless, being continuously provisioned from the north, Aurangzeb managed to take Bijapur in 1686 and Golkonda in 1687, albeit after long sieges. After these successes, Aurangzeb could not but persist in his attacks against the Maratha forts giving access to the western ports. In the early 1690s the Mughal general Matabar Khan succeeded in taking the northern Konkan, the fertile coastal strip including the Maratha hill forts to its east. But in 1683–4 as well as in 1701–2, the Mughals tragically failed to take a more permanent hold over the more southern coastal strip because of the tremendous logistical problems caused by both the surrounding mountains and the excessive humidity of the area.[62] At the turn of the century, however, the Mughals had found another solution to their logistical problems in the Deccan by heading towards the far more accessible and wealthy fields and ports of the Coromandel Coast. After taking Gingee in 1698, the Mughals appeared to have rounded off their southern conquests. A few decades later, however, all these southern terminals of Mughal expansion had become the almost autonomous seats of the Marathas in the Deccan, the Nizam in Golkonda–Hyderabad and the Nawayats in Arcot, to name just the most important amongst them. Once again, an empire was falling apart at the height of its expansion.

Taking another look at the geographical map of India, it appears that Mughal expansion was most successful in Arid India and in those parts of Monsoon India that were accessible by riverboats. Although we find in this region several inner frontiers demarcating differing degrees of settled agriculture or administrative control, all of it remained within the radius of action of the Mughal armies. Many of the dry areas served as de facto outer frontiers of empire because these were not interesting enough from the economic and administrative point of view, or because, in logistical terms, they were too far from the Mughal heartland, as for example in the case of Balkh and Qandahar, Mysore and the southern Coromandel Coast. Part of the sub-continent, however, remained outside the Mughal pale because it was beyond the natural terrain of Mughal armies. Without exception, these natural outer frontiers consisted of the humid, malaria-

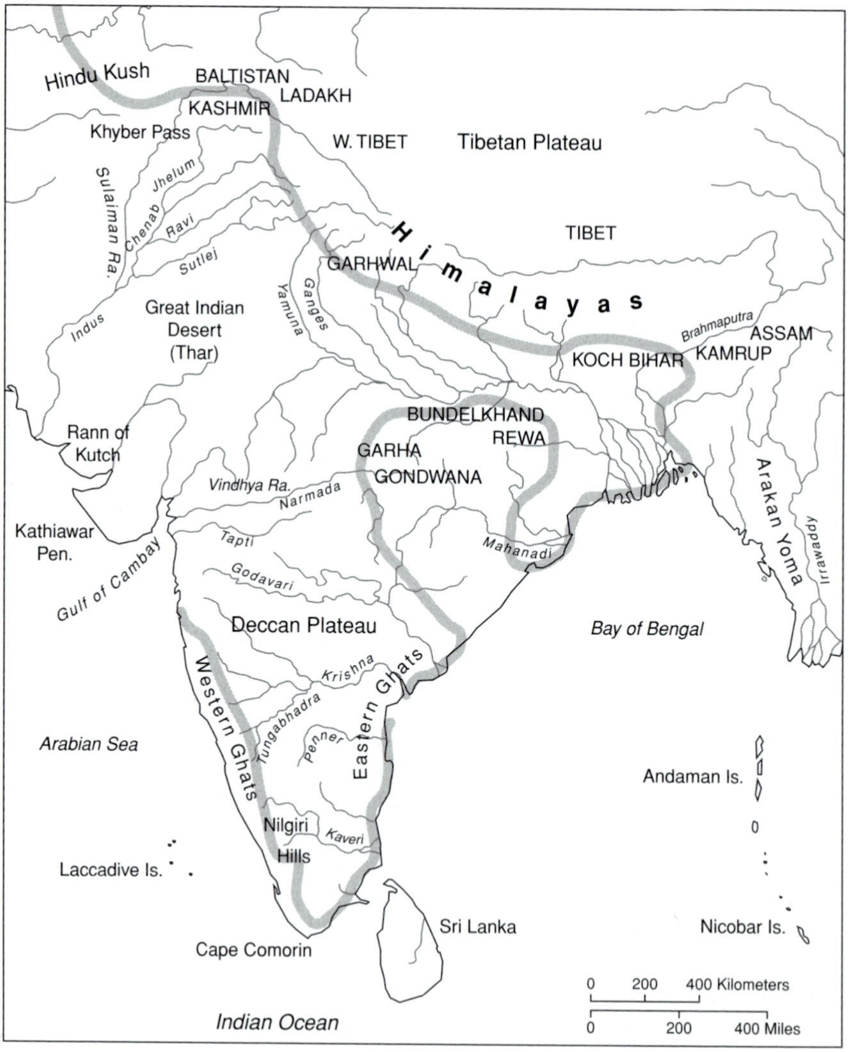

Map 1.6 Mughal India: physical features and natural outer frontiers

infested, dense forests and swamps of Gondwana, eastern Bengal and Assam, and along the foothills of the Himalayas and the Western Ghats.

Along their fringes there were several little kingdoms that could successfully resist Mughal incorporation since they could easily retreat into these dense wildernesses. Most of these principalities were neither poor nor primitive. On the contrary, their reputation was one of being extremely wealthy, most of their riches reportedly being buried or hidden at the bottom of secret wells and caves. In a way, they had become the natural depots of the dregs of Indian bullion streaming along the major highways of Hindustan. In addition, many of these states could build on the revenues from intensive paddy cultivation, the sale of elephants and, in some cases, the exploitation of important pilgrimage routes. For example, according to the *A'in-i Akbari*, the cultivators of the Gond state of Garha paid the revenue in golden mohurs and elephants. Their produce alone was considered sufficient to fully supply both Gujarat and the Deccan.[63] Hence, although these areas never became entirely integrated into the empire, the Mughals had a great deal of interest in them as may be witnessed by their various plundering raids.

One example of this is Shah Jahan's punitive expedition of 1635 against Jujhar Singh Bundela, the ruler of Bundelkhand, which was one of those peripheral regions linking the drylands to its north and west to the more humid and dense forests of Gondwana to its south. After chasing Jujhar Singh from his capital Orchha (see Figure 6.1), the Mughal cavalry pursued him into the neighbouring forest state of Chanda, where he was killed by a party of Gonds. More importantly, though, the Mughals took the opportunity to extort a great deal of money and many elephants from the Chanda raja, to plunder the Bundela treasure at Orchha and, apparently in a mood of sudden religious fervour, to demolish the local temple.[64]

Clearly, these kinds of Mughal razzias were not aimed at establishing solid Mughal rule on its periphery, but were merely meant to raise money. In most of these cases, the local ruler and population temporarily left their villages and fields, taking refuge in the nearby forests. At other times, such as in the case of the campaign into the Himalayan state of Garhwal in 1655–6, the raja acknowledged Mughal suzerainty, and agreed to pay tribute and send his sons to serve as hostages at the imperial court.[65] But all these rulers knew that, in the end, after they had eagerly hunted treasures and elephants, the Mughals were not in a position to stay and would soon leave again for fresh supplies and pastures.

In a way, Mughal expansion towards the northeast, towards Koch Bihar, Kamrup and Assam, is another example of this short-term aim to catch elephants and to bring into renewed circulation the sterile riches of these places. These campaigns neatly followed the lateral limites of the Karatoya and Brahmaputra rivers but, as the Mughals experienced in 1663, the limited, seasonal navigation of the latter river could not sustain a prolonged campaign under a climate that, according to one witness, 'agrees with the natives, while it is rank poison to foreigners'.[66]

Finally, the Kashmir case appears to be an interesting exception. Although clearly at the Himalayan periphery, it became more thoroughly integrated into the empire. Every time the Mughal emperors decided to enter this mountainous valley, mostly against the advice of generals who thought its location too eccentric, they could not but leave the bulk of the army behind in the plains of Hindustan. After Akbar conquered it in 1588, it could easily be controlled by a small Mughal contingent because of the flatness of its plateau as well as its pleasing climate. Indeed, the Mughal attachment to the valley is often related to its being a kind of pre-modern tourist and health resort for burned-out emperors. But, apart from these more personal reasons, we should not forget that the Kashmir valley was of considerable commercial weight because of its shawl trade, which was closely linked to the mountainous meadows of Ladakh and Western Tibet. To protect the Kashmir monopoly in the trade of Tibetan shawl wool against the expanding Dzungar Empire, the Mughals even launched a war for this almost empty Himalayan tableland. In 1683 it was agreed that the latter was to be annexed by Tibet in return for continuation of the Kashmir wool monopoly.[67] The Mughal–Tibetan war should remind us of the fact that even the Himalayas were not entirely impenetrable for Mughal armies. Of course, these mountainous expeditions into places like Kashmir (1561, 1585, 1588), Garhwal (1635, 1656), Baltistan (1637), Ladakh and Tibet (1679–84) present the military historian with jewels of Mughal logistics, in which the invaders had to carry all the provisions for a campaign that had to be terminated within the two or three months that the passes remained open. They also show that it was not so much the high relief but the moist climate and dense vegetation at the foot of the eastern Himalayas that served as the natural frontier of the Mughal armies. But even these most unhealthy frontiers were not rigid but continuously shifted, albeit less readily than the arid, inner frontiers of empire which provided mobility.

To sum up the main conclusions of this chapter, the natural, outer frontiers in the north and east contrast sharply with the open, inner frontiers situated along the Indian limites of Uttara- and Dakshinapatha. The first represents not only a natural, geographical barrier but also within the extent of the Arid Zone, a compromise between the range of conquest and the economy of rule. Conquest was governed by the marginal costs of imperialism, always considering whether the local food supply or the long-distance provisioning could sustain the army without it becoming an intolerable logistical or economic burden. In addition, the cavalry armies and their trains of numerous camels and bullocks needed the space and the extensive pasturage provided by the Arid Zone. Hence, although the

Mughals were permanently drawn into the rich and well-populated centres of the river valleys and the coast, they always had to keep an eye on logistical considerations. The ideal centres of political power combined the characteristics of limites and inner frontier; or, to state it differently, the Mughals looked for regions along major commercial highways, at the interface between rich arable land and extensive jungle. In the end, of course, at all these places, there was always the danger that centripetal gain was converted into centrifugal loss, which was indeed what happened during the eighteenth century.

Plate 2 Mughal court: Shah Jahan receives his three eldest sons and Asaf Khan during his accession ceremony, 1628. This scene by Bichitr (*c.* 1630) illustrates the importance of courtly ritual in making the various chiefs and landlords of the country the participants and sharers of the Mughal body politic (see also M. Cleveland Beach and E. Koch (1997), p. 38).

Source: *Royal Library, Windsor Castle, Padshahnama,* f. 50B

CHAPTER TWO

War-band and court

As we have seen in the previous chapter, the Mughals built their empire on the exploitation of the inner frontier. By having stakes on both sides of the frontier, collecting revenue from the agrarian heartland and assembling the army from the marchlands, they took the best of both worlds. The frontier aspect of the Mughal Empire compares well with the other great Islamic empires of its day, those of the Ottomans in the Middle East, the Safavids in Iran and the Uzbeks in Central Asia. Although to differing degrees, all these mighty empires emerged at the frontier of settled and nomadic worlds, the first being most productive in India and Anatolia, the latter two being most vigorous in Central Asia and Iran. What we see is a dual society not only based on two different economic systems, but also on two different social structures and two different cultures. The sedentary parts consisted of an urban and rural population which essentially preferred more or less peaceful relations. This peace was threatened though by the population of the mawas: nomads, warriors and ascetics who were driven by their search for pasture, booty, glory or by religious vocation. In India, the social cohesion of these fringe groups was neither based on the consanguinity of tribes nor on the endogamy of castes, nor on the orthodoxy of religions. On the contrary, the basic social ingredient of the mawas was the inclusive war-band consisting of people with shared interests. Of course, these open groups could take a tribal or communal identity, but in principle their recruitment was not ascriptive but conscriptive.

This phenomenon of the war-band is best studied in the case of the Ottomans, who appear to have started their careers as so-called *ghazi*, or warriors of the faith.[1] These bands of ghazis, however, were not like modern-day fundamentalists, relentlessly attempting to spread their own untarnished version of Islam, but consisted of open status groups articulating a religious or tribal idiom. In fact the word 'ghazi' itself does not refer to some kind of holy war at all, but merely to the more opportunistic razzia, or raid, whether or not sanctioned and rendered meaningful within the framework of a higher cause.[2] In India also, we find the same frontier people raiding and plundering in the name of jihad or some other higher principle. Taking shifting identities of tribe, caste or creed, the war-band was a community of 'lion-like' men of the sword, restless elements who offered their services wherever a holy war was in progress and, more importantly, wherever booty might be expected. Of course, the continued vigour of these ghazis was a permanent liability to Mughal peace. They were perfectly aware that they themselves had started as a petty war-band from the mawas, and it was one of the Mughals' prime challenges not to suppress and destruct these groups, but to recruit and redirect them and to turn them into an imperial asset. In other words, the key to Mughal success was to harness the mobility and fluidity of the frontier to their own ends, while shaping and taming it to conform to their stability-seeking, centralising vision.

Against the image of the ghazi stands the more refined *mirza* or Rajput of the settled palaces, cities and estates of the countryside, mostly having extensive rights over land or other immobile goods. This was a group that often had risen from the mawas but had gained landed rights and had become a more rooted gentry of land-holding zamindars who, in addition, could mobilise an enormous number of armed peasants to easily undermine Mughal rule. The interests and outlook of the settled mirza and Rajput were different from those of the ghazi, since the first primarily aimed at legitimising his elevated status in local society as well as the fixed distribution of landed rights. Hence, we find a much greater emphasis on ascriptive criteria of tribe, caste and religion. This means, for example, the construction of extensive genealogies, marriage relations becoming more endogamous, and religion finding a more material expression in the construction of sumptuous mosques, tombs, madrasas and temples. Hence, next to the rootlessness of the wilderness, we find a society committed to settled wealth and status. We should not forget, though, that the gentry of India was not as settled as that of its feudal European counterpart. The nearness of the frontier implied that even the most settled landholders were never sure of their position. At any time, their status and honour could be undermined by rivalling groups from within or from outside the local community. Besides, the Mughals themselves were reluctant to recognise a rooted aristocracy with inheritable distinction, since this would immobilise their own operations. Hence, even in the more settled regions of empire we find a gentry that is never sure about its position and, in case of need, is ready to shift habitation, allegiance and identity. As a result, the distinction between ghazi and mirza is not a rigid one but represents the two opposite ideal types in a continuum of shifting values and mentalities. Anyway, for the Mughals to gain access to India's immense resources of rural production and military labour, they had to come to terms with the powerful Indian zamindars who mediated the payment of the land revenue. Again, the Mughals' prime aim was not to suppress but to accommodate and incorporate this landed gentry into their realm.

As a result of all this, we find the Mughals again situated at the frontier, faced with the challenge of finding common ground between the mentalities, the values and expectations of the ghazi warriors of the mawas and the gentlemen warriors of the more 'civilised' and settled centres of society. It was, in particular, Akbar who succeeded in incorporating the settled gentry, both Muslim and Hindu, in a newly created imperial ideology and ritual. But his success was also very much the result of his ongoing commitment to the eclectic and pragmatic spirit of the ghazi, perhaps most clearly articulated in the concept of *sulh-i kull*, i.e. 'peace with everyone' who was willing to join the Mughal standard. To some extent, it was this open ideology of the frontier that made the massive recruitment of military slaves, as in the case of the Ottomans and Safavids, superfluous, as it opened the Mughal ranks to all and sundry with sufficient man- and horsepower to be of interest. As we will see in this chapter, all these armed groups were held in a precarious check, partly by instilling in them a sense of spiritual devotion to the emperor (*din-i ilahi*), and partly by making them 'sons' of the imperial household (*khanazadagi*) through a complex system of ritual incorporation. In the next chapter, we will look at some other means of keeping some kind of control over these various warrior groups, primarily involving their smooth incorporation into the flexible and meritocratic ranking system of the Mughals, the so-called mansabdari system. Only the last chapters will highlight the purely military instruments of warfare to be used as the last resort.

While stressing the ongoing dichotomy of the inner frontier between mawas and ra'iyati, it will be necessary to warn the reader of three important modern dichotomies that are clouding our understanding of Mughal warfare. First of all, there is the highly sensitive, communal distinction between Muslims and Hindus. Although not without relevance, I would suggest that, in terms of warfare, this was hardly a crucial distinction. Although at times Muslims and Hindus publicly pledged to fight each other, in practice they were more usually fighting amongst themselves in one or the other pragmatically inspired alliance. Hence, in this chapter we will not set Muslims against Hindus, but ghazis and sadhus against mirzas and Rajputs. It is my contention that the outlook of ghazis and sadhus was closer to that of each other than to that of their religious brethren, since they were speaking the same language of mawas adventurism. In religious terms, we find a similar separation between the more mystically oriented and more ascetic sufis and sannyasis, and the more literate and orthodox ulama and Brahmans. Again, this is far from being a clear-cut separation, but rather reflects two opposite ideal types. Much earlier India had already witnessed a convergence of the political idiom focused on the cosmopolitan ruler, Hindu rajas being styled as *suratranas* or sultans, Muslim sultans as *maharajadhirajas*. The Mughals further elaborated and optimised this kind of royal eclecticism, in which Muslim and Hindu warriors shared a common mentality of imperial service.

The second, more or less anachronistic, dichotomy is that between private and public. The Mughal army belonged to what Stephen Blake has called a patrimonial-bureaucratic empire. In such empires, the ruler governs on the basis of a personal kind of traditional authority whose model is the patriarchal family.[3] Hence, within the political organisation there could hardly be a separation of the private and the official sphere, which is so characteristic of modern states. The Mughal state was based on patrimonial officialdom in which the administration of the empire was treated as a purely personal affair of the ruler, and political power was considered part of his personal property. Although the emperors remained dedicated to the idea of the personal household, the empire as a whole was far too extensive to make this work well in practice. Therefore, a great deal of power had to be delegated to numerous administrator-warriors. The latter had extensive households of their own, apart from numerous armed retainers, and also employed numerous accountants and clerks to take care of the financial management. Hence, we arrive at the third false dichotomy, that between civic and military functions. Mughal administration was military in origin, and though in time it became more and more detached from military affairs, it very much retained its military features.[4] For example, every higher official had to be enrolled in the army list as he was given a *mansab*, or rank as the nominal commander of a certain number of horsemen, which determined his pay and status. But for these military rank-holders wielding the pen was considered at least as useful for military purposes as wielding the sword.[5] As visualised in that showpiece of Mughal administration, the *A'in-i Akbari*, it was this army of officials-cum-soldiers that served as the crucial middle ground between Mughal household and empire.[6]

Taking all these false distinctions, it would hardly make sense to write the military history of Mughal India purely on the basis of military aspects such as weaponry, strategy and tactics. These will be dealt with in the second part of this volume. For now, we should take account of the fact that warfare was not merely a matter of technology but, first and foremost, a matter of mentalities and organisation.

Ghazis and sadhus

Although a great deal of the Indian sub-continent is part of the Arid Zone, it was ecologically unable to sustain the kind of extensive pastoral nomadism characteristic of Central Asia or Iran. Although widespread in many areas, in terms of the range of movements as well as the quantity of flocks pastoral nomadism in India was comparatively limited, consisting of short-distance transhumance, mostly in combination with crop cultivation and permanent settlement. Between the pure forms of the full-time pastoral nomad and the fully settled peasant we find various mixed forms of occupancy; for example, we find both pastoralists and peasants engaged in long-distance trade and soldiering. Hence, although India could not sustain extensive forms of pastoral nomadism, a large part of its population was permanently on the move, be it as herders or as migrant workers, traders, pilgrims or mercenaries. In fact, well into the eighteenth century, the mobility of Arid India is not represented by tribes of pastoral nomads, but by wandering bands of warriors looking eagerly for employment on the huge Indian military labour market. Sometimes they were highly professionalised groups of mercenaries but, more usually, they combined soldiering with other means of living, like horse-trading or raiding. Even at the height of the empire, and even very close to the Mughal capitals, we find these roaming bands of freebooters both protecting and undermining the safety of the imperial routes and the production of the agrarian fields.

For the Mughals it was crucial to accommodate as many as possible of these migratory, armed bands, either by giving them a place in their own armies or by channelling their martial activities into areas beyond direct control. Indeed, in order to understand the logic of Mughal expansion, one should be aware that it was heavily governed by the constant urge to incorporate or canalise this enormous potential of irregular military power. Incorporation was facilitated by the booming Mughal economy, but in the case of lacking cash revenues, these groups often participated in official Mughal campaigns, taking their part of the booty or possessing revenue grants of countries still to be conquered. Hence, in many ways, the operations of the Mughal armies always retained certain elements of their *qazzaqi-ha*, i.e. their early days of wanderings and banditry. Indeed, through the refreshingly open memoirs of Babur, we get some idea of the outlook of these cossacks. Of course, the *Baburnama* is not entirely a work of the mawas, since Babur had always been a member of the well-established Timurid elite of Central Asia. Before coming to India, he had become the ruler of Kabul and, as such, should not be considered a free-floating ghazi without any settled interests. Nevertheless, his autobiography clearly depicts a different world to that in the more formalised accounts of the official panegyrics of his successors.[7] Especially during his various raiding campaigns into Hindustan, we get the typical picture of the wandering ghazi, fighting both Hindu and Muslim adversaries, and on the lookout for booty to be equally distributed among his friends and followers. In fact, booty was the most important ingredient that held the war-band together and opened up new vistas of political success. In other words, Babur's following consisted mostly of those who were true to the salt (*namak*), the marketable pay of the soldier.[8] Their true leader was the most talented warrior who maintained his position by distributing booty.

Not surprisingly at this early stage, the hierarchy within the Mughal army was not well developed, ranging from individual troopers or *yikitlar*, household troopers or *ichkilar*, to chiefs or *beglar*. To achieve the position of *beg* it seems that one had to mobilise a following consisting of kith and kin (*biradaran-u-khweshan*) and retainers (*naukaran*).[9] In fact, not kinship but the latter phenomenon of *naukari* appears to have been the most important ingredient for the social coherence of Babur's band. Naukar was originally a Mongolian word meaning retainer, comrade, a soldier in the service of a Mongolian clan he did not belong to by birth, a free warrior. Later in India it took the more general meaning of honourable service related to long-distance soldiering, also with strong ascetic overtones of leaving one's family behind in the village and the field.[10] Clearly, like Osman's group in the case of the Ottomans, Babur's war-band was not an ascriptive tribe but an open status group of various warriors and their families. Their camaraderie stemmed from a togetherness of deeds sealed in various plundering expeditions and raids. Prominent in the *Baburnama* are the many bouts of heavy drinking and taking of *majun*, which was a mild narcotic concoction made into a chewable pellet. All of these were casual, unpretentious and egalitarian social gatherings of Babur and the main chiefs. As well as the enjoyment of playing games, singing songs and composing poetry, these parties were full of unembarrassing emotional outbursts and physical contacts. At times, even sufi dervishes participated freely in them. Babur writes about one of his many wine parties:

> Darwesh Muhammad Sarban was there. Although he was a warrior and a soldier, he was abstinent and did not drink wine. Qutlugh Khwaja Kukaltash had long since given up soldiering and become a dervish. He was fairly old too and had a white beard. He was always a good drinker at these parties. I said to Darwesh Muhammad, 'Qutlugh Khwaja's beard shames you! He's a dervish and an old man with a snow-white beard, but he always drinks wine. You are a soldier and a warrior with a black beard, but you never drink. What's wrong?' Since it was not my habit to offer wine to someone who did not drink, this was just a joke. He was not offered any wine. The next morning we had a morning draught.[11]

Of course, drinking or drug-taking as such was not characteristic of the war-band. Babur's first experiments with alcohol started during his visit to the highly civilised court of his Timurid uncles in Herat. It is more the relaxed, egalitarian atmosphere of the drinking bouts that appears to be so typical of the war-band.

Apart from Babur's memoirs, a similar picture emerges from the contemporary, but often ignored, Indo-Afghan works, which once again stress the importance of togetherness, this time illustrated by the band enjoying shared meals. From these sources, one gets the impression that the most successful chief is he who has the best *langarkhana*, or public kitchen, from which each and every soldier may be lavishly fed.[12] Clearly, all these cases of shared consumption established a bond of comradeship and alliance and declining to attend such gatherings was an affront and a clear sign of dissociation.[13]

As seen already in Babur's anecdote, sufi saints could also be part of the ghazi band. In fact, we find various accounts describing how early sufi-warriors fought their way with other ghazis along the shifting frontiers of Islam.[14] During the more settled times of the Mughal Empire, we still find them in the midst of the armies. In the seventeenth century, for example, we come across the Naqshbandi saint Baba Palangposh who is reported to have used his spiritual force of *tawajjuh*, or concentration, also in religious sense, to bring luck to the battlefield. According to saintly lore, the Baba was generally believed to go before the advancing bands of the army, loosing his arrows along the way. Also, at the height of the battle each band used to see him fighting beside them. It appears that many soldiers were fanatic *murids*, or disciples, of such fighting saints as Baba Palangposh.[15] For example, we find war-bands consisting entirely of disciples venerating their commanders as *pirs*, or spiritual masters, such as the Mahdawis and Raushaniyyas, respectively the armed devotees of the would-be messiah Saiyid Muhammad of Jaunpur (d. 1505) and the 'divinely illuminated pir', Bayazid Ansari (d. 1573). At a later stage, these chiliastic connections continued to serve as major recruiting networks for the Mughal army. Looking at these sufi-warriors, we find once again that, in the open air of the military camp, the social distinctions between sufi and soldier were porous. Some who entered the sufi life in young adulthood had previously embarked on careers in the Mughal imperial service, usually as mounted soldiers. Vice versa, Mughal soldiers could choose the life of a dervish by selling their horses and effects or presenting them as an offering. It was one of the main achievements of Sher Shah Sur, the Afghan rival of Humayun, that he was able to convince a great number of his brethren to leave behind their lives as wandering mendicants and, instead, become his soldiers.[16] On various occasions, we find ulama as well as sufis sanctioning Sher Shah's sudden u-turns or broken promises, for example at the battle of Chausa and at the siege of Raisen.[17]

The Afghan sources further illustrate that, even during the heyday of their power, various Afghan tribes, including women, children and flocks, retained a great deal of their migratory habits.[18] But in contrast to most of their pastoralist fellows at home in Roh, in India their unit of movement shifted from the nomadic encampment or *da'ira* to that of the military camp or *urdu*. A similar transformation may be witnessed in the rapid careers of Afghan horse-dealers who turned into mercenary captains or *jamadars* and, with some luck, even carved out their own little kingdoms along the various inner frontiers of the sub-continent. These more settled Afghan dynasties often attempted in vain to base their polities on the solidarity and cohesion of the Afghan tribe (*qaum* or *ulus*). Hence they tried to build a new awareness of common descent (*nasab*), mainly by collecting and rearranging the widely scattered traditions of their tribe and by constructing new genealogies that could legitimise their newly won positions. Paradoxically, though, highlighting Afghan consanguinity also automatically implied the articulation of their common background as egalitarian warriors of the faith. Hence, while sponsoring a new Afghan Great Tradition, they continued to sit and dine together with their tribesmen, keeping up the roguish appearances of an idealised past.[19] In practice, of course, their option of tribal cohesion could only work as long as they remained true to the ethnically open recruitment of the mawas, where it was still possible to *become* an Afghan. Here, loyalties and identities were always shifting, mostly towards the winning side or the one which promised the biggest spoils. But at the time they started to construct a more rigid mould of Afghandom, it became increasingly difficult to find broad acceptance of their authority. Hence, although we find Afghans gaining power relatively easy, their pre-Mughal polities remained inherently unstable and extremely liable to fall apart at the death of the first ruler.

Interestingly, at the time Babur conquered India we see a similar dual tendency on his part of, on the one hand, distancing himself from the open and informal outlook of the war-band and, on the other hand, taking one of its imagined features as the central legitimising principle of the new empire. Babur's ideal was not the tribal cohesion of the Afghans but the solidarity of ghazis. As in the case of Afghan nasab, Mughal ghazidom was transformed into a highly idealised concept more suitable for settled kings. Having risen to become the new Padishah of Hindustan, Babur solemnly decided to let his beard grow and to give up his drinking habits.[20] He now took the title of Ghazi, this time not referring to the many lucrative razzias of the past but to celebrate his defeat of the Rajputs at the battle of Khanua (1527): 'for the sake of Islam I became a wanderer; I battled infidels and Hindus. I determined to become a martyr. Thank God I became a holy warrior.'[21] Paradoxically, though, at the time he composed this quatrain, he had become more settled than ever before in his restless life as a most successful leader of a war-band. Obviously, Babur's bearded, totally abstaining ghazi was a caricature. The eclectic ghazi of the mawas had turned into the devout ghazi of the *dar al-harb*, the juristically defined 'war zone' requiring jihad against infidels. Unfortunately, since Babur died three years after Khanua, we are kept in the dark about the consequences of this sudden transformation, but since the vast majority of his empire's population was not Muslim, Mughal ghazidom could hardly be the promising option it had proved to be for the Ottomans. As we will see, it was only under his grandson Akbar that the Mughals fully established a more workable compromise between the mentalities of the mobile war-band and the settled state.[22]

While the phenomenon of the ghazi war-band is clouded by the prevailing image of Islamic jihad, its Hindu counterpart is often misrepresented as a result of present-day tendencies to idealise the concept of *ahimsa*, or non-violence. Notwithstanding its popular image, mostly informed by Mahatma Gandhi and propagandists of neo-Hinduism, it appears that classical Hinduism even misses a tradition of anti-militarism.[23] This is also the general impression of those Sanskrit texts and inscriptions that refer to the earliest confrontations with Islam. Here, we find champions of Hindu dharma fighting the impure *mlecchas*, or barbarians, who cause all kinds of calamity by harassing Brahmans, by ending the recitation of the Vedas, by destroying temples, and so on. Obviously, in this context, fighting the Muslims becomes meritorious, although the category of mlecchas is not reserved for Muslims alone, but is used as an almost timeless category for all outsiders of the Brahman social order of *varnashrama-dharma*, mostly 'wild' people beyond the agrarian frontier. But this voice of confrontation is only one of many others that appear to be far more compliant. For example, Muslims are rarely described as *musulmanas*, but mostly with labels referring to their ethnic or geographical origin, such as Turushkas (Turks), Parasikas (Persians) or Yavanas (Greeks). At other instances, they are called *ashvapatis*, or 'lords of horses', which refers to their military skills as mounted archers. Other texts even manage to provide Muslim rulers with a Hindu past or myth, looking at them as the outcome of a long natural sequence of regional rule. Hence, as in the case of jihad, we find instances of irreconcilable hostility and religious toleration next to each other, their usage mostly depending on changing political and socio-economic circumstances.[24]

In our period, the most obvious counterpart of the ghazi war-band appears to be those armed groups of spurious Rajputs as described by Dirk Kolff. Being different from the settled Rajputs of western India, these were mobile, open-status groups like the war-band. Under vague ethnic or geographical labels such as Bundelas, Ujjainiyas or Purbiyas, they were well adapted to recruiting the tremendous numbers of armed peasants looking for military employment at the end of the agrarian season. Although under Mughal pressure, these mercenary bands of armed Rajputs were increasingly relegated to the jungly fringes of the Mughal realm, especially towards Bundelkhand and Rewa, their tradition of military service, of naukari, continued to play a crucial role in providing the Mughals with irregular but well-trained footsoldiers, their jobbing commanders becoming gradually absorbed as minor mansabdars in the Mughal army. For many of these Rajputs, the act of leaving their fields and families behind was also a religious expression of social dissociation, coming very near to the Hindu ideal of the world-renouncing sannyasi.[25] In practice, this form of part-time asceticism was accessible to all and sundry. Apart from offering splendid opportunities for enrichment, it was a way to achieve social improvement, in other words to become one day a Rajput with an honourable pedigree and with extensive rights over land. Of course, as in the case of the Afghans and Babur, achieving such an elevated status of agrarian lordship also required a new social and cultural outlook, in which there was hardly any place left for former ideals of mobility and asceticism.

Perhaps corresponding more to the mentality of the sufi-warrior is that of the Hindu armed ascetic, or *sadhu*.[26] Sects and groups of such armed sadhus first arose some time after the establishment of the Delhi sultanate, but became a significant political and military presence during the fifteenth century. From that time onwards we find a number of different sectarian groups, of which the Dasnami Nagas, or Gosains, and the Dadupanthi Nagas, the Vaishnava Bairagis and the Sikh Akalis are the most notable examples. All these groups were organised into *akharas* or regiments which, although starting as part of a religious order, gained prominence as mixed groups consisting of mercenary soldiers and bandits, as in the case of the ghazis and Rajputs, most conspicuously in the border areas of the Punjab, Rajasthan, Bengal and the Maratha territories. According to their own folklore, these akharas are certainly not represented as sacred fighters against Islam. More prominent are clashes with rival groups, of which Abul Fazl gives an interesting example:

> While he [Akbar] was encamped at Thanesar, a dispute arose among the Sannyasis which ended in bloodshed. The details of this are as follows. Near that town there is a tank which might be called a miniature sea. Formerly there was a wide plain there known as Khurket which the ascetics of India have reverenced from ancient times. Hindus from various parts of India visit it at stated times and distribute alms, and there is a great concourse. In this year before H.M.'s arrival, the crowd had gathered. There are two parties among the Sannyasis: one is called Kur, and the other Puri. A quarrel arose among these two about the place of sitting. The asceticism of most of these men arises from the world's having turned its back on them, and not from their having become cold-hearted to the world. Consequently they are continually distressed and are overcome of lust and wrath, and covetousness. The cause of the quarrel was that the Puri sect had a fixed place on the bank of the tank where they sat and spread the net of begging. The pilgrims from the various parts of India who came there to bathe in the tank used to give them alms. On that day the Kur faction had come there in a tyrannical way and taken the place of the Puris, and the latter were unable to maintain their position against them [see cover illustration].[27]

In most of our sources, the sadhus are generally disputing the policing of the great religious fairs and the collection of pilgrim dues.[28] As may be illustrated in this anecdote, Akbar's policy was not about suppressing such conflicts but rather about balancing and supervising them as a neutral arbitrator.

In various ways, the customs of sects of armed sadhus are reminiscent of those of the wandering bands of sufi-warriors. First of all, both recruited openly, irrespective of ethnic or social background. The sadhus adopted children as so-called *chelas*, or disciples, after which they lost their caste status. Both easily transmuted the ideal of devoted service to a spiritual master into that of dedicated military service to a charismatic warrior chief. The Sikh Guru Govind Ray provides the most dramatic instance of this development. At the Baisakhi festival of 1699, at the advent of the harvest, the Guru shocked his followers by demanding the heads of five loyal Sikhs. His insistent demand finally produced a volunteer who was led into a nearby tent. A thud was heard and the Guru, emerging with a blood-stained sword, called for the next head. After the fifth candidate, the Guru drew back the side of the tent, dramatically revealing five living Sikhs and five decapitated goats. The five were the *panj piare*, the 'cherished five', who had so convincingly demonstrated their total trust and loyalty. Thus, he instituted the ceremony of initiation or baptism called *pahul*. Apart from the five outer attributes of having uncut hair (*kes*), and wearing a wooden comb (*kangha*), a steel bangle (*kara*), a sword or dagger (*kirpan*) and a pair of short breeches (*kachh*), the new identity was publicly confirmed by adding the suffix Singh to the name of every consecrated Sikh warrior.

Although the Sikhs are famous for their valiant resistance against Mughal rule, some of the wiser emperors tried to incorporate them into the ranks of the army. For example, Aurangzeb's successor Bahadur Shah sought to conciliate them by making their leader the military commander of the Deccan.[29] Much later, after the Mutiny (1857), the British chose the same option, as the Sikh territories of the Punjab were turned into the army barracks of the Raj which, incidentally gave the Sikh ideology a new lease of life.

In other ways, the sadhu stood close to the sufi. Both subscribed to an eclectic image that was dreaded by the settled representatives of the more orthodox strands of Islam and Hinduism. Commensal rules, as well as prohibitions against the eating of meat and the taking of narcotics, seem to have often been ignored by the sadhus. In addition, they found no moral inconsistency in combining their asceticism with extensive business relations all over the sub-continent. Nevertheless, others were to criticise their various worldly engagements. Such criticism was poignantly voiced by the famous poet Kabir:

> Never have I seen such yogis, brother.
> They wander mindless and negligent,
> Proclaiming the way of Mahadeva.
> For this they are called great mahants.
> To markets and bazaars they bring their meditation,
> False siddhas, lovers of maya.

When did Dattatreya attack a fort?
When did Shukadeva join with gunners?
When did Narada fire a musket?
When did Vyasadeva sound a battle cry?
These make war, slow witted.
Are they ascetics or archers?
Become unattached, greed is their mind's resolve.
Wearing gold they shame their profession,
Collecting stallions and mares and
Acquiring villages they go about as tax collectors.[30]

Despite Kabir's criticism, though, the armed sadhus remained closely associated with the so-called Sant tradition, of which Kabir and also Guru Nanak were prominent exponents. From about 1400 this evolved into an important literary-cum-religious movement in northern India. As in sufism and bhakti, it was built on the spiritual devotion of a disciple to his master. It also openly expressed a disdain for Brahmanical knowledge and ritual, and it had an outspoken disregard for idols and images, as well as a dedication to egalitarian poetic verse, mostly in vernacular, full of fierce criticism of the existing caste hierarchy.[31]

The sants being a frontier phenomenon in the north of India, in the dry western parts of the Deccan and the Carnatic we find similar iconoclastic movements with a martial tradition. One example is the sect of Virashaivism, or the Lingayats, who again transgressed existing distinctions of caste and creed, and dissociated themselves from the Brahmanical values of ritual purity. Most of them being true nomads, they lacked a geographical point of reference, their only shrine being the emblem of the *linga* carried with them around the neck. This phallus served as the moving abode of Shiva. It was also a social leveller, enabling the wearer, theoretically at least, to achieve social equality with other Lingayats, despite the rank of the caste from which he had converted. All Lingayats had to adhere, however, to a *matha*, or monastic order, and had to have a guru.[32] In the same dry regions of the southern mawas, we find such highly eclectic folk deities as Khandoba, who was the family deity of the Holkars and the Gaikwads, two important branches of the Maratha gentry. He was venerated like a well-armed king, protected by Muslim guardians, dressed up like an Afghan horse warrior and adopted Muslim names, such as Mallu Khan or Ajmat Khan.[33]

Taking all these martial factions of armed sadhus together, it appears that their prime identity was closely related to the ideal of renunciation, *gosain* meaning 'in control of the senses', *bairagi* 'bereft of emotion', *sanniyasi* 'one who renounces', and *naga* 'naked'. Apparently, this culture of self-abnegation also served well to transform an individual recruit into an effective and unselfconscious member of a military regiment. Besides, the intense devotion to their spiritual masters allowed for violent sacrifices, not only as a reflection of their renunciation but also as a token of their intimate love for their guru. But beyond the intimate ranks of the akhara, the same ideals of renunciation made the armed sadhus notoriously 'faithless', 'unscrupulous' and 'selfish' as allies on the military labour market. Of one of their best-known chiefs, Himmat Bahadur, it was said that 'he was like a man crossing a river who kept a foot in two boats, ready to abandon the one that was sinking'.[34] But although they were not trusted on the battlefield, they served all the better as guerrilla soldiers, in surprise attacks and in man-to-man fighting. More importantly though, they were often eagerly enlisted because of their wide-ranging connections, thus giving access to a ready supply of well-trained troops and to intelligence from all over the sub-continent.

Mirzas and Rajputs

Many features of the vagrant life of ghazis and sadhus in the mawas lived on in the constantly moving camp of the Mughal army. However, ghazidom is only one aspect of India's military culture. Equally important were the values and expectations of the nobility, mostly settled in India's numerous cosmopolitan cities. Although many of these gentlemen warriors originated as spurious ghazis or Rajputs, at some stage they had acquired landed lordship that required more refined norms of comportment than the unpolished habits of the wilderness. Many of them began to consider themselves as mirzas. Initially mirza – from *mirzada*, or 'son of a prince' – had been a royal title of the Timurids, but gradually found a more general meaning as a gentleman of taste and culture, a manly person held in high public esteem. Thanks to two seventeenth-century manuals of conduct, one of them apparently a parody of the other, we can get an impression of the prevalent mentalities of these mirzas.[35] Although all of them were, one way or the other, tied to the imperial court, they also convey an independent, self-conscious outlook that appears representative of the middling Muslim nobility of the north-Indian cities. Of course, their sophisticated culture was nothing new, but part of a long-held tradition of Indo-Islamic urbane society. In the end, the Mughals could only absorb this culture into their own courtly society.

Who was entitled to call himself a mirza? First of all, the mirza should have a pure and well-known pedigree. Second, in the eyes of the people the mirza should have a position of dignity. Therefore, in the third place, he should have either capital or a considerable mansab. But apart from these basic prescriptions of descent and wealth, the character and temperament of a mirza are essential, as is his elegant and well-dressed appearance. Mirzas dread the rapid careers of *homines novi* who do not know how to behave as gentlemen. Being one of the latter involves knowing about *fiqh*, Islamic jurisprudence, and *tafsir*, Quranic exegesis, since 'an irreligious mirza is even more insignificant in the eyes of the accomplished ones than an impecunious mirza'. He should also study works of history and be well versed in poetry and literature. He should know how to write letters (*insha*) and to express himself properly. In addition to Persian, he should know Arabic, Hindustani and Turkish. In public, he should show restraint and not become prey to his passions. Hence, it is not proper to exhibit spontaneous emotions like singing or dancing. Drinking should be limited and done as much as possible at home. With friends, he should not join in circulating the bottle but keep to his own bottle. Even more so than drinking, eating and clothing are very much subject to complex rules of etiquette.[36] In sum, the picture that emerges is that of a refined, self-controlled, dandy-like mirza who knows about the rules of good society and good manners.

Taking a look at the martial requirements of the mirza, these appear to have been limited. For example, the mirza was not expected to use a matchlock musket, because the unpleasant smell of its fuse could reach his nose. At the same time, though, it was admitted that:

> A soldierly mirza is better than an unsoldierly one. He should not be inclined to enjoy watching marksmanship. On the day of battle he should not choose the ignominy of running away; at the time of action he should remain firm like a soldier, even though he be killed. One who claims to be a mirza welcomes such a death; for an honourable death is better than a dishonourable life.[37]

As appears from the parodied version of the other manual, this advice was the ideal; day to day reality looked different:

> He must value life and should not go near war. If he happens to be in a battle-field he must keep out of the reach of musket-balls. If victory takes place, he should not pursue the defeated and flying army; on the contrary if his party suffer a defeat, he must run away as fast as possible.[38]

Anyway, as we shall see in the next chapter, this latter picture compares well with the observations made by various European witnesses. It is also the impression produced by the manuals' other requirements: although the mirza should be an expert in judging horses, for travelling he should prefer the palanquin (*palki*) and not a horse or elephant, since there is always the risk of falling off. The latter danger is also the reason why one should not indulge excessively in hunting. Only during the rains, the mirza should prefer elephants, since with a horse or palanquin he would certainly become filthy.[39] But despite this gentle, but fairly unheroic, model, it was still very well possible that such mirzas would take high office in the Mughal army. For example, of one Itiqad Khan Mirza (d. 1671) it was said that 'he was of an independent disposition, of a careless nature, and a lover of comfort and pleasure [who] spent his life in a delightful manner and had a sufficiency of the means of enjoyment.' These characteristics could not prevent the mirza from becoming the Mir Bakhshi, or military paymaster and chief recruitment officer of the Mughal army.[40] It generally appears that the mirza was less ready to act in the front line of battles and sieges and more willing to join the administrative branches of the army.

All in all, the refined requirements of the mirza stand in sharp contrast to the rustic manners of the ghazi. In fact, the various liberties of the latter, such as drinking, joking, singing and dancing, were either suppressed or, at best, relegated to the private apartments of the mirza. For the Muslim warrior, ghazidom and mirzahood offered two paradigms of behaviour that represented the two sides of the frontier. The contrast between the two is not that of tradition versus modernity but that of war-band versus the sedentary household, and mawas versus ra'iyati. As we shall see in the next section, a somewhat similar distinction can be made between the spurious, mobile Rajputs mentioned before and the fully settled Rajput having extensive landed rights in his own *watan* or homeland. The fact that one of these Rajputs, Jai Singh Kachhwaha (d. 1667), received the title of Mirza-Raja may again remind us that, at least in the eyes of the Mughals, rajputness and mirzahood represented consonant models of excellence.[41]

According to Hindu Dharma, to wage war was a prescript for the ruling class of kings and warriors as embodied by the Kshatrya varna. The martial ethos of the Kshatrya is at least as old as the Indian epics of *Mahabharata* and *Ramayana*, but it appears that it experienced a marked revival during the eleventh and twelfth centuries,[42] probably in the wake of intensified processes of settlement and state formation in India's Arid Zone. From this time onwards, India, like Europe, was developing an assertive new aristocracy based on landed lordship. Although this process of gentrification was an all-Indian phenomenon, it is most clearly visible in the rise of the Rajputs in northern India and the Nayakas in southern India. For now, I shall concentrate on the first group, since the Rajputs became crucial elements in the Mughal army, in particular the Kachhwaha rajas of Amber–Jaipur and the Rathor rajas from Marwar–Jodhpur. The repeated emergence of new groups of Rajputs, i.e. 'sons of kings', reflects an ongoing process of rajputisation that involved the gradual transition of mobile, open, exogamous war-bands into settled, closed, endogamous castes who recognised little else than unilineal kinship. Those war-bands that had grown into local dynasties, particularly in Rajasthan, commissioned Brahmans or bardic pastoralists to construct a new Rajput Great Tradition, equipped with numerous heroic narratives and with fixed, but highly fictitious, genealogies. The past of the new Rajput dynasties was probably not much different from that of the spurious Rajput war-bands, as they were both mobile and open to various outsiders, but now this was strongly idealised and formalised.[43] In many ways, it was a pattern we have described already for the settling Afghans and Mughals, who also romanticised, and by this transformed, aspects of their tribal past as ghazis of the mawas. During the sixteenth and seventeenth centuries, Mughal patronage could only crystallise further the internal Rajput hierarchy, facilitating an even more codified construction of their history.

In many ways Rajput Great Tradition reproduced typical Kshatrya ideals, such as violent sacrifice and devotion. As we have seen already, both aspects had been present in the life of wandering war-bands of Rajputs and sadhus, albeit in the more pragmatic forms of raiding and military service. In the new situation, violent sacrifice was an idealised option in case the honour of the Rajput and his family was at stake. Apart from his physical prowess, the Rajput was primarily recognised by his position in the social hierarchy and by his landed rights. Time and again, we find descriptions of battles in which heroic acts become represented as acts of personal sacrifice. We see Rajputs immolate themselves in fire or deliberately seek death in battle, especially when faced with a particularly humiliating defeat. Well known is the suicidal rite of *jauhar*, in which the wives of Rajput soldiers shared their husbands' fate on the battlefield by having themselves burned to death at the stake. One of the last times this happened was in 1568 during Akbar's siege of Chitor, when the Sisodia chiefs burned their families to save them from dishonour in defeat. The Rajput's honour was closely related to marriage, which also represented his various relations outside his own kin or brotherhood (*bhaibandh*). Those who became his clients also gave their sister or daughter to their patron, often in exchange for land. More generally, to engage in connubial relations provided means of gaining access to land, rank and prestige, and made alliances more durable.[44] Rajputs, however, did not have a monopoly on jauhar, as there are various examples of Afghan and other Muslim chiefs whose wives and daughters were killed to prevent further humiliation after they themselves were killed or were to be killed in battle.[45]

The place where the Rajput's honour was communicated best was on the battlefield. Here, the Rajputs neatly followed the prescriptions of the Indian epics, where the worst thing that could happen to martial giants was to die at home, in bed with the ailments of old age, or to return from battle without wounds. As Krishna tells Arjuna in the *Mahabharata*: 'either slain you shall go to heaven, or victorious you shall enjoy the earth'.[46] In the same spirit, the Rajput ethos extolled man-to-man fighting, preferably on foot with a sword (the curved, one-edged *talvar* or the double-edged *khando*) or short spear (*barchhi*), whereas the more detached, cowardly means of mounted archery and gunpowder weapons were abhorred. *Pace* John Keegan, it appears that the ethic of the battle to the death on foot is not an exclusively Greek phenomenon.[47] Characteristic of the Rajputs' prowess in battle is the following anecdote given by Bada'uni of the battle of Samel (1544) between the Rao Malde Gangavat of Jodhpur and Sher Shah Sur:

> After striving to the utmost of their powers, when they had abandoned all hope of life, at the very moment when the army of Sher Shah came in sight, as a result of their own stupidity, by the good luck of Sher Shah or by the superior fortune of Islam, the infidels in a body dismounted from their horses, and renewing their vows and singleness of purpose and mutual assistance, binding their sashes together and joining hand to hand, attacked the army of the Afghans with their short spears, which they call Barchha, and with their swords. . . . [Sher Shah then] ordered the elephant troops to advance and trample them down. In the rear of the elephants, the artillery and archers gave them a taste of the bowstring. . . .[48]

Although such fighting on foot remained the norm, it was only used as a kind of ritualised self-destruction as a last resort. Most of the Rajputs in Mughal service appear to have been part of the heavy cavalry employing unrestrained shock tactics against the enemy. Usually, consuming lots of opium considerably enhanced their bravery.[49] According to the Jesuit priest Monserrate, their Muslim counterparts were not very much impressed by these doped Rajputs who certainly knew 'how to die, but not how to fight'.[50] Aurangzeb, in this case an unsuspected source, appears to have been more balanced in his judgement. In advice to his successor he contrasts the frequent Turani retreats from the battlefield:

> [with the] crass stupidity of the Hindustanis [i.e. most probably Rajputs] who could part with their heads but not leave their positions [in battle]. In every way, you should confer favour on this race, because on many occasions these men can do the necessary service, when no other race can.[51]

Sacrifice is also often presented as being the result of intensive devotion. According to the Rajput self-image, it was through devotion to his god or goddess that he had obtained the necessary power to conquer and to rule a kingdom. We find a similar exaltation about the Rajput's devoted service to his political overlord. For example, we find a very early tradition of so-called 'companions of honour', groups of servants or slaves who were associated with the persons of Indian monarchs to the death, often by voluntary self-immolation.[52] In Rajput tradition itself, service (*chakari*) to one's local patron or *thakur* was seen as a form of worship, expressed through acts of devotion and self-sacrifice, which involved both a willingness to support a superior and to offer one's life in battle on his behalf.

Clearly, the Rajput tradition of devotional sacrifice to one's patron was something to be cherished by the Mughals. Although increasingly self-conscious about their honour and descent, the Rajputs themselves found no trouble in seeing the more powerful Mughal warriors as a part of their own caste (*jati*). The Muslim emperor, in particular, held a position of high rank and esteem, at times even equated with the Hindu god Ram, the pre-eminent Kshatriya cultural hero of the Rajput. What basically distinguished the emperor from local Rajput rulers was simply his possession of greater sovereignty and power and his greater ability to grant favours and rewards. Within Hindu Rajput cultural conceptions, service to the Muslim emperor or one of his subordinates was thus not different from service to a local thakur. In exchange for his devoted service, the Rajput received rich rewards in cash and revenue rights.[53] Simultaneously, the Rajput notions of honour became more and more expressed in the ritual of the Mughal court. One can imagine that, under these circumstances, salvation through death became increasingly less attractive. In other words, the Rajput willingness to sacrifice his life became implemented only rarely and was more often negotiated against other means of acquiring honour, such as Mughal rank, money and landed rights.

Court society

It was mainly emperor Akbar who managed to bring together the differing mentalities of ghazis, sadhus, mirzas and Rajputs into the fabric of imperial service as expressed in ideology and ritual. In terms of ideology, there emerged a new dynastic cult that was designed to legitimise and propagate the newly gained power of the Mughal dynasty. This sovereign cult articulated Akbar's special Mongol and Timurid ancestry, as well as the divine sanction reflected in the Iranian notion of enlightened glory, or *farr*. Although more sophisticated than ever, this was done before and was consistent with the Turko-Persian standards of imperial rule.[54] The most interesting aspect of Akbar's sovereign cult was, however, not the tendency to emphasise the exclusive position of the Mughals, but its almost all-inclusive capacity to incorporate all those willing to serve them. It was this open, assimilative aspect of the Mughal ideology that built a strong group solidarity, similar to Ibn Khaldun's concept of *asabiya*. It even seems that Akbar or his ideologists fully understood the implications of Ibn Khaldun's other message that this asabiya was strongest in the mawas.[55] Anyway, it is striking that Akbar's imperial apparatus retained the pragmatic openness of the war-band, so cogently proclaimed in the imperial concept of sulh-i kull, peace with everyone, irrespective of ethnic, social or religious background. Within this free-for-all in which various talents could rival each other as in an open market, it was necessary to establish some kind of hierarchy, which should of course be highly flexible in order to accommodate outsiders and to reward excellence. Hence, there were no clear lines of command, not even in the military. One way some kind of hierarchy was established was by the means of an elaborate system of mansabs, i.e. a hierarchy not of command but of ranks to which we shall turn in the next chapter. Equally important, however, was the classification through ritual. Again, this was nothing new but only found new, amplified forms. All members of the imperial nobility or amirs were expected to visit the court regularly and undergo a ritual, which, through a complex gradation in gestures and presents gave expression to rank and honour.

One could assess the amir's dignity, mainly on the basis of two central criteria: proximity (*taqarrub*) to the emperor and, closely related to this, love (*mahabbat*) for the emperor. Both ideals find all kinds of other expressions: in the case of proximity one also finds intimacy or related expressions that show the king's generosity (*sakhawat*), magnanimity (*hilf*) or favour (*lutf*); in the case of love we find similar terms conveying devotion (*mawaddat*) or the closely related notion of friendship (*dosti*). Thus, in return for the love of his servant the king granted proximity, intimacy or, very possibly, his love.[56] These values should certainly not be confused with modern connotations of sentimental love or sexuality, but are more consonant with European medieval notions of, respectively, *familiaritas* or *fides*.[57] In Akbar's ideology, proximity was conveyed in the idea of *khanazadagi*, i.e. 'being son of the house', which entailed incorporation into the emperor's household. The highest standard of devotion was reached in Akbar's *din-i ilahi*, or divine faith, the spiritual tie between the emperor and his disciples. Of course, this came close to the relationship we have already described in the case of the sufi and the sadhu, but, as we have also seen, its political implementation was nothing new and rather typical for the war-band. In fact, the Safavids of Iran are the foremost example in this regard, as they started their political career as ghazi-like pirs. It was an achievement for Akbar that he transformed the virtues of the mawas into the highly formalised and ritualised ideals of sulh-i kull, khanazadagi and din-i ilahi. More than ideals of nasab or jihad, these eclectic, open and all-inclusive principles were the perfect building blocks for constructing Mughal asabiya.[58]

How did all this theorising look in practice? Of course, nearest to the emperor were those men who were born in his household, called *khanazadas*, the sons of the house or the house-born ones. First of all, these were the members of his close family, most notably his brothers and sons. In fact, they were so close to him as to become an ever-present threat to his authority. Hence, we find a whole range of wars and conflicts between the male members of the family, mostly contesting the succession of their father, who at times is still alive; an example is Shah Jahan being toppled by his son Aurangzeb during the latter's fight with his brothers. Next to the real family members are the emperor's so-called foster-brothers (*kokas*) or foster-mothers (*anagas*) and foster-fathers (*atagas*). These are the relations of the specially selected wet-nurses of the emperor.[59] Especially, their sons developed a special tie with the emperor because they had known each other as playmates and had shared the same milk; as Akbar said one of Aziz Koka Muhammad Khan Azam, the son of Jiji Anaga: 'there is a river of milk (*juy-i shir*) which cannot pass away'.[60] At times, the physical intimacy with the emperor brought them considerable political influence as, for example, in the case of Akbar's alleged nurse Maham Anaga and her son Adham Khan.[61] But, as with the emperor's own family, there was a great deal of envy among the members of the foster-family. Adham Khan, for example, was put to death by Akbar because he had killed Akbar's ataga Shams al-Din Muhammad Khan out of jealousy. His son, the already mentioned Aziz Koka Muhammad Khan Azam, was known to have become extremely envious of the exalted position of Abul Fazl.[62] As with many other kokas, his frank speech and passionate behaviour in public was often the cause of considerable embarrassment.[63] In general, however, the kokas, including their brothers and uncles, were considered loyal intimates of the emperor and, as such, rose to prominent positions in the army.[64]

Another way to become closely attached to the emperor's household was to bestow one's daughters on the imperial harem. This was the option chosen by most of the Rajput rajas of Rajasthan, especially those of the Kachhwahas of Amber and the Rathors of Marwar. As we have seen already, this was in entire agreement with their own customs and ideals but, perhaps more importantly, it strengthened their position at home. As in the case of Raja Bihara Mal of Amber, who became the father-in-law of Jahangir, it was his clear intention to 'emerge from the crowd of landowners and to be enrolled among the special intimates of the court, and so [he] expressed a desire that his daughter might enter the harem.'[65] In due course, next to the foreign elements such as Iranis and Turanis, the Rajputs became the mainstay of the Mughal army.

Khanazadagi referred not exclusively to members of the family, the foster-family or the in-laws, but to all who had actual residence in, or who had some connection with, the imperial court. According to John Richards and Douglas Streusand, it even came to have a much wider meaning of pride in hereditary imperial service alone, without the necessary impetus of an initial personal relationship with the emperor. As such, it permeated downwards to the middling and lower nobility.[66] Therefore, we find a whole range of titles, gestures and presents, which one way or another symbolise and classify the amir's nearness to the emperor and his incorporation in the household. Some of these are fairly obvious in their intention, for example the bestowing of kinship titles such as *baradar*, brother, or *farzand*, son. Also indicating a father–son relationship was the practice of escheat, carried out by both Akbar and Jahangir in regard to treasuries, mansions, armour, stables and other property of their deceased servants. At times, the emperor was expected to approve the marriages of his amirs or to give names to their newly born sons. An interesting example is given by the Italian traveller Manuzzi, restyled Nicolao Manucci, who reports of Aurangzeb's brother, Dara Shukoh, that, in order to get support from one Raja Rajrup, he allowed his wife to receive the raja in her apartments, and treat him as her son by offering him water to drink with which she had just washed her breasts, not having milk in them.[67] This kind of physical nearness was also the aim of gestures, by which the emperor selected amirs to join him in the private apartments or during dinner or private parties. It was considered very honourable to get access to the royal harem or, as in the case of one Barkhurdar, Jahangir's envoy to Iran, to be kept in the emperor's bedchamber and be bestowed with his own blankets.[68] Sometimes, such privileges could lead to extreme forms of personal devotion, as in the case of Shah Quli Khan who castrated himself after Akbar had taken him inside the palace and into the harem. In gratitude Akbar bestowed upon him the title of *mahram* or confidant.[69] Indeed, as may be witnessed by the presence of various eunuchs in the more intimate apartments of the court, castration was a well-trodden path into the imperial household.

More generally speaking, in Mughal India power relationships were indicated by the image of near and far, in and out, or movement in either direction, less so by the modern western metaphor of up–down and front–back.[70] In the same spirit, physical contact was an act of political attachment and incorporation. Gestures such as the emperor approaching the amir, or laying his hand on the amir's back, or even embracing him, were all signals of the amir's special ties to the emperor's household. It appears that even emotional outbursts like weeping were part and parcel of the staged, courtly protocol and an expression of special favour. Weeping mostly occurred during official farewells, such as in the case of the leaving of Khan Jahan Lodi. He was a prominent and intimate amir of Jahangir who had repeatedly taken him into the female apartments and treated him 'as a friend'. In 1609 the Khan was sent to the Deccan and, at the time of his departure, the king descended from the public and private balcony and placed his own turban on the Khan's head, took his hand and set him on his horse. An order was also issued that, as he went, he should beat his drums. On one side the king and on the other side Khan Jahan indulged in 'unrestrained weeping' on account of the impending separation.[71]

Obviously such favours of tears and grief were reserved for the highest and most intimate nobles of the court, but there were other ways in which imperial incorporation could be achieved for almost every single serving amir of the empire. This was the almost routine bestowal of *khilats*, or dresses of honour, by the emperor upon his amirs, hence the importance attached to the public wardrobe. In principle, the khilats had been worn by the emperor himself and, therefore, their acceptance symbolised the incorporation of the amir into the body of the emperor who incarnated the empire. As dramatically expressed by F.W. Buckler, the amirs became the *membra corporis regis*, in other words, participants and sharers in the body politic.[72] Another example of routine submission was the practice of bowing, in which the amir offered his body to the emperor. Every amir who presented himself to the emperor was honoured by executing one or more *taslims*, which involved laying the palm of the hand on the ground, raising it gently till standing erect, then laying the palm of the hand on the top of the head.[73] In fact, the taslim was a poor substitute for the *sijda* or *zaminbos,* which involved full prostration. Since this was considered against Islamic prescription, Akbar banned the sijda from public audiences but continued the practice in his private apartments. It appears that the latter allowed such indulgences, as well as a more spontaneous and casual conduct, which were not allowed any more in public.[74]

Again, all these staged gestures and presents conveyed proximity to and intimacy with the emperor or his household. They also expressed a clear political message. Those who became near to the emperor could only submit to him; anything else was considered outright rebellion. Two examples may illustrate this point. The messages of courtly ritual were most difficult when communicating with foreign powers that had their own autonomous claims to sovereignty. This was certainly the experience of prince Aurangzeb during the Balkh campaign in 1647. Shah Jahan had ordered him to deliver Balkh and Badakhshan to the Uzbek ruler, 'that descendent of Chinggis Khan', Nazr Muhammad Khan, provided the latter agreed to have an interview with Aurangzeb in which the two regions would be conferred on him. As the Uzbek ruler knew that such an interview would mean submission to the Mughals, he preferred to keep some distance, the more so because the Mughal army was in dire straits and had to leave before the winter snows blocked the southern passes. In order to speed up Nazr Muhammad's approach to Balkh, Aurangzeb accepted almost all the Uzbek conditions. On his part, while tarrying in the direction of Balkh, Nazr Muhammad threw up all kinds of new demands, which were all eagerly accepted by Aurangzeb. When the meeting was at last arranged, Nazr Muhammad failed to be present as he had fallen victim to a sudden ailment. Instead, he sent his son who Aurangzeb folded in a fond embrace, a gesture which, in the case of Nazr Muhammad himself, would have clearly symbolised Uzbek submission to the Mughals. But, since the winter was close at hand, grain scarce and time short, Aurangzeb had no other choice than to leave Balkh and deliver it to Nazr Muhammad in his absence.[75]

Another example of failed incorporation is the treatment of the famous Maratha leader Shivaji, again by Aurangzeb. After protracted negotiation with Aurangzeb's general Jai Singh, Shivaji had finally decided to submit to Aurangzeb in the expectation that he would be restored to the emperor's favour. But on his arrival at court something went terribly wrong. Shivaji was brought forward in audience and duly offered 1,000 gold mohurs and 2,000 silver rupees as *nazr*, or tribute, to the emperor. The latter, however, neither spoke to him nor acknowledged his presence. Shivaji was then made to stand with relatively low-ranked nobles at some distance from the throne. Failing to become nearer to Aurangzeb, he made a scene, refused the emperor's khilat and stalked out of the audience hall. Thanks to bribes, Shivaji was only captured and not killed. While negotiations about his rank and honour dragged on, he decided to escape. As Stewart Gordon rightly stresses, it is hard to overestimate the opportunity that the Mughal Empire lost at this point of conciliating one of the major powers of the sub-continent.[76] Perhaps more than any military shortcomings, it was Aurangzeb's failure to ritually incorporate the Maratha leader that engendered the decline of empire at the end of his reign. Meanwhile, Aurangzeb himself had embraced the settled, exclusive version of ghazidom which rationalised this failed attempt to assimilate the Maratha 'infidels'.

The Mughal ritual and idiom of incorporation and submission were reminiscent of the pir-murid relationship in sufism.[77] For example, the sijda and the khilat, in sufi jargon the *khirqa*, were well known to sufi practice. But the whole concept of coming nearer to one's master through different stages of love and devotion is a common theme. Not surprisingly, during his early reign, Akbar showed a great deal of interest in the Chishti order, which, in various ways, he tried to incorporate in the imperial fold. But perhaps inspired by the Safavid example, he decided to start a kind of imperial sufi order of his own. This din-i ilahi was meant for those amirs whose devotional service to Akbar required them to give up their life (*jan*), property (*mal*), religion (*din*) and honour (*namus*), for which in return they received Akbar's seal and portrait (*shast wa shaba*).[78] Although only a few amirs actually became disciples of Akbar, the general way of expressing one's loyalty and service to the emperor became very much influenced by the sufi idiom of love and devotion, even, in the emperor's absence, by seeking his proximity in their dreams.[79] Even the slaves in the imperial households changed their names from *bandas*, slaves, to *chelas*, meaning disciples as used in the Hindu mystical idiom of bhakti.[80]

The idiom of love was, however, not exclusively reserved for those looking for spiritual guidance from the emperor but was a most striking element in all relations of the court, between the emperor and his amirs and also among the amirs themselves seeking 'affectionate companions' and 'caring friends' who could help in one's daily struggle to survive.[81] These networks of *amici* helped the amirs through the many insecurities in the life of an amir. This kind of social networking was a source of increase in 'prestige and exhilaration', the more so since fidelity and faithfulness were rare. As Muhammad Baqir, one of the leading amirs under Jahangir, expressed it: 'expecting people to keep their word is like joining the star Canopus with the Pleiades. To hope for faithfulness from the people is akin to planting a rose shrub in the fire of a furnace.'[82] According to the same amir, love was considered to be of two kinds: first, spontaneous love and friendship with complete, intense desire and absolute sincerity, and lacking any semblance of self-interest or hypocrisy; and, second, the temporary affection for worldly power and wealth.[83] That the second was the more usual appears in his advice that one should acquire wealth since 'a person without money is without friends', and with wealth 'one could achieve any level of ascendancy in this world'. Moreover, money means honour since 'every quality for which the wealthy are admired and praised evokes condemnation and ridicule in the case of the impoverished'.[84] It should, however, not be saved but generously spent on one's friends and intimates. As another source has it: 'to win hearts one must lavish gold freely'.[85]

Money was also a kind of insurance against the dangerous aspects of love, in particular the love of the emperor. Although being near to the emperor was an important favour and gave political influence and standing, it was also extremely dangerous. Of Aurangzeb it was said that 'through this policy of affection he continues to destroy'.[86] Muhammad Baqir also admitted that imperial service was perilous and demanding, since rulers should be compared to 'lofty mountains, although there be in it a mine of precious gems, it is arduous to pass over and difficult to stay atop'.[87] He added that, whoever is closer to fire is more exposed to danger.[88] Other sources confirm the anxiety of being in the imperial service.[89] Every amir knew that he was constantly being screened, not only by the emperor but also by all the other amirs who were jealously taking stock of each other's latest ranking, as expressed in the daily ritual at court.[90] For example, rulers themselves were known to organise various games in which their servants could be tested.

> Outwardly they keep them in playful mood, but in reality they are testing them. It is therefore essential for courtiers, both while at work and in play, never to ignore the rules of respect and obedience, and a close study of the dispositions of their superiors, who are easily offended, must be regarded as a matter of paramount importance in all dealings.[91]

To get an impression of someone's character was also one of the prime functions of the extensive intelligence department of the emperor. It was considered his duty to keep track of amirs' 'sincerity, discernment, judgment and prudence' in order to better benefit from their services and to patronise them according to their talents.[92] As a result, most amirs were kept 'between fear and hope, caught between promises and evasions and between apprehension and expectation'.[93] Clearly, there was no social security; there were many drop-outs and many burn-outs. He who rode high today could be cast down tomorrow. Or as Baqir expressed it, 'closeness to rulers lacks permanence. Every action is followed by inaction and prosperity by adversity'.[94] Hence, for the amirs to survive it was extremely important to know what was going on in and outside court, what were the latest rumours, who was who and who was with whom, and how to read gestures and faces (*firasat*), etc.[95] Obviously, all this could only be achieved through extensive networks of influential and wealthy lovers and friends. Finally, it should be stressed that the emperor himself could never be sure about his own position, since there were numerous rivals who could topple him if he neglected his own networks or the rules of etiquette and ritual. Being part of a system in which the rules were known but the future was highly insecure because of the ever-shifting circumstances, he should not be considered an oriental despot but, as expressed in the various rituals of incorporation, merely the prime shareholder of the realm dependant on the willing cooperation of the other co-sharers.

All in all, although surrounded by the love of the emperor and one's friends, life at court was not peaceful. Amirs pressurised each other, as 'job-hunters and seekers after advancement'.[96] They struggled for prestige, for their place in the hierarchy. The affairs, intrigues, conflicts over the proximity to and affection of the emperor knew no end and caused a lot of anxiety. In a way, this may remind us of what Norbert Elias has described as the 'courtisation of warriors' (*Verhöflichung der Krieger*) by the *ancien-régime* courts of Europe. This implied that warriors were disarmed and coerced into courtly behaviour.[97] This taming of the warrior's passion is indeed also one of the characteristics of the Mughal court. To some extent, courtly ritual replaced the battlefield as the locus of conflict. As honour and wealth became increasingly attached to imperial service, it was the court where amirs sought means of improvement and enrichment. It was also thanks to the court that the emperor could manage the empire through conflict. Perhaps even more important, through the means of a highly eclectic ideology and of standardised ritual, the Mughals could build a kind of corporate identity prescribing uniform standards of conduct. Crucial for understanding their success in incorporating the major powers of the sub-continent was the openness and pliability of the Mughal system, which enabled them to respond to the values of a wide range of different groups. In this chapter we have highlighted the refined world of mirzas and Rajputs expecting the enhancement of honour and lordship in their respective regions. More than any other group, these became fully integrated into the imperial system through marriages, revenue grants and presents. Meanwhile, through extended patronage, the Mughals had set a new standard of Persianite high culture, which sprang from and appealed to the tastes and talents of the mirza.[98] In due course, the honour of both Rajputs and mirzas was expressed in their imperial rank.

What about the expectations of the members of the war-band, the ghazi and the sadhu? Some were assimilated, many others continued to be outside the empire. Of course, those who were integrated in the system lost a great deal of their mawas temperament as they gained lordship over land, as for example the Afghans in Rohilkhand or the Sikhs in the Punjab. But what is even more important, the Mughals adopted the war-band's system of the open, conscriptive household, pragmatically ruled by merit and power. That they also adopted the equally open principles of khanazadagi and din-i ilahi is another indication of their ongoing liability to the mawas. In the end, it was the openness of sulh-i kull that had made the incorporation of so many different groups possible.

This brings us back to the frontier. As stressed already in the first chapter, the Mughal Empire never became a fully settled polity. For the Mughals it was imperative to have their feet on both sides of the frontier. As stressed in this chapter, this internal duality is also reflected in their ideology and ritual, which continued to refer to the ways of the mawas but formalised and standardised them to make them suitable for the more settled parts of the empire. In the next chapter, I shall turn to the actual manpower of the Mughal army, its organisation in theory and its operation in practice. As I hope to demonstrate, the latter was again well adapted to rallying the forces on both sides of the frontier.

Plate 3 Seven recruits from Haryana. This drawing by William Fraser (*c.* 1815) identifies three Rajput Muslims, two Brahmans, one Gujar and one unidentified 'Sada', but, according to Fraser, they are 'now all troopers'. It illustrates the integrating capacity of the multi-ethnic military labour market in Mughal India (see also M. Archer and T. Falk (1989), p.4).

Source: *BL:OIOC, Skinner Album,* Add. Or. 1262, no.4

CHAPTER THREE

The military labour market

The Mughal Empire evolved out of Babur's nomadic war-band. As we have seen in the previous two chapters, the Mughals never made the transition into a fully settled Indian state, as they remained dedicated to the mawas and the outlook of the nomadic camp. This chapter will highlight yet another phenomenon that precluded them from fully putting down roots. To put it more positively, the ephemeral, pragmatic and meritocratic world of the Central Asian war-band lingered on in the highly competitive Indian military labour market.[1] To a large extent, Mughal power hinged on its capacity to exploit this enormous market by mustering a maximum number of what Joseph Fletcher called 'surrogate nomads', in other words, highly talented, movable warlords and their mounted following.[2] For about two centuries, the Mughals successfully managed to seduce these people with imperial ranks (mansabs) into becoming dedicated co-sharers in their realm and taking part in its prodigious wealth in cash and land.

Supply

In a peculiar way the Indian military labour market was like a seller's market. This was not the result of any scarcity of supply but it followed from the strategic need, on the part of the Mughal state – by far the single largest, but far from being the only employer of military labour on the sub-continent – to incorporate, in one way or another, a large portion of the total supply into the army. Abul Fazl himself expressed it without too much ceremony as: 'the number of men brought before His Majesty [for service] depends on the number of men available'.[3] Here supply determined demand to the extent that the Mughal state could not afford to leave the bulk of military labourers to competing employers or, equally inadvisably, to let them start their own military enterprise and, as it were, to create their own demand. In other words, the prime challenge of the Mughals was to link the Indian military labour market to the Mughal apparatus of empire. It was a challenge indeed, since this labour market consisted of a sheer mass of warriors, ranging from the highly professional warlord or jamadar to the part-time armed peasant looking for mere subsistence. As a consequence, mustering soldiers alone never raised any problems. As Manucci observed, 'a thousand at a time will attend to take service, and of these the best are chosen'.[4] It was far more difficult, though, to bring some kind of order to these enormous numbers of labourers and to keep them in check. But before going into the details of Mughal military organisation, let me first draw a more general picture of the composition of military supply itself.

Generally speaking, the military labour market consisted of two broad interacting segments of supply. At one end, one finds those groups that had no vested stakes in land. Many of them were immigrants from Turan (Central Asia), Iran or Roh (Afghanistan), often but not necessarily with a nomadic background. These tribal groups were highly mobile war-bands offering their temporary military service to the highest bidder. For the Mughals it was of crucial importance to recruit the chiefs of these floating war-bands, the jamadars, and to incorporate them into their army. Following their enlistment, the Mughals retained the inherent mobility of these chiefs by upgrading them into a readily summoned military service elite of mansabdars, or rank-holders. Although channelled by the imperial imperative, the jamadar turned mansabdar could hold on to many of his old habits. For example, he continued to recruit his own retainers, often from his own homeland. He also kept relying on the familiar ways of mounted warfare, further stimulated by a moving Mughal court and frequent hunting expeditions. Of course, many jamadars remained even more autonomous, often developing into condottiere-like entrepreneurs. These independent mercenary captains are an almost permanent phenomenon of the Indian military market but they became particularly prominent at the earliest and latest stages of the Mughal Empire, at those times when the real value of mansab was still, or had become, too insecure.

At the other end of the Indian military labour market stood the representative of the Indian gentry, the so-called zamindar and his following of a few mounted retainers, often light cavalry, but mainly comprising armed peasants, artisans and other local folk with a more restricted radius of action. In contrast to the mobile jamadar, the zamindar was strongly rooted in local Indian society. Hence, his readiness for distant imperial service was much more limited. But as with the jamadar, the empire could not do without the cooperation of the zamindar as the chief mediator between the court and the village. Hence, as with the jamadars, the Mughals attempted to co-opt the zamindars into the mansabdari system. Concomitantly, it was hoped that mansabdari service would stimulate them to widen their perspective beyond their local background. In the long run, however, Mughal hopes proved futile as more and more zamindars managed to become mansabdars without abandoning any of their local ties, or to put it differently, mansab increasingly became an instrument of zamindari instead of imperial policy. At the same time, an increasing number of mansabdars, of all backgrounds, tended to trade their military assets for stakes in settled agrarian lordships, thus becoming zamindari landlords themselves. Starting from the second half of the seventeenth century, this zamindarisation or gentrification, as some have called it, of the military apparatus engendered the long-drawn-out crisis of empire that continued into the eighteenth century. Paradoxically, imperial decline naturally followed from the earlier successful incorporation of the military labour market into the military structure of empire. In the end, the empire succumbed to its own success.

The supply side of the military labour market is usually understood as comprising ethnic or caste groups of which the Turanis, Iranis, Afghans, Rajputs and Marathas were the most significant.[5] These labels should not be considered as rigid, ascriptive categories indicating inbred loyalty or cohesion. For example, during the numerous succession struggles of the empire, these groups never closed ranks against each other. In fact, political coalitions generally cut across these lines, and the promises made by each prince to individual warlords, or the personal associations of warlords with individual princes, were the chief factors determining their formation. Likewise, looking at the racial fabric of their military contingents, there was a great deal of intermixture, Rajputs serving Afghans and Muslims serving Hindus, etc.[6] More significant than definitions of race or caste was the fact that the real building blocks of the military labour market consisted of the chief's or warlord's household, which, apart from his military retainers, contained his own extended family and numerous personal servants, ranging from accountants to sweepers.[7] In addition, the household often served as the centre of an extensive network of patronage of relatives and friends, either near to home or spread all over the country. Hence, a Turani warlord often commanded a network that was most likely, but not necessarily, connected to Central Asia. To a large extent, this determined the Turani label. But this should not distract us from the fact that even such recognisable Turani households were mostly highly assigned categories, in which one could become a Turani by joining a Turani chief or warlord. Actually, all retainers, whatever their ethnic or caste origin, were loyal to the one 'whose salt they ate'. Here, the patron's salt (namak) that 'nourished the flesh and skin' of the servant, represented, as it were, the marketable pay of the soldier.[8] This may illustrate once again the pragmatic nature of military recruitment. As we have seen, this had already been the case among the nomadic war-bands of Central Asia and, as such, was not much different from the situation in the Indian military labour market. The difference between the two was only one of degree, to the extent that the monetary incentives for joining or leaving someone's company, in particular mansabs, were far more exciting in India than in Central Asia. Given the lack of any automatic tribal cohesion, Mughal policy to enlist warlords from different ethnic backgrounds was less instigated by the need to divide and rule than by their willingness to exploit as many recruitment networks as possible from all over India and, preferably, from beyond the sub-continent, where the best-trained and most reliable warriors, mounted on the best-bred horses were to be found.

All this does not mean that distinctions of race or caste were entirely irrelevant. They did reflect a mixture of market-oriented prejudice and image-building, which at times gave rise to some sort of common group behaviour, generating, as it were, a fair degree of recognisable product differentiation. For example, Turanis were generally seen, but by the Iranis in particular, as somewhat uncultured, rustic men of the sword and experts in military tasks such as making charges, raids, night attacks and arrests. Most significant, of course, was their nomadic record as well-trained horsemen and archers. Aurangzeb himself considered the Turanis superior to the Rajputs:

> [The Turanis] felt no suspicion, despair or shame when commanded to make a retreat in the very midst of a fight, which means, in other words, 'drawing the arrow back'; and they are a hundred stages remote from the crass stupidity of the Hindustanis, who could part with their heads but not leave their position [in battle].[9]

Thus the emperor preferred Turani discipline to Rajput bravery. In contrast to the disciplined Turanis, Iranis were considered as more civilised men of the pen, to be used as excellent administrators and accountants, also being far more 'cunning' and 'ease-loving' than the Turanis.[10] All this made the Iranis far from being unfit for military service as this required military talent as well as a great deal of administrative acumen. Hence, it appears that Iranis were hardly less involved in purely military functions than the Turanis. The prime asset of both foreign groups was the fact that they served extremely well as a kind of deracinated military elite detached from local society. At the same time, though, both were known for their vanity and self-esteem, which could become extremely dangerous when they were not sufficiently flattered as grand nobles of the state. The Iranis, for example, often confronted the Mughals with the rather embarrassing fact that both Babur and Humayun had heavily relied on Safavid support against their erstwhile Uzbek and Afghan enemies. Only after Akbar's dismissal of his Irani regent Bairam Khan in 1560 and the promulgation of the so-called infallibility decree (*mahzar*) in 1579, did the Mughals begin to free themselves from their inferiority complex vis-à-vis their former Irani overlords. Nevertheless, the successful invasions of Nadir Shah and Ahmad Shah Durrani during the mid-eighteenth century once again reminded the Mughals of this old Persian claim of suzerainty.[11]

While the self-esteem of the Iranis was primarily based on these early memories of Safavid patronage, as well as on their ascribed skills in courtly etiquette, good manners, poetry and literature, Turani pride was vested in a relatively egalitarian political style that attached great value to autonomy and the right to share in the spoils and conquests of their Mughal patron, the latter merely being the first among equals. In addition, many Turani warlords were proud of being descendants of either Chinggis Khan or Amir Timur. Being Turanis themselves, the Mughals found it extremely difficult to cope with the self-conscious behaviour of their Turani 'brothers'. In 1564 Akbar was faced with a major uprising of some of his early Turani followers, who revolted against his increasingly autocratic tendencies, also finding common cause with Akbar's half-brother and imperial shareholder at Kabul, Mirza Muhammad Hakim. The leaders of the revolt were Shaibani Uzbeks who were straight, paternal descendants of Chinggis Khan, whereas Akbar could only boast direct descent form Amir Timur, having just a maternal connection to Chinggis Khan. Almost simultaneously, a group of Timurid nobles bearing the title of Mirza also rose against Akbar. Its leader was descended from Amir Timur's second, most favoured son Jahangir, Akbar merely springing from Timur's third son Miranshah. Although Akbar crushed these revolts, they certainly may have made the Mughals wary of recruiting Turanis on a massive scale.[12]

Apart from the Turanis and the Iranis, the Afghans were the third important source of foreign recruits. They had a somewhat ambivalent market reputation. On the one hand, they were known as rather uncivilised but ferocious fighters, on the other hand, they were notorious for their unfaithfulness and their proclivity to defect. The Afghan hero Sher Shah Sur was a reputedly gifted spoil-sport who knew 'all kinds of machinations, deception, duplicity and stratagem which are never treated as forbidden in war and . . . he knew how to begin the fight and how to conclude it.' One such example was his behaviour at the battle of Chausa (1539) when Sher Shah and Humayun had agreed that they would fight each other only for show: the Afghans were to vacate the ford of the local river (the Karamnasa) in order to allow Humayun to cross and make a show of pursuing the Afghans by two or three stages before retracing his steps. The Afghans won the battle, though, as Sher Shah suddenly changed his mind and attacked scattered Mughal troops by complete surprise.[13] But despite this kind of unfaithfulness, more than any other tribe Afghans were also known to feel a certain loyalty for their brethren, especially when the latter were in the camp of the enemy. Be that as it may, their preference for employing men from their own ethnic background was considered exceptional. According to an apocryphal tradition, Shah Tahmasp of Iran had advised Humayun to recruit Rajputs instead of Afghans because he would never be able to win the latter's friendship.[14] As in the case of the Iranis and Turanis, the Afghan tendency to go their own way was partly the consequence of their prestigious past. Long before the arrival of the Mughals, the Lodi and Sur Afghans had established their credentials as perfectly able sovereigns of Hindustan. Although early Mughal propaganda attempted to ridicule the Afghan antecedents of Mughal rule, even after the fall of the Sur state at the second battle of Panipat in 1556, the Afghans remained an ever-present threat to Mughal rule, not only from Afghanistan proper, but primarily from their little kingdoms in eastern Bengal and Orissa and, to a lesser extent, from their numerous power centres in the sultanates of the Deccan. From all these places, the Afghans kept dreaming of an Afghan *risorgimento*. In 1629–30, Khan Jahan Lodi, one of the most trusted Afghan nobles of the Mughal Empire, generated a new renaissance of Afghan culture and, once again, attempted to rally Afghan support against their eternal Mughal adversaries. Obviously, on their part, the Mughals were extremely reluctant to incorporate a large number of such obstreperous Afghan warlords, the more so because their Indian past made them relatively well connected to local society.[15]

Although confronted with all these various uprisings, the Mughal emperors continued to rely on their foreign warlords, together comprising about half of the rank-holding nobility of the empire, the Iranis being its largest, the Afghans its smallest segment. It should be kept in mind, though, that an increasing number of these so-called foreign mansabdars were born in India, only their parents or even grandparents having actually immigrated from Turan, Iran or Roh. This trend of Indianisation increased during the second half of the seventeenth century, which saw a new influx into the imperial service of well-assimilated Afghans, Iranis and a handful of Habshis from the Deccan.[16] But even in their policy to recruit an increasing number of Indian warlords, the Mughals always showed a certain preference for military men without roots in Indian soil. Many of the Indo-Muslim mansabdars belonged to the group of so-called *shaikhzadas*, i.e. the true or claimed descendants of sufi-saints such as the well-known Shaikh Salim (d. 1571) of the Chishti order, or Muhammad Ghauth (d. after 1635) of the Shattari order.[17] Before they became settled as Mughal nobels, many of them had lived as itinerant dervishes, such as the prominent Akbari amir, Shahbaz Khan Kamboh, who claimed to be a descendant of the famous Makhdum Baha'uddin Zakaria of Multan.[18] These sufi-warlords could exploit the extensive religious networks of their orders as well as the exceptional devotion of their disciples. The Saiyid Abul Fath and Rashid Khan Ansari, leading figures of, respectively, the Mahdawi and Raushaniyya sects, are two other such cases in point where warlords built their military careers on their religious connections and charisma.[19] Again, as with the foreign mansabdars, the shaikhzadas could not be deterred from gaining settled holdings in land, as may be witnessed in the quintessential example of the Saiyids of Barha, who became big landlords in the upper doab region between the Ganges and the Yamuna and even rose to imperial fame as powerful king-makers during the early eighteenth century.

Highlighting such inbred tendencies of zamindarisation and Indianisation brings us automatically to the zamindari segment of the military labour market. First of all, the most noteworthy group of zamindari warlords were the Rajput princes from the most arid western parts of the sub-continent, who formed about fifteen per cent of the Mughal nobility. Some of the most prominent generals of the empire originated from the families of these relatively small landlords, such as the Khachhwahas from Amber or the Rathors from Marwar. As we have seen in the previous chapter, after they had negotiated their entry into the imperial elite, they offered their daughters as marriage partners for the Mughal emperor. Like the foreign warlords, the Rajput chiefs obtained employment for their kinsmen as well as non-kin retainers and organised them into cavalry contingents, armed and equipped for active military service. In exchange, the Mughals turned their ancestral lands into non-transferable holdings, the estimated revenues of which were offset against their assigned salaries. Under Mughal patronage, Kachhwaha chiefs like Man Singh (1592–1614) and Mirza Raja Jai Singh (1625–67) or the Rathor chief Jaswant Singh (1638–78) built impressive careers as imperial mansabdars, amassing enormous riches along the way, often to be invested in huge building projects in or beyond their homelands.[20] Although their marketable image was one of complete self-sacrifice and devotion to their master, in day-to-day practice the Rajput attitude was often embarrassingly rational. In fact, their political behaviour had much in common with the image of zamindari commanders in general: highly unreliable, prone to endless negotiations with the enemy, and always keeping a hidden agenda of their own.[21] In fact, heroic Rajput generals like Man Singh and Jaswant Singh proved to be excellent political arithmeticians comfortably waiting to see which way the wind would blow during the succession struggles of, respectively, Khusrau against Jahangir in 1605 and Aurangzeb against Dara Shukoh in 1658–9. Likewise, Jai Singh's campaign into the Deccan in 1665 was hardly remarkable from the purely military point of view, but was highly impressive in terms of diplomacy and intrigue. Besides, not unlike the Uzbek Turanis or the Lodi Afghans, the Rajputs played their part in the warlord's resistance against Mughal centralisation. Their rebellion in Marwar and Mewar against Aurangzeb in 1678, continuing well into the 1680s, is the best-known example of their growing assertiveness as regional zamindars of Rajasthan.

Apart from the Rajputs there were many other local zamindars who made it into the imperial nobility, such as the Ujjainiya chiefs Narayan Mal and Rudra Pratap or the Bundela chiefs Bir Singh Deo and Jujhar Singh.[22] Like the Rajputs, they primarily aimed at expanding their existing landholdings or converting them into officially acknowledged, hereditary holdings (*watan-jagirs*). Many of these petty zamindars built their careers on tapping into the enormous supply of armed people all over the Indian sub-continent. The extent to which Indian society was an armed society may be gathered from the many travel accounts that speak of a countryside that was 'protected' by a multitude of armed bands and studded with little forts or fortified temples.[23] Whether peasant, artisan or trader, it appears that almost every Indian male had some kind of experience with arms and combat, either as a part- or full-time soldier. As mentioned already, the state authorities had no monopoly whatsoever on the use of violence. Even very near to the imperial centres, daily agrarian routine could not do without an almost permanent armed alertness, as in the case of the village Malkusah near Agra: 'no one there, whether peasant or soldier, goes without weapons so that even the cultivator at the time of ploughing has his loaded gun fastened to the plough, and his match burning'.[24]

Another indication of the enormous military potential of the Indian countryside may be provided by the *A'in-i Akbari*, which gives the number of zamindari retainers for each district.[25] This imperial inventory from the end of the sixteenth century gives the modern historian some insight into the lower echelons of the military labour market. The sheer quantity is staggering. According to its author Abul Fazl, there were more than 4.4 million people with a military qualification in the Mughal Empire. The figures are supposed to represent the local militia and not the troops enlisted by the mansabdars, although there may have been considerable overlap between the two. Obviously, the Mughals could not come anywhere near to engaging, whether directly or indirectly, such masses of armed people. Table 3.1 shows the figures for each province of the empire.

Table 3.1 Zamindari retainers according to *A'in-i Akbari* (*c.* 1595)

Province (Suba)	*Horsemen* (Sawar) *Number*	*%*	*Foot soldiers* (Piyada) *Number*	*%*	*Total numbers*	*Horsemen as % of suba total*
Bengal/Orissa	23,330	6	801,150	19	824,480	3
Bihar	11,415	3	449,350	11	460,765	2
Allahabad	11,375	3	237,870	6	249,245	5
Awadh	7,640	2	168,250	4	175,890	4
Agra	50,681	13	577,570	14	628,251	8
Malwa	29,668	8	470,361	11	500,029	6
Gujarat	12,440	3	61,100	1	73,540	17
Ajmer	86,500	22	347,000	8	433,500	20
Delhi	31,490	8	242,310	6	273,800	12
Lahore	54,480	14	426,086	10	480,566	11
Multan	18,785	5	165,650	4	184,435	10
Kabul	46,954	12	330,360	8	377,314	12
– sarkar Kashmir	*4,892*	*1*	*92,400*	*2*	*97,292*	*1*
– sarkar Qandahar	*13,875*	*4*	*25,260*	*1*	*39,135*	*35*
– sarkar Kabul	*28,187*	*7*	*212,700*	*5*	*240,887*	*11*
Total	384,758		4,277,057		4,661,815	8

If we consider the horsemen only, the western provinces are most eye-catching, obviously because these areas were the most conducive to breeding and keeping warhorses. But apart from the northwestern concentration, it is also striking to find most cavalry forces based around the major imperial capitals, such as Lahore, Delhi and Agra. The highest figure, though, is given for Ajmer, primarily representing the various Rajput principalities. Most probably, in all these provinces we could also find the main Indian centres of recruitment for the mounted contingents of the mansabdars.

Looking at the total figures, thus including the much higher numbers of foot soldiers, then we get an altogether different picture, especially if we relate the numbers of zamindari retainers to the assessed revenue (*jama*) and to the size (in *bigha*) of the measured areas (*arazi*). As worked out in Table 3.2, this gives us some idea of the military density of each province.

Now it shows that the largest military density is to be found in those areas that were not closely administered, or in areas where the chiefs were allowed a semi-tributary status.[26] Bihar and Malwa come out as provinces with the highest military density, obviously representing a big potential for both military recruitment and armed revolt. Not surprisingly, these provinces are exactly those areas that are so prominent in Kolff's study of the military labour market. Here we come across the numerous networks of those so-called spurious Rajputs, such as the Ujjainiyas, Bundelas, and Baghalas who recruited the bulk of their manpower from the Purbiya areas, i.e. the Awadhi and Bhojpuri Hindi-speaking areas of present-day eastern Uttar Pradesh and western Bihar. They established their political power, however, in the more peripheral areas of eastern Malwa, Bundelkhand and Rewa, all along the northern foothills of the Vindhya Range and into the dense forests of Gondwana.

Table 3.2 Density of zamindari retainers according to *A'in-i Akbari* (*c.*1595)

Province (Suba)	*Jama per soldier* (*in* dam)	*Measured area per soldier* (*in* bigha)
Bengal/Orissa	726	–
Bihar	482	5
Allahabad	852	16
Awadh	1,147	58
Agra	869	44
Malwa	481	9
Gujarat	5,975	230
Ajmer	665	78
Delhi	2,197	59
Lahore	1,164	34
Multan	1,180	17
Kabul	–	–

South of the Vindhya Range, this belt of relatively high military density stretched along the Satpura and Satmala hills into the dry eastern slopes of the Western Ghats. Here one entered just another zone of military entrepreneurship, this time dominated by the Maratha zamindars, or *deshmukhs*, of the western Deccan, who supplied most of the military manpower to the sultanates of Khandesh, Burhanpur and Bijapur.[27]

As we have seen in Chapter 1, the Maratha landlords, or deshmukhs, had built their power on the Mavals, the frontier zone between the rich

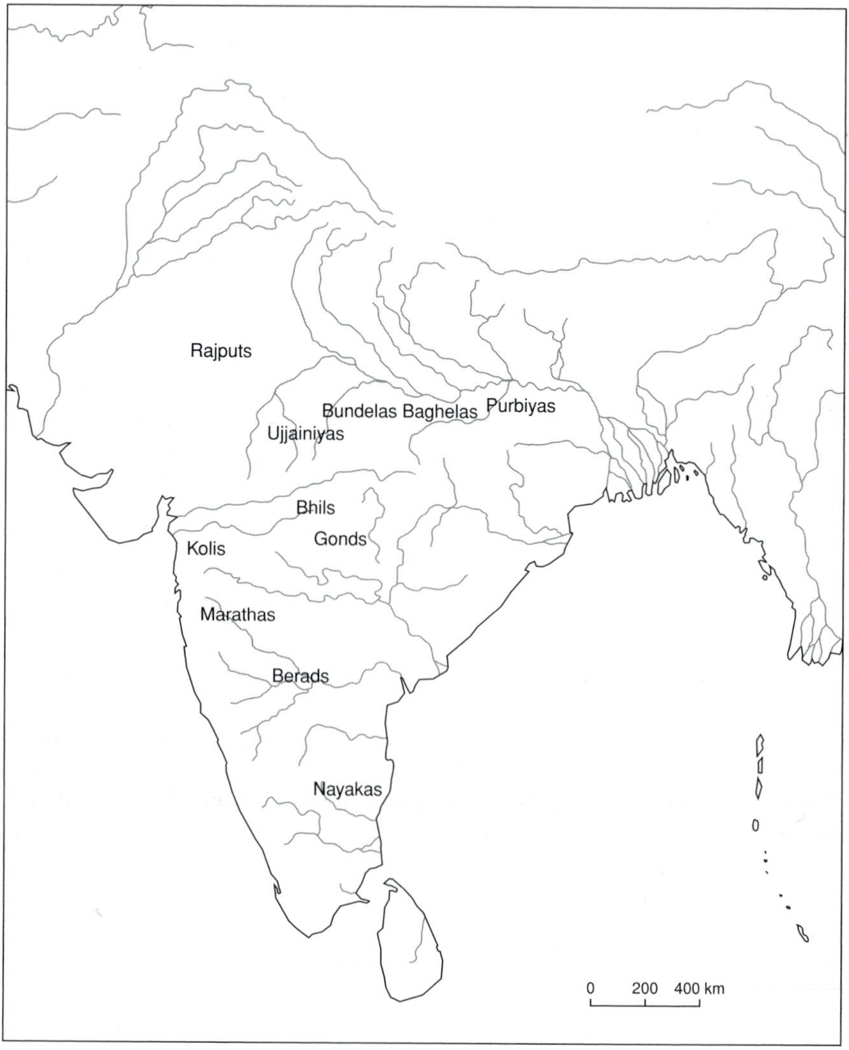

Map 3.1 Mughal India: zones of zamindari military entrepreneurship

and fertile coastal areas of the Konkan and the dry savannahs of the Deccan plateau. Although clearly beyond the coverage of Abul Fazl, the latter was another area of high military density, emphatically claimed, not so much by an armed peasantry, but by bands of militarised nomad herdsmen, such as the Kolis, the Bhils and the Gonds. One of these groups was the Berads who became well known for their excellent musketry. They had started as a forest-based community of savage marauders from the western hills, who raided villages and carried off cattle and women. In due course, these Purbiyas of the south, as we may call them, settled down, establishing small principalities of their own, such as the one in Sagar at the confluence of the Bhima and the Krishna rivers. Probably in a bid to enlist them into the imperial army, Aurangzeb presented the leading Berad chiefs with mansabs, which could not, however, prevent them from cooperating with the Marathas and from persisting in their old habits of 'ravaging villages and waylaying caravans'. One of their chiefs, Parya (or Pidia) Naik, had entrenched himself at his hill fort of Wagangira from where he collected about 15,000 foot soldiers and 5,000 horsemen. Khafi Khan sums up the usual procedure of bringing local chiefs such as Parya Naik into the Mughal fold:

> Whenever an army was sent against him, he relied upon the forces which he had collected, the fortification of his stronghold, the influence of the money spent in bribery, for he had become aware of the ways and methods of the Imperial Court and had become audacious. By sending bags of *huns* and jewels, he used to close the doors of negotiation and used to mention himself among the taxpayers (*malguzar*) and loyal zamindars.[28]

It was Parya Naik's bad luck, however, that his little kingdom was relatively close to the imperial camp. As a result, he sadly overplayed his cards and, after a long and bloody siege, escaped, but not without surrendering the fort to Aurangzeb in 1705.[29]

For many modern historians, the Mughal campaigns into the Deccan overstretched the empire and brought about its ruin in the eighteenth century. The gravest charges are against Aurangzeb who, because of his supposed bigotry or parsimoniousness, failed to assimilate the Marathas as Akbar had assimilated the Rajputs.[30] Another line of thinking accuses him of exactly the opposite. In his eagerness to annex the southern kingdoms, Aurangzeb lavishly awarded high positions in the imperial service to all those Deccani warlords who were willing enough to defect. This not only exhausted the limited resources of the empire but also estranged the long-established mansabdars, because they heavily lost much of their salary assignments to the southern newcomers. This caused widespread conflict and demoralised the established Mughal nobility.[31] Although this is not the place to resolve the issue, it may be helpful to zoom in briefly on three exemplary cases of Mughal recruitment in the Deccan.

First of all, it is clear that the initial success of Mughal conquest hinged on their capacity to entice the Deccani warlords away from their Adilshahi (Bijapur) and Qutbshahi (Golkonda) patrons, in particular by offering them exciting salaries, both in cash and *jagirs*, the latter being assignments of land revenue. The showpiece of this policy was Aurangzeb's enlistment of Golkonda's major warlord, the Irani entrepreneur Muhammad Saiyid Ardistani. This Indian Wallenstein was one of those typical great jamadars who combined military enterprise with all kinds of commercial interests such as diamond mining, shipbuilding and overseas trade. Apparently, he had started as a horse-trader in the early 1620s but had risen to chief minister of the Golkonda sultanate in 1638, later receiving the title of Mir Jumla for which he is best known in the history books.[32] Under his leadership, Golkonda annexed large parts of the Carnatic, which further contributed to his personal status and wealth. In 1655, he defected to the Mughals. This move won him high rank, and he even became the wazir of the empire. He contributed tremendously to Aurangzeb's early success in the Deccan and was of crucial assistance during the latter's succession struggle against his brothers. From 1660 to his death in 1663, he was sent to the highly lucrative province of Bengal, where he staged large-scale military expeditions into the eastern parts of that province as well as into Assam. Mir Jumla's main asset was his well-paid and very disciplined army, equipped with European-trained light artillery. According to the Dutch account of one P[ieter] v[an] d[en] B[roeck], Mir Jumla had enlisted fourteen to sixteen German soldiers and sailors who had served the Dutch East India Company at Pulicat. They introduced German order and discipline and the European art of making all kinds of trenches, bastions and batteries (*aprocheeren, loopgraven, trencheen, katten en bataryen*).[33] Apart from his military expertise, Mir Jumla was equally important because his Deccani connections made him the perfect medium for intrigue at the Deccani courts, or as Jadunath Sarkar puts it, 'he knew the exact prices of all the chief officers in Golkonda and Bijapur'.[34]

Mir Jumla's defection is the major success story of Aurangzeb's expansion in the Deccan. What appears to be crucial is the Irani warlord's preparedness to shift with his entire establishment to the north, ready to do active military service in a province far away from his original holdings in the Carnatic. His readiness to move and to be moved made Mir Jumla the ideal mansabdar. He proved, however, the exception to the rule that most Deccani mansabdars focused attention on the consolidation and expansion of their regional settlements in the south. This zamindari attitude may best be illustrated by the Afghan Panni and Miyana warlords who, after exchanging Adilshahi for Mughal employ, went on to establish their zamindari power in the southern Deccan, often in close cooperation with the Marathas. In 1682, Da'ud Khan Panni moved into Mughal service and, under the patronage of the powerful Irani general Zulfiqar Khan, laid the foundations for the nearly autonomous principality of Arcot, later to be ruled by the nawabs of the Nawayat and Walajah dynasties. His brother, Ibrahim Khan, took a more permanent hold of Qamarnagar, or Kurnool. Similarly, the Miyana Afghans who, under the leadership of Abdul Karim Khan alias Bahlul Khan, had been the leading commanders of the Adilshahi army, shifted into Mughal service, just to carve out their own zamindari holdings in Savanur and Cuddapah. Thus, the establishment of a string of little Afghan kingdoms in the southern Deccan was an unanticipated but important side effect of the Deccan conquests.[35]

Apart from about sixty Muslim warlords from the Deccan, the Mughals enrolled almost a hundred Maratha chiefs, who were the core of the Bijapuri forces, mainly in the lower ranks of the mansabdari system. Most of them were regional deshmukhs who enlisted out of enmity towards each other or were just driven by expediency. The Maratha share of the total number of mansabdars increased from a mere 5.5 per cent at the beginning, to about 16.7 per cent at the end of Aurangzeb's reign.[36] This open policy put a strain on the imperial resources and forced Aurangzeb to restrict admissions and to reduce salaries. Here we may recognise the two opposing lines of thinking of the modern historians mentioned above. Perhaps more striking than the changing degree of Mughal openness is the phenomenon that more and more Maratha warlords were not interested any longer in joining the Mughal service. Shivaji is of course the best-known example of this, but most of his Maratha colleagues were already well entrenched as deshmukhs in hill forts that could be rather well defended against Mughal cavalry.[37] Besides, Mughal cavalry could not isolate the Maratha strongholds from their fertile hinterlands in the Konkan since its humid climate proved equally as detrimental to cavalry logistics as that of the higher Mavals. Hence, from the beginning of the Deccan campaigns, the strategic position of the Marathas had been different from that of the Rajput princes. Equally significant was the fact that, following their earlier careers as military warlords of the sultanates of Ahmadnagar and Bijapur, the Marathas had already taken firm zamindari roots in the area. As the most powerful landlords of the western Deccan, they were not as keen as Mir Jumla had been to risk their territorial possessions in the south for an insecure future in any remote corner of the empire. In other words, for the Mughals the critical situation in the Deccan was not far removed from the one they had faced in Hindustan at the time they began their campaigns into the south. As we have hinted at already, the northern territories also witnessed a growing assertiveness on the part of the zamindars. At the end of the seventeenth century, zamindari revolts became more frequent. Although this was partly a reflection of zamindari dissatisfaction with the increasing imperial pressure on their agrarian resources, whether or not following the expansion of the mansabdari organisation, the revolts were first and foremost another demonstration of the increasing zamindari share in the land revenue.[38] More and more powerful zamindars made it increasingly difficult for constantly moving mansabdars to realise the salaries from their far-off assignments. As the actual collection of assigned salaries could not be assured, Mughal service gradually lost a great deal of its earlier appeal, both in the Deccan as well as in Hindustan.[39] During the eighteenth century, not the mansabdari but the zamindari status had definitively become the most attractive option for any ambitious warlord in the county. At that stage, the Mughals could only reconcile themselves to the changed situation by increasing the zamindari share of the imperial army, obviously to the cost of the more pliable, foreign mansabdari segment.

The zamindarisation and Indianisation of the Mughal army is somewhat reminiscent of what the Ottoman historian Halil Inalcik has called the *levendisation.* This followed the Celali peasant revolts during the second half of the sixteenth century, when groups of disbanded infantry soldiers, or *sekbans* – originating from the *levends*, the landless vagrant peasants of Anatolia – roamed the Anatolian countryside on the lookout for plunder and ransacked its towns and villages. These wandering companies of paid infantry soldiers contributed significantly to the decentralisation of the Ottoman Empire, as they were the principal source on which local men could and did build their military strength in the seventeenth and eighteenth centuries. According to Inalcik, levendisation was the result of the fact that, due to the growing need for a soldiery with firearms in the Central European battlefields, peasants had invaded the military institution and replaced the foreign slave segment.[40] Levendisation and zamindarisation appear to have many elements in common. In both cases, the companies of armed peasants play a prominent part in bringing about the disintegration of the empire. On the other hand, it should be stressed that levendisation as such hardly deviates from the normal situation of the Indian military labour market, which had always been packed with itinerant companies of peasant-soldiers eager to find suitable employment, or in case of need, to plunder. In the case of Mughal India, the increasing unrest during the second half of the seventeenth century was merely the result of a shifting balance in favour of the zamindars vis-à-vis the Mughal emperor and his mansabdars. In many ways, this was the natural outcome of the fact that a pre-modern state such as that of the Mughals could not but cooperate with the local elite of zamindars who traded their local knowledge and control of the land revenue against ever increasing levels of autonomy. Anyway, zamindarisation was certainly not a consequence of the introduction of handguns. If there was a relationship at all, it appears it was rather the other way round, zamindarisation giving rise to increasing infantry warfare. But, before engaging the issues of military technology more thoroughly in Chapters 4 and 5, we first have to ask ourselves how the Mughals came to terms with zamindari power at all. How did they ever manage to build and sustain their power in the midst of a military labour market with more than four million armed labourers? Abul Fazl knew part of the answer as he opened his explanation of the mansabdari organisation with the remarkable piece of wisdom that: 'if that which is numerous be not pervaded by a principle of harmony, the dust of disturbances will not settle down and the troubles of lawlessness will not cease to rise'.[41] It is to this 'principle of harmony' that we shall turn in the next section.

Army organisation

All conquerors establishing large empires, in particular those surrounding the Central Asian steppes, in this period the Ottomans in the Middle East, the Safavids in Iran, the Mughal in India and the Manchus in China, were faced with the problem of how to transform their efficient but relatively small war-bands that had made the conquests into the much larger imperial armies that could sustain them. The Manchus, for example, had recourse to the so-called banner organisation, with which they rearranged the tribal composition of the military elites into large units, or banners, that combined military and administrative functions commanded by chiefs who remained very close to the imperial household. By shuffling tribal groups into mixed military contingents, old tribal loyalties were superseded by loyalty to the new military units. The Manchu banner system appears not too far removed from Timur's use of the *tümen*, which originally referred to a large military formation but later also became a term signifying an administrative region. Apparently, both echo the Central Asian tradition of distributing spoils and conquests, i.e. territories and peoples, among the followers of the war-band. In the succeeding Turko-Persian empires of Ottomans, Safavids and Mughals the situation was somewhat different. Here the conquerors were confronted by a more or less well-established revenue system based on the so-called *iqta*. Every holder of an iqta had the right to collect the revenue of an assigned piece of land in exchange for certain military or administrative services. In principle, it was not about the equal division of conquests, as had been the case of the tümen, but involved, at least in theory, conditional and temporary rights to accurately assessed revenue proceeds. Anyway, the iqta system enabled the rulers to keep some sort of remote control by sophisticating and individualising the exploitation and redistribution of the agrarian resources. As a result, the Turko-Persian armies were organised to match the iqta system, in which each military unit, be it the great warlord or the individual horseman, received the proceeds from an earmarked territory.

But despite the sophistication of the iqta system, Ottoman, Safavid and Mughal armies retained the dual structure of the war-band consisting, on the one hand, of an inner circle of relatives and personal retainers who were companions and friends (*nököd*; sing. *nökör*), and, on the other hand, of numerous tribal allies whose loyalty was more conditional on the success of the leader.[42] Despite the repeated attempts to co-opt the leaders of the second group into the inner circle, for example by stretching the idiom of kinship or by the *nöködisation* of the tribal fighting forces (see Chapter 2), the dual structure remained visible in the distinction between the troops of the imperial household and the 'tribal' or 'provincial' levies of enlisted warlords-cum-officials. The Ottoman army, for example, consisted mainly of tribal elements supported by *timar* land grants, the Ottoman version of the iqta. These timariot troops were a seasonally mobilised, provincial cavalry that complemented the sultan's standing and cash-paid army of so-called *kapu kulu*, the 'servitors of the gate', or household troops. These comprised free cavalry regiments as well as janissary units of military slaves, the latter being primarily infantry.[43] Like the Ottomans, the Safavids maintained a royal bodyguard of *qurchis* – Mongolian for archers – along with the more autonomous units consisting of Turkoman, Kurd, Chaghatai and other tribal allies. Some of these allies developed into the so-called Qizilbash contingent, a tribe that was considered particularly close to the imperial household and from which most qurchis were recruited. The latter were paid directly from the imperial treasury, while the tribal leaders received more or less permanent *tiyuls,* the Safavid version of the iqta. At a later stage, during the rule of Shah Abbas (1587–1629), the household segment of the Safavid army was widened to include a group of military slaves. Both these *ghulams* and the qurchis represented the standing army of the Safavids but, as in the case of the Ottomans, the majority of the imperial armies remained tribal levies.[44]

In the Mughal case the war-band dual structure is clearly recognisable in Babur's distinction between his house corps of so-called *yikitlar* and his tribal allies of *ichkilar* and *beglar.* To create some kind of hierarchy within the tribal corps, an early difference was made between the tribal beglar and the somewhat inferior, intermediate position of the ichkilar. In practice, it was somewhat more complicated, as there were Baburi and Andijan Begs as well as so-called *mehman* Begs, or 'Guest Begs': those Begs who had already enjoyed the status of Beg under various Timurid and Mongol rulers before joining Babur. Later, the personal unit of yikitlar lived on in Akbar's standing army of a few thousand *ahadis* who were equipped with several horses and had a reputation for being excellent archers.[45] These gentlemen-at-arms, as Moreland calls them, were single men (from *ahad*, one) having no following of mounted retainers themselves.[46] Apart from the ahadis, the household troops of the Mughals were composed of large numbers of *ahsham*: all sorts of rag-tag foot-retainers (*piyadagan*) comprising clerks, runners, gate keepers, palace guards, couriers, swordsmen, wrestlers, slaves and palanquin bearers, etc. These included infantry consisting of a few thousand musketeers (*banduqchis*) commanded by 'captains of ten' (*mir-dahs*). In addition, there was the important elephant establishment as well as the imperial stables for warhorses and animals for transport. Last but not least, the artillery was also part of the imperial household, as was the case in the Ottoman and Safavid armies.[47]

Strikingly missing in the household segment of the Mughal army was a substantial number of military slaves. Military slavery had been an important element during the early Delhi sultanate, but began to disappear again during the fourteenth century. And although Akbar held a few chelas – those household slaves that were relabelled as disciples – these should not be confused with the mamluk phenomenon of janissaries or ghulams. The chelas were only few in number and had no regular military function.[48] One European observer refers to a unit of 4,000 slaves, but he probably mixes them up with the so-called *walashahis*, the most trusted bodyguard of the emperor and often associated with the ahadi contingent.[49] Indeed, for any European observer, the precise difference between slaves and free retainers must have been rather obscure. For example, the ascribed practice of escheat, i.e. the royal claim to the entire inheritance of the imperial servants, must have reminded many of them of straightforward slavery. As we have seen already, much of the phraseology of imperial service concerned that of 'slaves' devotedly serving their master. But although the legal differences with slavery should not be overestimated, all this remained a matter of mere rhetoric and style belonging to what was, in principle, a form of free military service, whereas the real thing remained a Safavid and Ottoman phenomenon.

How can we explain this striking Mughal exception of what seems to be the rule within the Turko-Persian ecumene? In Chapter 2, I referred to the significance of Akbar's courtly culture. Here I can only repeat that concepts of khanazadagi and din-i ilahi may have served as attractive alternatives to that of military slavery. Recently, Kolff and I have suggested that the institution of military slavery was drowned, so to speak, in the huge military labour market that was India. Slave identity tended to mutate and to assume features that were vaguely defined, merging into other, more permanent categories.[50] But, referring to the highly volatile conditions of the military labour market, one could equally argue that slavery could serve as an excellent antidote to prevailing tendencies of defection and sedition. Perhaps more important than the fluid characteristic of the Indian military labour market is its gravitational force. In other words, why have recourse to such an expensive and burdensome institution as slavery when there already existed a substantial flow of foreign military immigrants into India? Similar to slaves, these foreign warriors could also serve as an excellent deracinated elite without any local attachments. Decisive in this respect was the Mughal capacity to attract and to enlist these foreigners into their army, mainly through offering them substantial shares in Indian wealth, as ostentatiously epitomised in mansab.

Coming back to the Mughal army's organisation, apart from a few thousand household troops under the personal command of the emperor, the bulk of the Mughal army was under the command of a few hundred great mansabdars or amirs who recruited a total number of between 100,000 and 200,000 mounted retainers. Hence, the main job of recruitment was delegated to a military elite, which was partly financed in cash through the imperial treasury but mainly through the assignment of *jagirs*, the Indian version of the iqta. Here we should once again stress that the mansabdars not only served as military commanders but also represented the ruling class of the empire at large. As a consequence, to become a mansabdar not only required military talent but also, and more importantly, political, administrative and economic skills.

How could one become a mansabdar? In practice, every candidate for mansab needed the political and, as we shall see, financial backing of an already influential, high-ranking patron at court. The latter introduced the candidate and proposed a rank to the emperor, sometimes through the Mir Bakhshi, the main recruitment officer. After a personal assessment in public audience by the emperor, who was reportedly able to see 'through men at the first glance', the candidate received a fitting mansab to be followed by a lengthy bureaucratic procedure of registration and confirmation. Invested with dignity and nobility, the new mansabdar was now responsible for the enrolment and the equipment of a number of mounted retainers in accordance with his rank, mostly to be paid from jagirs for which he entered into another elaborate selection procedure involving another set of rules controlled by different officials. Thus an important element of the mansabdar's quality was his function as a kind of military employment agency. For each and every mansabdar it was crucial to command extensive networks of patronage and other connections involving both the court and potential sources of recruitment, either in their homelands or elsewhere. The more extensive the mansabdar's network, the more important it was for the emperor to enlist him, the higher his price on the military labour market and the higher his mansab. From this angle, the well-known rivalry between factions of Turanis and Iranis does not primarily reflect ethnic antagonism, but rather a form of market competition between two rival employment agencies eagerly looking for imperial contracts and commissions. From the Mughal point of view, bestowing mansab could hardly be restricted to purely military criteria of strategy or tactics, as it primarily ensued from the need to link the most important recruitment networks to the court.

Under Akbar the mansabdari system started off as a rather effective, practically oriented ranking system. From its early beginnings, roughly between 1573 and 1596, it aimed at incorporating free warlords into the Mughal army by 1) fitting them into a flexible imperial hierarchy, 2) granting them cost-based salaries, and 3) promoting the military strength of their contingents.[51]

Later it evolved into a highly formalised scheme indicating inflated ranks, accounted salaries and paper armies, which, however, hardly made it less effective as an attractive instrument of recruitment.

From its very beginning, the mansabdari system took the form of a decimal ranking system that was reminiscent of, but not identical to, that of the Central Asian tümen, the latter referring, at least in principle, to units of 10,000 men to be further broken up into smaller units of 1,000, 100 and 10. Although mansab created a hierarchy of amirs that was linked to the emperor at its apex, it was certainly not a hierarchy of military command. In fact, the Mughals dispensed with a clear command structure as this was to be determined by the emperor as the commander-in-chief for each and every military operation. Mansab indicated, however, the degree to which its holder stood in the emperor's favour. As such, mansab was an accurately calibrated kind of honour, to be conveniently raised and reduced by the emperor pending the almost permanent assessment of the mansabdar's performance. Coming to its second purpose, mansab also aimed at ending the arbitrariness of past recruitment when, according to Abul Fazl, 'honour was bartered for silver and gold'.[52] From now on, mansabdars were supposed to receive rank and salaries in accordance with the real number of mounted retainers offered for imperial service. Of course, this required a sophisticated system of inspection, monitoring and auditing. For this purpose, Akbar revived the system of horse branding (*dagh*), which had already been in use during the Delhi Sultanate. Apart from registering the horse's breed, colour and marks on its body, etc., each and every horseman was also described in rolls (*chehra*), which laid down his name, father's name, tribe or caste, place of origin, complexion, features, any identification marks, stature and age.[53]

But, as the degree of the mansabdar's honour could vary with his real military stature, one single rank could hardly meet both criteria at the same time. This was even more so because, as we have stressed already, the mansabdari organisation included all government services, without any official subdivisions into military, financial and executive branches. Therefore, after two decades of working with single ranks, Akbar introduced the system of double ranking in which mansabdars were granted a personal rank (*zat*) and a military one (*sawar*). Zat indicated the holder's position in the hierarchy of imperial honour. It was always higher than, or equal to, second, sawar rank, which represented the number of mounted retainers the mansabdar was supposed to maintain. The salary of the mansabdar was calculated on the basis of both ranks, each requiring different tables of conversion.

The third purpose of the mansabdari system was to promote the size, as well as the optimal composition, of the mansabdari contingents. One way to achieve this was to retain a certain link between the zat and sawar scales, by which those mansabdars who maintained a relatively high number of retainers, that is, had a high sawar rank in proportion to their zat rank, also received higher zat salaries. Ranking itself must have stimulated mansabdars to maximise their contingents in order to move up the scales. As Bada'uni claimed, those performing well at inspection clearly had the prospect of promotion:

> It was settled that every Amir should commence as a commander of twenty . . . and when, according to the rule, he had brought the horses of his twenty troopers to be branded, he was then to be made a *sadi*, or commander of hundred, or more . . . When they had brought to the musters their new contingent complete, they were to be promoted accordingly to their merits and circumstances to the post of *hazari* [or commander of thousand].[54]

In addition to these measures, a sub-scheme of premiums and incentives was built into the system, particularly aimed at attracting well-trained soldiers mounted on well-bred horses, and at keeping the ideal ratio of horses to retainers at 2:1. Pending their assessment and registration, mansabdars were paid standard advancements (*bar-awardi*) per horseman. At this stage, highly sought-after commanders of foreign origin already received higher scales. Later, at inspection, additional pay was allowed for foreign horses and for those horsemen with more than one horse, and there were also allowances for maintaining transport animals – horses, elephants and dromedaries – and carts. All this was clearly targeted at the recruitment and maintenance of well-trained and highly mobile cavalry troops. As mentioned already, infantry and artillery were part of the household army and irrelevant for the mansabdari system.

In due course, the incentives to keep up one's mansab at inspection failed to ensure the military strength of the mansabdari contingents. Manucci, for example, said of the mansabdars during Aurangzeb's reign:

> these gentlemen have generally each in his stable fifty, a hundred and up to two hundred horses for show or service. On the day of the review they equip their servitors and mount them on these horses, and pass them off as soldiers, putting to the account of profits the pay these men draw. In every quarter of the empire there are officials who keep an eye on everything, or, at least, ought to do so, for being at a distance from the Court, they do not acquit themselves of their duty as loyal subjects ought. But they are negligent by reason of the presents given them to that intent by the person interested. Owing to these considerations they practice concealment, and never dream of enforcing the performance of duties.[55]

During the reigns of Jahangir and Shah Jahan, it appears that the working of the system was increasingly standardised and made less dependent on actual inspection. As the bar-awardi rate became the uniform rate for the sawar rank, a third rank was introduced, known as *do-aspa-o-sih-aspa* (two and three horse), which allowed extra pay for strong or sizeable contingents. In practice, however, this became increasingly irrespective of actual assessment and merely a matter of accountancy. Nonetheless, triple ranking was a convenient means of countering the ongoing inflation of ranks, since granting a third rank precluded the need to increase both zat and sawar ranks. For example, someone with a rank of 2,000/1,000 but offering a contingent of 3,000 retainers could be given a new rank of 3,000/3,000 but, in case one did not want to change the zat status of the mansabdar, one could also grant him a position of 2,000/2,000/1,000, the latter indicating that, of the 2,000 sawar, 1,000 were do-aspa-o-sih-aspa which warranted double rates.

Further standardisation was achieved through a system of fixed reductions. One of them was to compensate the court for the centralisation of some commissariat functions that were previously delegated to the mansabdars, such as keeping a certain number of animals for transport or providing fodder. Under Shah Jahan most of these levies were directly passed on to the mansabdars by lowering the bar-awardi scales. Generally speaking, one may say that the policy of standardisation and formalisation was probably a consequence of the rapid expansion of the empire. The incorporation of more and more mansabdars at growing distances from the court made the inspection of the sawar ranks increasingly cumbersome. At times of mobilisation, however, inspection remained in general use. Nonetheless, even the dagh procedure appears to have been considerably simplified following the new, so-called monthly rates. Albeit on a reduced level under Aurangzeb, these standardised rates continued to stimulate a high ratio of horses to retainers.

The mansabdari system was a huge success. This may be judged from its rapid growth after its introduction in 1573–4. More and more warlords were enlisted and received higher and higher ranks. Whereas under Akbar there were only about 150 mansabdars with a rank of 200 zat or more, under Shah Jahan this number increased to about 450 mansabdars of 500 zat or more, reaching a level of about 575 mansabdars during the later years of Aurangzeb. To make another striking comparison, at the death of Akbar there were only eleven mansabdars holding zat ranks of 5,000 or more, while at the end of Aurangzeb's reign this had increased to seventy-nine! Although mansabs tended to go up, it appears that the standard bar-awardi rates remained more or less stable, i.e. twenty rupees per month per horseman. What made mansab less attractive during the second half of the seventeenth century was not the rates themselves but the decreasing ability of the mansabdars to realise them from their jagirs. Already during Akbar's reign the total salary claim against mansab was a staggering 80 per cent of the total revenue (jama), that is 30 per cent from the zat and 50 per cent from the sawar ranks.[56] Mansab always represented a claim (*talab*) on cash (*naqd*) or, more frequently, on jagirs. Thus most mansabdars were temporarily granted an area that was assessed to yield in revenue an amount equivalent to their salaries. In practice, however, the assessed revenue, or *jamadami* – the revenue assignment expressed in terms of copper dams – was liable to become outdated, the more so because many jagirs were only partly under direct imperial assessment (*zabt*), a considerable part remaining rebellious (*zor-talab*).[57]

Obviously, this was a deliberate device by the Mughal authorities to stimulate imperial control and agrarian expansion, but it also reflected the almost perennial problem of effectuating registered salaries on the ground. It became a particularly pressing issue during the second half of the seventeenth century, when a growing number of mansabdars complained about the inadequate collections (*hasil*) in their assigned jagirs, most probably following the growing zamindari rake-off. Shah Jahan and Aurangzeb introduced reductions to pass on these failed hasil figures into the salaries and military requirements of the mansabdars. For example, the recruitment of the Deccani warlords was almost entirely against reduced rates. Here again, we are faced by the repercussions of zamindarisation. As we have seen already, the position of the zamindar vis-à-vis the mansabdar had grown tremendously, the former siphoning off an ever growing part of the land revenue and thus of the mansabdars' salaries. It was a strength of the mansabdari system, however, that many zamindars still aspired to become honourable mansabdars. In fact, the growing standardisation of the system made its working more pliable, which might have enhanced its capacity to incorporate a growing number of zamindars. At the same time, though, mansab became less an indication of the mansabdar's real military force and more a clue to his current stock in the military labour market. As such, mansab became a commodified object of permanent speculation and negotiation requiring, of all participants involved, a great deal of business acumen.

Military marketing

Apart from creating hierarchy, fixing salaries and promoting military strength, mansab was primarily meant to attract military labour even though the mansabdar would be mostly called on to perform administrative tasks. Basically, the Mughals could not afford to leave the most powerful Indian warlords to alternative employers or, equally detrimental, to allow them to create their own demand by beginning a military enterprise of their own. For this reason, the Mughals attempted to dominate the top segment of the labour market by granting the most attractive and most exciting incentive on offer: mansab. Eagerness to acquire and augment mansab instilled competitiveness in all players in the market, which was even further enhanced by the highly meritocratic and flexible nature of mansabdari service itself.

In a way, entering the mansabdari system resembled investing money in a business enterprise, bearing various risks to be balanced by the future proceeds of the mansab. For example, every potential mansabdar required a starting capital, which, if not paid by the candidate himself, could be borrowed from his patron or from a professional moneylender. This capital was not only needed for the enrolment and equipment of his own contingent, but also for paying a surety (*zamin*) or a nazr to the emperor. In return for financial backing, sponsors often obtained a share in the forthcoming profits. For foreign adventurers from Turan or Iran, moving to India came close to being a commercial venture, as may be illustrated by the Irani mansabdar Danishmand Khan of Yazd:

> in order to obtain a maintenance in an honourable way [he] took a sum of money from Persian merchants on the arrangement of a participation in profits, and came to the spacious land of India which is the capital of profits for the owners of hope, and the possessors of desires.[58]

The more mansab came to represent access to Indian wealth, the more it became an important instrument in the expansion of the empire. This is most forcefully demonstrated in the well-known dispatches of the Mughal field commander in the Deccan, Jai Singh Kachhwaha. His strategy against Shivaji was primarily based on offering endless promises of high mansab and money to all his chief officers and allies. After he had capitulated, Shivaji was allowed to keep part of his estate as a zamindar, while his young son Sambhaji was granted the rank of 5,000 zat. Later, Jai Singh succeeded in enticing Shivaji to court, but ongoing negotiations about his standing ended in the tragic outcome mentioned in the previous chapter. It was one of the first indications that zamin was tending to become more attractive than mansab or, to put it in a different way, that mansab was increasingly seen as a key towards a wealth-promising position as zamindar. Anyway, this was the general outlook of the Maratha zamindars after Jai Singh had come to a settlement with Shivaji. As he observed himself:

> All the zamindars of the Karnatak and the wild people of Barkol and Kanul etc. have sent their agents, just as one captured deer draws many wild and forest deers. And they are waiting for hints and signs and for the sake of the Bijapur expedition it is absolutely necessary to conciliate them and give them hope to get their watan (homeland).[59]

Jai Singh's subsequent campaign against Bijapur in 1666 was also basically about bringing disorder and disunion to the camp of the enemy, again lavishly scattering mansabs, jewels and cash. His first aim was to win over the Afghan, Habshi and Mahdawi leaders: 'Their hand of courage would be held back by the payment by way of *tankhwah*, or something in cash and grant of many jagirs from our old territory for the maintenance and sustenance of their children.'[60]

For the mansabdars themselves, this kind of warfare could be extremely lucrative, as it opened splendid opportunities to extend their patronage network, which helped to improve their standing at court and could only be reflected in a higher mansab. This also explains the behaviour of mansabdars during the numerous sieges in the Deccan, where many of them furthered their interests by negotiating settlements with the besieged party. Apart from gaining the honour of having defeated them, it was even more important to take the opportunity to become their mediators and sponsors at the imperial court.[61] Hence it was not only employment as such that gained the Deccan its reputation as 'the bread and support of the soldiers of Hindustan', but also the chance it opened to exploit new sources of recruitment. To a large extent, the Deccan campaigns are representative of the usual Mughal way of warfare, combining carrot with stick, not to destroy but to incorporate the enemy. In most of these cases, mansab was the prime incentive, giving access to ready cash, exciting careers and, even more so during the seventeenth century, to hereditary rights over land.

Bargaining for mansab could only have its full effect on the military labour market if the mansabdari system itself was, to a high degree, open to talented outsiders. Indeed, almost without exception, European observers were struck by the lack of hereditary succession among the Mughal nobility. According to Bernier, most of the amirs were adventurers of low descent, destitute of education, who enticed one another to court.[62] Nobility itself was an achieved status following from somebody's mansab.[63] This meritocratic feature of Mughal service is corroborated by the Mughal sources that also stress the importance of rewarding the quality of the product. Akbar, for example, considered it:

> the sine qua non of the high office of sovereignty in matters of retribution that no consideration should be shown for friends or foes and relations or strangers, and to administer justice to the oppressed, so that royal associates and government officials might not use their positions as a means for oppression and tyranny.[64]

It is true that, during Aurangzeb's reign, Mughal sources, especially those inspired by the established mansabdars, increasingly complained about the growing tendency to enlist so many new recruits who had 'neither honour nor descent' – a well-known literary cliché to explain the fall of empires. Nonetheless, it had always been official Mughal policy to muster people on the basis of their talent and quality, irrespective of their ancestors and with a certain preference for those without independent means of existence.[65] According to Abul Fazl 'every one who wishes to join the army is taken before His Majesty, in whose presence his rank is fixed'.[66] This is more or less confirmed by Bada'uni's complaint that Akbar's recruitment resembled a bazaar attracting lots of 'low trades people, weavers and cotton cleaners, carpenters and green-grocers, both Hindu and Musalman'.[67] Compared to the military elites of Europe, Mughal mansabdars were liable to almost permanent assessment by the court.[68] Hardly ever did the sons of high mansabdars inherit the mansab of their father and they were lucky to be allowed to start anew from sharply reduced ranks. To continue an elevated position at court for more than a hundred years was considered exceptional.[69] Hence, a son taking over the entire mansabdari establishment of his father was also a rare phenomenon, which contributed to making military employment at the lower levels of the market also extremely volatile.[70] Even during their lifetimes, mansabdars could be reduced in rank or even dismissed as, for example, after the hasty enlistments during the Deccan campaigns of 1667–8.[71] Nevertheless, it was this insecurity of rank and wealth that acted as a powerful incentive for individual distinction.[72]

The problem during the latter part of Aurangzeb's reign was not so much the incorporation of too many upstarts, but rather their zamindari background. More than their more mobile foreign colleagues, mansabdars with stakes in settled landlordism found themselves in an ideal position to turn their de facto hold on villages and land into hereditary watan-jagirs. Their outlook was one of settled ease and certainly not one of standby readiness to serve the emperor at every corner of the empire. Exemplary of this parochial mentality is the ascribed attitude of the Afghan mansabdar Husain Khan Khweshgi, who lived at the end of Aurangzeb's reign and had gained zamindari rights in the town of Qasur in the Punjab. 'Although he nominally held a mansab, yet he never stirred from his home, and what others obtained by hard endeavours he received, in double and quadruple measure, by merely sitting in his house.'[73] For the long-term survival of the empire it was crucial to counteract such leanings towards zamindarisation, the more so because it endangered the smooth realisation of mansabdari salaries, which was mostly mediated through the zamindars. The result was inflation of mansab and, thus, a decreasing capacity to attract military labour. Consequently, it was sound Mughal policy to keep mansabdars on the move and to disperse 'wherever a large number of people of one mind and language are gathered and there are signs of crowding and commotion'.[74] The employability and flexibility of the mansabdars had to be stimulated by promulgating the mansabdar's cosmopolitan image, which was to contrast sharply with the parochial, rustic reputation of the gentry. The *Mirror for Princes* of the Irani mansabdar Muhammad Baqir is a case in point, as it appeals to this ethos of globetrotting mansabdars. He explains that travelling must lead to wealth, discipline and refinement:

European observers at the time were struck by the efficiency of Mughal intelligence. According to Manucci, spies were the Mughals' best means for the good regulation of their kingdom. They reported what went on in the realm but chiefly amongst their officials.[84] According to Hawkins, the king had spies upon every nobleman.[85] Others draw an equally telling picture of generals embroiled in reading reports and newsletters. Among the greatest of generals, Mir Jumla was reported to have followed the custom of the country:

> [he had] the intervals between his toes full of letters, and he also held many between the fingers of his left hand. He drew them sometimes from his feet, sometimes from his hand, and sent replies through his two secretaries, writing some also himself.[86]

A similar story of a data-processing commander is presented by Herbert de Jager's report of his visit to Shivaji in August 1677. When the Dutch agent arrived at the camp, Shivaji could hardly find time to meet him, according to de Jager, because he received so many letters and reports from the more than 1,000 spies in his service. At long last, the Dutch succeeded in drawing Shivaji's attention, but only after they had loudly played their drum and horns (*tabalingo en cromhoorns*) in a tour around the camp. Even then they could hardly get down to serious business as Shivaji was diverted every minute by the arrival of one spy or another with some letter or news report.[87] For Mir Jumla and Shivaji, as well as for any other successful general, this kind of information gathering was not only crucial for reasons of purely military intelligence, but also helped to determine someone's current position in the political arena as well as his 'price' on the military labour market. As we have seen already, Jai Singh expected to conquer the Deccan by buying every officer 'at his own price'.[88] More and more this market price was to determine the warlord's mansab on entering Mughal service.

Finally, to understand the gravitational force of mansab, one can hardly overestimate the corresponding aura of Mughal wealth. This is particularly true for the Turani and Irani warriors, who must have gazed with wonder at the unequalled pomp and circumstance that clothed the Mughal court and that promised them exciting careers and rapid riches. According to Pelsaert, the riff-raff of Khorasan could become big men in India if they had only one relative or acquaintance at the Mughal court.[89] At every opportunity, the Mughals ostentatiously demonstrated their splendour to the outside world. According to one European observer they preferred camp to capital because the first provided more space for proper display.[90] Another example is the well-known weighing ceremony (*wazn*) during Nauruz when the emperor's weight in money and other valuable goods was lavishly distributed among the public. Commensurate with this munificent image, at audiences the emperor always sat next to a heap of gold coins that he could grasp and award to attendants.[91] According to Mughal propaganda, the wealth of India dwarfed the resources of the Uzbek state in Turan or the Safavid state in Iran. Public bookkeeping served to demonstrate that the Mughal state was the single most resourceful employer of the Islamic world,[92] or as one source puts it:

> The revenues of the Princes of other countries do not amount to what the servants of the Indian government receive. The revenues of Imam Quli Khan and Nazr Muhammad Khan, who held the whole of Transoxania and Turkistan, even to Balkh and Badakhshan, were from land revenue and taxes in cash and grain and also in enhancements and tithes one crore twenty lakhs [12,000,000] of khanis, which are equal to thirty lakhs [3,000,000] of rupees. The assignment for every officer of 7,000 with 7,000 horse, do-aspa-o-sih-aspa is a crore of dams (250,000 Rupees), not to mention Yamin al-Daula Asaf Khan who each year collected from his fiefs fifty lakhs (5,000,000) of rupees.[93]

Another Mughal source reckons the revenue of Balkh and Badakhshan under the Uzbek ruler Nazr Muhammad Khan to be not more than 2,500,000 rupees, which was considered equal to the income received by mansabdars of 5,000 zat who had a like number of sawar of the do-aspa-o-sih-aspa levels, while those of higher grades received a still greater sum.[94] The message to put across is clear: it was better to become a wealthy servant in Mughal India than to remain an autonomous but poor king in Central Asia.

There was much veracity in Mughal propaganda. Looking at Iran, the conditions for service were certainly better than in Central Asia, but still below the usual Mughal level. Considering Ottoman salaries as well, it appears that the regular payment for a mounted trooper rose from west to east: the Ottomans paying about a quarter, and the Safavids about a third of the usual Mughal level, ranging from 200 to 500 rupees annually, even without considering the fact that the Mughal rupee was more stable than either Ottoman or Safavid currencies.[95] In order to induce more foreigners into Mughal service, Turanis and Iranis could count on a standard 25 per cent bonus, which reflected their skill as superior horse-warriors. Since the salary rates were also linked to the quality of remounts, they often received an additional premium on their Turki and Irani horses. It further appears that higher officers and officials received considerably more in Mughal India than in either Iran or Turan. Mughal propaganda is corroborated by the reports of European travellers, like von Mandelslo and Ketelaar, who visited both the Mughal and the Safavid courts. The first even thought that the annual costs for maintaining the Mughal elephants were about equal to half of the total expense of the Safavid king.[96] Indeed, looking at the available figures, public expenditure in Iran was a mere one-fifth of that of Mughal India, that is, before the conquest of the Deccan sultanates. And, although Mughal payment was always kept in arrears, six to eight months pay for one year of service appears to have been common practice,[97] the Safavids had a particularly bad reputation for their lack of ready money, often leading to massive defections.[98] By contrast, the Mughal army was known for its sumptuous spending, which may be illustrated by the early-seventeenth-century account of Manrique. Encountering some Irani troops on the way from Farah to Qandahar, the Christian friar noted that the Irani warriors were not at all impressed by their decadent Mughal adversaries:

> Mogol horse, which though great numerically, is in fact not very formidable, most of it being merely good for show. For the Mogols were weaklings, and luxurious and enervated, rather than fighters or warlike soldiers. Their cavalry, therefore, owing to excessive luxury, is more suited to contests of tilting at the ring than for the martial activities of war and battles.[99]

The same feeling reverberates in the mid-eighteenth-century view of the learned Azad Bilgrami who observed that the exceptional wealth of India 'has kept the people of this country away from practicing the art of warfare. It has plunged them in a life of ease and luxury'.[100] Nonetheless, Mughal prodigality was hardly less effective than Safavid valour, as may be judged from a report by Cornelis Speelman made in 1652, in which he recorded that 6,000 Irani troops at Qandahar had defected to the Mughals as every horseman received not more than only one toman for the entire year, for himself, his servant and two horses, which was indeed a mere 10 per cent of the common Indian level.[101]

For the Indian warrior, Mughal wealth was perhaps only slightly less awe-inspiring. But from the very beginning they tended to be more distracted by their keenness to gain and assert zamindari rights. For Rajputs and Indian Muslims alike, mansabdari service could temporarily make surrogate nomads out of them but never kept them from dreaming of their own little kingdoms in their homelands. To a large extent, the late-seventeenth-century rise of the zamindars was the natural outcome of what may be called a pre-modern case of Indian state formation, in which the state itself could only survive through the continued cooperation of the local landlords. As long as their assistance was ensured, preferably by an attractive system of ranks and other incentives, the empire could survive. Ultimately, though, the zamindar's dream had to become the emperor's nightmare.

Coming back to the meaning and workings of mansab, it has been shown that it contained four overlapping ingredients. First, it served as a rather rough indication of imperial hierarchy. As such it did not signify a rigid command structure but the unequal distribution of imperial honour. Second, it was meant as a personal salary irrespective of the holder's services. The latter constituted the third element that was reflected, in particular, in the sawar component of the rank. For the 'men of the sword' it involved a highly flexible system of earmarked subsidies to meet the costs of recruiting and equipping an agreed number of mounted troops. Fourth, as mansab was increasingly commodified, it conveyed the marketable value of its holder on the military labour market. In all its four different meanings, mansab played a crucial role in the ongoing success of Mughal warfare. In general, only in those rare instances when offerings of mansab and money were insufficient to accommodate the enemy, primarily during the beginning and the end of empire when there was uncertainty about the mansab's value, did the Mughals have to fall back on the use of violence. This, their second-best option, will be the subject of the second part of this book.

Plate 4 Mughal battle of Shibarghan, 1646. This miniature by Hunhar (*c.* 1650) was meant as a study for the *Padshahnama*. On the right are the Mughal forces under Asalat Khan (top) and Bahadur Khan (bottom); on the left are the Uzbek forces under Nazr Muhammad. The picture illustrates the ongoing importance of mounted archers. Apparently, compared with their Mughal counterparts, the Uzbeks employed relatively light armour and more archers (see also S. Gahlin (1991), pp. 35-6, and this book, p. 184).

Source: *Foundation Custodia, Paris, 1989-T.5*

CHAPTER FOUR

Camp, warhorse and elephant

> The splendours of this king are scarcely to be believed: . . . when he travels through his country he takes fifteen hundred thousand human beings, horsemen, soldiers, officers, women, children, with ten thousand elephants, and with a great deal of artillery even though it is of no use except through its grandeur.
>
> (Augustin Hiriart about Jahangir's court[1])

As we have arrived at the middle of this book, let me recapitulate the argument so far. The first two chapters accentuated the dual make-up of the Mughal state in which the ideal-typical characters of ghazi and mirza confronted and complemented each other on the ecological frontier between wild mawas and settled ra'iyati. Chapter 3 focused on yet another closely related ideal-typical dichotomy: that between the cosmopolitan mansabdar and the local, more rustic zamindar. In fact, mansabdari aimed at civilising the ghazi, not by destroying but by canalising his martial ethos and, at the same time, by keeping him from striking root in Indian soil, in other words, by stopping him from becoming a little king in his own right. As a consequence, mansabdari combined the mobility and flexibility of the ghazi with the refined manners of the mirza, or, to use the catchy phrase of Sumit Guha, although in a different context, it was to turn the noble savages of the mawas into the savage nobles of the empire. Hence, the model Mughal mansabdar was supposed to stand Janus-faced between the ghazi's and the mirza's world.

This chapter will highlight yet another way in which the Mughals attempted to bridge the inner frontiers of their empire. As I will try to demonstrate, ruling India implied travelling through India. From Babur to Aurangzeb we come across an almost permanent urge on the part of the emperors to move and to keep moving. Movement was considered healthy, not only for the Mughal mansabdars, but also for the emperors themselves, and actually for the entire Mughal body politic. Constant mobility could only be realised, though, by exploiting the enormous locomotive potential of warhorses, elephants, dromedaries and oxen. Indeed, more than any gunpowder weaponry, the mobility and striking power of these animals lay at the root of Mughal power.

Camp

The Mughal emperors always had a strong awareness that travelling with court and army across the realm was somehow crucial to their survival. This is also illustrated in the rhetoric of mobility used in the Indo-Islamic chronicles, in which the king is recurrently warned that he 'ought not to keep his tent pitched at one place for two days even with a view to enjoying ease and comfort'.[2] This is perhaps most clearly publicised in one of Aurangzeb's own councils for kings:

> Next this, an emperor should never allow himself to be fond of ease and inclined to retirement, because the most fatal cause of the decline of kingdoms and the destruction of royal power is this undesirable habit. Always be moving about, as much as possible: It is bad for both emperors and water to remain at the same place; the water grows putrid and the king's power slips out of his control. In touring lie the honour, ease, and splendour of kings; the desire of comfort and happiness makes them untrustworthy.[3]

Aurangzeb's advice that kings should never rest was even used to charge his father with political negligence, as he chose to stay at Delhi and Agra instead of being constantly on the march.[4] Later, during the eighteenth century, the idea reverberates in the political testament of Nizam al-Mulk, the Mughal viceroy of the Deccan:

> Consider your life and the proper administration of the country as depending on travel. The pleasure to be gained in experiencing change of climate and change of water by making a habit of moving under the tents should not be given up by you. God has ordered in the holy book, the interpretation of which points to the necessity of travelling. The administration of the country is dependent upon touring.[5]

Of course, Aurangzeb's and Nizam al-Mulk's perception that political fitness required movement was not new. On the contrary, it may even be seen as a fairly late illustration of a long-established Indian tradition going back to the ancient horse sacrifice in which the sacrificer-king repeatedly set out on a conquering circuit in order to follow and protect the horse that later, on its return from this perambulation around the realm, was immolated.[6] It may also be interpreted as a continuation of a Central Asian tradition inspired by the world-conquering campaigns of Chinggis Khan and Amir Timur. In the spirit of these famous ancestors, the sixteenth-century Uzbek ruler Shaibani Khan of Bukhara could only declare when asked about his capital: 'let our capital be our saddle.'[7] As we shall see, the attitude of the Mughals of India was not much different.

According to most contemporary chronicles, Akbar is represented as the ideal, standby ruler who 'plans expeditions all the time, for which there are always in attendance before his court 500 elephants, a hundred rows of horses and camels, consisting of ten in a line to carry his baggages and camp equipments'. Indeed, this 'ever-growing planner' had been able 'to capture the country by means of travelling through it'.[8] Abul Fazl stresses this picture of an ever-marching Akbar who was known to be fond of 'travelling and hunting', and who does never 'fix his heart to one place', gathering 'new affluence from every quarter'.[9] He also recurrently boasts about the speed of the imperial army, most spectacularly demonstrated by Akbar's swift expedition to Gujarat in August–September 1573. In this blitzkrieg, Akbar with 300 to 400 troopers reportedly defeated more than 20,000 rebels after he had covered the *c.* 800 km from Fatehpur Sikri to Ahmadabad in nine days, a journey for which caravans would need at least two or three months.[10] Despite the rhetoric of speed, marching was usually much slower of course, coming down to a mere 10 to 20 km for a day-march, as it was less about military campaigning than about administering justice, or, to adapt a less abstruse phrase from the chronicles, 'to drag every chief and leader by the hair to do homage to the sublime Court and to exalt them by eternal auspiciousness'.[11]

But before taking up the question of whether and why supremacy depended on the ruler's ability to move, we should first determine the extent to which this ideal of *perpetuum mobile* was actually realised on the ground. In other words, to what extent should the Mughal state really be considered an itinerant monarchy? This question is all the more important because the Mughal Empire is usually depicted as a highly settled, agrarian state ruled by a top-heavy, stable bureaucracy.

According to Stephen Blake, the Mughal emperors spent nearly 40 per cent of their time in camp, on tours of one year or more.[12] Blake's figure is roughly corroborated by my own calculations, as based on the reports of the official chronicles, and as summarised in Table 4.1.

From these calculations it appears that the four emperors Akbar, Jahangir, Shah Jahan and Aurangzeb were, for about 65 per cent of their reign, settled, i.e. staying for more than six months in one place, short trips not being counted. For about 35 per cent of their rule, they were migratory, be it on tour, on military campaigns or long hunting expeditions. Although based on different criteria and being extremely approximate, it strikes one that these calculations come very close to Melville's figures for Shah Abbas I

Table 4.1 Settled residence of Mughal emperors

	In capital	*In centre*	*In north*	*In south*
Akbar	55	35	20	–
Jahangir	75	40	10	25
Shah Jahan	60	45	10	5
Aurangzeb	70	35	5	30
Average	65	40	10	15

Note
Based on periods of > 6 months of unbroken residence in and around one place (but excluding sieges), in central, northern and southern parts of the empire, in round quinary percentages of the total period of regular government.

(1587–1629). The Safavid king was travelling for about one-third of his reign, resident in a capital for one-third, and static in other locations for the rest.[13] The Safavid and Mughal figures are certainly much higher than those for the Ottoman rulers, who stayed for much longer periods in the capital. Here one should add that, like the Safavids, the Mughals repeatedly shifted their capital, or rather, the capital shifted to wherever the emperor was. In Table 4.1 it is shown that the Mughal emperors stayed for about 40 per cent of their 'settled' time in central capitals, that is, Delhi, Agra and Fatehpur Sikri, about 10 per cent in northern capitals, that is, Lahore, Kashmir, Kabul and Hasan Abdal, and about 15 per cent in southern capitals, that is, Ajmer, Mandu, Burhanpur or the 'permanent' camps of Aurangzeb in Galgala and Islampuri in the Deccan. The mobility of the emperor himself, as well as his permanent tendency to look for new capitals, clearly evokes a restless picture of an ever-moving Mughal court.

But the striking thing about these figures is not only that they differ from the current image of an entirely settled, agrarian empire, but that they also convey some unexpected differences between individual emperors. For example, despite his exhausting Deccan campaigns, Aurangzeb appears to have been much less of a traveller than Akbar, or even Shah Jahan, who is usually seen as the most secure and settled ruler who built the new 'fixed' capital of Shahjahanabad in Delhi. Although Aurangzeb may have covered a lot of kilometres, this was mostly during the last stage of his reign and mainly in the Deccan, far away from the geo-political centre of his realm. During his later years, Aurangzeb preferred to be present at every single siege or battle that took place. This kind of eagerness had already been witnessed in the younger Akbar, whose personal command at sieges such as Chitor and Ranthambor helped to establish his reputation as an invincible warrior. Later, however, Akbar preferred to leave most of the actual fighting to his sons and commanders. Instead, he used to follow them at a strategic distance to keep an eye on them or to urge them into action.[14] Both Jahangir and Shah Jahan adopted the strategy of their father and also chose to follow the main campaigns from a certain distance. But, far from being settled rulers, they shifted headquarters depending on the current campaign. With an eye on the Deccan, Jahangir stayed for relatively long periods in places like Ajmer and Mandu. Shah Jahan, though, was more focused on northern expansion and settled for relatively long spans in places like Lahore and Kabul. With hindsight, all this appears to have been sound policy, as it ensured that the whole empire remained within the emperor's radius of action. As a result, it was not Aurangzeb's endless campaigning as such, but his growing habit of settling for long periods at the empire's periphery – for more than twenty-five years he was away from the central capitals – that must have considerably undermined the power and reputation of the Mughals and stimulated the zamindarisation of his officials and generals during the late seventeenth and early eighteenth centuries.

Of course, the same could have happened to Aurangzeb's predecessors if they had given in to their inclination to stay for long vacations in wonderful Kashmir. For example, Abul Fazl reports that Akbar was ill advised to go there as he was considered to be putting himself 'in a corner' of the realm. Fortunately, though, wisdom prevailed and Akbar decided to leave 'that ever-vernal flower garden which leads every one else to self-indulgence'.[15] Abul Fazl was very much aware that, as the empire 'took a year to traverse',[16] the emperor should never waste too much time on the outer limits of the realm and, instead, should focus on striding along its inner limites.

Indeed, it appears that the itineraries of the emperors neatly followed the Uttarapatha and Dakshinapatha pattern as described in Chapter 1. The heaviest imperial traffic occurred along the line Kabul – Lahore – Delhi – Agra – Ajmer – Mandu – Burhanpur. Remarkably, the eastern route from Agra to Bengal was much less in use, which may have had something to do with the relatively easy communications provided by the Ganges and Yamuna rivers, which facilitated political integration and rendered the relatively problematic necessity of marching through these rather well-populated areas somewhat superfluous.[17] As we have seen already for the western routes of Gujarat, areas of intensive settled agriculture were much less conducive to extensive marching than the northern and southern routes, where we still find lots of uncultivated waste as well as the main royal hunting grounds.[18] In the north, the need for space, grazing, firewood and, in particular, running water often urged the Mughal emperors to take the route to the Jalandhar doab along the Siwalik mountains, somewhat to the north of the main highway between Sirhind and Lahore. Not surprisingly, this northern route along the Himalayan foothills had also been the trajectory of the invading armies under Timur and Babur.[19] Similarly, the southern campaigns through Rajasthan and Malwa deflected from the main caravan routes connecting the various urban markets. Instead, in constant search for suitable pasturage and hunting grounds, they both crossed and paralleled the main highways from a certain distance. These movements of the court, zigzagging instead of neatly following the main road, remind one of the pastoral movements as analysed by Jean Aubin for Iran in the eleventh to thirteenth centuries.[20] As such, it raises the question whether, or to what extent, Mughal mobility should still be seen as a manifestation of transhumant migration.

First of all, it would be too easy to ascribe Mughal mobility to their nomadic heritage. Like the nomadic rulers of Central Asia, the medieval kings of Europe remained itinerant as late as the sixteenth century.[21] Although this was not a result of the need to look for new pasturage, it could certainly be caused by logistical considerations. As in the European case, the court often thought it much easier to take men and horses to their food than to bring their food to them. Not unlike the much smaller European courts, the Mughal royal camp steadily ate its way round the empire. Although these considerations must have played a role, in general it appears that the Mughal court in India was extremely well served by both high levels of regional food production and by excellent logistical facilities over long distances. Only a few places, such as Kabul and Kashmir, were known to be incapable of sustaining the Mughal court for long periods of time out of their own resources. As we will see in more detail in Chapter 6, imperial campaigns to southern India and Qandahar could only be successful by living off the country, by building many fortified magazines (*thanas*) along the way, or by being supported by Banjara hauliers bringing food and fodder from far-off places.[22] But as long as the camp remained in the northern and central parts of India, it appears to have been very well provisioned by a relatively sophisticated and highly monetised market system.[23] Also, in comparison with Europe, there appears to have been less need to carry animal fodder, as dromedaries used to browse in the surrounding meadows. Fodder grasses for the other animals were often cut, beaten and washed along the way.[24] Apart from this, the diet of the common Mughal soldier appears also to have been much less demanding than in the European case. To quote the French traveller Tavernier:

> One hundred of our European soldiers would scarcely have any difficulty in vanquishing 1,000 of these Indian soldiers; but it is true, on the other hand, that they would have much difficulty in accustoming themselves to such an abstemious life. For the horseman as well as the infantry soldier supports himself with a little flour kneaded with water and black sugar, of which they make small balls; and in the evening, whenever they have the

> necessaries, they make khichari, which consists of rice cooked with a grain of the above name in water with a little salt. When eating it they first dip the ends of their fingers in melted butter, for such is the ordinary food of both soldiers and poor people.[25]

But the key factor in Mughal logistics was the ready availability of money. As Abul Fazl knew perfectly well, the latter 'enabled men to travel'. Indeed, without money 'how difficult would it be to carry provisions for several days, let alone for several months or years'.[26] Merchants, bankers and accountants were always conspicuously present in the camp to mediate in the numerous financial dealings of the emperor and to assist the nobility, who had to manage all kinds of landed estates throughout the country. These financial people not only provided credit to the pillars of the state, but also to the simple soldier, whose pay was usually held in arrears.[27] As money was the fuel of the camp's mobility,[28] access to it was ensured by carrying treasury and by strategically distributing it along the main arteries of the empire. Although Agra fort served as the central depot of the state treasury, secondary depots were at Gwalior, Nanwar, Ranthambor, Asirgarh (Burhanpur), Rohtas, and Lahore.[29] The emperor also took a great deal of his treasury with him on tour, for, as one of his principal generals knew, 'if the treasury is with the army, the merchants following the army also have a sense of security'.[30] Trusting Manucci, on his way to Kashmir, Aurangzeb used 300 camels carrying 56,000 pounds of silver, and 28,000 pounds of gold.[31] One of the advantages of the open camp, either in the fields or in a garden outside the city, was that it offered excellent opportunities for exhibiting the vast resources of the state and, thus, for showing its ongoing creditworthiness to the outside world.[32] In practical terms, the actual presence of the imperial treasury was not always a necessity, as excellent credit facilities could build on an extensive and efficient transfer system of bills of exchange (*hundis*).[33] At least before the latter part of Aurangzeb's reign, money was only rarely in short supply. Perhaps even more important, as the remittance needs of hundreds of Mughal nobles depended upon the commercial exchange between the camp and India's various regional economies, it also acted as a stimulus to the integration of these economies.[34] As it moved right across the sub-continent, the camp 'sublime' dragged with it a whole web of long-distance financial relations. Anyway, in contrast with the somewhat shabby, penurious European kings, it appears that, for the wealthier Mughals, there were no logistical reasons to move.[35]

Still, Mughal movements show a certain seasonal rhythm. Although they did not have specific winter and summer quarters, they generally preferred to stay in the north during the heat of summer, and in the south during winter. For example, the Mughal emperors after Humayun always stayed at Kabul between May and September, which was also the best time to buy warhorses from the northern tribes. Likewise, Kashmir was usually favoured during the summer. Because of the oncoming heat, southern campaigns rarely started after December. Besides, there was not much movement during the monsoon, although the rains could not always prevent campaigning, even into the wettest, eastern provinces, as is found in Akbar's campaign against the Afghans in 1574. In order to cover longer distances, the Mughal marching season often started somewhat before the end of the monsoon. Starting too early, though, could keep the peasants from sowing the kharif crops, which became essential for feeding the army after the monsoon. Although, in these instances, ecological circumstances clearly affected the overall rhythm of the Mughal circuit, the main incentives for moving around were of a different nature.

First, marching implied surveillance and road building. During the advance, time and distance were precisely registered. As the camp often travelled through jungly and mountainous areas, the advance of the army could only proceed by levelling the ground or clearing the jungle in advance. For example, to facilitate the approach of the imperial camp to Kabul, in 1585 Akbar ordered one Qasim Khan, also the builder of Agra Fort,[36] to level the roads up to the Indus river, to make a bridge over it, and to make the Khyber Pass passable for carriages. According to Abul Fazl, this road-building activity caused such uproar in Central Asia that 'from fear of a rapid march of the World's Lord, the gates of Balkh were generally kept close.'[37] Somewhat later, the same engineer opened up the road to Kashmir by employing 3,000 stonecutters, mountain-miners and splitters of rock, and 2,000 diggers. As a result, 'mountains which pedestrians could not traverse were crossed by His Majesty with a large army and numerous elephants'.[38] Later, Akbar boasted of this extraordinary piece of road building in a letter to the Shah of Iran.[39] In all these cases, Abul Fazl almost reads like Isaiah's boast that: 'ev'ry valley shall be exalted, every mountain and hill made low, the crooked straight and the rough places plain' (Isaiah 40:4). Abul Fazl is no exception though. We come across jungle-clearing and road-levelling activities throughout the other Mughal chronicles, especially in those areas that were unfit for large-scale operations of the imperial army, such as along the Western Ghats and into Gondwana or Orissa, and in such places 'where there was no path through it, but the coming and going of the army formed a track.'[40] Hence, one very important reason for marching was to keep the main arteries of the empire open and to construct new ones.

Perhaps the most obvious reason for extensive royal marching was the need to keep in touch with local power. As noted in Chapter 2, physical contact between the emperor and his many co-sharers of the realm was extremely important for forging bonds of loyalty. Sheer distance often determined the effectiveness of Mughal power or, as one European observer remarked:

> Sometimes the conquest of one part of the kingdom is the loss of another, for that rajah who without reluctancy submitted to the Mogul's power, while his camp was near, immediately disclaims it, when he knows it at a distance; which commotions bring on the Mogul endless troubles and expense.[41]

In this light, it should once again be stressed that the royal camp was not a wandering horde of nomads. Although the word 'horde' itself is derived from the Turko-Mongol *ordu,* or camp, in Persian it became the *urdu-i humayun* or *urdu-i mu'alla*, the imperial or sublime camp of the Mughals. This was not a nomadic tribe but a well-organised wandering army, the imperial army being the capital. Even stationary capitals like Agra and Delhi derived their chief support from the presence of the army. Bernier, for example, saw Delhi merely as a military encampment with a few more conveniences than are usually found in such places.[42] Outside Delhi, the layout of the imperial camp accurately copied the structure of the settled court, from the most public to the increasingly private spaces near the emperor in the centre. The princes and great amirs, accompanied by their wives and retainers, had to pitch their tents in fixed locations, separated from, but facing, the square for public audiences. The colour, space and height of the tents all followed a clear hierarchy, in which the largest, highest red tents were exclusively reserved for the emperor. In camp, the daily rhythm of prayers, darshan, public and private audiences was supposed to go on as usual. Even the marching order appears to have been based on the basic arrangement of the court. Military objectives appear to have played only a minor role, for example sending the heavy artillery as well as hundreds of scouts a day or two ahead of the main train. Over the breadth of one-and-a-half miles,[43] the emperor with all his belongings in the centre of the procession was preceded by the musical band and the imperial standards, immediately followed by the princes and the great amirs, the whole entourage protected by about 8,000 horsemen on each side. In their wake followed the bulk of the camp, which, apart from a minority of actual soldiers, consisted of a multitude of menial servants, porters, accountants, merchants, powder-makers, grass-cutters and prostitutes, etc.

The existing figures are staggering indeed. Bernier probably exaggerates when he speaks of about 100,000 horsemen and 300,000 animals in Aurangzeb's camp on its way in the Punjab. He also mentions the total figure of 300,000 to 400,000 people in camp, adding that the whole population of Delhi was collected in the camp, because, as it derived its employment and maintenance from the court and army, it had no alternative but to follow them in their march or to perish from want during their absence.[44] The camp Careri saw in Galgala counted 60,000 horse and 100,000 foot supported by 50,000 camels and 3,000 elephants. In addition there were huge numbers of supporting personnel and other followers such as merchants and artisans, altogether amounting to 500,000 souls. With its 250 bazaars, he compared it to a moving city with a circumference of about thirty miles.[45]

Under these circumstances, speed could only be limited. The average speed was about 16 km on the march, together with resting days, making about 8 km a day, of course depending on season and territory, which seems to be considerably less than the usual speed of about 35 km per

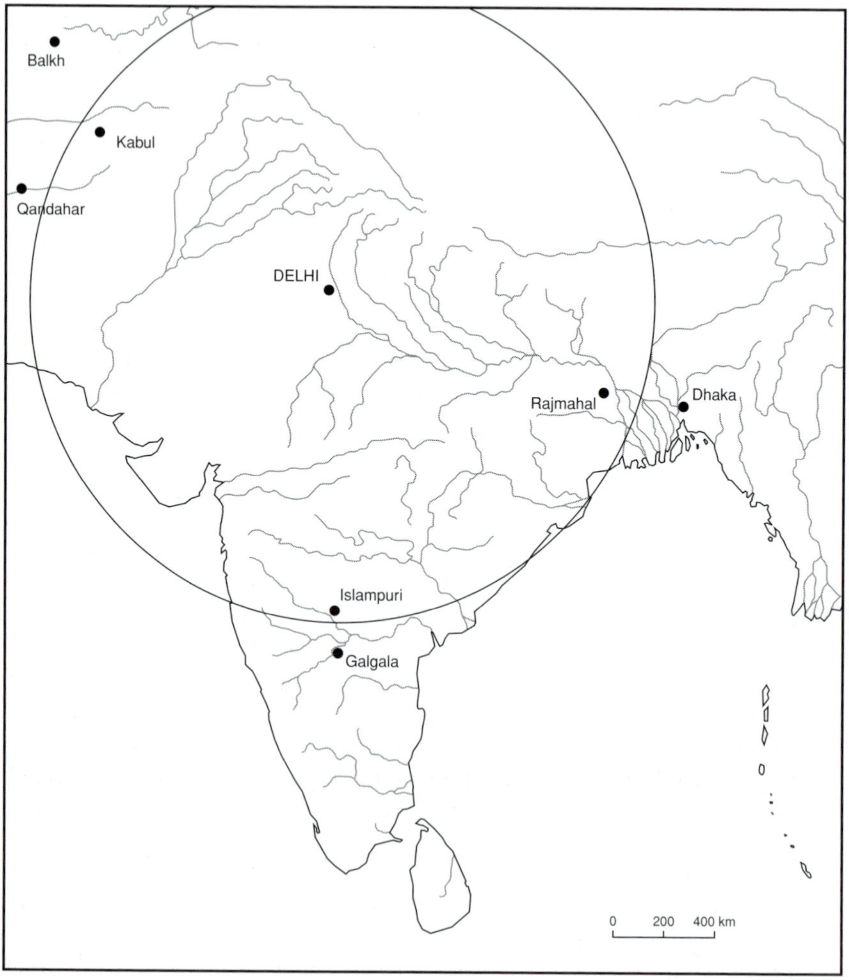

Map 4.1 Mughal annual radius of action. Based on the assumption that the court has to return to Delhi within one year, with an average speed of about 8 km, and travelling about 9 months. This comes down to a radius of roughly 1,200 km from Delhi.[46]

march of the much smaller court in Iran.[47] Of course, apart from the royal camp, other army units could be much quicker. Mansabdars who were summoned to court were expected to travel at least 30 km a day, post-runners even making 125 km a day.[48] But as far as the radius of action of the court is concerned, Abul Fazl's statement that the empire took one year to cross, comes fairly close to the actual extent of the empire as seen from Delhi (see Map 4.1).

Thus what we see at the court is an enormous quantity of people and animals moving around very slowly, doing business as usual. Marching was not to disrupt the daily routine of ritual and administration. To facilitate the unrestricted routine two fully identical sets of camp equipment were kept in order to be able to set up the next camp in advance. In general, it seems that the court's mobility did not endanger the routine working of Mughal bureaucracy. The royal record office always accompanied the court and, according to Manucci, required eighty camels, thirty elephants and twenty carts to carry all kinds of registers and papers of account. As a result, officials were always ready to provide detailed descriptions of the territories through which the court passed.

One of the main reasons behind all this marching was to circulate the entire organisation and paraphernalia of the imperial capital around the realm. With all the dust, smell and clamour surrounding it, the moving imperial camp was a permanent reminder of Mughal sovereignty and, as such, a constant threat to any obstreperous zamindar considering disobedience or revolt. Since the camp showed the imperial grandeur on permanent display all over the empire, actual fighting could often be avoided. The pending arrival of the court was usually more than enough to bring people into submission. Indeed, neither the city nor the palace, but camp in open fields was the ideal setting for stately ritual, such as welcoming ceremonies (*istiqbal*), paying homage (*kornish*), grand receptions and banquets of reconciliation, and giving robes of honour (khilats) and other presents.

Another example of public ritual moving with the camp is the royal pilgrimage, which in itself is used as a distinct incentive for travelling. We have noticed already the recurrent pilgrimages of Akbar to the shrine of Mu'in al-Din Chishti in Ajmer. Equally telling is the way Akbar founded his new capital Fatehpur in 1572 after visiting the Chishti shrines at Ajmer, Pakpattan and Sikri, apparently in gratitude for the birth of his sons Prince Salim and Murad. This almost one-year pilgrimage neither kept him from subduing oppressors and administering justice, nor from the usual feasting and hunting as 'worship was performed under the veil of pleasure'.[49]

Perhaps even more important than such public, political and religious processions was the fact that the camp represented a culture and mentality of its own. Actually, the Mughal camp combined the cosmopolitan ethos of mostly foreign mansabdars with the more parochial outlook of mostly indigenous zamindars. In the Mughal camp emerged a new, highly eclectic culture that was neither purely Persian nor purely Indian, neither purely Islamic nor purely Hindu. It was certainly non-sectarian and relatively liberal, as well as free from local attachments. The atmosphere in camp was probably not much unlike the atmosphere as described by one of the Mughal amirs: 'though there was much praying and fasting in the camp, gambling, sodomy, drinking and fornications were also prevalent.'[50] But despite the usual association with all kinds of licentious behaviour, the Mughal camp also served as a repository of knowledge, providing a vast system of schooling.[51] Camp society was relatively literate and both practical accountancy and news-writing, as well as all kinds of belles-lettres were well represented. Not surprisingly, the lingua franca of the imperial camp, *zaban-i urdu-i mu'alla,* gradually evolved into Urdu, being a mixture of Persian and various forms of Hindawi or the languages of the region. By constantly staying under canvas, entire generations of the nobility and many of its retainers were born and grew up in an environment that focused on imperial patronage that was relatively free from strong regional, religious or ethnic group feelings.[52]

Both the military and the administrative objectives of imperial mobility converged most visibly in the practice of hunting. Hunts could be organised when the court was temporarily settled in the capital and also when the army was on the move. Often we find the emperor hunting or hawking 'as he went', 'on the way' or 'along the road'. In all these cases, the bulk of the imperial troops were left behind and continued on their own route at their own pace. The hunting party accompanying the emperor usually included a few personal retainers and never exceeded the number of 1,000 horse and foot. At every stage of the hunt, special friends could be selected to join the emperor. Away from the tight ritual of the court, the excitement of hunting created a more convivial atmosphere, reminiscent of the one in Babur's erstwhile war-band, in which new relations of friendship and loyalty could be forged.

But apart from being an enjoyable pastime, hunting was an essential instrument of Mughal government. Under the veil of hunting,[53] the Mughals both rallied and suppressed the enormous military potential of the country surrounding the imperial hunting grounds. Hunting expeditions were often organised to inconspicuously mobilise troops or inspect mansabdari contingents. For example, Akbar's campaign against Chitor in 1567 started with a hunt in the Bari district, 'in order that the loyal and devoted leaders might come without the notoriety of being sent for, while others, either their servants or not, would, seeing that there was no prohibition, readily assemble in order to pay their respects.'[54] Hunting expeditions were also important for practising cavalry manoeuvres. Most prominent in this respect is the *qamarga.* From an area that could be as large as about 100 km in circumference, all the wild game was driven together into a small, enclosed circle where the king started the actual hunt.[55] Since the rounding up of wild animals involved similar manoeuvres to those on the battlefield, i.e. skirmishers in front of the centre with two flanks wheeling around the enemy, it was a most useful training camp.[56]

Similar to what we have seen for marching in general, hunts were also useful for making surveys and for gathering local intelligence as well as for subduing unruly areas, some of which were very close to the imperial centres, be it capitals or hunting grounds.[57] Abul Fazl himself admirably summarised the objectives of hunting as follows:

> The sublime thought of the wise Khedive in the enjoyment of hunting is that he may, without the awe inspired by royal majesty and without the intervention of prattlers – whose skirts are mostly stained with self-interest – acquire a knowledge of the events of the world, put down oppressors, and exalt the good who sit in the corner of contempt.[58]

Notwithstanding the fact that prescriptions of Islam and *adab* could warn against the unnecessary or excessive killing of game,[59] hunting remained one of the cornerstones of sixteenth- and seventeenth-century Mughal rule.[60]

Given the objective and capacity of perpetual movement, it is all the more surprising to find modern historians often disqualifying the Mughal army for its lack of speed and the lumber of its non-fighting masses. This criticism heavily underestimates the enormous success of the Mughal camp in integrating the empire, be it by hunting, by courtly ritual and pilgrimage, by propagating an eclectic cosmopolitan political culture, by surveillance and road building, or by its endless commercial and financial transactions. It also ignores the fact that cavalry remained by far the most important instrument of warfare in Mughal India. Similar to the camp, the ongoing prominence of the warhorse once again reminds us of the Mughal capacity to keep moving. Although horses did not really speed up the movement of the bigger camps, they certainly enhanced the striking power and reach of Mughal troops operating from these camps. Thus, it was not the long-term, strategic speed, but the temporary, tactical radius of action of the horse that made it such an effective instrument in bringing relatively large areas, at relatively long distances, under central control.

Warhorses

Although horses were to be found all over the sub-continent, the ecological conditions for horse breeding in India were far from ideal.[61] Only throughout the Indian extensions of the Arid Zone, stretching from Sind, the Punjab and Rajasthan into the dry shadow-zone of the Western Ghats and into the Deccan, could good warhorses be produced. But even here, horse breeding still to a considerable degree relied on the regular input of foreign breeds from Arabia, Iran and Central Asia. But what circumstances made India so much less suitable for horse breeding than its neighbouring areas in the west and northwest?

First of all, it appears that India's main drawback was the lack of extensive grazing areas, as well as the lack of suitable green and dry fodder crops. Although horses can do without hard feed such as all kinds of grain, they cannot dispense with grass or hay.[62] Overall, Indian grasses suffer from the extreme differences between rainy and dry seasons, which often make the soil at one time a swamp and at another hard, parched and cracked. Grass fields grow rapidly during the rains in late summer but, before the end of the year, the subsequent dryness again renders them unsuitable for pasture. Although continuous moisture and high temperatures tend to cause vigorous growth, the nutritive properties of grasses are low by being expended in the formation of this luxuriance. Since India has a relatively short natural grazing season, haymaking has to be done within a relatively short time, i.e. at the beginning of the grazing season, from about September to October. Actually, it is often too wet for haymaking when the grass is high towards the end of the rains, and after that the peasant is too busy with the kharif harvest of rabi sowing. Where rainfall is too light to inhibit haymaking there is precious little to make hay with, and in any case – probably as a natural consequence of these conditions – the Indian peasant has been a grass-cutter, but never a hay maker, and he always finds it hard to begin.[63]

Under these conditions, early British veterinary specialists considered so-called *dub* grass (*cynodon dactylon*) to be by far the most suitable Indian fodder for horses. Dub fared best in the drier western provinces where it was usually gathered and beaten by grass-cutters instead of being grazed. Other suitable grass species such as *dhaman* and *sewan* also fared best in the west and northwest of India.

The Indian alternatives for grass and hay were not very attractive either. Until the nineteenth century, India did not produce oats, the main fodder crop in Europe, while barley, the main horse feed in Arabia, was also in short supply. Not surprisingly, the Indian methods of feeding horses raised feelings of bewilderment on the part of Middle Eastern and European visitors. The French travellers Thévenot and Tavernier both confirm that India's horse-keepers must have faced real problems when feeding the huge numbers of incoming horses from Arabia, Iran and Central Asia.[64] The usual food for horses in Mughal India consisted of a mixture of soaked or boiled gram (*chuna*) or beans (*moth*) in summer, and green wheat and some barley (*khavid*) in winter, often supplemented by a mixture of flour, coarse brown sugar (*khand*) and clarified butter (*ghi*). Although all this served well as a supplementary ingredient to grass or hay, as an almost exclusive basis for feeding it was considered deficient, since it could not fully substitute for the nutritional value of grass and hay and it kept Indian horses small.

Indo-British breeders commonly considered the Indian diet not only insufficient but also detrimental to the horse's health. Apart from this, India's excessive heat and humidity made horses succumb to fatal diseases not met with in the Occident.[65] As a consequence, the best breeding grounds of India were to be found in relatively cool areas with modest levels of rainfall and, as horses require an almost continuous supply of fresh water, always near rivers and streams. All these features were more or less present at all the important breeding grounds of the Indian sub-continent, such as the Lakhi Jungle and other doabs of the Punjab as well as the Marathas studs along the Bhima river in the Deccan.

In a stimulating, recent study on Mongol ponies and Mamluk, i.e. Egyptian, horses, Masson Smith Jr suggested that the latter were larger by being supported on fodder rather than on grasses. Hence, although the Mamluk horses were fewer, they were stronger than the more numerous but lighter ponies of the Mongols. In other words, horses raised in more settled, agrarian circumstances enabled cavalry to be equipped more heavily: with armour and shield, lances and curved swords, in addition to bows and maces.[66] Earlier, Western Europe had already produced the *grand cheval*, which could carry the heavy knight of European feudalism and which successfully confronted the light cavalry of the Magyars. Although Masson Smith's thesis may have been true for the Middle Eastern and European cases, the Indian warhorse always retained a fairly bad reputation throughout history. One obvious reason for this may have been the Indian lack of oats and, according to Tavernier (see note 64), also barley as alternatives for grasses. But apart from deficient fodder crops, it appears that breeding methods played an equally important part. Obviously, good breeding depends on selecting the best stallions and mares. In the case of India, it was considered necessary to import strong foreign stallions to keep up the quality of the indigenous breed. Arab stallions had the best reputation in this regard, which is also supported by modern fact. For example, we know that, when an Arab stallion is crossed with another horse of a different breed but similar in size to himself, the offspring is frequently very much larger than either parent.[67] Perhaps this also partly explains the continued eagerness of rulers in South and Central Asia to stimulate cross-breeding with Arab stallions. It also suggests that the reduced size of the Mongol horse was due to a lack in the supply of Arabian stallions in the steppes of Inner Asia.

Now, for understanding the range of the Mongol armies, it appears that the size or strength of the Mongol pony is less relevant than the logistical problems raised by the transition from a nomadic breeding and feeding complex, i.e. based on extensive grazing, to a more intensive, stationary complex in which horse breeding is combined with settled agriculture supporting large populations. The latter situation was prevalent in the eastern and southern parts of the sub-continent. Here, horse breeding appears to have been a relatively small-scale enterprise. Although the courts often stimulated the practice, it very much remained a matter of individual landlords and peasants, who combined breeding with all kinds of other agricultural activities. Also significant is Abul Fazl's remark that the horses at the Mughal court could do with the fodder of three *bighas* of cultivated land, which is a mere 1.5 to 2.5 per cent of the grazing area needed for one horse in Mongolia.[68] Although during the eighteenth century horse breeding was to become an important state enterprise, as for example in Mysore and Rohilkhand, states mostly preferred to import foreign horses.

Still, India's dry and open western and northwestern regions produced a fair amount of good-enough warhorses.[69] In terms of horse-breeding criteria, regions such as Sind, Rajasthan and parts of the Punjab are much closer to Central Asia and Iran than to India. Not surprisingly, these areas also demarcate the furthest stage of thirteenth-century Mongol expansion. Actually, horse breeding in these places was known to have been stimulated by the successive invasions of cavalry armies from the northwest. Despite the common liking for foreign breeds, throughout India's medieval history rulers procured a great number of their cavalry mounts from the various indigenous breeding grounds of Sind and the Punjab. Even the Mughals, who took most of their horses from Central Asia, could hardly dispense with the nearby supply of the Indian-bred horses from these areas.

Although the Mughals considered the best breeds to come from abroad, that is, Arabia, Iraq, Iran, Khorasan and Central Asia, they also kept lots of mixed breeds, called *Mujannas* in the case of Arab blood, and *Yabus* in the case of Turkish blood. Less precious were the home-bred Indian horses: the best kind called *Tazis*, the middling *Janglas*, and the inferior *Tattus*. The best Indian breeds were the Arab-like horses from Sind, Baluchistan and especially Kachchh, the *Sanuji* from the Punjab, and the *Pachwarya* from Rajasthan.[70] Small but strong Indian horses included the *Gut* from the western Himalayas and the *Tanghan* from the eastern Himayalas. Actually, none of these breeds were fixed classes and, in the course of time, their reputation could change considerably. For example, the *Tazi* horse originally referred to a horse from Iran but, as noted, was included later under the lesser Indian breeds. In general, there existed two ideal types: 1) the Arabo-Persian breed, relatively small, lively, active and vigorous horses with great speed and fire, requiring intensive training and control; and 2) the Turkish breed, slower in its movements, but in height, docility, durability and perseverance surpassing the Arab. The stamina and staying qualities of the Turkish horse rendered it particularly valuable on long marches and for heavy duty, which also made it the best horse for military service under the Mughals.

The early Mughal court stables supported about 12,000 horses, of which about one-quarter consisted of Arabo-Persians and about one-half of

Turks.[71] As Abul Fazl mentions that the common Janglas and Tattus were thrown out of the imperial stables, it appears that the quality of Mughal horses was improved under Akbar. The latter also attempted to attract good horses by paying the horse-dealers high prices with ready money, as well as by giving premiums on the maintenance allowances of foreign horses.[72] During Shah Jahan's reign, about one-half of the Mughal troopers, most of them Turanis and Iranis, were mounted on Turkish breeds, the other half, mostly Rajputs and Marathas, on various Indian species.[73] According to a later, eighteenth-century source, the common Indian cavalry horse was a Tattu.[74] Probably this does not indicate any decline of the breed during the eighteenth century, but merely points towards the different quality levels of the Indian cavalry. For example, the household contingent of the emperor possessed by far the best horses, including a fair number of Arabs. Mansabdars used mostly Turkish mounts, whereas the common Mughal troopers and zamindars had to content themselves with Tattus and other indigenous breeds.

Considering the fact that the Mughal cavalry largely depended on foreign imports of Turkish breeds, it was crucial to control the trade routes through Kabul to Central Asia. Earlier though, India had procured a great number of its foreign horses by the overseas supply lines bringing so-called *bahri* horses from Hormuz and Aden, via the ports of the Konkan and Kanara Coasts, to the various courts of the Muslim sultanates and Vijayanagara. The latter state, especially, did much to entice a great number of Arab, Persian and Portuguese horse-traders to southern India.[75] As Sewell expresses it, its ruler Krishnadevaraya (r. 1509–30) 'wanted horses, and again horses' for his perpetual wars against the Deccan sultanates.[76] Many of the Portuguese horse-dealers used to exchange horses for the well-known diamonds of the mines of the Carnatic.[77] After the fall of Vijayanagara (1565), there appears to have taken place a northward shift of the transpeninsular trade routes, from Bhatkal/Goa – Vijayanagara, to Dabhol/Chaul – Golkonda – Masulipatam and Surat – Burhanpur – Golkonda.[78] In a way, this late-sixteenth-century shift paved the way for the restoration of the old Dakshinapatha following the Mughal conquest of Khandesh and Ahmadnagar (*c.* 1600–35). More relevant in this context is the simultaneous drying up of the overseas horse trade. Although the Portuguese continued to bring a few horses to Ikkeri, the trade in general shifted largely to the overland routes, mainly through the various fairs of Rajasthan and Malwa.[79] Only during the late seventeenth and early eighteenth centuries, was part of the overseas connection, especially with Arabia and Kachchh, restored due to the rising demand of the Maratha cavalry.[80] In general, though, it would probably not be too bold to observe that, as much as the fall of Vijayanagara state coincided with the decline of the overseas horse trade, so the rise of the Mughal state was concurrent with the domination of the overland supply lines.

Taking a closer look at the main characteristics of the overland horse trade, it is remarkable that, although most Mughal horses came from Turkistan and were bred by Turkoman and Uzbek nomads, Afghan intermediaries dominated the horse trade with India. After the Afghan dealers had bought the horses at low prices from the nomadic tribes, they were fattened for one or two months in the various meadows around Kabul. During October and November, the horses were brought to India and sold through an extensive network of horse fairs or *melas*, which, according to an intricate timetable, reached Indian markets as far south as Tirupati in the Carnatic or as far east as Hajipur in Bihar. Although it is very difficult to size up this trade, figures range from 25,000, as mentioned by Bernier, to Manucci's 100,000.[81] The eighteenth-century figures have about the same range.[82] Babur himself mentions that in the early sixteenth century, about 7 to 10,000 horses were imported through Kabul into India.[83] Based on the statistics of the *A'in-i Akbari*, Moosvi calculates that about 16,000 horses must have been imported annually to replace the existing number of Turkish horses in the Mughal army, arriving at an Indian total of 1,000 Persian and 21,000 Turkish horses. This would result in a massive trade volume of at least three million rupees.[84]

Obviously, the horse trade was important not only in terms of horses delivered for the army but also in terms of taxes that could be raised. According to Abul Fazl, Akbar enforced a tax of two to three rupees on every horse imported through Kabul and Qandahar.[85] According to Manucci, horse-dealers had to pay 25 per cent of the value of their horses on crossing the Indus.[86] In the end, however, overtaxing could always endanger supply itself or force dealers to look for alternative outlets.

Although most of the contemporary figures may have exaggerated the numbers of horses imported, they still illustrate the close association between the Central Asian horse trade and Mughal power. This was nothing new though. The Afghans, especially, had a widely acclaimed reputation for using the horse trade as a springboard to gain political power. For example, it was told of the Lodi sultans of Delhi – the Afghan predecessors of Babur – that they had started their careers as horse-traders from the northwest.[87] Of course, horse-traders like the Lodis could easily trade their horses for revenue assignments or pose military threats by mounting their horses with warriors. Horse-traders were often hard to distinguish from horse-raiders. Thus we have several examples of armies that approached their adversaries under the guise of horse-traders.[88] The military threat posed by horse-traders is also demonstrated in one of the anecdotes of Aurangzeb, in which the emperor reprimanded Amir Khan, his governor in Kabul, for letting into the country 11,000 horses fit for service but accompanied by one groom for every two horses. According to Aurangzeb:

> It is a very strange act of negligence on the part of Amir Khan who has been trained by me and knows my mind. It is as if 5,500 brave

> Turanis have entered the imperial territory from foreign parts. Well such [was the number of the] men who wrested the kingdom of Hindustan from the hands of the Afghans. . . . In future, he should know it to be his duty to avoid this sort of action, and he should remedy the past in this way, that whenever the droves of horses arrive, he should allow only one groom to every 20 horses, and that groom should be a useless old and helpless man.[89]

This fairly common pattern in which the horse trade ushered in, directly or indirectly, political power and even state formation, once again repeated itself during the eighteenth century when we see the emergence of a string of Afghan chieftaincies along the major horse-trading routes from Kabul to southern and eastern India.

Considering the significance of the horse trade, we have to raise the question as to what lay at the root of such ongoing high levels of demand. Or to put it more bluntly, what made the horse such an attractive instrument of war in India? When considering the effectiveness of the warhorse in India, we should first of all point towards the quantities involved. As had been shown by the Mongol armies, horses appeared to be most effective when used in great numbers. Now, despite the fact that the Indian climate did not favour widespread horse breeding, the Mughal army, including its mansabdari contingents, could still employ between 100,000 and 200,000 mounted warriors using between an equal and a double quantity of warhorses. Within the semi-arid reaches of the Uttarapatha and Dakshinapatha, these quantities of horses really must have acted as a kind of steamroller, hard to withstand by any number of badly drilled infantry or badly manufactured artillery. Whereas, in European battles, cavalry numbers usually went into the thousands, the quantities of horsemen in Indian battles always went into the tens of thousands. The ideal Mughal trooper was supposed to have at least two horses, which considerably enhanced his radius of action both in campaigns and in battle. In day-to-day practice, it appears that only the ahadis and the mansabdars who were close to the emperor employed more than one horse. Nonetheless, as in the case of the Mongols, the sheer numbers of horsemen the Mughals could muster and bring into actual battle operations must have been as decisive as any advantage in tactics or weaponry.

Coming to the latter two aspects, the strength of the Mughal cavalry on the battlefield lay in the combined employment of heavy cavalry in the centre and light mounted archers on the flanks. In the tactic called *taulqama* the latter wheeled around the enemy, firing volleys of arrows. This had to be done repeatedly from about 250 metres maximum, every archer having about forty to fifty arrows in his quiver. The tactic was used to wear out the enemy's troops, to lure them into uncoordinated and untimely action and, in other words, to make them easy victims of the oncoming charge of the heavy cavalry. Recently, Douglas Streusand has rightly stressed the pre-eminent role of mounted archers in winning battles for the early Mughals.[90] Here we should take account of the fact that effective employment of mounted archers was far from easy, as it not only required excellent horsemanship but also the capacity to construct, maintain and use the small but penetrating composite bow. All of these talents combined were only present in the Turkish horse-warriors from Central Asia, many of them endowed with a (semi-)nomadic background and long-time practical experience with horses. Although India did not fail to produce archers of its own, horse archery never really struck deep roots as it lacked a strong tradition of nomadic horse breeding.

Indian bows, mostly made of bamboo, were of lesser quality than the Central Asian or Persian composite ones.[91] Similarly, the composite bows of the Mughal army were supposed to have much greater range and penetration than those of the Marathas.[92] The Indian climate, however, was known to harm the bow's effectiveness. Babur, for example, dreaded the Indian monsoon rains because the humid air ruined his precious bows made of horn, wood and sinews.[93] The construction of the composite bow itself was time-consuming and, to a certain extent, based on the Central Asian climate. Its construction took about one year: the slow drying of the glue required about three months of cool weather, to be followed by warmer weather in which sinew could be applied. To protect the bow from the Indian climate, it was often completely covered with leather or lacquer to protect the glue. Later, the Mughals even turned to steel bows. The penetration of the bow depended on the distance, its size, the arrow-head and the angle of entry. Within 100 m an average bow of about 30 kg would have penetrated any mail or armour if equipped with a steel arrow-head and if squarely hitting the surface. The heavier bow could use a heavier arrow to achieve a higher penetration. All in all, mounted archery was not a technology that was easily adopted whenever needed. On the contrary, it was a highly specialised discipline requiring the highest levels of horsemanship and archery, again only to be provided by experienced horse-warriors with a nomadic background, preferably from Central Asia.

In contrast to the mounted archers, the tactics of the heavy cavalry usually consisted of charging into the enemy's rank, mostly with swords, and with or without leather shields. Although charging required some cohesion, it was usually without much discipline or order, often resulting in uncontrolled one-to-one combat. The Mughal charge should not be confused with the shock charge of the medieval knights of Europe. Even the heaviest of Mughal troopers sat loose in their saddles, raising themselves to mow down their enemies, perfectly able to cast a spear and take it up again from the ground at full speed. They were able to stop their horses with a jerk and laughed about the European ways of 'taking their horses up by degrees as well as riding with our feet at length'.[94] Despite the lack of order, well-known Mughal cavalry movements included sudden turns and manoeuvres, such as the *courbette* and the *oran,* especially designed to confront elephants. Individual horsemanship was important and was exercised in the tremendously popular *chaugan*, the Mughal variety of polo. The ideal Mughal cavalryman rode his mount on a loose rein but using 'thorn bits' and in a saddle that gave closer contact with his horse's movements than the European war saddle.[95]

Despite the high level of individual horsemanship, Mughal cavalry lacked the collective manoeuvres of European cavalry contingents. Here it is interesting to cite Manucci, who once demonstrated to the Mughal general Jai Singh the mode of European cavalry warfare. With three Europeans he demonstrated what must have been a kind of European caracole:

> We rode out with our carbines, two pistols in our holsters and two in our waist-belts, and carrying our swords. We rode two and two and began to career about, our horses being excellent. Then first of all we skirmished with the carbine, and after some circling and recircling, letting off our pistols, we made pretence of flight and pursuit. Then turning round and making a half-circle, the fugitive attacked the pursuer and let off his pistol. Thus we went on till all our charges were fired off, of course without bullets. Then laying hand upon our swords we made gestures as if giving sword-cuts, which the other parried.

Upon this spectacle, the raja mounted on his elephant and asked Manucci 'several times if really they fought like this in Europe?'.

> I answered that this was only a small specimen. We would show him sport when it came to reality, observing the same order; and if there were on the field dead men or horses, we would ride over them as if riding on a carpet, and make no account of them.[96]

What the amazed raja did not know, of course, was that such disciplined cavalry tactics proved rather ineffective on the European battlefield. Collective drill was fine for infantry but for the heavy cavalry it was of limited use. In general, as well as in the Mughal case, heavy cavalry appears to have been most effective when freely charging together, preferably using great numbers.

Apart from the mounted archers, heavy cavalry made the Mughals superior in the open field, especially in their confrontations with the lighter, but also speedier, horsemen of the Deccan sultanates or the Uzbeks. The body armour (*bagtar*) of the heavy Mughal horse-warrior consisted mostly of a helmet (*khud, dabalgha, top*) covered with iron or copper mail (*mighfar*), steel vambraces (*dastana*) and greaves (*ranak*), and a plated cuirass, either worn over or integrated with a coat of mail reaching to the knees (*zirih*), and maybe worn over a quilted jacket (*qabcha*) or under a quilted cotton coat (*chilta*).[97] Like Indian steel in general, Indian armour had a certain reputation for being pierced neither by swords and lances nor by musket and arrow shots.[98] The Mughals, however, used, neither the lamellar armour of the Mongols nor the scale armour of the Europeans. Fryer contrasted India with Europe, where it was the custom 'to appear all armed cap-à-pie'. Insufficient Indian armour may have accounted for the ongoing popularity of slashing with a broad sword instead of stabbing with sharp-pointed sabres that could pierce 'the junctures of the harness, or the plates of a coat of mail'.[99] According to Geleynssen de Jongh, the Indian heat made European harnesses or helmets too uncomfortable.[100] Monserrate even claims that the Mughals had no heavy cavalry at all.[101] It seems, however, that Mughal body armour was designed to find the best possible combination of protection and flexibility. Hence, it was heavier than the usual south Indian outfit consisting of thick quilted tunics that the Portuguese called *laudees,* but probably lighter than the scaled suit of armour of Europe. Anyway, it was certainly much cheaper than the latter.

Although the Mughals used mounted archers and heavy cavalry to great effect on the Indian battlefield, in terms of tactics and technology there was hardly any innovation. Long before the coming of the Mughals, mounted archers and heavy cavalry appear to have been common elements in every major Indian army.[102] Hence, the success of Mughal cavalry was hardly one of technological or tactical innovation. What really made the difference was the Mughal capacity to reinvigorate an already well-proven technique of Central Asian warfare and to use it on an unprecedented scale on the Indian sub-continent. In terms of cavalry warfare, there was nothing new, but there was certainly more, under the Mughal sun. Only during the later stages of empire did mounted archery become somewhat less prominent, possibly following the reduced recruitment of Central Asian troopers. All this confirms that the Mughal success story was not only a matter of military superiority.

Apart from its purely military aspects, the horse derived a great deal of its appreciation from being an important marker of fine manners and nobility. Of course, India had a long tradition of equine literature, going back to the *Ashvashastra* of the legendary Salihotra and to part of the Indian science of statehood or *Arthashastra.* Part of this tradition continued in the Indo-Persian genre of the *Faras-nama*, which also incorporated the Arabo-Persian tradition of *Furusiyya* literature. Basically, a Faras-nama was a small encyclopaedia of facts relating to horses. The contents usually included a preface explaining the importance of horses, with sayings and anedoctes of equine heroes, such as Salihotra, Ismail, Solomon, Muhammad, and various Persian kings. This was followed by chapters on the recognition of the horse's age by its teeth; nomenclature of horses of different types and colours; good and bad qualities of horses and indications of their presence or absence;

shortcomings of horses and ways to rectify them; proper methods of breeding, training, controlling and caring for horses; and, most important of all, ill health in horses, with prescriptions of treatments and drugs appropriate for different diseases and injuries.[103] From the point of view of modern horsemanship, it was somewhat impractical and esoteric. As a literary achievement it served well to bolster the horse as one of the prime symbols of royalty. In the Faras-namas the horse was often presented as the mount of kings, while knowledge of the horse distinguished kings and nobles from the common man.[104] The Mughals themselves often used equine terms such as 'the imperial stirrup' (*rikab-i humayun*) as metaphors of their authority; hence, to be at court was often described as 'present with the stirrup' (*hazir-i rikab*). White or other stallions at court, as depicted on Mughal miniatures, also evoked images of royal authority but, for the Mughals, the horse meant much more than just a very effective instrument of power. For them it was a token of royalty, nobility and chivalry. As may be seen from the highly propagandistic battle scenes on Mughal miniatures, good wars were always fought on horses.

Elephants, dromedaries and oxen

Even more than the horse, the elephant had a huge ceremonial standing at the royal courts of India, but, in contrast to the horse, it lost considerable ground on the actual battlefield during the Mughal period. Apart from its ritual and propagandistic function, it remained important as a beast of burden, as such complementing the main task of dromedaries and oxen, the other two animals that made the Mughal ideal of perpetual movement such a daunting reality.

Unlike the horse, the elephant was very much at home in India. Whereas horse breeding gravitated towards the dry northwestern and central parts of India, the natural breeding grounds for the elephant were the moist and thick jungles of the east and south. In general, one may say that the elephant is sensitive to cold and dry areas, as well as to a rapid change of climate, when it becomes liable to diseases.[105] During the reign of Akbar, many wild elephants could still be found in the various extensions of the huge eastern forests, even near to the settled centres of the provinces of Agra, Malwa, Allahabad, Bihar, Bengal and Orissa. According to Abul Fazl, the best elephants came from Punnah in Bundelkhand. Despite this gravitation towards the humid east, we find elephants as far west as eastern Gujarat, as well as along the Western Ghats. About one century later, however, it appears that most of the elephant stock had retreated into the thick forests of Gondwana proper, of eastern Bengal, and along the eastern Himalayan foothills.[106]

Although under Akbar the Mughals started to breed a few elephants themselves, elephant breeding was generally considered too costly, since elephants became fully grown only between the ages of twenty and twenty-five years, while training could only start at the age of ten.[107] Apart from the high initial expenses, the maintenance of elephants required lots of servants and huge quantities of fodder. Moosvi calculates these costs at an average of about thirty rupees per month for a male, and seventeen rupees per month for a female.[108] Anyway, a mature elephant would spend about eighteen hours eating at least 200 kg of green fodder and 100 l of water. Tavernier thought that the maintenance costs of elephants would amount to a staggering 500 rupees a month. The keepers attempted to reduce costs by taking them daily out of court to the jungle to eat the branches of trees, sugar cane and millet, to the detriment of the peasants.[109]

Given these enormous expenses, the Mughals preferred to procure most of their elephants at a mature age. They were often accepted as tribute, taken as plunder or caught in a wild state in hunting expeditions. Elephants as tribute were mainly gathered from chiefs near the natural hunting grounds of Gondwana, Nepal and Bengal. For example, during the Mughal campaign in Berar in 1637, the Mughals forced Kukia, the zamindar of Deogarh, to pay all of his 170 elephants as tribute to the court,[110] and during Shah Jahan's reign, the rulers of Bijapur and Golkonda regularly sent elephants, many of them Ceylonese, as tribute. The Raja of Nepal sent one elephant in tribute annually.[111] To buy elephants on the market was considered extremely expensive; in early Mughal times it ranged from *c.* 100 rupees to even 100,000 rupees.[112] The most valuable, not being the largest but the most courageous elephants, were supposed to come from Ceylon, although these were less suited for mountainous terrain.[113] At the end of the seventeenth century, Ceylonese elephants would cost less than 1,000 rupees at Jaffnapatam, that is, without the travel expenses for overseas transport to Golkonda and Bengal.[114] Initially, the Mughals imported Ceylonese elephants through Golkonda and Bengal, but after the conquest of the Deccan sultanates they could procure them directly from source. For example, in 1703, the Mughal general in Coromandel, Da'ud Khan Panni spent 10,304 hun for what must have been thirty to fifty elephants from Ceylon.[115]

Apart from tribute and trade, the emperor himself caught many elephants in large hunting missions. The best season for hunting elephants was from December to March. There were various ways to capture elephants. The simplest but also crudest method was called *gad* and caught individual elephants in covered pits. More usual was the so-called *kheda* in which elephants were brought into an enclosure surrounded by a ditch or fence work. In this the wild elephants were either driven by hunters in the manner of the *qamarga*, by making noise and fire, or were seduced with fodder or tame females. The next stage often involved wearing out the captured elephants by continued noise or by provoking fighting with the tame females that were sent into the enclosure. After they were thus worn down, elephants could be caught with a rope, either from the ground or by hunters at the back of the females. Subsequently, the taming of elephants was achieved by manipulating the elephant's sleeping and eating habits or by having them tied to tame females.[116]

According to Hawkins there were about 40,000 elephants in the service of Mughal army.[117] The Mughal emperor himself kept a maximum of about 5 to 7,000 elephants in his *fil-khana*, of which about 100 of the very best were reserved for his personal collection (*khassa*).[118] This number is certainly impressive, the more so because the Delhi sultans at no time appear to have had more than 3,000 elephants.[119] Later, the Mughal numbers appear to have come down again, to less than 1,000, most of them used for transportation purposes, with only about 100 males ready for war.[120] At court, the elephants were arranged in accordance with their strength, each class sub-divided into large, middling and young ones, the last containing ten different kinds. The strongest of them were allowed the most and the best fodder as well as the most attendants, all of whom appear to have been indigenous Indians.[121] Apart from one or two drivers (*mahawats*), maybe accompanied by an assistant (*bhoi*), there were one to three servants (*meths*) for fetching fodder and caparisoning the elephants. Training was in charge of the *faujdar* who was also superintendent of troops (*halqa*) of ten, twenty or thirty elephants. The most important element of training was to teach elephants to stand firm at the sight of fire and at the noise of artillery and rockets. In the battlefield, elephants performed best when being *mast*. This was a wild, rutting state that could take several months. Mast was a sign of superabundant physical energy and vitality but mast elephants also proved extremely difficult to handle.[122] Much of the elephant's harness was intended to keep control over mast elephants, while drugs and arrack were also used to keep them under control. The care and maintenance of the halqas was further delegated to the mansabdars.

Coming to the elephants' function in Mughal warfare, one may say that they performed three major tasks.[123] First of all, the elephant had an impressive appearance. With its elaborate make-up, rings, bells and necklaces, it was one of those really exciting wonders of India that struck every outsider with awe, be it in processions and organised fights at court, or in the actual heat of campaigns and battle. Even more than in the case of the horse, the elephant was an ancient symbol of Indian royalty, its use being considered the prerogative of kings. Very much like the science of the horse, elephant husbandry in India could build on the long tradition of *Gajashastra* or elephant science, going back to the mythical founder Nilakantha, the author of the *Matanga-lila*. But in contrast with Ashvashastra, Gajashashtra was not transmitted into any comparable Islamo-Persian tradition of elephant management and thus very much remained an Indian expertise. Nevertheless, the pomp and circumstance displayed by elephants made them a conspicuous part of the whole plethora of good-looking arms surrounding the Mughal army.

In its purely military role, the position of the elephant declined during the seventeenth century. Much earlier, from the eleventh to thirteenth centuries onwards, the horse-archers of Islam had already driven the elephant from its pre-eminent military position – at least in those parts of India that were conquered by the Turks.[124] But there also seems to have been a remarkable revival of the war-elephant during the sixteenth century, as large numbers of elephants appeared, not only in the Indo-Afghan armies of Hemu at Panipat (1556) and Da'ud Karrani at Tukaroi (1575),[125] but also in the Mughal army under Akbar.[126] It was only under Akbar's successors that their numbers fell off again and that they almost disappeared from the front line of battle. At this stage, they mainly served as high platforms from where the commanding generals could watch, and be watched from, the battle scene. Obviously, the visibility of the commander was of the utmost importance for his troops. If he was killed or, more frequently, just disappeared, the army lost its employer and, in no time, all fighting men left the battle scene and the battle was lost, the more so because Indian armies were often held together by a precarious network of temporary alliances, often culminating in just one man.[127] Exactly this happened to Rana Sanga at Khanua (1527), Hemu at Panipat (1556), Dara Shukoh at Samugarh (1658), Prince Shuja at Khajwa (1659) and Prince Azam Shah and his son Bidar Bakht at Jajau (1707).[128] Although the elephant's platform or *hauda* could be made of high and strong metal plates, the leader remained extremely vulnerable by being a clear and visible target for the enemy's archery and musketry. Thus, there was always a kind of ambivalence on the part of the commanding generals: although riding an elephant in battle offered them status and authority, it also very much exposed them to unfriendly fire.

To account for the decreasing military role of the elephant, André Wink recently stressed the diminished availability of elephants as well as the gradual shift to a warhorse economy from as early as the twelfth and thirteenth centuries. The latter involved the outmanoeuvring of elephants by tactical horse movements of the Central Asian type.[129] But given the major drawbacks of elephants against mounted archery, as explained by Wink and others, how can we explain the revival of the elephant in the Indian armies of the sixteenth century? Here one can only speculate.

Perhaps there was a temporary decline in mounted archery in India. This had happened earlier to the Byzantines who knew mounted archery before, but failed to maintain their skill against, their Turkish adversaries.[130] As we have stressed already, mounted archery could not do without ongoing close contacts with the Turkish steppes of Central Asia. It is also possible, though, that the diminishing availability of elephantss had merely been a temporary phenomenon following massive hunting. In any case, during the sixteenth century, elephants were again abundant all over northern India. Although the shift to a warhorse economy was important enough, it could hardly have prevented the ongoing use of elephants, which had an entirely different ecological habitat. Looking at possible military explanations, it is plausible, of course, that elephants became better equipped during the sixteenth century and were protected by leather, mail and plate armour, while their haudas were not only covered with high iron or brass plates, but were also adjusted to hold one or two heavy muskets (*gajnal*). But perhaps more important than these technological improvements was some kind of tactical shift in the employment of elephants. It appears that they were no longer expected to stand in front of the battle line ready to break the rank of the enemy.[131] In the earlier Hindu armies, elephants were employed as a standing wall in defence or as a moving wall in attack, i.e. in the front rank and centre, preceding the infantry in order to attack at the outset of the battle.[132] Obviously, fast-moving and evasive cavalry made this tactic much less effective. Although elephants retained their traditional function of breaking through the enemy's ranks, to stiffen their own ranks and to confuse the charge of cavalry,[133] during the sixteenth century, it appears elephants were more often kept as a reserve in the rear. According to one Jesuit observer:

> Elephants thus equipped are not placed in the front line, as they would shut out the enemy from the view of the soldiers, and would, when wounded, break the ranks of the soldiers, and throw the army into disorder. They are kept in the rear of the force; and should the enemy penetrate so far, this formidable troupe is brought suddenly into action, to bar his further progress.[134]

Abul Fazl maintained that experienced men of Hindustan considered the value of a good elephant as equal to that of 500 horses; and they believed that, when guided by a few bold men armed with matchlocks, such an elephant alone was worth even double that number.[135] But as Babur had shown, even when using slightly different tactics, elephants remained extremely vulnerable to the massive employment of horse-archers.

With the onset of gunpowder weaponry, elephants definitively lost their position at the front line of battle to the artillery. As elephants had a natural aversion to excessive fire and noise, cannon and rockets were particularly effective in frightening elephants, often driving them into friendly ranks.[136] Nevertheless, elephants fitted with rams and battering equipment continued to be used in sieges, for ramming gates, doorways, or even walls and buildings.[137] In retrospect, it appears that only the very best Central Asian armies, equipped with the best-trained mounted archers, could really play havoc with the Indian elephant. This had been the case during the early Islamic and Mongol invasions, as well as the early Mughal conquests. But it was only in the seventeenth century, following the increasing use of gunpowder weapons, that elephants became fully obsolete.

They remained important, however, as beasts of burden carrying exceptionally heavy weights or bulky goods, such as cannon or tenting gear. Under peaceful conditions, elephants were more tractable and docile than dromedaries or bullocks and, although very expensive, were perfectly suited to crossing marchlands, streams and, rivers, as well as creating tracks through dense vegetation or thick jungle (see Plate 6).[138] Also, in the hills they often served better than carts or dromedaries.[139] Albeit on a limited scale, transportation remained an important function of the Indian elephant, even in the nineteenth-century Indo-British armies.

The two animals that really sustained Mughal mobility in the field were the dromedary and the ox. The moving court and army could never do without the thousands of dromedaries and oxen, endlessly carrying the court's belongings and its provisions from one place to the other. First, the dromedary, within the southern Arid Zone of the Middle East, Iran and northwest India, may be considered by far the most efficient beast of burden. It was not only capable of going for several days without drinking, it could also carry relatively heavy loads (150–200 kg) at a speed of about 30 km a day. Unloaded it could travel for many days at double that speed. With the campaign in Gujarat in 1573, Akbar's she-camels were supposed to have made 200 km a day.[140] Unlike cattle, camels were economical feeders that never overgrazed the vegetation and kept moving while feeding. On the march, they didn't need any extra fodder. Moreover, as beasts of burden they were capable of keeping pace with the rapid movements and long marches of cavalry units. Dromedaries were, however, only fit for relatively flat and dry terrain and in general were not able to survive in the very humid conditions of eastern India. Still, according to Modave (1971, p. 328), in the four cities of Faizabad, Lucknow, Agra and Delhi there were at least as many as 100,000 camels. During Mughal campaigns, we find dromedaries in action as far east as Assam and as far south as the Coromandel Coast.

Although the dromedary was already domesticated before 1000 BC, it was only around the beginning of our era that it became the most efficient means of transport in the Middle East. According to the pioneering work by Richard Bulliet, this was partly the result of the invention of the new, more convenient north-Arabian saddle, and partly due to the increased integration of camel-breeding nomads into settled society. The spread of the dromedary entailed the gradual disappearance of transportation on wheels and on Bactrian camels. The latter retreated to the equally arid, but colder climate of Central Asia. Later, in Khorasan, where the habitats of dromedaries and camels overlapped, strong and cold-resistant hybrids (*bukhtis*) could be bred that were able to link Central Asia with the Middle East. Apart from these hybrids, a new breed of one-humped camel was developed that could resist the colder conditions of Iran and southern Central

Asia. According to Bulliet these developments in Khorasan took place well into the Islamic period. He also believes that it seems more than likely that, in South Asia, the one-humped camel became known in significant quantities only after 1000 AD, which suggests that the introduction of the dromedary occurred simultaneously with the expansion of Islam. Thus, it appears that Indian dromedaries, mainly those from Baluchistan and Rajasthan, had a fairly late start on the Indian sub-continent.[141]

The best camel breeds in India were the small but strong Afghan or Pahari dromedaries that were also fit for the cold and hilly conditions of Central Asia. The Mughals were very well aware that good bukhti dromedaries could be produced from interbreeding one-humped female dromedaries (*arwanas*) with two-humped male Bactrian camels (*bughur*).[142] In northwestern India, excellent camel breeds were found around the Thar Desert in Rajasthan and in Sind, Kachchh, Kathiawar and Baluchistan. The availability of these dromedaries was, however, closely tied to the rhythm of transhumancy. Along the Indus valley, for example, it was difficult to find suitable dromedaries during the summer when they would be off to the higher and cooler mountains. At the same time, dromedaries could not be used indiscriminately under all circumstances. In general, they were highly sensitive to the vicissitudes of climate, and to the stresses of bad weather and change of country.[143] Apart from being less at home in the more humid east, all the sub-varieties appear to have had their own limited radius of action. For example, dromedaries from Sind were not at all suitable for travelling the mountain passes towards Qandahar, which fact both the Mughals and the British experienced to their dismay during their various Afghan campaigns.

Although Akbar's army maintained about 6 to 7,000 camels and dromedaries of its own, in case of campaigns a great deal more had to be hired from Baluchi and Raibari nomadic breeders and transporters. Probably thanks to their crucial role as transporters, some of these tribes had achieved a considerable political standing. For example, during the late fifteenth century, the Dodai-Baluchi chiefs migrated to the central Indus valley, establishing their own semi-autonomous chiefdoms in Dera Ismail Khan, Dera Fatah Khan and Dera Ghazi Khan.[144] Although other camel breeders may have achieved a status as Rajput chiefs, many others preferred to stay aloof from local politics. Nomadic camel breeders, such as the Charans and Bhats, played an important role as protectors of caravans and cattle, as well as peacemakers and bardic genealogists at the various Rajput courts.[145] In more practical terms, though, their main asset was their specialised knowledge of the dromedary. As Abul Fazl knew, the Raibaris were 'a class of Hindus who are acquainted with the habits of the camel [i.e. dromedary]', and who 'teach the country-bred *lok* camel [i.e. the male dromedary] so to step as to pass over great distances in a short time'. Besides, they served well as camel-mounted messengers and were often put in charge of herds of breeding camels.[146]

Apart from its important role as a beast of burden, the dromedary even makes a remarkable appearance on the battlefield, thanks to the development of a small swivel gun (*zamburak, shutarnal, shahin*) that was attached to the saddle of the dromedary. These zamburaks were first mentioned by Bernier, who reports that Aurangzeb took two to three hundred camel-guns with him on his expedition to Kashmir in 1663.[147] Although probably an Indo-Mughal innovation, zamburaks were more systematically employed by the eighteenth-century Afghan armies of the Ghilzais against the Safavids, and of the Durranis against the Marathas, their use subsequently spreading to Iran and the Middle East. More than the gajnal, which was attached to the elephant, the zamburak could adapt the increasing use of gunpowder to the existing mobility of Indian warfare. Hence, it could be smoothly integrated into the cavalry-oriented armies of the Mughals and the Afghans. The zamburak had the size of a double musket, was fixed to the saddle of the camel, and could be fired from the camel's back. The swivel ensured an increased flexibility in firing. To control the fire and to protect the animal against the shock of discharge the camel was usually made to kneel on the ground. To prevent its rising and moving each leg was fastened with a cord, but even under attack camels proved extremely stolid and relatively unperturbed by gunfire. Obviously, on the part of the camel-drivers all this required a great deal of training and drill.[148]

Finally, we come to the ox. Unlike the horse and the dromedary, but much like the elephant, and as the official name indicates, the *Bos Indicus* was very much an indigenous species. But, in contrast to the elephant, the ox fared well under both dry and humid conditions. As such, it was the ideal intermediary between the two different ecological zones of India. Tavernier's report is revealing in this respect:

> It is an astonishing sight to behold caravans numbering 10,000 or 12,000 oxen together, for the transport of rice, corn, and salt – in the places where they exchange these commodities – carrying rice to where only corn grows, and corn to where only rice grows.[149]

Although the ox travelled much more slowly and could carry only about a third of the dromedary's burden, besides taking much more food on the way, the main advantage of the ox was its all-India reach and availability, the only restriction being, perhaps, the need to shoe in rough and mountainous places.[150] For example, on his trip from Surat to Masulipatam (1617), the Dutch factor Pieter van den Broecke witnessed that the oxen of his caravan were shoed at Yacktien, a place along the Dudna river, which also happened to be the frontier town between the territories of the Mughals and Ahmadnagar.[151]

Although some ox breeds, for example the large, white breeds from Gujarat and Mysore, possessed a distinctive reputation, most Indian oxen were of a mixed breed. There is much evidence to suggest that cattle from different regions were continuously exchanged, both for breeding and rearing purposes. From nineteenth-century observations it appears that one may distinguish between two interacting spheres of cattle husbandry. First, there was the breeding of so-called village cattle, often unattended and freely grazing and mating on the local commons of waste and fallow land. Although this inbred variety constituted the bulk of the agricultural stock and was the main source of dairy supply, it was unfit for heavy ploughing and transport services over long distances. The stronger variety of cattle, however, was produced and raised by professional pastoralists, both nomadic and settled, on the basis of selective breeding and extensive grazing in the open and broken jungles of the sub-continent. The main ingredients for successful breeding were the keeping of large herds of cows, often supplied by the village breeders, the selection of superior bulls, often dedicated to a regional temple, and the castration of the lesser ones, often sold at the regional market. Clearly, the grazing of selected cattle across extensive pastures considerably improved the stamina and strength of the breed. This second, more extensive, breeding system served as the major supplier of the beasts of burden for the army on the march.[152]

According to Abul Fazl, Akbar had about 7,000 oxen in his service, but many thousands more were needed during military campaigns. As in the case of camel transportation, the cash-and-carry business by oxen was in the hands of a highly professional group of transporters called Banjaras. Although some of the Banjaras appear to have operated from a settled base in Malwa, they were always on the road, accompanied by wives and children. These Banjaras bred and kept thousands of oxen that could cover thousands of kilometres across the entire sub-continent. Both Mughal and British sources acknowledge that the success of their military campaigns in the interior of the sub-continent hinged on the willingness of the Banjaras to supply their armies with grain and other necessities. For both, it was of crucial importance to link up with this extensive transportation network. Although the latter appears to have been very much in place before the coming of the Mughals, it is certainly possible that, in the slipstream of the Mughal armies, the network expanded further south during the seventeenth century.

Although Indian transportation was dominated by pack-dromedaries and pack-oxen, wheeled transportation never disappeared entirely, as had been the case earlier in the Middle East. Ox-drawn carts remained important on the relatively level ground of the northern plains, where they were much more common than in the south of the continent. In purely military terms, oxen became increasingly important for drawing cannon, as will be seen in the next chapter. Like wheeled transport, river transport was only important in the north, but even here the army accompanying the emperor always kept to the road, only the immediate retinue of the emperor going by boat.

Bringing this chapter to a close, we may conclude that India's enormous resources, both in ready transport and ready cash, tremendously facilitated the mobility of the Mughal army and court. However, only on the peripheries of its empire, was the Mughal army like a nomadic horde living off the country. Usually, it was a well-lubricated moving capital, smoothly facilitated by a huge network of enterprising hauliers and bankers, and integrating the empire on its way. In the context of a constantly moving court, the warhorse continued to be the mainstay of Indian battle. The next chapter will address the question as to what extent Mughal mobility, sustained by the warhorse and other animal power, was threatened by the introduction of new gunpowder technology.

Plate 5 Mughal siege of Ranthambor, 1568. This painting by Miskin (outline) and Paras (*c.* 1590) illustrates the difficulty of moving and siting heavy siege guns against the various hill forts of Mughal India. Although the Mughals produced excellent heavy bronze cannon, it was difficult to integrate these into an army based on mobility and cavalry.

Source: *Victoria and Albert Museum, London; Akbarnama, IS 2:72–1896; 22/G2*

CHAPTER FIVE

Forts, guns and sails

Forts, guns and sails always rise to the occasion when stories are told about the rise of the West. Indeed, military historians have always been eager to depict the three as hallmarks of a more modern kind of warfare, at times even heralding the final victory of western civilisation over oriental barbarism. For one of the first world historians of the West, Edward Gibbon, it was, in particular, fortification and cannon that formed the impregnable barrier against the Tatar horse and secured Europe from the irruptions of nomadic barbarians. From that 'glorious' moment in history onwards, the barbarians could only conquer by ceasing to be barbarous, in other words, by adopting the modern military techniques of fortification and gunpowder weaponry.[1] Gibbon's early views still reverberate in the recent debates about the so-called military revolution and the making of the so-called gunpowder empires during the early-modern era.

Since Michael Roberts launched his thesis on the military revolution, it has been vehemently debated among military historians. His revolution occurred in Western Europe during the century after 1560. Basically, it came down to the replacement of relatively small, undisciplined cavalry troops by huge, well-disciplined and drilled gunpowder infantry armies.[2] More recently, Geoffrey Parker has complemented Roberts' thesis by stressing the radical development of European fortification, the *trace italienne*, as a response to the increased challenge of artillery. Parker's main contribution, though, was his successful attempt to extend the Roberts debate to Asia. Hence, it was Roberts' gunpowder infantry and Parker's edged bastion that came to represent the European military *Sonderweg* that would ultimately pave the way for the rise of the West. According to Parker's subtle formulation, the native peoples of America, Siberia, Black Africa and Southeast Asia lost their independence to the Europeans because they seemed unable to *adopt* western military technology, whereas those of the Muslim world apparently succumbed because they could not successfully *adapt* it to their military system.[3]

The impact of gunpowder technology in Asia had been discussed before. The Chicago historians Marshall Hodgson and William McNeill applied the term 'gunpowder empire' to the large sixteenth- and seventeenth-century Muslim states of the Ottomans, the Safavids and the Mughals. These empires were supposed to owe their long-term stamina to their effective and exclusive use of firepower, employed by both infantry and artillery. Hence, as is often claimed for the European case as well, the coming of gunpowder to Muslim Asia blew up the old feudal order of forts and heavy cavalry.[4] This idea was also implicitly present in David Ayalon's pioneering work on Mamluk Egypt, in which he claimed that the traditional, cavalry-oriented Mamluks were defeated by the more innovative Ottomans, who made effective use of infantry equipped with modern matchlocks. Here again, modern gunpowder, in this case employed by a disciplined infantry of military slaves, or janissaries, stood at the base of rapid imperial expansion.[5]

Combining the debates on the military revolution and the gunpowder thesis raises the paradox that, although a stagnant Muslim East was believed to have failed to adapt gunpowder, it was nevertheless able to exploit it for impressive imperial expansion. Of course, it may be argued that their gunpowder weaponry was good enough for their Asian rivals, but failed to impress those from the West, but this argument has never been explicitly made. Interestingly, a similar contradiction appears in the discussion on military fiscalism, where historians have stressed the enormous fiscal pressures exerted by the state's urge to adopt modern gunpowder armies. Whereas in Europe this is claimed to have stimulated the emergence of highly centralised states, in Muslim Asia the results appear to have been more ambiguous. For example, in the case of the sixteenth-century Ottoman Empire, military expansion and state-wide decentralisation went hand in hand. According to Halil Inalcik, the spread of modern firearms provided the local elites and peasantry with the military and financial means to withstand the central authorities.[6] In the case of fifteenth- and sixteenth-century south India, a similar paradox appears in the influential work of the late Burton Stein. Although Stein stressed the prominent role of modern gunpowder in the making of the Vijayanagara Empire, he also rightly observed a fundamental contradiction between, on the one hand, military fiscalism leading to centralisation, and, on the other, the ongoing existence of vigorous regional chieftaincies.[7]

As far as the Mughal Empire is concerned, Douglas Streusand recently tested the Hodgson–McNeill thesis. He doubted its validity, in particular on the basis of his study of the early Mughal sieges. Although the Mughals could take the strongest forts in Hindustan, gunpowder could not alter the usual pattern of difficult and prolonged sieges. Gunpowder, whether propelling balls or exploding a mine, did permit them to breach the walls of fortresses, but hardly nullified such strong hill forts as Chitor, Ranthambor and Asirgarh. It took so long, and maintaining a siege was so difficult, that the defenders had always reason to hope that the siege would end before the walls were breached. More than this, the Mughals did not perceive fortresses primarily as bases for disloyal provincial governors as the latter did not control them. Mughal forts, with relatively insular commanders under direct Mughal supervision, were seen as obstacles to local revolts. Hence, in general there was no need at all to upgrade fortification, because their natural location already made them unapproachable for artillery and because the Mughals had no reason to expect that their fortresses would face a major siege, with the exception of the forts of Afghanistan. Here Streusand could not but support Irfan Habib's earlier view that Mughal superiority in the field outweighed their ability to take or defend fortresses.[8]

In the open field too, Streusand continues, gunpowder was not the sole element of Mughal military superiority, as they effectively combined the use of firearms, mainly artillery, with mounted archers. Nevertheless, gunpowder contributed to centralisation in a more complex way: the military changes in the sixteenth century greatly strengthened the central government as long as it retained control of the infantry and the artillery. Its combined strength could always defeat the mounted archers from the provinces. For Streusand, this fact accounts for the greater coherence of the gunpowder empires as compared with their predecessors.[9]

All in all, Streusand's measured objections to the gunpowder thesis appear to be valid as long as he stresses the ongoing tactical weight of mounted archers. His reformulation of the thesis is less convincing, however. When he rightly suggests that Mughal superiority stemmed from the combination of gunpowder technology with mounted archers, where does this leave this superiority when the latter is lacking? In fact, as I have stressed in the previous chapter, the imperial armies used to be better equipped, not only and primarily in terms of artillery and infantry, but mainly in the supply of horses for mounted horse-archers as well as for heavy cavalry. Actually, more than the imperial troops, the regional zamindari forces relied on infantry equipped with firearms. Even the use of cannon did not remain the monopoly of the central state, but became a prominent tool of zamindari expansion, in particular during the later stages of the empire. Confrontations of the sort Streusand imagines – i.e. imperial infantry and artillery against provincial cavalry – simply never happened. In addition, Streusand *over*-estimates the level of long-term control the Mughals possessed over their provincial forts and *under*estimates the decentralising effects of fortification as witnessed, for example, during the long decline of the empire in the eighteenth century. Actually, as with gunpowder weaponry, strong forts could underpin as well as undermine the authority from the centre, or, as far more elegantly formulated in a sixteenth-century Telugu poem:

> The battle, the fortress,
> diplomacy and robbery,
> doctoring, serving the kings,

trading in ships on the ocean
and powerful spells –
if they work for someone,
then the fruit will be very great.
But if control is lost
and the wrong things happen,
all that wealth will disappear
and the man's life will hang in the balance
O God of Kalahasti.[10]

Having said this, though, this chapter cannot but corroborate Streusand's main arguments, especially when he stresses the disappointing effectiveness of early gunpowder weaponry, be it against walls or in the open field. To avert the danger that this rekindles the old but simmering picture of a static and outdated oriental art of warfare, the following section will attempt to trace the military architecture under the Mughals to a somewhat earlier period, in which the art of taking and building forts changed dramatically, also paving the way for the well-known early Mughal successes against such forts as Chitor and Ranthambor. But, first of all, we should ask ourselves the question as to what extent such forts were part of the strategic and tactical considerations of the Mughals. In other words, how should we situate forts in the geo-political context of the Mughal Empire?

Forts

Geo-political context

As seen already in the case of Gibbon, forts and fortification have often been defined in their oppositional capacity to a supposed or real nomadic threat. This is most clearly visible in the case of the Chinese Wall, or actually walls, which were supposedly meant to keep the nomads out of a settled and orderly China. Also, for someone like Ibn Khaldun, walls protected the people of the city against nomads but, at the same time, undermined the people's cohesion. For him, walls ate into the strength of a people desiring to gain control, very much breaking the impetus of its efforts in this respect.[11] In a similar spirit, Machiavelli's unyielding prejudice against fortification may be explained. Witnessing the early spring of the trace italienne, Machiavelli supported the idea, inspired by the classical example of Sparta, that to build a wall usually causes a softening of the soul in the inhabitants. He forcefully argued that forts are not needed by peoples or kingdoms that have good armies, for good armies suffice for their defence without fortresses, while fortresses without good armies are incompetent for defence. Hence, a prince, who can raise a good army, need not build any fortresses; and one who cannot should not build any.[12]

For both Ibn Khaldun and Machiavelli walls pertained to the city. As such, they served in a dual capacity: as a defence against outside invaders and as a check on the urban population inside. Hence, city walls may be interpreted as symbols of the city's autonomy, as for example in the case of Western Europe, but equally well as tokens of the city's subordination to the state, as in the case of the Middle East and, perhaps, China. In fact, both kinds of thinking are present in the ambiguous Mughal attitude towards forts, which saw them as stepping stones as well as thorns on the way to state centralisation.

In general, the building of forts in India was closely connected to the building of roads, especially at the start of the empire. One case in point is the energetic road-building activity under Sher Shah Sur (r. 1540–5), which really set the example for the later Mughal policy under Akbar. Most of the Sur and early Mughal forts were located along the main trade arteries of the empire. Sher Shah's road-building programme included the foundation of as many as 1,700 caravanserais along the imperial roads, all of them provided with mosques and wells. One of his roads commenced in his newly built fortress of Rohtas (Punjab) and ran up to the port of Sonargaon in Bengal. Two other routes radiated from the capital city of Agra, one to Burhanpur in the south, and one to Jodhpur and Chitor in the southwest.[13] Apparently, Sher Shah retraced the pattern of the old imperial limites of Uttarapatha, Dakshinapatha and the Aparanta(patha) once again. In a way, the establishment of forts along the road was also a function of the logistical need for a string of supply stations or magazines – often called thanas – supporting an army on the move. According to the Afghan historian Sarwani, during his marches Sher Shah always left behind 'earthly' fortresses with a mud-plaster thereon'.[14] Similarly, the Marathas, famous fort-builders themselves, were well aware that expansion implied the construction of thanas. According to one of their councils for kings, a ruler should gradually conquer the country unprotected by forts and strongholds by building new fortified places from the boundaries of his kingdom onwards. If there was no protection of forts and strongholds the army could not continue fighting in another's territory.[15]

But forts were not only means for building or controlling trade and supply routes, but also important instruments for pacifying the surrounding countryside. Following Sarwani again, Sher Shah was always keen to

> construct a fort in each *sarkar* [district] after taking into account its requirements so that it may become a refuge for the oppressed and a centre for humbling the rebels, and that I will make of all the mud sarais converted into brick-built ones.[16]

This dual function of forts may already be implied in the categorisation of forts given by the Arthashastra, which makes a distinction between the river and mountain fortresses of frontier chiefs (*antapala*), meant to protect the country, and the desert and jungle fortresses of forest-dwellers (*atavi*), meant as places of retreat in times of calamity.[17] Anyway, both considerations converge in Sher Shah's fort at Rohtas, which, apart from being situated on the main road to Kabul, was constructed with a view to keeping the country of Kashmir and the Ghakkar zamindars in check. The name of the fort was to mirror Rohtas in Bihar, that other strong fort on the opposite end of the imperial highway.[18] History repeated itself when Akbar built Attock at the empire's western extremity, again emphasising its linear connection with Katak Benares, the fort on the eastern extremity. According to Abul Fazl, Attock was to serve as a 'noble barrier' (*barzakh*) between Hindustan and Kabulistan, and to enforce the obedience of the unruly inhabitants of that border. Indeed, in his own majestic words, at Attock 'the helpless obtained a means of subsistence, the seekers of traffic obtained confidence, and world travellers had security'.[19]

Thus the building of forts was partly the outcome of the imperial policy to control trade, to secure military supply lines and to check regional landlords. These aims also account for the way the Mughals tended to fortify their cities. As Streusand has stressed already, for the Mughals there was hardly any need to build strong city ramparts, as there was hardly any serious threat from enemies who were able to maintain protracted and costly sieges. At the same time, Mughal superiority in the open field required relatively open, accessible cities, often provided with extensive gardens to accommodate the imperial camp. Usually the frail outer walls of Indian cities were good enough to keep roaming bands of robbers and plunderers at a distance and also served well as a convenient means of channelling and controlling in- and outgoing traffic. But city walls hardly ever played a prominent role in resisting sieges. Most of the more memorable Indian sieges were directed against forts that were either attached as citadels to cities or situated on steep hills or in thick jungle far from the main urban centres. Perhaps contributing to this apparent neglect of urban fortification was the authorities' awareness that cities and other examples of settled life in India were relatively unstable geographical configurations and thus not worth a big investment in immovable real estate such as city walls. As trade routes shifted almost continuously – albeit within the broad perimeters of the limites pattern – cities also tended to have a chequered history of rapid rises and equally rapid declines. Babur himself was struck by the ephemeral existence of Indian settlements:

> In Hindustan, the destruction and building of villages and hamlets, even of cities, can be accomplished in an instant. Such large cities, in which people have lived for years, if they are going to be abandoned, can be left in a day, even half a day, so that no sign or trace remains. If they have a mind to build a city, there is no necessity

> for digging irrigation canals or building dams. Their crops are all unirrigated. There is no limit to the people. A group gets together, makes a pond, or digs a well. There is no making of houses or raising of walls. They simply make huts from the plentiful straw and innumerable trees, and instantly a village or city is born.[20]

Obviously, for any Indian ruler, spending money on building walls for such highly disposable cities always involved a great deal of risk.

Finally, and also closely connected to the elements mentioned previously the city authorities lacked the long-term autonomy to act for themselves. Usually, a small but relatively strong citadel *inside* the city worked as a check on the urban elites and constantly reminded them of the proximity of the central authorities. Functionally, it appears that urban citadels were not much different from the forts along the highways, as both were primarily forts of transit used as checkpoints to oversee and exploit the trade and main production centres of the realm. For the state authorities it was crucial to keep the command of forts and towns separate. According to Manucci, all Mughal fortresses were commanded by selected and loyal officers to whom the king gives 'a secret countersign, by which only they are to make the place over when superseded by his orders.' They were not allowed to interact and to leave the fort during their term of office.[21] In a similar spirit, Babur's near contemporary in southern India, Krishnadevaraya of Vijayanagara (r. 1509–30) insisted that forts should be commanded by Brahmans.[22] Again, the Marathas considered local landlords and officials, who occupied the surrounding territory as not suitable for the command of a fort.[23]

An interesting case in this respect is the port of Surat. The *qiladar*, or commander of the fort, appears to have been fully isolated from the other authorities and communities in the city. His citadel, or *qila*, was ideally situated between the harbour and the central market place, or *maidan*, the latter also serving as the main military assembly place of the town. In other words, the Mughal citadel was well placed to control the maritime and continental termini of the inter-regional trade. More unusual in the Indian context, however, was Aurangzeb's order to build strong bulwarks to protect part of the outer city. This occurred in reaction to the Maratha raid of 1664, which had laid waste to the earthen outer walls, but had left the citadel, moated by the river and well protected by thirty of forty pieces of heavy artillery, fully intact.[24] At about the same time, again instigated by a Maratha raid, Aurangzeb decided to build new stone walls around his southern headquarters of Aurangabad. Indeed, Aurangzeb's whole reign may be called exceptional as it signalled a new thrust in fortification, also illustrated by his later mania for attacking the fortresses of the Marathas.

Arriving at the end of the seventeenth century, forts and other strongholds were increasingly turned into centres of local development and autonomy. As mentioned already, the Mughal lack of attachment to settled strongholds had always been partly informed by their fear that these could easily be turned into hotbeds of local rebellion. Hence, they generally discouraged zamindars from building forts or, occasionally, took active measures of defortification.[25] For, as every local landlord knew perfectly well, the long-term possession of a fort stood at the root of successful regional state formation. For example, it enabled him to store treasure and keep relatives from the clutches of rivals or of the central state.[26] Many of these forts were built in thick forests, wet marches and hilly areas, far from the open plains still dominated by the imperial cavalry. Not surprisingly, we find most of these forts in Bundelkhand and in southern India, especially on the hills of the Western Ghats, and in the Carnatic. Manucci guessed that, in the whole of Hindustan, from Kabul to Bengal, there were about 100 fortresses and, in the whole of the Deccan and the Carnatic, about 380.[27] Hence, particularly in the south of India, the building of local chieftaincies was directly linked to the possession of fortresses. This is demonstrated, for example, in the careers of the Maratha and Nayaka chiefs commanding various hill forts for their distant superiors in Bijapur and Vijayanagara. The Nayakas became known as Poligars, or Palaiyakkarars, which indicated their prime capacity as the lords of small, fortified centres called *palaiyam*s in Tamil. As early as the late sixteenth century, especially after the decline of the Vijayanagara Empire, fort-building activities in these areas increased, giving rise to the emergence of new regional states and launching a new round of rural expansion.[28]

In the Mughal north, the close connection between fort-building and zamindarisation manifested itself most vigorously during the eighteenth century. According to the Jesuit Father Wendel, the inability to bring local fortification to a halt was one of the main weaknesses of Mughal rule at that time. Under the pretence of assuring the safety of the local population against outside attacks, zamindars were left free to make mud walls. To protect the walls against the rains, bastions were added, and a moat created from where the sand had been removed.

> Finally, by each monsoon amassing soil on soil, the local official (often in league with the zamindar) neither obstructing it nor warning the court, there emerges the zamindar, in a few years time surrounding his residence with four bastions and a solid, cannon-resistant wall, with hundreds of matchlockmen at his disposal and with as many sabres as there are peasants inside, ready and determined to support his revolt. A thousand times one has seen how the court had been forced into a siege, formally to reduce the rebels, often only achieving this under conditions that were more advantageous to the rebels.[29]

Obviously, this kind of unrestricted fort-building enabled mansabdars and zamindars alike to strike local roots and to carve out autonomous homelands for themselves. It was the most visible beacon of Mughal decline. It followed from the Mughals' failure to keep up their earlier strategy of permanent movement, in which they had opted for the mobility of the horse and not for the stability of walls, for ruling India from the camp and not from the fort. As forts were not their priority, the development of military architecture under the Mughal was not very remarkable and merely built on the earlier tradition of their predecessors, in particular of the fourteenth- and fifteenth-century Tughluq and Bahmani dynasties. Hence, in order to understand the Mughal fort architecture it is necessary to make a short excursion among its antecedents.

Architecture and siege technology

Fort-building under the later Delhi sultanate developed mainly in response to radically improved siege technology, both during the Crusades and the Mongol invasions. At about this time, northern India began to follow the pattern of the Middle East and Central Asia, in which huge territorial conquests, by increasingly effective horse-warriors generated a new, revolutionary style of fortification. In India, the southern raids under the Delhi sultans Ala al-Din Khalji and Muhammad Shah b. Tughluq not only highlighted the improved range and logistics of cavalry armies but also showed the growing impact of new siege technology.[30] Prominent in all these sieges was the recurrent reference to extensive groundwork, involving earthen battlements (*pashib*) and mines (*naqb*), as well as sophisticated engineering involving the construction of wooden siege towers (*gargaj*), mangonels and trebuchets. The latter is mainly referred to as *manjaniq-i maghribi*, i.e. western mangonel, which is the so-called counterweight trebuchet as introduced from the Middle East. The maghribi was a great technological advance on the earlier catapult (mangonel). The latter was a mechanised bow, either in the form of a big crossbow (*qaus al-ziyar* in Arabic, or called *charkh* in India) or a torsion ballista (*arrada*). These engines drew their energy from the elastic deformation of twisted ropes or sinews. The trebuchets, however, relied on human traction or gravity or both, which was vastly more effective. Most probably, Islamic armies had already introduced the traction trebuchet from China as early as the seventh century. Its variation, the hybrid trebuchet – in which gravitational force was primarily utilised to counterbalance the beam at discharge when the sling was loaded with a heavy stone shot, but which contributed little to the acceleration of the beam – was introduced at the beginning of the eighth century and was one of a number of military innovations made under the impetus of Islamic conquest movements. From the twelfth century onwards, the slower but most effective counterweight trebuchet was introduced from Byzantium. It could launch heavier missiles – from 200 to 1,000 kg, as opposed to 50 to 200 kg for the traction or hybrid trebuchet – and could cover greater distances – 200 m, as opposed to 75 m for the traction and hybrid types.[31] From the few existing sources, it appears that the modified trebuchet did not fail to have its impact on the Indian ramparts of the day and remained an important siege weapon, even one century after the introduction of cannon.[32] Its effectiveness is illustrated by Amir Khusrau's description of the siege of Warangal (1310) by the Muslim forces under Malik Kafur, in which the poet-historian contrasts the effectiveness of Muslim maghribis against the weakness of Hindu arradas:

> The stones of the Mussalmans all flew high, owing to the power of the strong cable, and hit the mark, while the balls of the Hindus were shot feebly as from a Brahman's thread, and consequently went wrong.[33]

Most probably, Amir Khusrau's arradas were the now somewhat outdated torsion engines. In the Muslim armies of the north, however, arradas began to refer to light, quick-firing traction machines, primarily used as anti-personel weapons.

Apart from trebuchets, it appears that better mining techniques played an increasingly decisive role in breaking walls. Of course, mining was a system of siege warfare that had been known for many centuries, but which had been used quite rarely before the twelfth century, reaching the peak of its success in the late twelfth and in the thirteenth centuries.[34] Mining appears to have been effectively used by Timur against Bhatnir and Meerut (1398). Before the gunpowder era, mining implied that galleries were built under the part of the wall to be breached, which was supported by wooden frames while the excavation was in progress. After a sufficiently large cavity had been formed, the wooden frames were set on fire, and were therefore no longer capable of supporting the wall, which fell in, producing the breach. Apart from mining, the introduction of new incendiary technology, such as explosive and fire-throwing bamboo tubes, may also have contributed to the sudden impetus of besieging armies. Possibly, some of these were Chinese proto-guns reaching India through Mongol channels.[35]

Rapidly developing siege technology triggered off a revolution in military architecture all over the Islamic world, but in particular in the Middle East.[36] Its salient changes involved measures to counter the easy approach of sappers. For example, walls were provided with round towers that could give flanking fire, while more loopholes and machicolations were used to throw down nafta and other anti-siege incendiaries.[37] Most of the adaptations of the Middle East started to influence Indian fortification during the Tughluq era (1320–1414). At about this time, a notorious generation of iconoclastic, fort-breaking conquerors of the twelfth and thirteenth centuries was replaced by a new generation of fort-building patrons. As ghazi-like veterans of the Mongol frontier, the Tughluqs showed a remarkable passion for defensive architecture that had to stem the ongoing Mongol raids from the northwest. The staunch defensive vocabulary of the day even manifested itself in non-military buildings, such as the bastion-like tombs of Ghiyath al-Din Tughluq (r. 1321–5) in Delhi and Rukn-i Alam at Multan. Both made use of massive projecting buttresses with an almost unbroken surface, but with all kinds of merlons, turrets, crenellations and pinnacles on top.[38] The most striking example of Tughluq military architecture is the fort of Tughluqabad, built between 1320 and 1325 by the Rumi architect Ahmad b. Ayaz. Tughluqabad with its masonry ramparts, sloping walls, and bastions with prominent battlements of rounded elements and box-like machicolations, is a clear manifestation of the earlier Middle Eastern developments.[39]

Tughluq military architecture spread gradually towards the Deccan, mainly thanks to the adaptations introduced by the Tughluqs in the southern city of Daulatabad, which became their capital during the reign of Muhammad Shah b.Tughluq (1325–51). Here the ramparts were replaced with a double line in lime-mortar masonry, and provided with round bastions and gun turrets. The moat in front was deepened and widened, a counterscarp was built and a glacis was provided for.[40] From Daulatabad, the Tughluq style influenced the Bahmani dynasty (1347–1538) in building their strong new capitals of Gulbarga, Firuzabad and Bidar. As mentioned

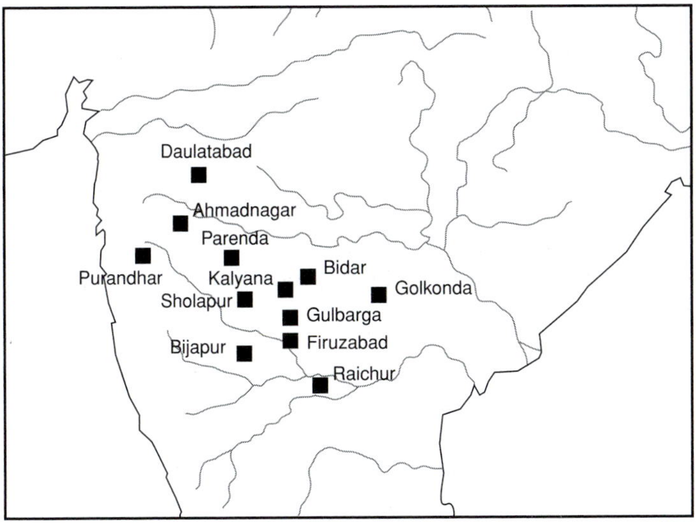

Map 5.1 Fort-building in the Deccan: 1300–1500

already, sustained by extensive networks of aqueducts, channels and pipes, these new cities consolidated the opening up of the Dakshinapatha by the raids of the Delhi sultans. The new fashion of fort-building was also evident from the construction of various smaller strongholds at places like Purandhar, Kalyana, Sholapur, Parenda and Raichur.

By and large, the style continued to flourish under the sixteenth-century Deccani successor states of Ahmadnagar, Bijapur and Golkonda.[41] Its general features were a double line of projecting ramparts with prominent battlements of rounded elements and box-like machicolations, alternated with round or polygonal bastions. At some places, earlier massive walls were provided with inner vaulted chambers that improved the ability to provide counter-fire against attackers along the walls. To compensate for the inclusion of these inner depots and gangways walls became thicker and more solidly built. Often the dry-stone masonry was exchanged for lime-mortar masonry protecting a rubble core. Also, more and more forts were built on steep, rocky hills and in the midst of dense thorny forests, hard to approach by sappers and other engineers.

It is only from the late fifteenth century onwards that we get the first evidence of gunpowder playing a more prominent role in Indian sieges, in particular through mining. Among the first to employ gunpowder for mining in India was Mahmud Gawan (1458–82), the Persian newcomer (*afaqi*) and minister under the late Bahmanis, who apparently used an explosive mine during the siege of Belgaum in 1472.[42] From that time onwards we come across several other examples of underground explosives being used, for example at the sieges of Mandasor (*c.* 1520) and Raisen (*c.* 1532) by besieging armies from Gujarat, as well as at the siege of Gwalior (1518) by an army of the Lodis.[43] At about this time, we also see cannon appearing although not yet having much of an effect on the besieged.

It was also at this time that the Mughals arrived on the Indian scene. Their siege technology partly built on the expertise and experience of their predecessors. But although they continued to rely heavily on mining, as did other Indian rulers, they also introduced cannon, which gradually replaced the earlier maghribis and arradas. Although this may have had some impact on the numerous mud-built zamindari forts of the day, cannon could hardly destroy the stone bastions erected during the Delhi and Deccan sultanates. In these cases, cannon could at best be used to ravage the battlements, which prevented the enemy's gunners and matchlockmen from discharging their pieces.[44] In addition, mortars were used to bombard the interior, as had been done previously by the trebuchet. Hence, despite the growing use of cannon, the Mughals could not radically alter the existing balance between besiegers and besieged. They continued to rely on the traditional methods of their predecessors based on making underground tunnels, covered passages and high battlements (*naqb wa sabat wa sarkub*).[45] Even Akbar's much acclaimed successes against the reputedly impregnable

Ranthambor and Chitor were nothing unusual as both forts had been taken several times before, for example under Ala al-Din Khalji between 1301 and 1304, and under Sher Shah Sur between 1542 and 1544.[46]

More important than the purely military means of taking forts was the ability to buy their surrender. Although the besieged could be supposed to withstand the siege technology of the day, they could not be reasonably expected to reject endless offerings of cash and mansab. Occasionally, lack of food supplies forced the capitulation of the besieged, but scarcity was equally challenging to the besieging army ever struggling to tackle the enormous logistical problems of providing food and munitions for the soldiers, as well as fodder for the horses, camels, oxen and elephants. As we have stressed earlier, for a very long time the dry conditions surrounding the Deccani forts made any siege directed from the north extremely precarious.[47] Actually, all sieges were deemed to failure if not sustained by well-organised logistics, without which, all military and monetary means would be of no effect whatsoever.

Returning to fort-building, cannon and other firearms only marginally modified military architecture under the Mughals. For example, forts were extended to enclose possible sites for bombardment, such as in the cases of Vellore, Ginjee and Golkonda. Most modifications could be noticed in the structural form of the parapet or walls. Embrasures were filled up and replaced by small musket-holes. In addition, ramps were made to move cannon more easily upon the battlements. Somewhat at the back, platforms (*burz*) were made for long-range artillery to fire over the merlons.[48] In general, though, the Mughals did not bring about major improvements in the construction and the design of forts and were perfectly happy to elaborate on the already sophisticated style as developed under their predecessors. Ruling their empire on horseback, the Mughals had no need of a trace italienne, which in India remained a rarity confined to the European settlements at the coast. Although India definitely had fewer nomads and more forts than Iran, the Mughal position came fairly close to the situation under the Safavids, where ill-fortified towns competed in importance with the marches. The latter remained the prime recruiting ground of the cavalry-based army of the Safavids; an army, by the way, that also failed to build up a machinery of artillery.[49] In this light, it is all the more interesting to investigate the adoption of firearms under the Mughals and ask ourselves to what extent cannon and firearms changed their proven ways of mobile warfare based on the horse and the bow.

Guns

Although the scholarly debate about the introduction of gunpowder in South Asia has a long history, it is currently not strongly contested, since it is dominated by only a few historians, all of them originating from the

Aligarh Muslim University in India. The work of Iqtidar Alam Khan, especially, has made an important contribution, not only in rectifying and synthesising the earlier views of scholars, such as M. Akram Makhdoomee, A.Z. Nadvi and Yar Muhammad Khan, but also in opening up new avenues of research by paying closer attention to the sources of the Mongol and early Timurid rulers.[50] One of the big problems facing the discussion about the introduction of gunpowder in India, as elsewhere, is the complicated and ever-changing nomenclature of the weaponry involved. The distinction between so-called 'co-viative' throwers of projectiles and true guns – i.e. where a bullet or cannonball fills the bore of the barrel in order to use the maximum propellant force of the gunpowder charge – is not always evident from the terminology used in the primary sources.[51] This is aggravated by the fact that we have only very few Indian sources that are more or less contemporary with the introduction of either gunpowder or guns, none of these sources referring directly to such an event. Even worse, later sources that describe earlier events, tend to use technical words like *tup* (cannon) and *tufang* (small arms) anachronistically, giving the false impression of an early appearance of these weapons. As a result, even imaginative modern scholars like Iqtidar Alam Khan have to construct a tentative argument, on the basis of highly circumstantial evidence, that true guns were introduced during the second half of the fifteenth century, which would be roughly about a half to one century later than the Mamluks and the Ottomans in the Middle East and more or less simultaneous with Iran. For Iqtidar Alam Khan, the essential reference is found in the word *kaman-i rad* (literally, thunder-bow) as used in Persian texts from fifteenth-century Central and South Asia. In his view, these references demonstrate that the Timurids and Bahmanis employed heavy mortars, on one occasion capable of throwing a stone projectile of about 1,200 kg! As in some of his other attempts to make one-to-one connections between Chinese and Persian terminology, the results are certainly stimulating but not (yet) convincing.[52]

It should be kept in mind that gunpowder not only pertains to the true gun but also relates to other gunpowder-related devices, such as pyrotechnical fire-lances (Ch. *huo chhiang*), grenades (Ch. *huo phao*; Pers. *huqqa*) launched by trebuchets or crossbows, or rockets (Ch. *liu hsing*; Pers. *ban*), all of which are mentioned by the Indo-Persian sources that often without much distinction label these as *atishbazi*.[53] As mentioned already, from about 1200 these weapons entered India from China, probably through Mongol channels. They were used as incendiary weapons, setting fire to forts, arsenals and ammunition wagons. The rocket, especially, became very popular in Mughal India, as it turned out to be very effective against elephants and cavalry. It consisted of an iron tube, 15 to 25 cm long and 5 to 8 cm in diameter, loaded with explosive gunpowder and tied with leather straps to a bamboo stick, about 2 to 3 m long. Some of the rockets had a chamber and burst like a shell. Others had a serpentine motion and, on striking the ground, rose again and bounced along till their force was spent. Although the delivery was inaccurate, rockets had a range of about 1 km. Above all, more than much heavier cannon, rockets suited the mobility of Indian cavalry. During the nineteenth century, the Indian success story of the rocket was continued in Europe, where it was adopted as the so-called Congreve rocket equipped with explosive warheads. As such, the Indian ban launched a great development of military rocketry in the West.[54]

Returning to the issue of the introduction of true guns, so far there is no univocal evidence that ascertains beyond doubt that firearms were used in India before the sixteenth century. It is only at the start of that century that we find the first clear references to the production and use of both cannon and handguns. For example, the earliest Indo-Portuguese sources suggest that, just before the Portuguese conquest in 1510, European and Muslim gunmakers manufactured guns in Goa. When the Portuguese entered the city, they found storage space which, following the report of the Viceroy's later secretary Gaspar Correia,

> the Turks had filled with all the materials necessary for ship-building, and lots of iron and mortar artillery, large and small, and also two of our camel cannons and eight cradles and mortars which the Turks had brought from the defeat of Dom Lourenco at Chaul, and other metal pieces in their fashion and a great number of metal guns, and a large quantity of gunpowder, saltpetre and utensils used in the making of these, and an enormous quantity of all kinds of weapons.[55]

This report is more or less corroborated by Duarte Barbosa who claims that the Bijapur authorities in Goa began to produce iron and copper ordnance after the Ottoman defeat at Diu in 1509.[56] Other early-sixteenth-century reports also appear to suggest that artillery was present at the ports of Gujarat but not yet in the interior.[57]

Although the occasional cannon or handgun may have reached the Indian interior before,[58] the first clear evidence of the use of true gunpowder weaponry on the battlefield comes from the *Baburnama*. When in 1519 the Mughals used their matchlocks against the people of Bajaur, in the extreme northwest of the sub-continent, the latter 'showed no fear of the sound of matchlocks, and even made fun of the noise with obscene gestures when they heard it'.[59] Six years later, during the famous battle of Panipat, Babur made effective use of *tup-i firangi* and *zarbzan*, which both clearly refer to light cannon, following the contemporary Iranian vocabulary.[60] The first is evidently a gun of European make, the latter probably a kind of falconet having an exceptionally long barrel.[61] Apart from light cannon and handguns, Babur refers also to the *kazan*, most probably a heavier mortar which was most effectively used in sieges.

After the Mughal victory of Panipat, Babur's successors, both Humayun and his Afghan rival Sher Shah, were keen to adopt firearms. At Kanauj (1540), Humayun is said to have employed as many as 700 zarbzan. These guns had a 4.75-pound calibre of stone shot and were mounted on simple carriages drawn by four pairs of bullocks. In addition, he used twenty-one heavy 47.5-pounders that shot bullets of molten brass and were drawn by eight (?) pairs of bullocks.[62] The same source claims that zarbzan and *dig* formed the mainstay of Sher Shah's fighting power.[63] Although dig often refers to a mortar, it also often refers, like *tup*, to cannon in general, as for example in the 4,000 *digha-yi atishbazi* used by Sher Shah during the siege of Kalinjar (1545), which weighed 4 mann, i.e. approximately 100 kg,[64] which would be a mere quarter of a bronze 3-pounder.

Simultaneous with, but also independent from, their entry through Mughal channels, was the rapid introduction and extensive use of firearms by the army of the sultanate of Gujarat. Again following the inside information of Gaspar Correia, in the 1530s the army of Bahadur Shah of Gujarat could count on 4,000 musketeers, and 200 field guns mounted on wheels, including thirty heavier guns.[65] At the battle of Mandasor (1535) the Gujaratis were equipped with more artillery than their Mughal counterparts.[66] In both cases, however, the production and expertise of firearms was negotiated through Portuguese and Ottoman (Rumi) specialists.[67] The short-term lead of the Gujarati army over the Mughals is not surprising considering their alliance with the Mamluks and Ottomans against the Portuguese and given their easier access to the large Portuguese supply along the coast.[68]

Given the evidence from the early sources, it appears that all the armies concerned primarily adopted light artillery, which goes against the cliché that oriental powers had an irrational preference for heavy pieces.[69] Both the Surs and the early Mughals had an artillery park that was dominated by light bronze cannon, most of them mounted on, and used from, carts (*arabas*). Heavy pieces were preferably used in sieges as in the case of the Gujarati siege of Chitor in the early 1530s.[70] From the sixteenth-century point of view the use of bronze was sound policy and very much in accordance with the European *communis opinio* at that stage.[71] It also appears that Indian armies were quick to follow the European trend in improving the transport facilities of guns. Whereas the guns of Babur were still loosely mounted on carts from which they had to be taken when brought in action, Akbar and the later Mughal emperors introduced better gun carriages.[72]

All in all, one may conclude that the first effective use of true firearms in India dates from the early sixteenth century, when it spread from the western coast and the northwestern overland routes, via Ottoman and Portuguese intermediaries, into the interior. The process of proliferation took less than thirty years and could even be called revolutionary if its military impact had not been considerably less enduring. But by saying this, we should not fall into the trap of accepting the all too well-known views of the eighteenth-century European accounts and adapt them uncritically to the sixteenth and seventeenth centuries. Based on the eighteenth-century accounts, colonial observers like Robert Orme, as well as more modern historians like William Irvine and Bruce Lenman, too easily disqualified Mughal artillery in general as using much outdated, extremely heavy bronze or wrought-iron firearms, operated by inexperienced and, at best, foreign gunners.[73] To test this view, I will focus on the three main elements that influenced the effectiveness of Mughal firearms: the manufacture and quality of Mughal powder and firearms, and the tactical use of guns in actual military operations.

Powder

Pre-modern gunpowder, or more properly black powder, in India as elsewhere, was a mixture of roughly 75 per cent saltpetre (KNO_3), 15 per cent charcoal and 10 per cent sulphur. Seventeenth- and eighteenth-century European accounts tend to rate Indian black powder as being much weaker than the European equivalent.[74] It appears that this kind of criticism became increasingly relevant from the late seventeenth century onwards, when new powder mixtures with more explosive power came into vogue in Europe, reducing the size of powder charges from two-thirds of the weight of the shot in the early seventeenth century to a mere one-third by the mid-eighteenth century.[75] How can we explain the lesser quality of Indian black powder and what were the consequences for its effectiveness in the field?

Taking the ingredients of black powder first, the sources give no indication at all that either charcoal or sulphur raised problems in the production process of Indian powder, although the best quality sulphur had to be imported from Afghanistan, Persia, Europe or from various places in Southeast Asia. In the case of saltpetre, both Indian quality and supplies were far superior to anything outside the sub-continent. Earlier, during the fifteenth and sixteenth centuries, Europe had compensated for the inferior nitrate quality of its domestic saltpetre, first by the so-called corning process, and second, by the potash process that substituted potassium nitrate (KNO_3) for the inferior calcium nitrate ($Ca(NO_3)_2$).[76] By the seventeenth century, though, India delivered the bulk of saltpetre used for European black powder and, until well into the nineteenth century, it remained the single largest producer and exporter in the world. Saltpetre was produced in India mainly in Bihar, Awadh, the Punjab, Ajmer and the Coromandel Coast. During the seventeenth century, Bihar became by far the largest producer, as it was virtually the only supplier of saltpetre for the growing

European market. At the end of the seventeenth century, Bihar produced about 4,250,000 kg of refined (i.e. *dobara*) saltpetre, more than half of which was carried away by Dutch and English companies. Less than 20 per cent was for consumption in Bihar and Bengal, leaving about 25 to 30 per cent for the Asian trade. India's main saltpetre grounds were in the districts of Bihar, Champaran, Hajipur, Saran and Tirhut.[77] Given the high natural quality of Indian saltpetre, one may again question the bad reputation of Indian powder.

One possible solution to this problem is to be found in the saltpetre production process. This started between November and the middle of June, when a particular caste called *lunias* scraped the inch-thick saline surface off old mud heaps and waste grounds. This earth was then dissolved and filtered through bamboos and grass mats. Next, the saltpetre liquor was evaporated to a crystallised state, which was done in earthen pots fixed in two rows over an oblong cavity dug in the ground, the interstices between the pots being filled up with clay. The product of this first stage of refining was called *kachcha* as it was still in raw condition and contained only 45 to 70 per cent of pure nitre. This raw saltpetre was often sold to a group of thirty to fifty *asamis*, literally tenants or peasants, who supervised another stage of filtration and crystallisation in separate refineries, which produced the so-called dobara saltpetre with a purity of 80 to 85 per cent.[78] From the point of view of the European companies, though, this was still less than the required 95 per cent of the so-called *qalami* or *dobara-qabasa* quality used for making gunpowder. This third stage of refining was extremely expensive, probably because it required copper vessels for crystallisation instead of the more usual earthen vessels of the lunias and asamis. Although qalami saltpetre could be supplied locally, the European companies preferred to take this final stage of refinement into their own hands, either by exporting dobara saltpetre to Europe or by building their own refineries in India.[79] Given the European complaints about the difficult supply of qalami saltpetre in India, it is very well possible that Indian powder-makers were content to use the inferior dobara saltpetre, which may explain the lesser quality of Indian black powder.

Except for the production of saltpetre, the Indian way of manufacturing actual powder should also be taken into account. In general, Indian powder-making was based on relatively small-scale production units. It appears that numerous small powder-makers were active in villages, some of them following the army camp, the women of families often manufacturing the article for the matchlocks of their husbands. Although some reports suggest that Indian powder-makers could only produce very fine, but rather ineffective, serpentine powder,[80] Indian manufacturing was not substantially different from the usual process described for contemporary Europe. In India, powder was produced by thumping a 'very wet' mixture of saltpetre, charcoal and sulphur and by passing it through catgut sieves to form grains.[81] Thus, at the time when effectiveness of black powder was primarily manipulated by the size of the grain, it appears that Indian powder-makers were perfectly able to do just that. But perhaps the Indian lack of large mechanised stamp or wheel mills hampered the proper incorporation of the three ingredients. Nonetheless, all the possible weaknesses of the Indian production processes of both saltpetre and powder, still do not explain why even gunpowder produced by European powder-mills in India continued to have such a bad reputation in comparison with powder manufactured in Europe.[82] One last possibility may have something to do with the relatively high moisture levels, especially in eastern and southern India, which must have made the drying process of powder problematic.[83] But the answer to why Indian gunpowder was inferior remains still somewhat inconclusive and more research is needed.

To what extent did the inferior quality of Indian powder really impair the use of Indian gunpowder weaponry? In this respect the recent, pioneering study by D.F. Harding suggests a few possible answers. First of all, the difference in quality of the powder was best revealed when used in small charges. When used in relatively large quantities, such as in cannon, bad powder could be as effective as good powder.[84] Hence, it appears that the question of effectiveness is only relevant for small arms. But even in muskets the negative effects appear to have been limited, since the form of breeching in Indian matchlocks suggests an automatic air space between powder and ball, which, as in pre-1600 European artillery pieces using serpentine powder, improved performance.[85] This implies that Indian powder was not affecting either artillery or musketry, but that it was only less suitable for muskets manufactured in Europe. Again, the evidence is still inconclusive and a solution to this problem still awaits the laborious investigation of the firearms' internal workings.

The Mughal authorities were only indirectly involved in the manufacture of saltpetre and black powder. Occasionally, the Mughal proclaimed a ban on European export or, in times of war, attempted to forcefully monopolise the saltpetre trade by confiscating supplies. The buying and transporting of saltpetre usually required a licence from the Mughal authorities.[86] In Bihar 22 per cent of the output of refined saltpetre originated from Mughal crown lands.[87] Here, the authorities attempted to control the trade by farming out the saltpetre districts to local officials or their financial supporters, who also acted as middlemen between the lunia and asami producers and the European Companies. In the 1730s, for example, the saltpetre production of Bihar was entirely dominated by the family of the governor of Bengal Alivardi Khan and his network consisting of Bania and Armenian traders who exported a great deal of saltpetre on their own account through the Bengal ports. Only after the battle of Plassey (1757) did the EIC begin to take full control over the saltpetre fields in Bihar.[88]

Firearms

As with powder, as much as the Mughals may have bemoaned the proliferation of firearms, they never attempted to really monopolise their production and use. In fact production appears to have been widespread and increasingly responsive to the demands of various local and regional markets. In evaluating the production process of firearms we should make a distinction between cannon and small arms. Usually, military historians point to two factors: the first relates to cannon and involves the failure to produce relatively cheap cast-iron cannon; the second relates to small arms and involves the failure to adopt the flintlock mechanism. Although both these deficiencies became increasingly important during the eighteenth century, it is my contention, that in the sixteenth and seventeenth centuries, they were not yet as relevant. Moreover, at that stage, Mughal cannon and small arms were not that inferior to those of European make. Let us start by considering the metallurgy of firearms.

In general, it appears that the Mughals were capable of manufacturing good bronze (i.e. an alloy of copper and tin) and brass (i.e. an alloy of copper and zinc) cannon. The reports about their quality are not unequivocal though. Terry, for example, is altogether positive, whereas Manucci, an experienced gunner himself, is more ambiguous. Although he praises the quality of metal of Akbar's artillery park, 'with the breech made plain just like a drum', he also concludes that they must be of Chinese origin, more than 200 years old, which was proved 'by the imperfection of the work'.[89] The English ambassador Thomas Roe is also a bit sceptical, considering the brass pieces he saw at Burhanpur as 'generally to shortt and too wyde bored'.[90] Thévenot reports that one weakness of the production of brass cannon in Mughal India was the tendency, also described in the *Baburnama*, to 'melt the metal in diverse furnaces, so that some of it must be better melted than others when they mingle all together, their cannon commonly is good for nothing'.[91] From this it appears that one of the main problems facing Indian gunmakers was their failure to work with large furnaces, something that was also hindering them in manufacturing cast iron.

Obviously, as with bronze and brass, India had a long tradition of making iron, which exists in great abundance in many parts of India. The equipment used to make wrought iron was as simple as the metal itself, consisting of a small furnace, or bloomery, heated by charcoal and with hand- or foot-operated bellows to fan the fire. Tongs were used to hold the hot metal while it was forged into shape. High-carbon cast iron, however, was produced in a blast furnace, which became well known in China and Europe, but not so in India. The blast furnace was in some respects like a bloomery and it still used charcoal as its fuel. Like a bloomery, the blast furnace needed a continuous blast of air to keep the fire burning, but its greater size demanded mechanical power to work the bellows. The major difference was that, because the furnace operated at a higher temperature and the ratio of charcoal to ore was greater, the iron absorbed a greater amount of carbon; therefore it produced, instead of a spongy piece of wrought iron ready for forging, much greater quantities of molten cast iron. Apart from making cast-iron guns, most of the iron made in European blast furnaces went through a second process for conversion into wrought iron with the help of a waterwheel-driven finery.[92]

As with the large furnaces producing bronze and brass, the absence of a sufficient power source denied to Indian smiths the ability to obtain high-enough temperatures in large furnaces. In other words, their failure to impart a sufficient amount of air to the furnaces meant that only small amounts of metal could be melted at one time in each furnace, and also affected the quality of the metal, be it iron or copper. One major element that may have contributed to this inability was the difficulty in keeping large furnaces supplied with enough charcoal, a problem not solved by the British, even in the nineteenth century.[93]

Following the Mughal failure to make cast iron, their guns were primarily of bronze and brass with a few wrought-iron ones. Unfortunately, the famous Indian wootz, also called Damascus steel, did not offer a suitable alternative. It was a high-carbon steel made, particularly in southern India, by packing small pieces of bloomery iron into a crucible with pieces of charcoal and organic matter, then heating this for several days until the mixture liquefied. It is possible that the furnaces used a wind-based air-supply principle dependent on the Indian monsoon.[94] Both finished arms and cakes of wootz were exported throughout the Islamic world, and even to Europe.[95] In centres of arms manufacture the latter were carefully forged, at an unusually low temperature, into small military items like sword blades, and plates to reinforce mail armour such as in the Indian char-aina. Its high carbon content, however, made the forging of solidified cakes of wootz extremely difficult (melting-point falls with increasing carbon content) and hardly possible for large items such as European plate armour or cannon. Hence, as with bronze metallurgy, wootz might well yield an individual product that was superior to any other metal, but it could not be made or used in mass production.[96]

Nonetheless, the Indian failure to produce cast iron became a major disadvantage only during the eighteenth century when the Europeans started to produce cheap, standardised and light cast-iron field guns. Earlier, it appears that the Mughals were perfectly happy with their own artillery, largely consisting of light bronze cannon, even though these somewhat deviated from the European standard, as illustrated by the comments of Manucci and Roe.[97] Although more expensive, the bronze pieces of the Mughals were certainly lighter and considered more reliable than any contemporary iron ones.[98] Even in terms of relative costs, iron may have been more expensive in India than in Europe following the need to locate its production near areas that could supply sufficient fuel. According to Moreland, in India it meant that smelting was a jungle industry, which could be carried on only at a distance from where the iron was needed, since the land near those centres was occupied by cultivation; and this in turn meant that the cost of production was increased by the very heavy cost of overland transport.[99]

In contrast to cannon, Indian metallurgy produced excellent iron small arms (*tufang* or *banduq*), which compared rather well with the European product. According to Abul Fazl, Akbar himself improved the forging of barrels. The earlier method had produced numerous accidents, as the barrels had been made by flattening pieces of iron with a hammer and anvil and joining the flattened edges of both sides. Now it was Akbar's 'inventive genius' that 'introduced' a production process that was more or less similar to current European practice:

> They flatten iron, and twist it round obliquely in form of a roll, so that the folds get longer at every twist; they then join the folds, not edge to edge, but so as to allow them to lie one over the other, and heat them gradually in the fire. They also take cylindrical pieces of iron and pierce them when hot with an iron pin.

As a result, 'matchlocks are now made so strong that they do not burst, though let off when filled to the top. Formerly they could not fill them to more than a quarter.'[100] Generally speaking, the relatively small bore and thick barrel, often made of superior wootz, allowed Indian small arms to be used with proportionate larger powder charges, probably filling relatively large powder chambers and giving them greater range and precision than European barrels. Like the Iranian one, the common early Mughal musket appears to have been relatively light at the breech and heavy at the muzzle, making the use of a prong or tripod necessary.[101] Of course, apart from the heavier musket there was the lighter arquebus, but both tended to be rather long – often about 1.80 m[102] – probably following the Mughal leaning towards accurate delivery.[103] Indeed, whereas the pistol made a considerable impact as a powerful new weapon of the new European *Reiter*, it hardly influenced then-current Indian cavalry tactics. Actually, both pistols (*tabanchas*) and carbines appear to have been rarely used by the Mughal cavalry. Although the invading Iranian and Afghan cavalries of the mid-eighteenth century successfully used short blunderbusses (*sherbachas*), probably equipped with firelocks, most Indian cavalry, as late as the early nineteenth century, continued to rely on long matchlocks, even using them on horseback.[104] But as mentioned previously, during most of the Mughal period, cavalry preferred to fight with composite bows and *armes blanches*.

The high quality of Indian muskets is altogether confirmed by the European accounts of Bernier and Tavernier. The latter is most outspoken as he observes that 'the barrels of their muskets are stronger than ours, and the iron is better and purer; this makes them not liable to burst'.[105] Against this statement, however, one can point towards Manrique's negative judgement that Indian arquebuses were poorly-made, awkward arms.[106] In general, though, it appears that, in terms of their metallurgy, Mughal handguns were at least equal to, but probably stronger and more accurate than, the European specimens of the day.

The critical point where failure occurred was in the making of an efficient trigger and lock. In Europe, by the second half of the seventeenth century, the matchlock had given way to the wheel- and snap-lock and these were brought together into the flintlock, which combined the steel and pan cover as one element. In addition, and much earlier, paper cartridges had been introduced in order to simplify and speed up loading.[107] During the early seventeenth century, the Ottomans were quick to adopt their own variety of the snap-lock, the so-called *miquelet*. The common Mughal soldier stuck, however, to his matchlock, which, in technical terms, was a descendant of the fifteenth-century German matchlock that had reached India through Ottoman channels. Its characteristic was a mechanism inside the butt with only the small head of the matchholder and a rectangular or curved plate for the trigger showing. It was different from the usual European matchlock, as the hammer moved from the back to the front position, and not backwards in the direction of the bearer of the gun. Indo-Portuguese, as well as Sri Lankan, Japanese and Malay matchlocks, were again different from the common Indian ones as they were based on the so-called Bohemian snap-matchlock, which used a mechanism whereby the match-hammer struck the charge by means of a spring and without returning, whereas the Indian and European match-hammers returned to their original position.[108]

As with the forging process for barrels, Abul Fazl again claims that Akbar himself was the inventor of the matchlock.[109] Of course, the mechanism was much older than that, but it is certainly possible that it was from Akbar's time onwards that the matchlock became the common musket of the Mughal army. Only during the second half of the eighteenth century do we find Indian rulers introducing flintlock muskets (*tufang-i chaqmaq*) into their infantry armies, but at that stage the latter were increasingly trained in a European style. One may speculate about the reasons why the Mughal army did not adopt the flintlock as early as the European or, for that matter, the Ottoman armies. It was definitively not because India did not have good flints as agate served the purpose well.[110] It is also extremely doubtful that the manufacture and repair of the mechanism as such was beyond the skill of the Indian smithy. Far more relevant than any technological deficiency was the lack of tactical urgency for the Mughals to introduce flintlocks. As their military thinking was based on the mobility and shooting power of large quantities of horse-warriors, the Mughals dispensed with the drilled infantry units that operated like the squares and lines of the Swiss and janissaries. For the same reason, they adopted neither the socket bayonet nor ball-cartridges, both of which had become the common equipment of the EIC army in Bengal from about 1700. All these innovations only made sense when used in a context in which cavalry was already pushed into the background by an increasingly disciplined and standardised infantry. This brings us to the third aspect involving the effectiveness of Indian firearms, namely, the question of how they were brought into operation on the actual battlefield.

The tactics of firearms

Already from about the fourteenth century, early gunpowder devices had played an increasingly important role in sieges. After the introduction of the true cannon, these weapons, especially mines, continued to be prominent in siege operations. Actually, if a Mughal siege was decided by purely military means at all, mining was mostly more effective than the use of cannon. While mining could really break the strongest of walls, the ideal siege artillery consisted of a combination of extremely heavy mortars to bombard the inside of a fort, and large cannon to do damage to the battlements. The latter were preferably used on high earthen *pashibs*, from where gunners could fire at the defenders on the walls or at specific targets inside. At the moment the pashib attained the height of the rampart, the siege had often reached a crucial stage where the besieged had to weigh the price of capitulation against the risks of staging a sortie to destroy the batteries.

One of the main problems facing a besieging army was transporting such heavy pieces to the place of the siege and then siting them appropriately, especially when the fort was located on a steep hill, in the middle of a march or in thick jungle (see Plate 5). As a result, the most heavy of mortars were often manufactured at the site of the siege. Problems of transportation urged Akbar to procure from the Turks the design for casting a barrel with screws to be dismantled into two pieces.[111] Although these devices may have facilitated mobility, they considerably harmed the trustworthiness of the barrel. Nonetheless, perhaps more than anything else, the approach, siting and firing of an extremely heavy gun, with all the accompanying fuss and noise, played on the morale of the defenders. This remained the case during the early years when guns were still something of a novelty, and when their size and metallurgy were seen as true wonders of the age. Later during the Mughal period, the use of extremely heavy siege-guns appears to have gone somewhat out of fashion but, like the increasingly obsolete elephants, heavy cannon remained part and parcel of the usual plethora of imperial weaponry. But, all in all, one can only agree with the conclusion reached for southern India that, despite the increasingly conspicuous role cannon played in sieges, it is hard to find more than the occasional instance of clear evidence that sieges were decisively affected by the use of artillery.[112]

The Mughal predilection for using cannon in sieges illustrates the fact that artillery was most useful when employed in static situations. In the field, it was particularly effective against multitudes of stationary infantry standing in line or in squares. Given its slow rate of fire, about once or twice every fifteen minutes, artillery was far less useful against cavalry, which, apart from tending to wheel around and out-flank the enemy, could overhaul and destroy the cannon after the first discharge. To counter the latter, cannon were often roped together by chains or placed behind carts, as in the first battle of Panipat. There evolved a purely defensive scheme in which well-covered light cannon and handguns awaited the attack of an enemy whose prime advantage lay in shock-cavalry and elephants. In the scheme's use of firearms, it came close to the one-century-old Hussite *Wagenburg*. The difference, of course, was that the Mughals combined the firepower from their covered centre with the use of highly movable flanks of mounted archers wheeling around the enemy, or enticing the enemy into the artillery fire by feigned retreats. These defensive tactics became the military fashion of the day, in India as well as in the Middle East and Central Asia. They were used by the Ottomans against the Safavids at the battle of Chaldiran (1514) and against the Mamluks at the battle of Dabik (1516). At the battle of Mohacs (1526), the Ottomans withdrew their cavalry to bring the Habsburg army under the fire of their cannon hidden behind the cavalry's back.[113] The Mughals adopted this so-called Rumi tactic against the Afghans at the battle of Panipat (1526) and the Safavids did the same against the Uzbeks at the battle of Jam (1528). Once the scheme was known, however, one became averse to rushing straight into the enemy's fire.

At the same time, flanking operations by the cavalry became more important, as is illustrated in the battle of Ridanieh (1517) where the Ottomans beset the static Mamluk artillery from the flank and the rear. Similarly, in India, the Mughal army under Humayun was able to defeat the Gujarati army at Mandasor (1535), although the latter was equipped with superior artillery. One archetypal Rumi Khan had the usual tactics in mind when he advised the Gujarati sultan:

> We have a grand park of artillery; when we have such a force of firearms, what sense is there in swordplay? The proper course is to make a bulwark of carriages and then having put a moat round this, let us first use those arms of long range so that the enemy may be diminished day by day and be dispersed. Fighting with arrows and swords has its own proper place.

Beveridge, the translator of these lines, was right to comment that Humayun had learned from his father's tactics and, instead of dashing himself to pieces against the entrenched camp, destroyed Bahadur's army by cutting off the supplies.[114] Nonetheless, and be it much less successful than during the earliest stages, the Rumi tactics of combining static firepower under cover with flanking cavalry continued to dominate battle operations until the second half of the eighteenth century, when the use of field artillery and drilled infantry radically changed the employability of firearms.[115]

The immobility of cannon during battles does not mean that they could not be moved swiftly before and after. As mentioned already, the heaviness and immobility of its cannon belong to the ineradicable stereotypes surrounding the Mughal army. The fact is, however, that after the early stages when guns had to be mounted and dismounted on carts, the Mughals managed to considerably improve the carriage equipment of the artillery.[116] In general, throughout the years, Mughal artillery tended to become lighter, simpler and more mobile. Bernier's reports about Aurangzeb's artillery should be conclusive in this regard. On the march, he reported, the heavy artillery consisted of seventy pieces of large, mostly brass cannon, accompanied by 300 dromedaries each carrying a zamburak.[117] The light artillery, also called artillery of the stirrup (*tupkhana-i rikab*),[118] always followed the king as a kind of household artillery.

> The stirrup-artillery is composed of 50 or 60 small field-pieces, all of brass; each mounted, as I have observed elsewhere, on a small carriage of neat construction and beautifully painted, decorated with a number of red streamers, and drawn by two handsome horses, driven by an artilleryman. There is always a third or relay horse, which is led by an assistant gunner. These field-pieces travel at a quick rate, so that they may be ranged in front of the royal tent in sufficient time to fire a volley as a signal to the troops of the King's arrival.[119]

It was also during Aurangzeb's reign that the Mughal artillery became less dependent on Ottoman and European expertise. From the various accounts one gets the impression that their services were less about manufacturing guns and powder, European supplies also becoming more easily accessible, and more about their skills in loading and aiming.[120] According to Bernier, Aurangzeb reduced the salaries of his gunners from 200 rupees a month, at a time when 'the Mughals were little skilled in the management of artillery', to a mere 32 rupees a month.[121] Although there may be some exaggeration in Bernier's figures, such an enormous reduction is certainly not an indication that artillery tactics were changing rapidly or that the Europeans were much in advance in this respect. In fact, the more important tactical developments were not occurring in the field of artillery but, in particular, in the use of small arms.

As with cannon, the Mughals preferred to use small arms in a defensive position behind cover or in ambush. As we have seen, Indian matchlocks were not inferior to the European muskets but were actually more accurate at a longer range. By contrast, the European development of handguns had been directed towards increasing their rate of fire. Hence, the introduction of the flintlock, bayonet and paper cartridges were aimed at maximising a rather inaccurate firepower. All this had been made possible by the earlier development of well-drilled squares of pikemen, meant to keep shock-cavalry at a decent distance. Together with the wheel-lock pistol, the tactics of the drilled square of pikemen had already begun to drive the mounted knight from the European battlefield.[122] Hence, in Europe the introduction of musketry involved its integration into the pike-square. In this situation, drill was needed to carry soldiers through the complicated movements necessary to change formation and to load and fire their guns amidst the noise, confusion and fear of battle. Both the design of the musket and the training methods involved discouraged musketeers from deliberate aiming. On the contrary, they were taught to load as quickly as possible, level the musket in the general direction of the enemy and, at least in theory, fire in simultaneous volleys.[123] To avoid being swept away by enemy cavalry, musketeers continued to require the support of pikemen, the latter disappearing only with the introduction of the socket-bayonet at the end of the seventeenth century.

In Mughal India, the tactical context of handguns was entirely different. In fact, the area lacked a long tradition of infantry warfare as it was perfectly happy, and rightly so, to rely on the nomadic cavalry tradition of the Arid Zone. The essential difference was the quantity of warhorses available as well as the combination of heavy shock-cavalry with mounted archers whose showers of arrows could destroy packed infantry, be it in squares or not, from a great distance. For a very long time during the development of infantry, pikes and the rather slow firepower of matchlocks would have made no impression at all against the massive numbers of horse-archers outflanking and wheeling around its position, be it in lines or in squares. Indeed, more than any difference in weaponry, two of the wittiest seventeenth-century European commentators were struck by the way current European battle practice was at odds with Mughal tactical common sense. It will be worthwhile to follow their observations in some detail.

The Dutchman Geleynssen de Jongh, for example, was surprised to find no pikes in the Mughal army:

> Here, in skirmishes and battles, one makes no use of pikes to prevent the cavalry from breaking in as usual in European warfare. In this country they do not keep ranks when marching, skirmishing or retreating as they do in the European quarters but everyone attacks and strikes wherever one feels fit or best to harm the enemy.

He was quick to add, however:

> Although they keep no fixed rule in their ranks, they take care that their troops or regiments, be it horse or foot, are not mixed up, and in attacking every one keeps to his duty, taking little notice of one being in the advanced or rear guard.[124]

Equally illustrative is Manucci's account in which he demonstrated European battle tactics to the Mughal general Raja Jai Singh.

> The foot soldiers were separated from the squadrons of horse, and all had their matchlocks and swords. Those who were mounted had good carbines, pistols and swords. When I was giving this account, finding some pikes or spears there, I exhibited how the spearmen stood in front of the companies to hinder the cavalry from getting in and throwing into disorder the well-ordered ranks of the infantry. Thus the battle would commence with great order and discipline, the cavalry helping wherever it was necessary to repress an onslaught of the enemy. Many a thing did we tell him of our fighting in the open country.

The raja's reaction was as understandable as the point when 'upon this he set to laughing, assuming us to have no horses in our country, and thus we could know nothing of fighting on horseback.'[125] Somewhat later Manucci reports of another Mughal commander, this time the governor of the Carnatic Da'ud Khan Panni. When visiting the English at Fort St George, this experienced Afghan general was astonished to find out that the company of soldiers were drawn up in single rank and in excellent order.

> Still greater was his amazement when, as they drew near the fort gateway, the soldiers and their officers, on catching sight of the governor, drew themselves up in line and went through divers movements which were quite unknown to him. They were only done in his honour and that of the governor. But being unaccustomed to all this military ceremonial, he was thrown into a state of confusion and apprehension. He believed himself to be already a prisoner. For this reason he spoke to me in a loud voice, requesting that all these men might be withdrawn. I reassured him, saying that it was nothing but the usual ceremonial and method among these troops; he should not be in the least afraid, or suspect anything. At the same time, I took care to cry out to the soldiers that they must retire.[126]

The same message is present in the account of the siege of São Tomé (1672–3) by the French Abbé Carré, which is all the more interesting because it is one of the first instances where European tactics turned out to be decisive in defeating an Indian opponent. Referring to the Golkonda infantry surrounding São Tomé, the Abbé articulately explains, albeit in a highly eulogistic sense, its recurrent defeat against the French squadrons.

> This was due to the fact that they were not accustomed to our pistols and bayonets at the end of our muskets, used after the shot had been fired, nor to our grenades and other fire-arms. They withstood us, however, with wonderful courage, having only steel weapons such as sabres, lances, and halberds, as well as large knives in their belts. Though they use a musket, they take so long over its loading and aiming that it is quite useless in close combat or in a melee, when they fight without order and have not time to be cool or to think of what they should do, such is the dismay and confusion into which they themselves fall through their howls, cries, and clamour.[127]

It is important to note though that the Golkonda troops were on the whole much inferior to the Mughal army, particularly with respect to the quality and numbers of cavalry. Hence, it remains extremely doubtful whether the French squadrons would have been equally successful against a fully equipped Mughal army. Anyway, at this stage, the Mughals felt no need to install a drilled infantry corps, neither on the basis of the European examples, nor inspired by the slave units of musketeers created under the Ottomans and the Safavids. Hence, until the mid-eighteenth century, the musketeer remained the least-valued and least-paid Mughal soldier, who could not but raise the compassion of the European onlooker:

> The musketeers cut a sorry figure at the best of times, which may be said to be when squatting on the ground, and resting their muskets on a kind of wooden fork which hangs to them. Even then, they are terribly afraid of burning their eyes or their long beards, and above all lest some Dgen [*jinn*], or evil spirit, should cause the bursting of their musket.[128]

Indeed, without his horse the Mughal soldier was a penniless as well as honourless figure. Besides, on numerous occasions, the Mughal horse-trooper had proven his superiority over numberless footsloggers. This does not mean that individual matchlockmen, even the emperors themselves, could not be praised for their excellent marksmanship. The crucial point is that matchlocks were used by individuals and not in drilled formation. In collective action, mounted archers and heavy cavalry had far more impact on the battlefield. Hence, there was no tactical need at all to shift to new methods. Infantry warfare with all its highly accessible skills and weaponry, remained something for small zamindars, tribal chiefs and Firangi pirates; those 'cowards' who entrenched themselves in hill forts, thick jungles or high carracks, and who knew neither how to deal with nor how to afford warhorses. Later, during the eighteenth century when the Mughal Empire was already dissolving, this zamindari kind of warfare became the new fashion. Significantly, it occurred only after the introduction of flintlocks, bayonets and cartridges had increased the firepower of drilled infantry and just at a time when lighter and standardised cast-iron guns improved the mobility and firepower of the field-artillery. Now, not these innovations as such, but their integration into the long European tradition of infantry warfare made the real difference. Although from the European point of view there was only gradual change, from the Indian perspective these innovations suddenly tipped the scales in favour of infantry and artillery against cavalry. Earlier the Mughals had felt no need at all to change their ways and now, all of sudden, they, for other than purely military reasons, had already passed the stage where they were fit to make such drastic technical as well as cultural adjustments. Their many regional successors, be it the Marathas, the Sikhs, the English East India Company or any other 'zamindari' power, were much better placed to take up the challenge by raising very effective modern armies based on drilled infantry and standardised field-artillery.

Oars and sails

Perhaps even more than forts and guns, the development in sails has always been closely associated with the rise of the West. Especially, the use of more cannon on board improved sailing ships is usually regarded as a crucial technological revolution with far-reaching repercussions in the sphere of state formation and overseas expansion. In Europe, the period from 1500 to 1650 saw decisive improvements in ship design, making battles with guns carried in sailing ships the dominant form of warfare at sea. In this period, albeit gradually and by fits and starts, the Atlantic maritime tradition of the full-rigged, round ship with square sails, firing a maximum number of guns mounted on the broadside of the ship, proved superior to the older Mediterranean ways of the galley with lateen sails and oars, and with only a few heavy guns in front and on the back of the ship, but having a maximum amount of soldiers available for boarding.[129] In fact, galley warfare was more or less an extension of the usual warfare on land, in which not the firepower as yet, but the numbers in the armies, counted.

It is a well-known story that the Portuguese exported this maritime revolution to the Indian Ocean. Although their operation did not militarise a thus far peaceful Indian Ocean, as often claimed, sea battles definitely occurred there more frequently after the entry of the Portuguese *naus* and caravels. On the high seas, these ships were undoubtedly superior in terms of strength, speed, manoeuvrability and, above all, firepower. Time and again, this was proved in the recurrent Portuguese victories over the galley-based Ottoman and Indian fleets.[130] But, as in the case of the Mediterranean, this sudden superiority of the round ship far from engendered the disappearance of the galley from the Indian Ocean. In fact, well into the eighteenth century, the galley, be it in its standard version (Pers. *jaliya*), in its smaller variety of the *fusta*, or in its larger, hybrid variety of the galleass (Pers. *ghurab*), remained the dominant warship along the coastal and riverine waters of the Indian sub-continent. In this respect, the development of Indian warshipping neatly follows the Mediterranean pattern.[131] In both cases, galleys continued to have a certain reputation for speed and manoeuvrability, at least as long as they operated over short ranges and in shallow waters. Hence, galleys were built and used by Indian and Portuguese navies alike.[132] Although the galley, as well as all varieties of the stitched Arabic *dhow* and the Chinese junk, continued to ply the high seas of the Indian Ocean, in terms of military capacity it was the European galleon, and later its taller adaptation the frigate, which definitely ruled the waves.[133]

Remarkably enough, the Portuguese domination of the Indian Ocean coincided with the Mughal conquest of northern India. Although aware that the Firangis had gained the upper hand along the overseas routes, the early Mughal rulers were not very much concerned with the radical changes occurring at sea. Why should they be? Initially the maritime confrontations between the Portuguese and the Gujaratis could only weaken one of their prime Indian rivals. But even after the incorporation of Gujarat and other maritime regions into the empire, the Mughals became hardly more bothered about the European domination of the seas. Of course, in their minds there was always the sensitive issue of ensuring the safe passage of the Hajj, but this was not an exclusive maritime concern as the land routes through Iran and the Ottoman Empire were also beyond their immediate control. Of course, in terms of trade, the sea-lanes were of profound importance to the Mughals as they brought goods and, above all, bullion into their territories. But given the structural trade surplus of their territories, trade and bullion would come in anyway, at least as long as there was a policy of laissez-faire and not one of fierce mutual mercantilism.[134] The Europeans on the coast, be it the Portuguese or the trade companies of the Dutch, English and French, were even more aware of this. Their trade could only be profitable when they were allowed to embark on the Indian shores and move relatively freely in the interior. For this reason, the period has often been described as one of mutual partnership in which the parties involved were very much aware of each other's different strengths and weaknesses. The few conflicts that occurred during our period were minor affairs and were mainly about renegotiating a slightly upset balance. Until the second half of the eighteenth century, for both the Mughals and the Europeans, the Indian littoral remained a natural, outer frontier, a nearly impregnable threshold beyond which expansion would require massive new investments, and involve the adoption of an entirely new technology and mentality.[135]

Of course, for the Mughals, the maritime activities of the Europeans were certainly not a matter of equal partnership, but rather the result of the benevolence and generosity they had shown to a subordinate community. In principle, their view of the maritime trading routes was not much different from that of the overland routes. Just as the latter were always threatened by the roaming tribes of the mawas, the former were always infested with all kinds of pirates criss-crossing the oceanic wilderness. Both required the payment of protection money, be it in the European form of *cartaze* or other payments for safe passage. In this light, the Firangis, as the Europeans were generally known, must have looked like a maritime tribe, having their nest (*nasheman*) on the *jaza'ir-i firang*, the Islands of the Franks.[136] Or, following a petition of the Portuguese Viceroy to Aurangzeb, they were the Mughal's unpaid servants. Populating a tract of worthless land, their main task was to suppress the mischief of the pirates on the coast. Anyway, be it for the Viceroy himself or for the Mughal historian Khafi Khan who reports the story, the Firangis were considered as merely nomads (*khana ba dush*) patrolling the seas (*muhafazat-i darya*).[137]

Although the Mughals were not in a position to safeguard the maritime routes, they were certainly eager to control the main maritime outlets along the empire's littoral, the latter also comprising the final termini of the Aparanta and Uttarapatha high roads radiating from the imperial capitals of Delhi and Agra. As a result, the coasts of Gujarat and Bengal stand out as areas attracting most of the Mughals' maritime attention. Beyond the ports, however, the Mughals, not much unlike the Ottomans, delegated the protection of the maritime routes, if not to the trading communities themselves, as in the case of the Companies, then to the highly specialised Abyssinian corsairs of Janjira on the western coast. These Sidis were authorised to protect Mughal shipping and to keep the other maritime powers at bay. They proved particularly effective in creating a second front at the Kanara Coast against the Marathas. During the Anglo-Mughal conflict of 1689–90 their fleet nearly wrested Bombay form the English East India Company. As long as they remained near the coast, their galleys proved not at all inferior to European shipping. In return for the services of the Sidis, the Mughals were satisfied to legitimise, finance and supply them.[138]

In Bengal the situation was somewhat different. To conquer its coast with all its many streams and rivulets, which became one big swamp (*jhil*) during the monsoon, was hardly a realistic option for a Mughal army based on cavalry.[139] To master this area, the Mughals needed to outfit an enormous fleet of riverboats. Under these circumstances, gunpowder weaponry, in particular light and heavy cannon that could easily be transported and sited on boats, became much more important than in the drier parts of the empire.[140] But as the Mughals had to spend time and money on making the necessary shift from their horses and bows to boats and guns, the conquest of eastern Bengal took much longer than that of Gujarat. Initially, the control of the Bengal delta was delegated to various regional lord marchers, the so-called twelve chieftains or *bara bhuyan*, each having a small territory of his own, and combining trade and shipbuilding with raiding and protection renting. At about 1600, this was still a typical frontier area attracting numerous, mainly Afghan and Portuguese, warriors who served in the numerous local fleets or engaged in the lively slave trade of the area. These marzban or 'wardens of the frontier' as they were called by the Mughals,[141] were supposed to supply ships and sailors to the Mughal river fleet (*nawara*) and in return received so-called *nawwara-jagirs*, often in still largely uncultivated territories.[142]

Over the years all these frontier chieftaincies were gradually conquered by successive Mughal campaigns. The biggest strides were made in 1611–12 under the governor Islam Khan Chishti (1608–13) against Musa Khan of Sonargaon and Raja Pratapaditya of Jessore, and in 1666 under Shaista Khan (1664–78) against the Arakanese forces in Chittagong. In all these campaigns, success depended on the firepower of hundreds of riverboats. Apart from the occasional round ship, the Mughal nawara consisted mostly of a few large ghurabs equipped with twelve to fourteen light guns, surrounded by four or five tall jaliyas equipped with four light guns, as well as hundreds of *kosas*, small but very manoeuvrable rowing boats with a few guns on board and with a crew of about thirty men.[143] Arakan, the main contender in the area, had a fleet that, in quantity and quality, was superior to that of the Mughals. Apart from its hundreds of galleys, large and small, it employed a few so-called *khalus* and *dhums*, which 'were so strongly made of timber with a hard core that the balls of zamburaks and small cannon could not pierce them'.[144] What appears to have made the difference in favour of the Mughals was the tactical support of the land forces, at times even mounted archers playing a role in outflanking the enemy's fleet.[145] Really crucial for the success of operations, however, was the logistical support that was made possible by digging canals and building new roads protected by numerous thanas. In this way, the Mughals managed, as it were, to extend the Uttarapatha, first to Dhaka under the governors Man Singh and Islam Khan, and later under Shaista Khan, then to Sangramgarh at the confluence of the Ganges and the Brahmaputra. The latter was an embanked road or *al* passable for horse and foot even during the monsoon. Sangramgarh itself was the ideal outpost to prevent the Arakanese and Portuguese from raiding the Bengal delta. Later, by cutting down the thick jungle along the coast, the road was extended to

Chittagong. Hence, it was again road-building that ensured the incorporation of the eastern Bengali ports into the Empire.[146]

Reassessing the impact of forts, guns and sails on Mughal India we may conclude that they could not really change the Mughal preference for the camp, the bow and the horse. Nonetheless, forts played a crucial role in extending and controlling the imperial high roads. There was no radical change in their architecture as their predecessors had made forts capable enough of withstanding the rather slowly improving gunpowder devices even during the Mughal period.

Coming to guns, from the early sixteenth century onwards, well-manufactured small arms and bronze cannon, both light and heavy, were widely available on the Indian sub-continent. Occasionally, cannon could decide the outcome of a siege or a battle. In tactical terms, firearms served best in a defensive situation behind cover, facilitating the flanking operations of the cavalry. As such, they merely replaced the elephants and the heavy cavalry in the centre at earlier battles. It was only in the eighteenth century that the European developments involving the production of cheap, standardised cast-iron cannon, flintlock, bayonet and cartridges began to dominate the Indian war scene. But this could only be achieved thanks to the tactical employment of firearms via the discipline of drilled soldiers. For the Mughals, this was a rare phenomenon only suitable for people without horses. For them drilling infantry troops had never made sense in a situation where warhorse and elephant remained the proven rulers of Indian battle. At the time the military balance was shifting towards infantry and artillery, the Mughal army had already been co-opted by the big zamindars and other regional warlords of the empire.

Plate 6 Mughal campaign to Orchha, 1635. This picture by Tezdast (*c.* 1637) depicts the capture of Orchha by the Mughal forces under Khan-i Dauran, Abdulla Khan and Saiyid Khan Jahan Barha (in front). Although Orchha is situated at the forested fringe of the Mughal high road, the rising dust of the imperial army storming through the dry jungle of Bundelkhand (at top, in the left corner) illustrates the achievement of the Mughal army campaigning both along the limits and limites of empire (see also M. Cleveland Beach and E. Koch (1997), pp. 88–9; 195–7).

Source: *Royal Library, Windsor Castle, Padshahnama,* f. 174A

CHAPTER SIX

The limits of empire

In principle, the Mughal realm was unlimited. In practice, Mughal territorial rule became stranded at various inner frontiers all along the imperial high roads. Paradoxically, however, crossing these frontiers became the routine business and the *raison d'être* of the imperial army. At the same time, though, as the empire was theoretically unlimited, conquest involved the extension of the Mughal high roads, that is, moving the termini along the main imperial axes of, in particular, the Uttarapatha, the Dakshinapatha and the Aparanta(patha). In Chapter 1, we saw how Mughal expansion started in Kabul and neatly followed the *longue durée* pattern of these Indian limites. This chapter will return to these high roads by concentrating on three major Mughal campaigns at the far ends of these roads. Since the (south)western road to Aparanta found an early and relatively final natural frontier at the Arabian Sea, the three campaigns involve the most eastern, most northern and most southern extension of the road network, respectively, the successful conquest of eastern Bengal between 1608 and 1613, the frustrated campaign in Balkh between 1645 and 1648, and the endless siege of the fort of Gingee between 1689 and 1697. These campaigns will illustrate how and to what extent the different geographical conditions determined the logistical outer frontiers of the Mughal Empire. They will also suggest that success and failure, expansion and contraction were closely related phenomena as the new, projecting high roads not only facilitated the outward expansion of the Mughals but also stimulated the inward encroachments of the Marathas, the Afghans and the European Companies.

Unlike the thematic approach of the previous chapters, this chapter will chronologically describe the main events as presented in a few contemporary Mughal sources. By looking at the Mughal army in its actual operation on the ground, the earlier analytical comments on geography, mentality, recruitment, strategy, tactics, logistics and weaponry will feature in its daily operation, albeit rather fragmentarily and often without the historical detail the military historian would wish for.

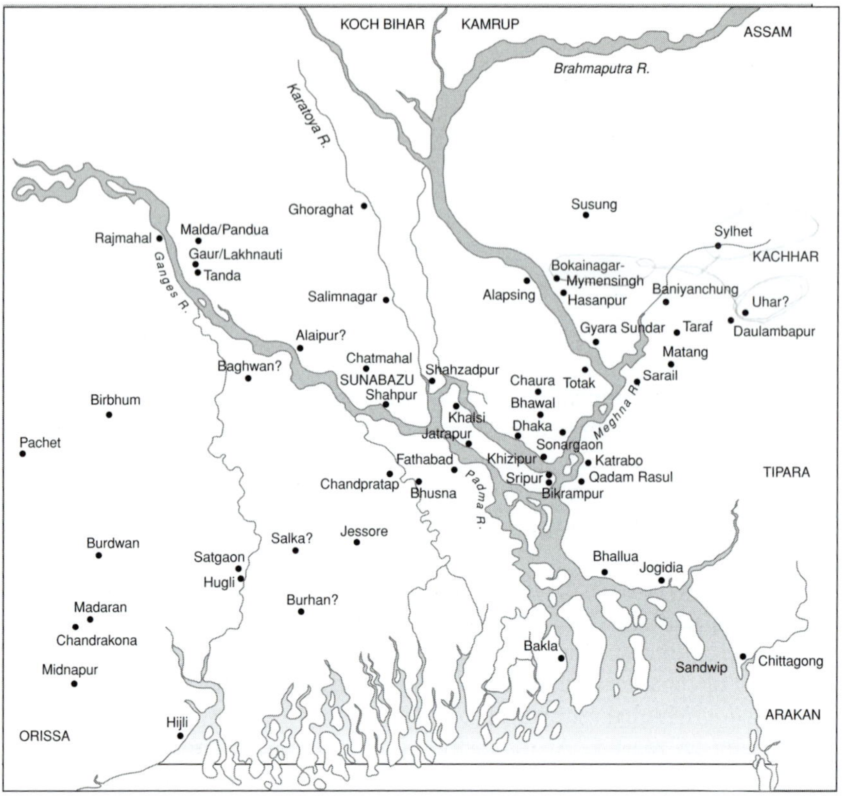

Map 6.1 Eastern front: 1608–12

The eastern front: Bengal 1608–12[1]

For the rulers of the Delhi–Agra region ruling Bengal had always been problematic. Apart from its mere distance, Bengal's humid climate combined with its countless rivulets and streams, its silted or stagnant swamps and marshes made the field operations of cavalry armies extremely hazardous. As we have seen already, the last stage of the cavalry was the relatively dry plain at the head of the Bengal delta, which also became the site of the medieval Bengali capitals of Lakhnauti, Pandua, Gaur, Tanda and Rajmahal. The lower-lying southeastern tracts of modern Bengal, also called Bhati, remained a dynamic kind of 'Wild East', attracting all sorts of free-floating warriors, settlers, preachers, ascetics and other pioneers keen to open up new ground for themselves. Many of them were Afghans from Bihar and Orissa, looking for a safe haven and new opportunities after being driven away by the Mughal armies. Some of them took service in the armed forces of the numerous lord marchers in the Bhati region, while others found a political niche of their own in the most eastern corner of Bengal, such as Khwaja Usman (Khan) Lohani in Bokainagar and Uhar, and Bayazid Khan Karrani in Sylhet. The supposed *jadu*, or witchcraft, in these regions only added to their reputation as the back of beyond of the East.[2] Apart from the Afghans, many Portuguese traders, renegades and other adventurers entered the Bhati area from the Bay of Bengal. Like the Afghans, they found a safe and often very lucrative refuge among the various principalities of the region. One of them, Sebastião Gonçalves Tibau, even managed to carve out a chieftaincy of his own on the island of Sandwip. The two most important principalities, however, were Sonargaon, under the chief Bhati marzban Musa Khan, and Jessore, under Raja Pratapaditya. These petty states thrived on a combination of activities, mainly involving trading, shipping, raiding and developing new land. Despite its reputation as a refuge for outlaws, obviously very much the Mughal view, the Bhati landscape showed a mixture of extremely fertile agricultural fields alternated with dense forests. This is neatly illustrated by a Jesuit account from about 1600:

> The way from Bacala [Bakla] to Chandecan [Jessore] is wonderfully pleasant. All along flow deep rivers of sweet clear water; on the one side are dense shady woods, and herds of stags and cattle roaming about the plains; on the other side fields covered with rice and displaying far and wide their joyful burdens. . . . Here and there plantations of the much-prized sugarcane were to be seen. But there were tigers too, and crocodiles which at times fed on human flesh.[3]

Apart from Sonargaon and Jessore, the 'Magh' state of Arakan, including its main shipping centre Chittagong, was a major player in the Bhati region. By showing a remarkable ability to connect agricultural expansion with extensive trading and raiding, Arakan and Chittagong fitted extremely well into the overall pattern of the Bhati region.

This was the situation in 1608 when Jahangir appointed his foster-brother Islam Khan Chishti, also the grandson of Akbar's chief spiritual guide Shaikh Salim Chishti, as the new governor of Bengal. About one decade earlier, under Raja Man Singh (1594–1606), the Mughals had begun to make the first inroads into Bhati, meanwhile making Dhaka their new regional headquarters in 1602. But it was only under Islam Khan (1608–13) that this far-eastern frontier region became more thoroughly incorporated into the Mughal realm. Actually, at the time the province of Bengal was conferred on Islam Khan Chishti it was still very much a region to be conquered. The governor's main task was to pacify the Bhati zamindars and to eliminate the last remnants of Afghan resistance, thereby crushing the last hope of a restored Indo-Afghan empire. One reason for bestowing

Islam Khan with the honour was his special tie of trust and friendship with the emperor. Also, the Chishti chief could build on an extensive network of about 20,000 loyal followers of his own.[4] On the one hand, this gave the necessary strength and cohesion to the Mughal army, but on the other hand, there was always the danger that, under a successful Chishti leadership, Bengal would break away from the empire. To curb this almost natural tendency of successful Bengal governors, Jahangir could build on a variety of trusted officers who acted independently from the provincial command structure. First, there were the imperial news-writers who reported directly to the court. Second, there were several mansabdars under Islam Khan's command who had close personal ties to the emperor, be it as khanazadas or as disciples in the imperial cult of din-i ilahi.[5] Apart from this, under the governor's supreme command there existed a dual hierarchy in which the personal and imperial officers were to be kept strictly separate from each other. At various instances, Islam Khan was accused of mixing the two contingents and of favouring his own officers to the detriment of the imperial ones. In general, though, Jahangir kept his trust in Islam Khan, knowing that his withdrawal would estrange the entire Chishti network from the imperial cause and, as such, jeopardise the military targets of the Bhati campaign.

In 1608 Islam Khan took charge as Bengal governor and moved to Rajmahal. After making various changes in the existing provincial administration, he attempted to win over as many local zamindars as possible, partly by threatening with the stick, but more often, by offering a carrot in the form of an official recognition of zamindari rights and of various other incentives like special honours and gifts. The Mughal commander Mirza Nathan gives an example of the usual Mughal procedure when facing a local zamindar:

> If he submitted he should be given the hope of imperial favours and brought to Islam Khan's presence; if he refused to submit and took recourse to war, he would have only himself to thank for his punishment. Then he should either be brought in chains or his head cut off and forwarded.[6]

This strategy was particularly successful in the early stages of the campaign when Islam Khan attempted to secure the southern and northern flanks of his coming march to Bhati. Although nominally part of the Mughal Empire, most of the zamindars in the southwestern and northern parts of the province were still liable to disrupt the army's ever lengthening supply lines. Even at the heart of the empire, local raiding could considerably undermine military operations, as was shown, for example, when the Mughal river fleet under Ihtiman Khan was attacked on its way to Bengal in Allahabad by the Gawar pirates of Chajuha. To avoid these kinds of harassments in the future, Islam Khan first sent part of his troops to the southern zamindars of Birbhum, Pachet, Hijli and Bhusna. After an initial show of force, the chief of Bhusna, Raja Satrajit, submitted to the Mughal commander Iftikhar Khan who honoured him with the designation of 'son' and brought him to the presence of Islam Khan. From that moment onward, Satrajit became an important and most active ally in the Mughal campaign in Bhati. The other three zamindars also submitted without much fighting. After they offered tribute (*peshkash*) and large gifts to Islam Khan they were allowed to return with honour to their respective zamindaris.

The procedure on the northern flank appears to have been somewhat different. As they controlled areas which were close to the marching route to Bhati, the northern zamindars were brought under more direct surveillance by bestowing their territories as jagirs on the mansabdars. Obviously, all these zamindaris became jagirs to be conquered. For example, the area surrounding the district of Sunabazu[7] was given as a jagir to the Mir Bahr, or commander of the imperial fleet, Ihtiman Khan and his son Mirza Nathan.[8] This implied that they had to collect their salaries, from which they had to pay for the equipment of the fleet, from territories controlled by well-entrenched zamindars unwilling to submit revenue. In Sunabazu, Ihtiman Khan, who himself commanded a fleet of about 300 boats, was faced with a zamindari force consisting of 200 boats, 400 horse and 4,000 foot. Similarly, the zamindars of Shahzadpur and Chandpratap forcefully resisted the *mutasaddis*, or revenue officers, sent by, respectively, Tuqman Khan and Mirak Bahadur Jala'ir, two other Mughal jagirdars. One last measure to take the area under closer control was the organisation of a massive kheda under the command of Islam Khan himself. This not only served to pacify the countryside but also delivered a large number of war elephants. Above all, it was an opportunity to exercise field operations of a newly composed army as well as to test the ability and social chemistry of its officers.

At about this time, Pratapaditya, the powerful Raja of Jessore, came to tender personal submission to Islam Khan. He promised to support the campaign by sending 400 war boats to join the imperial fleet under the command of his youngest son. In return, he received the revenue of the districts of Sripur and Bikrampur, as in earlier cases areas still to be conquered, this time from Musa Khan, the main Mughal enemy in Bhati. According to Mirza Nathan, in consideration of his high position, Islam Khan bestowed honours beyond measure upon the Raja. He was presented with a robe of honour, a sword, a bejewelled sword-belt, a bejewelled camphor-stand, five high-bred Iraqi and Turkish horses, one male elephant, two female elephants and an imperial kettledrum. 'Thus he was converted into a loyal officer'.[9]

After one year of preparations and with the rains approaching, Islam Khan decided to move his camp to the north to stay for the monsoon season, from roughly June to October, in Ghoraghat, one of the few 'ancient forts' in Bengal with fairly close links to the Rajmahal region.[10] Probably to alleviate the logistical problem of supplying a massive, stationary army, many of the Mughal commanders were given orders to go to their jagirs, to get ready for the coming campaign after the rains. Not all of them were happy with the situation. Ihtiman Khan, for example, complained to Islam Khan that he had been reduced from the level of a *darogha*, that is, a superintendent paid for his real disbursements, to that of an *ijaradar*, or leaseholder who had to equip his troops against a competitive rate on the military labour market. As another officer had offered cheaper rates, Ihtiman Khan had been forced to accept a reduction of his salary from 1,200 rupees per boat to a mere 400 rupees per boat.[11]

For the Mughal army the monsoon was a long period of waiting and preparation. This was due to the fact that, even in Bengal, the main asset of the Mughal army was its land force consisting of a relatively small number of horses and a relatively large number of elephants. As the latter were well accustomed to the humid climate, they figured prominently as beasts of burden, bringing men as well as guns safely across the region's many streams. In the absence of massive cavalry armies, they also served well as shock animals in pitched battles and as battering rams against wooden redoubts. Also, gunpowder weaponry, in particular heavy and light cannon, played a much more important role in Bengal than in other parts of the sub-continent. This was partly the result of less cavalry warfare, and partly thanks to the prevalence of river warfare, guns on boats being far more movable than those on land. In terms of boats and guns, though, the Mughals were far from superior. The local zamindars were well equipped with guns and had undoubtedly more boats, both well served by experienced European gunners and sailors. The Mughal fleet consisted of, at maximum about 500 boats, whereas the fleet of Raja Pratapaditya had twice as many, which was only slightly more than the fleet of Musa Khan and certainly less than the powerful Arakanese fleet.[12] During much of the monsoon, these zamindari navies were perfectly capable of military operations. Actually, extensive flooding enhanced the mobility and reach of flat-bottomed riverboats. Hence, at the time that the Mughal army had to remain in its camps, the monsoon was the high season for zamindari revolts. To counter these, the Mughals had patiently to await the arrival of the dry season.

Considering the military balance in Bengal, how can we explain the repeated successes of the Mughal army? From the available contemporary accounts, it appears that the Mughal ascendancy was due to the combined operation of land and river forces. In terms of numbers of elephants, horses and soldiers, as well as of capital resources, the Mughals appear to have had the upper hand. They could build on the almost permanent supply and reinforcements from northern India. To bring this enormous potential of military power into effective action, the movement of the army had to be slow, also to ensure that the land forces could keep pace with the fleet and vice versa. In the combined tactics of land forces and fleet, the latter served as a floating battery of heavy gun-platforms (variously called *katari*, *maniki* and *bathila*) equipped with both heavy cannon and light zarbzans. In the case of Mirza Nathan's fleet, the guns were attached to wagons that were moved up and down the boats and that, in case of need, could be brought ashore as well.[13] This riverine Wagenburg was usually assisted by numerous, more flexible, small riverboats, or kosas. Closely following the main fleet, there were always the boats of the *beoparis*, or traders, keeping up the necessary supply. Along the shore, mounted archers, musketeers and cannoneers enhanced the firepower from the flanks. Mughal cannon were preferably employed from quickly constructed wooden palisades. Indeed, as crucial as the purely military conditions was the Mughal ability to build strings of blockhouses and forts. As with the impressive engineering work of digging canals and building roads, this was not only to facilitate the approach of the army, in its fullest extent and weight, but also to secure the supply lines to the west. As such, the Mughal campaign in Bengal was entirely different from other Mughal operations. Instead of pace and mobility, it was the slow but sustained movement, as well as the concentrated employment of the Mughal army, that one by one rounded up the divided and spread-out forces of the Bengal zamindars.

After spending the monsoon of 1609 in Ghoraghat the Bhati campaign now began in earnest. Sending one contingent under Shaikh Kamal directly to Dhaka, Islam Khan with the bulk of the army turned southward in the direction of Musa Khan's forts of Jatrapur and Dakchara (3 miles northwest of Jatrapur. Thanks to the excavation of canals by Mirza Nathan's engineers the fleet could keep pace with the land army. Still, it was only in the summer of 1610 that the Mughal forces were ready to besiege Jatrapur. Again thanks to the excavation work of about 10,000 sailors under Mirza Nathan, the fleet with all its firepower was able to come close to the fort. This work was considerably facilitated by the material encouragement provided by the Mirza who lavishly distributed among the sailors 'copper coins, rice, bhang (Indian hemp) and opium'. Similarly, material incentives played an important role in the siege of Dakchara. In the midst of fierce fighting, the Mirza ordered his subordinate officials 'to lay a heap of 3,000 rupees on the ground, and he began to distribute them in handfuls among the wounded soldiers and the relatives of those who had been killed in battle, and thus made them all enthusiastic in their arduous task'.[14] Anyway, the Mughals' ability to generously reward their soldiers with money, food and intoxicants must certainly have contributed to the taking of both forts at a time when the monsoon rains had already started. After these two successes the army settled in Dhaka to make ready for the attack on Musa Khan's remaining territories on the eastern side of the Meghna river.

In February–March 1611, the Mughals turned towards the two main forts of Musa Khan, Katrabo and Qadam Rasul. As in the earlier sieges of Jatrapur and Dakchara, these forts were captured in combined operations of well-paid and well-fed land- and river-forces, which advanced en masse towards to the forts' defences. In all four sieges, elephants played a conspicuous role in crossing rivers and in breaking through the wooden entrenchments of Musa Khan's forts.[15]

After the Mughal victories of Katrabo and Qadam Rasul, the chief officer of Musa Khan, Shams al-Din Baghdadi, defected to Islam Khan and handed over to him the already evacuated capital city of Sonargaon. Many other allies of Musa Khan had already submitted to the Mughals, such as the zamindars Bahadur Ghazi of Chaura and Majlis Qutb of Fathabad. Musa Khan himself, with all his relatives and other supporters, followed their example in July. With the exception of Musa Khan, who was kept under surveillance, all of them were incorporated into the Mughal army and their estates were granted to them as jagirs. Meanwhile, carrot and stick also proved very effective in the flanking expedition of Shaikh Abdul Wahid against the zamindar of Bhallua. After bribing the zamindar's chief officer, the forts of Bhallua and Jogidia were easily converted into the most eastward thanas of the empire. As the Bhati zamindars were all either defeated or brought into the Mughal fold, the Mughals arrived at a stage in which all hands were free to rout their most sought-after enemies, the Afghans of Bokainagar and Sylhet.

Immediately after another monsoon sojourn in Dhaka, the Mughal army marched towards Bokainagar. Their hurry was aimed at the ongoing high water level, which could be used for the speedy approach of the Mughal fleet, the more so because the surrounding countryside was soon to become an almost impenetrable jungle of swamps and marshes. This time, after the incorporation of hundreds of zamindari boats, the fleet had become the Mughals' main asset. However, as they found out that the flooding of the rivers was not sufficient for their purpose, they decided to concentrate on a careful and gradual advance over land, raising fort after fort in which the artillery kept the enemy at a distance. According to Mirza Nathan, 'in every lofty fort, which was constructed, within a very short time with deep trenches around, they used to stop for four days. On the fifth day they would begin the work of another fort.'[16] After constructing nineteen of these forts in a row, with only Ramadan as a break, Usman Khan came to the conclusion that it was better to avoid a major confrontation, to evacuate Bokainagar and to withdraw to his other base in Uhar. At this far-eastern corner of Bengal where navigable rivers were lacking, he probably knew that, not boats, but elephants were to decide the final outcome of the Mughal–Afghan confrontation.

At Bokainagar, some problems arose that were due to the fuzzy Mughal command structure. In contrast to the campaign against Musa Khan, Islam

Khan had preferred to stay in and around Dhaka. After the taking of Bokainagar, the Mughal commanders were at a loss about what to do next: should they chase down Usman Khan or return to their headquarters in Dhaka? In addition, the question was raised: who is actually in charge in the absence of Islam Khan? Mirza Nathan, who was in favour of pursuing Usman Khan, was of the opinion that one should follow the imperial regulations and submit to the one who possessed the highest mansab. Apparently this was Qaza Khan who hesitantly inquired as to who was willing to accept his leadership? Not surprisingly, his decision to follow the Afghans was neglected by the other leaders who turned back to Dhaka after they had decided that they would collectively cover each other if Islam Khan was to accuse them of passivity. In Dhaka, Islam Khan was not amused and blamed his commanders for the escape of Usman Khan. In their defence, Ihtiman Khan pointed out 'that according to the orders of His Majesty, the governor ought to have remained behind at a distance of 30 kos from the field of battle'. He confessed the mistake but alleged that Islam Khan's lack of leadership had caused it. Ihtiman Khan considered himself not at all inferior to the governor, as every single officer was 'the slave of the master'.[17] He was fortunate that the conflict fizzled out, but the affair clearly shows the shortcomings of the Mughal command structure, which at all times required the nearby presence of the commander-in-chief. We should keep in mind, though, that this was most probably a deliberately built-in weakness of a highly flexible system of checks and balances aimed at stimulating the competition among the imperial mansabdars.

Confronted by the sudden finish of the northern campaign, Islam Khan kept his troops busy by sending one regiment ahead in the eastern direction of Taraf and the Afghan fort of Matang, and two other regiments in the southern direction of Jessore. The troops of Ghiyath Khan and Mirza Nathan were to approach Jessore through the forts of Salka and Burhan, while the troops of Saiyid Hakim were to advance via Bakla. As we noticed earlier, the Jessore Raja had already submitted to the Mughals in 1609. The reason for attacking his territories may have had something to do with the upcoming campaign against the Afghans. Perhaps Islam Khan thought that he could not afford to risk a revolt of Pratapaditya as this would cut off the supply lines of the army at the far-eastern front. It is also very possible that the Mughal army needed the reputedly rich material resources of Jessore to support the planned campaign against Usman Khan. Anyway, the expedition to Jessore was an easy success: the Raja submitted for the second time but could not prevent the Mughals from plundering his territories.

Immediately after the Jessore campaign, Islam Khan's leadership was again tested when he wanted to send Mirza Nathan to counter the Magh, or Arakanese, raids around Sripur. Mirza Nathan refused the honour since he wanted some rest and time to visit his father. But as the governor insisted, Mirza Nathan, together with 4,700 of his soldiers, decided to turn mendicant and threatened to leave for the imperial court. Only the emperor himself, 'whose favours nourish the humblest one' would be able to relieve him of his mendicancy. Islam Khan, of course, interpreted the Mirza's conduct as an act of open rebellion and could only keep him under suveillance and as far as possible from the eyes and ears of the emperor.[18]

Meanwhile, Jahangir, who may have heard about Islam Khan's tendency to stay aloof from the battlefield, had decided to give the campaign against Usman Khan a new boost by sending another Chishti commander to the province. Like Islam Khan, this Shuja'at Khan was a grandson of the great Salim Chishti. Assisted by another bunch of Chishti relatives and devotees, he was to take charge of the military expedition against Usman Khan. Islam Khan remained the acting governor and commander-in-chief.[19]

On his arrival, Shuja'at Khan forcefully headed towards Usman Khan's remaining fort of Uhar. He also took Mirza Nathan out of detention and made him part of his newly composed army. In March 1611, this army met its Afghan counterpart under Usman Khan near the village of Daulambapur. Although we are left without information about the size and composition of the Mughal forces, Mirza Nathan mentions that the Afghan army consisted of about 5,000 horse, 10,000 foot and, most importantly, 150 elephants. Usman Khan had selected a favourable position as he had raised a battery by fastening planks to some areca-nut trees on the shore of an extensive swamp. The confrontation started with the usual overtures of peace in which Usman Khan was offered a mansab of 5,000. But since he considered his position too advantageous, the negotiations came to nothing and on the twelfth of March the Mughals began to attack the Afghan positions. What followed was a mêlée of fighting soldiers in which the far-off Mughal artillery killed a great number of their own people. At the battle, a usual number of officers remained passive: whereas the Afghans in Mughal service declined to fight their brothers, some Afghan officers appear to have been in league with Islam Khan. Among the latter was Usman Khan's brother Khwaja Wali who failed to take up the command when Usman Khan, seated on an elephant, was fatally wounded by an arrow. Just before, the Afghans and their elephants had crushed both the right and left wings of the Mughals and killed their commanders. Even at the centre, the Afghans had broken the Mughal lines and isolated Shuja'at Khan. As hinted at already, the crucial reversal occurred when Usman Khan was killed by an arrow. As nobody was able to replace his leadership, the Afghans lost heart and gave up their winning position. They could not be prevented, though, from taking Usman Khan's dead body from the battlefield to be buried in a hidden grave. His wives and daughters, except one already betrothed and now given in marriage to his nephew Da'ud, were put to the sword and buried by the side of his false tomb.[20]

Daulambapur also turned out to be the end of the line for the other Afghan chiefs in Bengal. After hearing about the defeat of their brothers, the Karrani Afghans also capitulated and submitted to Islam Khan in Dhaka. At last, after a protracted campaign that took almost three years, the last credible remnant of Afghan resistance to Mughal power in the delta had been extirpated. Nevertheless, the final pacification of the province had to wait for another half a century until Shaista Khan managed to conquer Chittagong, the hotbed of ongoing slave-raids in the southern part of the province.

Nevertheless, as early as 1612, Mughal ascendancy in Bengal was symbolised by the fact that Islam Khan made Dhaka the new provincial capital. He embellished it with a new palace and new forts as well as new roads and canals.[21] Once installed, it developed into a cosmopolitan provincial capital increasingly attracting people and resources overland from the Mughal heartlands as well as overseas from the Dutch and English Companies.[22] In the long run, a booming centre like this could not fail to begin a life of its own. Indeed, at the beginning of the eighteenth century its governors became de facto autonomous rulers. Fifty years later, the British managed to turn the tables on the Mughals by making Bengal the hub of an entirely new imperial system. Once again in history, a frontier outpost had become an imperial centre.

The western front: Balkh 1645–8[23]

For the Mughal emperors the western front was special. Although in purely material terms, eastern and southern expansion was far more rewarding, the westward advance was more an emotional drive involving the honour and status of the Mughal dynasty. First of all, the Mughals had been forced by the Uzbeks to leave their pleasant homeland in Turan for the rich but 'inhospitable, uncivilised and heathen' Hindustan. Reading the Mughal sources, the success story of their Indian empire could hardly be a consolation for the painful loss of their hereditary kingdom of Samarkand. In the eyes of the early Mughal emperors, their empire in India was presented as the accidental result of a temporary, peripheral campaign. After straightening things out in India, the retaking of their homeland remained at the top of their agenda.[24] Apart from such feelings of *reconquista*, the Mughals were very much concerned about their prestige vis-à-vis their western neighbours. More than that by any other ruler, the recognition of Mughal rule by the kings of Iran and Turan really made that rule legitimate and worthy. As anyone knew, the Uzbeks were direct paternal descendants of Chinggis Khan, whereas the Mughals could claim a maternal connection only.[25] In their turn, the Safavids not only inherited that long Persian tradition of universal rule (*shahanshahi*) but they had also actively patronised the early careers of both Babur and Humayun. In this light,

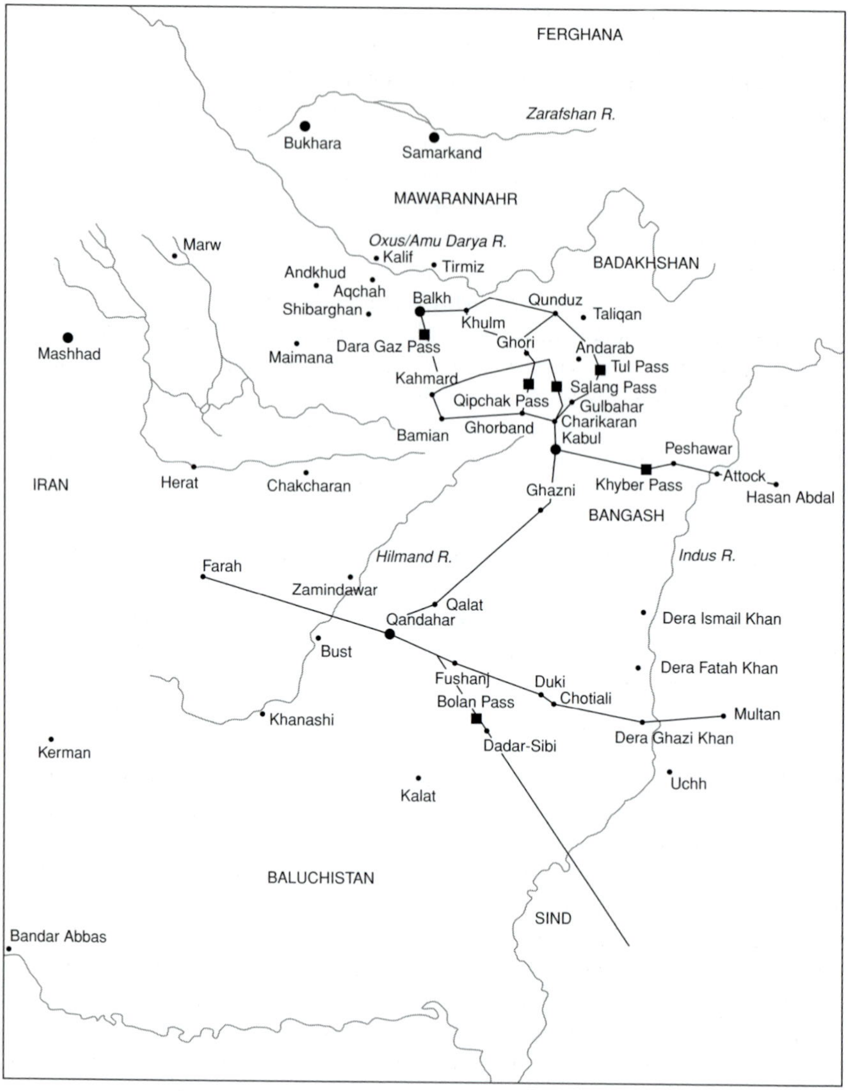

Map 6.2 Western front: 1645–8

the western drive of the Mughals may be seen as a reflection of a kind of Mughal inferiority complex in which they wanted to point out to their Uzbek and Safavid rivals that they had arrived as autonomous Muslim world-conquerors. Last but not least, the western front was of course crucially important for the supply of warhorses from Central Asia. Any neglect in this regard would not only affect the striking power of the Mughal army but also stimulate tribal revolts and foreign invasions from the northwest. Hence, securing Qandahar and Kabul, as the 'twin gates of Hindustan', was a vital strategic concern.

Although the theme of reconquista was prevalent among all the Great Mughals, it was under Shah Jahan that it really materialised. In 1639 Shah Jahan had already spent the summer in Kabul, this being only one year after the Kurdish turncoat Ali Mardan Khan had handed Qandahar over to him. But it was only six years later that Shah Jahan launched a full campaign against the Uzbeks. It was sparked off by a conflict between the Toqai-Timurid ruler of Balkh, Nazr Muhammad and his son Abd al-Aziz. After being expelled from Bukhara and harassed by the continued raids against his new capital Balkh, Nazr Muhammad saw no other alternative than to appeal to Shah Jahan for help. The latter, being at Lahore, appointed his son Murad Bakhsh as the commander-in-chief of the coming operations and, in February 1646, dispatched him with 50,000 horsemen and 10,000 foot soldiers to Kabul, from whence they had to march on to Badakhshan and Balkh. As usual, Shah Jahan himself wisely decided to follow the army and to keep a close eye on the campaign from Kabul.

In order to procure more supplies of grass and grain and to advance with greater ease through the rugged passes, the army used different routes to reach Kabul. Earlier, in August of the previous year, a few light contingents had already been sent ahead to survey the routes across the Hindu Kush, to enlist possible allies, and to make logistical preparations by procuring sheep, cows, horses and camels, and by laying out forward supply posts along the main routes, to the west through Kahmard, and to the east through the Tul, Salang and Qipchak Passes. In general, the Hindu Kush, with heights of over 4,000 metres, posed an enormous challenge to Mughal logistics. Its passes were extremely narrow and steep leaving no room for heavy artillery.[26] Even more of an obstacle was its impregnability during the winter months when thick packs of snow obstructed the passes, lasting from late October to March at the earliest. Even as late as May or June, snow could hinder the advance of an army, as is shown in the case of the Mughal approach through the Tul Pass in May–June 1646.

After the return of the reconnaissance missions, it was decided that at Charikaran the army would be split in two. While one part was to secure the western flank by a circular march through Kahmard and Ghori, the army's main body was to follow the long and winding road along the Tul Pass, crossing the Panjshir river as many as eleven times. At this stage, thousands of masons, carpenters and sappers were sent from Kabul to improve the road. Arriving at the foot of the pass it was mainly the snow that had to be removed in order to make a path at least wide enough for a laden camel. According to the Mughal sources, in one day the *bildars* (pioneers) managed to clear a road two yards wide and one *kos* in length. Impressed by the sudden Mughal approach, Khusrau, the Uzbek commander of Badakhshan and son of Nazr Muhammad immediately submitted to

Prince Murad without opposition. After taking control of Qunduz, the main Mughal army reached Balkh in mid-July, only one-and-a-half months after leaving Kabul and four-and-a-half months after leaving Lahore.[27]

Before continuing the account of the military operations around Balkh, it will be worthwhile to take a closer look at the composition of the Mughal officer-corps. In contrast to the Bengal command structure that was dominated by one family network, the officers at the western front had a much more varied background, and included Indian Muslims, Turanis, Iranis, Afghans and Rajputs. Apart from the successive Mughal princes at the top – Murad Bakhsh being replaced by Aurangzeb, who in his turn, was replaced by Dara Shukoh – the corps' composition remained more or less intact during the whole period of intensive Mughal campaigning in the northwest, i.e. from the beginning of the Balkh expedition in 1645 to the last of the three consecutive sieges of Qandahar in 1653. In the Balkh campaign, Prince Murad shared command with Ali Mardan Khan, the Kurdish noble who had handed Qandahar over to the Mughals in 1638. For the Safavids he had become a traitor, but for the Mughals he became the *amir al-umara* of the empire with a rank of 7,000/7,000 and, as 'he could not stand the heat of India', was entrusted with the northern provinces of Kashmir, the Punjab and Kabul. Probably because changing sides a second time was highly problematic, Ali Mardan became one of the most trustworthy Mughal officers, besides having a great deal of knowledge about, and connections with, the region.[28] The same goes for another important Mughal officer, Mirza Nauzar Safavi, who, apart from having Safavid blood, was a grandson of Mirza Muzaffar Husain, the Persian governor of Qandahar and the first to hand over the city to the Mughals as early as 1595.[29] As with these local defectors, Afghan officers like Bahadur Khan Rohilla could also be used to sow discord among the enemy and to build new regional alliances.[30] At the same time, though, their regional know-how was to be held in check by men from a different background and with interests in other parts of the empire. Hence, the other main officers included the two Turanis Qulij Khan[31] and Rustam Khan[32], the Irani brothers Asalat Khan[33] and Khalilulla Khan,[34] the Indian shaikhzada Allami Sadulla Khan,[35] a few Hindus such as various Rathor and Khachwaha Rajputs and the rajas of Kangra, Jagat Singh and his son Raja Rajrup. Also different from the eastern front, as described in the previous section, was that the loyalty of all these officers was enforced by the ever nearby emperor staying at his summer quarters of Kabul.

Despite the emperor's enthusiasm for it, the Balkh campaign was far from popular among his officers and troops. Actually, serving in the far northwest raised a spectre of horror and deprivation, not only because of the rigours of the Afghan winter, but also because the moderate agricultural production of the region promised only meagre returns for the individual soldier, be it from the regular land revenue or from incidental raiding. Indeed, to its dismay the imperial army discovered that it could live neither from the local revenue nor off the land. Beyond the Hindu Kush, they found no equivalent for the Indian grain-carriers, the Banjaras, who normally supplied them on their marches to the south of the subcontinent. Foraging was nearly futile because the continued raids of Uzbek war-bands, or Almans, devastated the generally productive but mainly artificially irrigated fruit orchards and grain fields of Balkh and Badakhshan.[36] In addition, the limited as well as different monetary infrastructure in the area north of the Hindu Kush made it extremely difficult to raise cash, either locally or from India through bills of exchange. As a result, enormous amounts of cash and bullion had to be carried across the long and arduous passes of the Sulaiman and Hindu Kush mountains, mainly to pay the troops, to procure supplies and to buy victories. Following the dire circumstances of the Balkh region, only ready cash and other relief measures could push the mansabdars up the Uttarapatha. Prior to setting out on the campaign, Shah Jahan had issued orders for the disbursement of three months' advance pay in cash. In addition, arrangements had been made for subsidies granted from the state exchequer for those jagirdars who held their estates by tenures entitling them to only a quarter share of the net revenue. A further incentive was introduced by making concessions with respect to the troop-muster required of the mansabdars. The usual reduction of one-third, when on duty in one's own province, and one-quarter when one was serving in another province, was increased to one-fifth of the usual muster when mansabdars were to serve in the Balkh campaign. Possible shortages were made up by the emperor who distributed 2,000 horses from his private stud among both the ahadis and the mansabdars.[37] Later during the campaign, we recurrently find Mughal caravans with lakhs of cash aimed at settling the financial claims of the troops. Clearly, the Hindu Kush not only posed a natural geographical obstacle to the purely military apparatus of empire but, more importantly, it also demarcated the limits of the logistical and financial network that sustained it.

Returning to our chronological account, when Murad Bakhsh arrived in Balkh his mind was set on orchestrating a suitable meeting in which Nazr Muhammad, that 'descendant of Chinggis Khan', would publicly submit to Mughal suzerainty. In an earlier letter to the Mughal Prince, Nazr Muhammad had already declared that he would go to Kabul to personally thank the emperor for his support, deliver his kingdom to him, and head on to Mecca for the hajj. Although Nazr Muhammad kept up this submissive appearance during the entire campaign, he also continued to avoid public interviews with any of the Mughal princes. At Balkh also, while Nazr Muhammad kept Murad Bakhsh out of town with intricate negotiations about the protocol of the forthcoming conference, he himself gathered together jewels and money and escaped, accompanied by his sons Subhan Quli and Qutluq Muhammad. Prince Murad, who took Balkh without any opposition, was furious about Nazr Muhammad's behaviour, sending Asalat Khan in hot pursuit. Although Asalat Khan won a fierce battle against the Uzbek forces near Shibarghan (see Plate 4), he could not prevent Nazr Muhammad from fleeing to Isfahan.[38]

Nonetheless, the Mughal march to Balkh had been another huge success for Mughal speed and logistics. Despite the enormous odds, an army of 60,000 soldiers had reached and conquered Balkh in about 120 days. As with the taking of Balkh, various other towns of the province, such as Andkhud, Maimana, Shibarghan and Tirmiz, were seized without much resistance. But in the midst of what must have been a Mughal flush of victory, Shah Jahan was struck all of a sudden by Murad Bakhsh's determination to leave Balkh. Apparently tired of the campaign, he had taken a great dislike to the climate, the water, the food and the people of the area. He also must have been disappointed about the real size of Nazr Muhammad's so-called fabulous fortunes, which were worth not more than 12 million rupees.[39] Another setback was the land revenue of the area. After the territory had been annexed by the Mughals the already modest regular sum of 2.5 million rupees per annum, for Balkh and Badakhshan together, amounted to between a half and a quarter of its usual value, being just about 10 per cent of the jama of provinces like Lahore and Delhi in Akbar's (!) time.[40] Even the enormous cash transports from India could not take away the deep feelings of misery and disappointment felt by Murad Baksh and shared by most of his commanders.[41] As the Prince could not be persuaded, Shah Jahan decided to send Allami Sadulla Khan as his ad interim successor. Once again, various pecuniary measures were to be taken by the latter to prevent the remaining commanders from leaving their posts. After he had settled the affairs of the new province in a few weeks, Sadulla Khan must have felt relieved that he was allowed to return to Kabul. Shortly afterwards, on 20 September 1646, Shah Jahan left Kabul for Lahore, leaving the newly conquered territories at the mercy of the fierce Afghan winter.

So far, the campaign had been more about diplomacy and marching than about actual fighting. During the next months, however, we see the extremely mobile Uzbek war-bands, or Almans, gaining the initiative by recurrent but unpredictable guerrilla raids at various locations along the long northern frontier marches south of the Amu Darya. From across that river, the Alman attacks were stimulated and probably directed by Nazr Muhammad's rival and son, Abd al-Aziz, also the ruler of Bukhara. If we trust the Mughal sources, at every instance the Alman mounted archers were beaten off by the fire of Mughal matchlocks, rockets and cannon, always to be followed by the capture of the previously raided cattle and goods. The rhetoric of the Mughal sources cannot conceal though that the Mughal troops were at a loss to counter the raids of these Alman freebooters aimed at destroying the productive countryside and the supply lines surrounding the main towns.[42] Meanwhile the situation in Balkh had been worsened following the Uzbek interception of a convoy of 30,000 oxen laden with food and money. The famine this produced was probably aggravated by an epidemic caused by the Uzbeks who had fouled the water of the Balkh river.[43] Trying to gain from the dire straits in which the Mughals found themselves Nazr Muhammad returned from Iran and began to besiege the town of Maimana.

These setbacks made Shah Jahan decide to head for Kabul again and to send one of his other sons, Aurangzeb, with a fresh army and with new funds across the Hindu Kush. As during the previous year's approach under Murad Baksh, Aurangzeb left Lahore in February 1647. This time, however, the Mughal army was at several instances confronted by the more confident and better prepared Uzbek army of Abd al-Aziz. As a result, in taking the western route along the Dara Gaz Pass, Aurangzeb had to fight several battles before he could more or less safely enter Balkh in June. The first confrontation was along the narrow and troublesome defiles of the Dara Gaz Pass where the Mughals used mass elephants to crush the enemy's attacks. Remarkably, hundreds of kilometres away from their natural breeding grounds, war-elephants continued to play a conspicuous role as shock instruments in the confrontations that were to follow.

More important than elephants, however, seems to be what becomes the standard phraseology of Mughal sources describing Mughal–Uzbek battles, in which the fire of Mughal guns, matchlocks and rockets rout the attacks of Uzbek mounted archers but cannot prevent the latter, however, from rallying again and again. In other words, it appears that the Uzbeks used the traditional Central Asian tactic of horse-archers wheeling around an army that was superior in numbers, armour and firepower.[44] Mughal superiority in firearms and light cannon counted only when defending towns or in pitched battles, whereas the mobility and speed of the Alman skirmishes could easily outmanoeuvre the much more heavily equipped Mughal army. One may even doubt if these Balkh battles were really the great events of war as depicted by the Mughal war propaganda. The Uzbek ability to keep fighting despite endless defeats suggests that these battles were mere skirmishes, in which the Uzbeks successfully avoided major confrontations and focused on wearing out the resolve and the supplies of the enemy. Indeed, at the end of this series of 'battles', Aurangzeb arrived at the conclusion that 'it would be impossible to punish the enemy in satisfactory style unless the troops left their heavy baggage and impediments at Balkh and marched unencumbered against their opponents'. Therefore he decided to move out of the city 'as lightly equipped as possible for the purpose of pursuing and engaging the Uzbeks'.[45] Although adopting this new tactic may have helped to chase away Abd al-Aziz's army across the Amu Darya – this is what the Mughals sources tell us –

it could not bring Balkh into secure Mughal possession. In due course, Aurangzeb followed in the footsteps of his brother Murad when he reported to his father that he desired to return to India and fight in the Deccan, 'where not only fame, but fortune might be gained'.[46]

At this point, with famine and epidemics reigning in Balkh and with a threatening new winter ahead, Shah Jahan could not but give in to Aurangzeb's anxiety and ordered him to deliver Balkh and Badakhshan to Nazr Muhammad and return to Kabul. This was not as easy as it sounds as the Uzbek ruler was expected to accept Mughal suzerainty in a public and personal encounter with Aurangzeb, thereby saving the blemished prestige of the retreating Mughals (see Chapter 2, p.60). As at the very beginning, the Balkh campaign ended with intricate negotiations about a suitable and face-saving meeting in which the Mughal overlord was to bestow Balkh on their Uzbek 'governor' (*wali*). This time, however, the Mughals were not swiftly approaching Balkh but slinking down the Hindu Kush passes before the onset of winter. After being repeatedly harassed by Uzbek and Hazara tribesmen, they reached Kabul on 9 November 1647. Meanwhile, Nazr Muhammad had taken Balkh without any opposition and without the need to make a personal submission to the Mughals.[47]

All in all, the campaign had cost at least twenty million rupees, in the end not even gaining the, at least, ten times smaller amount of the area's land revenue. Mughal caravans had carried about ten million rupees in treasure up the Uttarapatha to the northwest. The campaign was also a disaster in military terms. The initial successes of the Mughal army were due to its traditional strength in terms of movement and logistics. North of the Hindu Kush, however, the logistical and financial infrastructure proved much less sophisticated than in India. It should remind us that, although the Mughal army was a nomadic army, it was not one of tribal pastoralists following the rhythm of alternating grazing seasons, but one of professional soldiers depending on the logistical and financial assistance of the professional transporters, bankers and merchants who always followed the army's train. The meagre agricultural and financial resources of Balkh and Badakhshan proved insufficient to compensate for the failing supply lines. Looking at the other side, the Uzbek armies felt very much at home in the area and knew how to live off the land and how to use its grazing potential.[48] This had been just the kind of army that served Babur so well during the early years of his career. As we have seen, much of the mobility was retained under his successors, not by living off the land but mainly thanks to the assistance of the highly professional financial and logistical network that existed in India. As demonstrated in the Balkh campaign, the limits of this Indian network were also the limits of the Mughal army. Besides, since Babur's time, the Mughal army had also been thoroughly Indianised in terms of personnel. The Indian soldiery detested the living conditions in Balkh and eagerly looked for every opportunity to get back home. This is also illustrated by Murad Bakhsh's complaints about the weather, the food and the people of Turkistan, which mirror Babur's similar misgivings about Hindustan one century earlier. Anyway, at the very cradle of Mughal power, the Indianised Mughal army was overcome by the same Central Asian strategy and weaponry so effectively used by Babur at the beginning of his career. Even in the mid-seventeenth century, it was not modern gunpowder weaponry but mobility and its logistics that made the difference.

In the short term, the debacle of the Balkh campaign weakened the position of the Mughals in the northwest. The vulnerability of their position was shown as soon as the following year, when the Safavids seized Qandahar after a siege of merely two months. In the four following years history repeated itself when three consecutive siege operations failed due to the logistical problems caused by the long supply lines and the severe Afghan winter. Again lakhs of rupees were poured into the Afghan provinces without any positive result for the Mughals. For the next few decades Afghanistan was once again divided between the Uzbeks in Balkh, the Safavids in Qandahar and the Mughals in Kabul. As such, the area continued to attract the attention of these three dynasties, all of them investing in it considerable amounts of human and monetary resources. It generally appears that trade between India and Afghanistan did not suffer at all from the Balkh campaign, in particular because the Mughal generosity towards the local clergy and officialdom actually stimulated new commercial missions.[49] Not much different from the case of Bengal, the area's position as a frontier province contributed immensely to the breakout of Afghan tribes in the early eighteenth century, paving the way for the new wave of Afghan imperialism under the Durranis.[50] Actually, it was not the British from the east but the Afghans from the west who were the first to conquer Delhi as early as 1757, that is, only three years before the Marathas from the south managed to do the same. Not surprisingly, therefore, the Marathas are our next concern as we turn from Balkh to Gingee, and from the most western to the most southern terminal of Mughal expansion.

The southern front: Gingee 1689–97[51]

In the 1680s the Mughals were at the zenith of their power. In the south the Mughals were particularly triumphant: Bijapur was conquered in 1685, Golkonda in 1687 and the Maratha chief Sambhaji, Shivaji Bhonsle's son, was executed in 1689. Four new provinces were added, together comprising more than one-quarter of the whole empire: Bijapur and the Bijapur Carnatic, and Hyderabad and the Hyderabad Carnatic.[52] Although the Mughal frontier in the south was now coterminous with the furthest extent of Indian Muslim domination on the sub-continent, many areas within

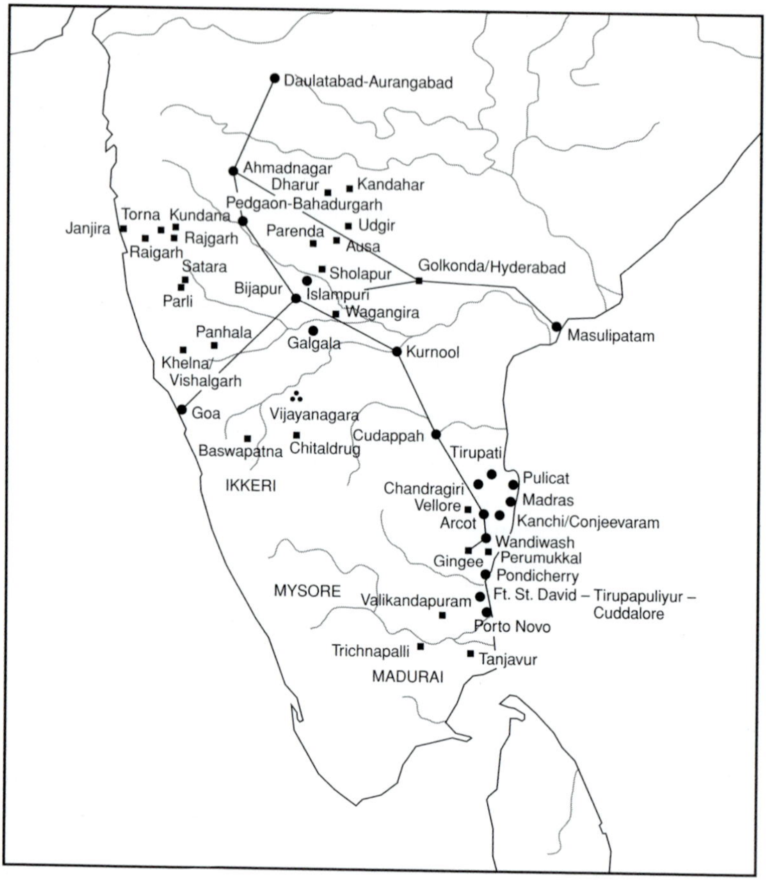

Map 6.3 Southern front: 1689–97

that frontier were still beyond the Mughal grasp. In the western Deccan, the Marathas managed to hold on to many of their mountain strongholds along the Western Ghats, their light horses still raiding the countryside far to its east and south. Hence, in order to eliminate the last remnants of Maratha power, Aurangzeb decided to remain in the Deccan for the next one-and-half decades. In fact, by fixing his camp, first at Galgala from 1690 to 1695, and then at Islampuri from 1695 to 1699, Aurangzeb diverted from the policy of movement of his predecessors. Only during the last years of his life did he take up travelling again, but instead of following the military operations from a strategic distance, he attacked each and every Maratha fort in person. Contemporary sources depict him as a kind of Mughal Don Quixote, a knight errant 'personally running about panting for some heaps of stone'.[53]

Aurangzeb's later animosity against Maratha forts was partly the result of his bitterness about the fact that, even after a long-drawn-out and costly campaign full of military victories, Maratha power in southern India was as strong as ever. Only one decade earlier it had appeared that the Marathas stood at the brink of being annihilated. After the Mughals had executed their leader Sambhaji Bhonsle, and captured his nine-year-old son Shahuji, the situation looked grim for the Maratha leaders who now could only turn to Sambhaji's younger brother Rajaram. After he was made king in a hasty coronation ceremony, the Mughals forced him to flee from the capital at Raigarh, from where, disguised as a yogi, he travelled south, about 800 km on foot, to Gingee. In the sixteenth century this celebrated triple hill fort developed into the political and symbolic centre of the Tondaimandalam region, displacing its sometime rival Padaividu. A Telugu Nayaka dynasty was installed there in the second half of that century and continued to rule till the late 1640s. At that time, Portuguese and Dutch contemporary observers were impressed by the strength and sheer size of this 'Troy of the East', 'the greatest city we have seen in India, and bigger than any in Portugal, Lisbon excepted', and 'a very populous city three times the size of Rotterdam'.[54] From 1649, when a Bijapuri army captured it, Gingee was contested among the various Maratha, Sidi, Nawayat and Deccani Muslim groups that had participated in the southern expeditions of the Deccan sultanates. In 1677 Shivaji asserted his superior rights over the area and, in 1689, when Rajaram arrived there, it was still under Bhonsle control.[55]

The fort of Gingee was one of the most strategically situated of all citadels in the Carnatic. On all sides it was surrounded by mountains that complicated the approach of a besieging army. The fort itself produced an impregnable spectacle of three independent rock forts at heights of 50–150 metres, each with granite walls encircling a natural outcrop. The walls running across the level ground between the forts enclosed a vast triangular area, no less than 1 km on each side. From about the late fifteenth and early sixteenth centuries, its first Nayaks, that is, the semi-autonomous governors of Vijayanagara, improved and enlarged the already existing fortifications, adding circular bastions and protective barbicans along the walls and gates. Under the Bijapuris (1649–77) and the Marathas (1677–98) the fort was further strengthened, the latter doubling the ramparts on the eastern side of the citadel. Later adjustments are also visible at the barbican of the main gate where the crenellations have been filled up and replaced by loopholes, to provide cover against, and defence by, musketry. Although the fort became noted for its insalubrity, mainly after the French and English lost a large number of men through malaria at the siege of 1761, its interior was well equipped to withstand a long siege. Apart from various well-covered granaries, there were two perennial springs of excellent water on the summit of the citadel, as well as three reservoirs for the reception and storage of rainwater below. Water, brought from a reservoir 200 metres

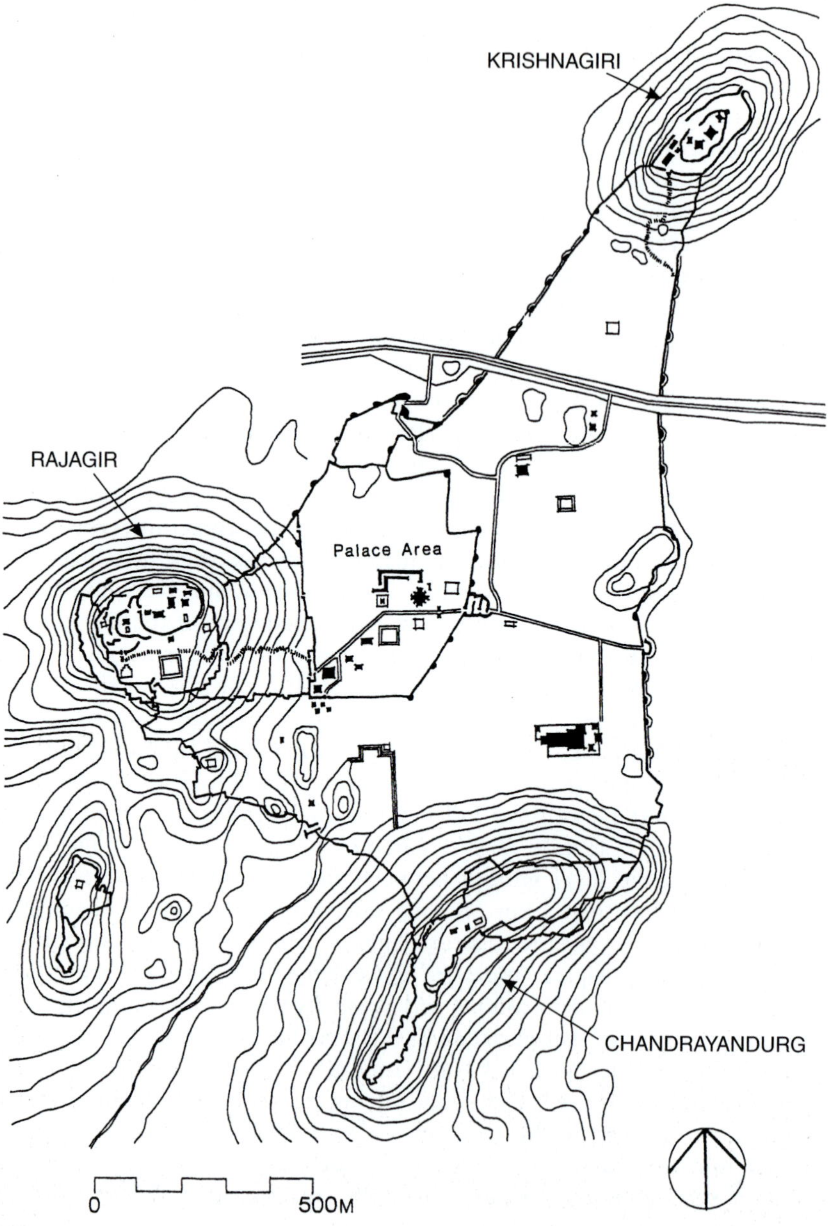

Figure 6.1 Plan of Gingee.

Source: G. Michell, *The New Cambridge History of India*, I, *6: Architecture and Art of Southern India* (Cambridge, 1995), p. 125. Courtesy George Michell

away and outside the walls, was supplied to the Kalyana Mahal in the palace area by an earthenware pipe. Perhaps it was not only propaganda when the Mughals claimed in 1698 that they had captured a fort that 'enjoyed the greatest fame and pre-eminence among the forts and strong places of Karnatak in respect of height and abundance of materials of war and defence'.[56]

For the next eight years Gingee was to become the benchmark of Mughal–Maratha confrontation. The Deccani campaigns, which so far had been characterised by constant movement, now, all of a sudden, became focused and fixed on just one stronghold. With hindsight, it appears that the siege of Gingee paralysed the Mughal army and kept the emperor himself from moving around and getting too far away from what appeared to be his final and most decisive frontier. It was generally thought that the taking of Gingee and the capture of Rajaram would be the deathblow to the Marathas and definitely open up the way for Mughal rule all over the Indian sub-continent.

One year after Rajaram had arrived in Gingee, Zulfiqar Khan, the Irani commander of the Mughal forces, started the siege in earnest. Apart from the emperor himself at Galgala, his father, the wazir Asad Khan, secured the long supply lines to the north by taking control of the towns of Kurnool and Cuddapah. After the fall of Vijayanagara, and in the wake of the southeastern expansion of Bijapur and the Marathas, these towns had emerged as important way stations along the Dakshinapatha. It had

Figure 6.2 Gingee (Rajagiri).

Source: Photo Jos Gommans, December 2001

been Maratha strategy to shift Mughal attention away from their homeland and to extend the Mughal supply lines southwards as far as possible. The strategy proved very effective as the Mughal army was regularly cut off from the imperial camp in the Deccan. The Banjara grain-carriers, who had been so crucially important during the Mughal sieges of Dharur, Kandahar, Udgir, Parenda and other Deccani frontier forts in Shah Jahan's reign, were not only confronted with ever-increasing distances but, more than ever before, with the continuous raids of Marathi and Bidari plunderers roaming the untamed countryside south and west of Galgala and Islampuri. To give an impression of the logistical challenge facing the Mughals at Gingee, according to French and Dutch sources Zulfiqar Khan's army at Gingee counted some 26,000 men, consisted of 10,000 Mughal horsemen, 8,000 Bundela musketeers and 8,000 soldiers from the Carnatic, the latter including 3,000 men from Mysore. This army was supported by about 100 elephants as well as 2–4,000 dromedaries for carrying tents and other heavy luggage. Countless porters and more than 200,000 cattle catered for the needs of the troops and the merchants who followed the army with their families, 'daily bringing in an abundance of food and fodder'. All this made foodstuffs such as rice and goats relatively cheap, at least for the regional soldiery who were reported to receive between 6 and 8 rupees per month in advance.[57]

This had been the situation just after the arrival of the Mughal army in October 1690. Shortly after the army had comfortably pitched its camp around the fort – erecting huts and houses and even embellishing a few of these with gardens – the logistical problems increased, however. Now, caravans consisting of as many as 10–12,000 draught animals were required for the transportation of cash, food, munitions and, in particular, forage and firewood from the north. As early as April–May of the next year, when the Mughals were faced by acute shortages, the situation became very critical. To relieve Zulfiqar Khan's isolation and to enforce a decisive assault, Aurangzeb sent Asad Khan, accompanied by Prince Kam Bakhsh, to Gingee. Meanwhile, Zulfiqar Khan launched a provisioning raid towards the southern chieftaincies of Trichnapalli and Tanjavur. The latter was under Maratha control, be it another branch of the Bhonsle family. Its ruler, Shahaji, had supported his cousin in Gingee with troops and supplies but was now forced to pay a huge levy under threat of his territories being pillaged by the Mughals. Later during the siege, in 1694 and 1697, each time during January–February, the Mughal army moved towards the productive south in order to raise money, food, fodder and cattle.[58] Each time, the local population, including the European factors at the coast, were gripped by apprehension as to the route that would be selected, and some of them stood ready with presents.

The Maratha troops in the fort consisted of about 7 to 8,000 men who did not content themselves with defending the walls but also regularly patrolled and raided the countryside to cut off Mughal convoys and hinder foraging. Actually, the enormous circumference of Gingee made it impossible to blockade the fort from each side. As the Mughal attacks concentrated on the northern, eastern and southern sides, supplies continued to refresh the Maratha garrison across the thick Vetavalam woods on the western side. As a result, the Mughal–Maratha conflict in the south developed into a nasty battle of attrition in which both sides attempted to ruin the supply lines and production centres of the enemy. Both armies regularly sent out contingents to roam and ravage the countryside, not only immediately surrounding Gingee, but all over the Carnatic and much of Tamil Nadu, all those areas that potentially provided the enemy with food, fodder and firewood.

Meanwhile, hard-pressed by the Mughals in their various homelands, the Marathas in Maharashtra attempted to cut off the Mughal supply lines from the Belgaum area in the west, mainly targeting the area surrounding Baswapatna and Chitaldrug. Apart from defending their headquarters at Vishalgarh and regaining the fort of Raigarh and Panhala in 1692, the western Marathas under Ramchandra Nilkanth managed to send two relief expeditions to Gingee, the first in late 1692 under the generals Dhanaji Jadhav and Santaji Ghorpade, and the second three years later under Santaji, Yemaji Malhar Mutalik and Hunamant Rao. In both cases, the Mughals were confronted by an extra 10 to 30,000 horsemen, which compelled them to pull their forces together. And after finding themselves besieged behind their own siege-works, they retreated twice to the logistically more convenient towns of Wandiwash and Arcot, about 50 km to the north. On one of these occasions the Mughals had to destroy their artillery before it would fall in the hands of the enemy. Given the recurrent uncertainty about who was actually besieging whom, both sides considered the countryside a potentially hostile no man's land, open for plunder. The scorched earth policy of both the Mughals and the Marathas devastated the regional economies that had just started a new phase of expansion following a new round of Nayaka state formation in places like Chandragiri, Gingee and Tanjavur, which had also attracted the various European trading settlements along the southern Coromandel Coast. More than ever during Mughal expansion to the south, the supply lines became overstretched and troops were forced to live off the land. By the time the siege ended in 1698, Gingee had definitively lost its position as the political and economic magnet of the southern Carnatic.

Apart from the unlikely possibility that the Marathas could be starved into surrender, it appeared equally implausible that the fort could be taken by force of arms. In 1690, the Mughal army was equipped with 130 cannon including at least eight heavy pieces and seventy light 1–4 pounders, besides some 1,000 zamburaks. The English factory at Madras provided 500 maunds of good gunpowder, as well as 300 iron shot.[59] In addition, about 100 European gunners were tempted by offers of high pay to join the Mughal army. Nonetheless, the sheer height and the rocky foundation of the fort's walls significantly reduced the impact of all gunpowder weaponry, be it as artillery or as explosives used in mines. On the part of the Mughals, two to four men were killed each day by hostile fire from the Maratha bulwarks at the base of the northern hill. The only option left for the besiegers appears to have been scaling the walls as repeatedly suggested by the Afghan and Bundela chiefs but as often forbidden by Zulfiqar Khan. Eventually, at the end of 1697, after the siege had dragged on for more than seven years, Zulfiqar Khan gave in to the growing pressure exerted by the emperor. Without the help of artillery or any other siege material, he took the fort after a few reckless assaults by his commanders Da'ud Khan Panni and Dalpat Rao Bundela.

Indeed, for most contemporary onlookers, it was neither logistical reasons nor any other military failure that accounted for the protracted duration of the siege, it was the sheer unwillingness of the Mughal commander to press ahead with it. At various instances, Zulfiqar Khan was accused of having a secret understanding with Rajaram that they would await the soon to be expected death of the elderly Aurangzeb, after which they would divide the newly conquered territories in the Deccan among themselves.[60] Another argument for keeping the siege going was the plausible but also horrifying prospect that, after bringing the siege to an early end, Aurangzeb would send Zulfiqar Khan and various of his generals on another miserable expedition to retake Qandahar.[61] Clearly, for every mansabdar, serving in the midst of the rich rice fields of southern India must have been like paradise compared to the barren hell that was Afghanistan. For Bhimsen, who served Dalpat Rao during the Gingee siege, it was 'the practice of all generals to protract operations', and usually the enemies 'fought in the day and entertained each other at night'.[62] Anyway, intentional or not, the long duration of the Gingee siege considerably undermined the Mughal determination to keep the mansabdars on the move, be it to Qandahar or elsewhere.

Somewhat surprisingly, during the entire siege Aurangzeb continued to rely on only one commander. Among the main officers of Zulfiqar Khan were various Iranis and Afghans, many of whom had previously served in the armies of the Deccani sultanates, either as major commanders like Da'ud Khan Panni and his brother Sulaiman Khan or as jamadars or captains of the local militia (*sihbandi*) like, for example, Isma'il Khan Makha. There were also some Hindu officers, such as Dalpat Rao Bundela, Kishor Singh Hara and his son Ram Singh of Kota, some local zamindars like Yachappa Nayak and a few Maratha leaders, such as Kanhoji Shirke and Nagoji Mane. Many of the Deccani officers were reputed turncoats who had negotiated their entry/re-entry into the Mughal army. For example, in 1689 when the Marathas took charge of the Gingee area, the local sihbandi zamindars Isma'il Khan Makha and Yachappa Nayak were quick to join the Marathas, only to change sides again a few years later – in 1692 and 1693 respectively – when the current political situation appeared to be in favour of the Mughals again. Similarly, Nagoji Mane had left Mughal service in 1691 but negotiated his re-entry in 1698. After Aurangzeb declined his initial opening bid demanding a mansab of 7,000/7,000, including payment of 70,000 rupees in cash and the possession of various forts in his homeland in southern Maharashtra, he eventually re-entered the Mughal army in 1698 by accepting Aurangzeb's counter-offer of a rank of 5,000/4,000, all to come from jagirs in Berar.[63] As we have seen in other instances, this switching of sides every few years was not at all unusual, but was all part of the reigning political arithmetic and military marketing of the time, which, apparently, had always been a feature of Indian ways of warfare.

Although Zulfiqar Khan himself was a Turkish-speaking Irani of the Qaramanlu tribe, the absence of a substantial Turani element in the Gingee command structure is striking. It is very possible that Aurangzeb's decision in 1691 to let his son Kam Bakhsh accompany Zulfiqar's father Asad Khan to Gingee was instigated by the need to keep an eye on the two Qaramanlu commanders. It is equally possible, though, that the prime motive of the emperor was to keep his son under the close surveillance of his most trusted officers. This is also suggested by the conduct of Aurangzeb himself, who sided with Zulfiqar Khan at the time Kam Bakhsh accused the latter of secretly conspiring with the Marathas. In their turn, Asad Khan and Zulfiqar Khan charged the Mughal prince with having a secret understanding with Rajaram, again in anticipation of Aurangzeb's forthcoming death. Especially at the times the Mughal camp was isolated from the outside world, it appears that the incessant rumours about the emperor's demise tended to stimulate negotiations between the various, increasingly nervous parties in the two camps. As with the lengthy siege, Aurangzeb's ongoing refusal to pass away only increased the anxiety and speculation about the future, which in turn could only encourage the volatility of the military labour market. In this tense situation, each and every player involved attempted to keep his stakes in as many scenarios as possible. All knew well that, as soon Aurangzeb died, all alliances and agreements of the past were to be renegotiated.

Looking at the relatively rare military confrontations in the open field during the siege, it appears that the Mughals were far superior, again, particularly because of their expertise in mounted archery. According to the shrewd French onlooker François Martin, the Marathas commonly carried:

> a half-lance and a sabre used for purposes of offence, and a shield for defence. Some of them use the bow and arrow but they are very much in a minority. The Moors possess an advantage over

> the Marathas. Apart from the musketeers who are to be found among their cavalry, some of their best marksmen exist among the ranks of their archers who can stop the Marathas from a distance by pelting them with arrows. The Moors are also better soldiers, 1,000 of their cavalry being able to withstand the challenge of 3,000–4,000, or an even larger number of Maratha cavalry. The Marathas score by their speed and mobility. They are men of great physical endurance who are content with very little. As I have said elsewhere in my relation, they move without baggage or train. When it comes to a hand-to-hand fight after their entry amongst the enemy corps, they can inflict terrible damage with their half-lances.[64]

Nonetheless, despite Mughal superiority in open battle, in several instances the Marathas were able to beat the Mughals in the open field. Often, the latter could only guess at the numbers and whereabouts of a constantly moving enemy. In several engagements, the swiftness of the Maratha light cavalry took the Mughals by complete surprise.[65] Their rapid movements were part of the usual Deccani way of fighting, which had become particularly prominent under the command of the Abyssinian general Malik Ambar (d. 1626) when serving the Ahmadnagar sultanate. It was a kind of guerrilla warfare based on a tactic of hit and run, avoiding major engagements in battles and sieges. The Mughal sources labelled this way of fighting as *qazzaqi* or *bargi-giri*; in due course *bargi* became synonymous with Marathas.[66] According to Manucci, however, the Maratha guerrilla tactics in which 'they prowled about on the frontiers, picking up here and there what they could; then made off home again' dramatically changed at the turn of the century when they began to move like real conquerors. 'They possess artillery, musketry, bows and arrows, with elephants and camels for all their baggage and tents. They carry these last to secure some repose from time to time as they find it convenient.' Far from being a military revolution, it was a sign of growing Maratha confidence, or as Manucci added himself, 'they are equipped and move about just like the army of the Mogul'.[67]

Apart from horsemen, the Marathas, like the Mughals, employed numerous musketeers, many of them being hired from the Berad region. These infantry troops were particularly effective in ambush and, as before, preferably behind the cover of trenches or walls.[68] Although artillery played an increasingly important role in sieges, it proved almost irrelevant at the siege of Gingee. As mentioned already, eventually Gingee fell by the fairly simple method of a few Afghan and Bundela climbers scaling its walls. In field manoeuvres and in actual battles, even in the far south and as late as the seventeenth century, cavalry remained the most decisive instrument of war.

After the seizure of Gingee in early 1698, the front shifted again towards Maharashtra. Although Aurangzeb captured fort after fort, mainly by means of negotiations, the Mughals had soon to give these up again and, after Aurangzeb's death in 1707, they gradually lost their hold over all the Dakshinapatha crossroads in the central Deccan. Here the Marathas managed to build a new state structure that was soon to incorporate large parts of northern and western India. To its east, Zulfiqar Khan's supposed dream of an independent territorial base in the Deccan was realised by one of his Turani rivals Chin Qilich Khan alias Nizam al-Mulk who, although officially a Mughal governor, established the practically autonomous Asaf Jahi dynasty in Hyderabad. At the new southern outlets of Kurnool and Cudappah Afghan chiefs of the Panni and Miyana branches carved out their own chieftaincies. Likewise, Arcot developed from being a temporary Mughal way station during the years of the Gingee siege, into a fully-grown regional capital ruled by the dynasty of the Nawayats first, and the Walajahis later. As in the case of Bengal and Calcutta, Arcot was to prove instrumental in the rise of Madras as the new imperial centre of the south.

Like the Bengal and Balkh campaigns, the siege of Gingee demonstrates both the success and failure of the Mughal army in the field. More than ever before in the history of the Indian sub-continent, one imperial structure controlled the entire network of Indian high roads; from their common crossroads near the capitals of Delhi and Agra to their most extreme outposts of Dhaka in the east, Balkh in the west and Gingee in the south. More than ever before, this network of imperial trade- and march-routes integrated the so-called ra'iyati, i.e. settled areas characterised by regulated agriculture, with the mawas, i.e. unsettled areas characterised by long-distance trade, nomadic pastoralism and seasonal raiding. Indeed, this simultaneous process of extensification and intensification makes the history of the Mughal Empire into an unprecedented success story. In all this, the Mughal army played a crucial role: while incessantly marching across the empire it connected outlying areas with each other and it incorporated a substantial part of its various populations.

The three campaigns dealt with in this chapter can only pay tribute to the enormous logistical capacity of the whole military apparatus of the Mughal Empire. The Bengal campaign was the most successful as its results were the most longstanding. Here the main challenge of the Mughals had been the transition from a cavalry-based land army to an infantry- and gunpowder-based riverine army. That they really made the transition is perhaps best illustrated by their decision to shift the capital from Rajmahal to Dhaka. From this new provincial centre, the Mughals gradually began to control the whole Bengal delta, also integrating it more closely with the Mughal heartland in Hindustan. From Bengal, extending the limites further was out of question: the high seas of the Bay of Bengal as well as the thick jungles of Burma and Gondwana created unbridgeable, outer limits to Mughal expansion. Their only remaining option for their new river-based army was to follow the Brahmaputra river north into Assam. But, as shown in various disastrous campaigns, its unhealthy climate and the restricted navigation of the Brahmaputra frustrated a long-standing occupation of this region.

Problematic communication also hindered the campaign towards Balkh. The cold Afghan winter, especially, made the Hindu Kush the prime hurdle. Although the Mughals repeatedly managed to cross its narrow and steep mountain passes, they failed to take root north of them. Here, the already insecure cultivation based on artificial irrigation was easily disrupted by the unrelenting raids of highly elusive Uzbek freebooters who also never stopped cutting off the long supply lines to the south. Nonetheless, in terms of mere logistics, the Mughal experience in Balkh was without precedent, as no Indian army had ever before managed to operate that far from its base into the northwest. And, as the British were to prove in the nineteenth century, even for a fully equipped 'modern' army, operations in Afghanistan from India remained highly problematic.

In terms of logistics, the Gingee campaign proved only slightly less challenging. Since the agricultural conditions in the south were much more secure and flourishing than in Afghanistan, the Mughal army around Gingee could hold on much longer than in the arid northwest, be it by collecting revenue, levying tribute or living off the land. More than any geographical or ecological circumstances, though, the Maratha opponent created the main obstacle to Mughal success. The Marathas had emerged as a well-entrenched gentry along the various routes and passes that crossed the Western Ghats and connected the Arabian Sea with the Dakshinapatha network. From hindsight, Rajaram's flight towards Gingee was a strategic masterstroke that diverted Mughal attention to the south and made their supply lines longer and thus much more vulnerable. The need to provision the Mughal army as far south as Gingee must have been one of the main reasons why Aurangzeb stayed in the Deccan for so long. After its capture, the Mughals realised again that their most vital strategic and economic interest were not in Tamil Nadu but in the various mountain strongholds in Maharashtra. In this sense, there was hardly any alternative to Aurangzeb's policy in the Deccan but it once again showed that, the further the empire expanded, the more vulnerable became its outer *and* inner frontiers. Hence, the eighteenth-century collapse was not only initiated at the most far-off termini of the main Mughal high roads – Kabul, Calcutta and Madras – but also, and perhaps mainly, at the new internal centres connecting these roads to some newly emerging regional economies. All this clearly paralysed the kinetic capacity of the imperial apparatus in general and of its army in particular. Here, it should be stressed again that the decline of empire during and after Aurangzeb's reign was neither the result of any shortcomings in the field of military technology nor so much of personalities, but was primarily the consequence of a pre-modern form of state formation, in which the imperial, regional and local elites were always on the lookout for long-term landed rights that usually tended to undermine the central organisation of extensive empires. As a consequence, ongoing processes of zamindarisation and regional centralisation were not instigated but merely stimulated by the military changes of the second half of the eighteenth century, which, indeed, through the domination of infantry, brought about the colonial conquests of the British.

Conclusion and epilogue

Frontier empires

The following inscription of the Maurya emperor Ashoka, alias 'the Beloved of the Gods', dates from about 250 BC. Its message is to disseminate Righteousness, or Dharma, across the whole civilised world, although Ashoka singled out two kinds of 'neighbouring' peoples:

> The Beloved of the Gods even reasons with the forest tribes (*atavi*) and seeks to reform them. But the Beloved of the Gods is not only compassionate. He is also powerful, and he tells them to repent, lest they be slain. For the Beloved of the Gods desires safety, self-control, justice and happiness for all beings.
>
> The Beloved of the Gods considers that the greatest of all victories is the victory of Righteousness, and that [victory] the Beloved of the Gods has already won, here and on all borders (*anta*), even 600 leagues away in the realm of the Greek king Antiyoka, and beyond Antiyoka among the four kings Turamaya, Antikini, Maga and Alikasudara, and in the South among the Colas and Pandyas and as far as Ceylon.[1]

With the Mughals, the Mauryas often figure as the only dynasty that ruled the whole of the Indian sub-continent before the colonial period. Although almost two millennia apart, Ashoka's concept of his realm appears not much different at all from the common Mughal perspective as outlined in Chapter 1. Both Maurya and Mughal realms should not be considered as rounded-off territories with neatly demarcated boundaries defining clear in- and outsiders. Their empires were, rather, open and fluid patchworks in which closely controlled areas of more or less settled agriculture alternated with uncultivated wastes and marchlands at best occupied by hard-to-administer nomadic tribes, but all tied together in networks of pastoral and commercial roads that, through the foremost urban centres, connected them to each other as well as to the outside world. In other words, both were imperial configurations with manifold inner frontiers inhabited by forest tribes of the types we come across in the first section of Ashoka's inscription. But, as illustrated in the second section of the inscription, the imperial boundaries also radiated deep into neighbouring realms much beyond the Indian sub-continent.

Does this imply that the overall structure of Indian states remained unaltered from the Mauryas to the Mughals? For a long time this was exactly what some orientalists wanted us to believe, mainly in order to stress the desired contrast between dynamic Western states and stagnant Eastern empires, thereby also underscoring the blessings of colonial rule. Obviously, there *was* enormous change in the organisation and reach of Indian polities throughout the intervening ages. Nonetheless, it is my contention that this always happened within the long-term, ecology-based perimeters of India's limites and inner frontiers. As such, most pre-colonial Indian empires were polities that emerged on the roads and crossroads of commercial and nomadic interaction. What changed throughout the ages were the precise location, the dynamics and the impact of this interaction. Crucial for the relocation of the agrarian frontier, for example, was the introduction of new and better crops at the end of the first millennium AD. Somewhat later, the military revolution of the horse-warrior reinvigorated the nomadic frontier, giving rise to the more powerful and more centralised frontier empires of the Turks. In this light, the Mughal Empire, and with it the Safavid and Ottoman Empires, may be considered the highpoint of a six-century-old frontier-imperial development. More than any of its predecessors, the Mughal Empire managed to deploy the massive mobile resources of its high roads and frontiers, mainly money and horsepower, to achieve an unprecedented degree of agricultural, commercial and political expansion. In Chapter 2 we have seen that, even in terms of ideology and ritual, the Mughal state reflected as much the world of the settled court as that of the nomadic war-band.

But as the Mughals needed and exploited the empire's inner frontiers, the latter remained in place and, as before, caused centrifugal tendencies to re-emerge, as may be witnessed in the process of regional centralisation and in the foreign invasions of the eighteenth century.[2] In many ways, this was a natural development stemming from the logistical incapacity of all pre-modern empires to control each and every village from a distance. As we have seen, one temporary antidote was to keep the court, the bureaucracy, the army and the nobility on the move. When Aurangzeb departed from this policy nothing could really prevent the whole imperial structure of high roads and marches from collapsing. All this had happened before on the sub-continent, the last time in the fifteenth century when the Delhi sultanate broke apart and opened the way for Babur's conquests in the following century. In both cases, regional groups had increasingly succeeded in carving out their own autonomous homelands leaving the imperial authorities in Agra and Delhi with the mere ceremonial residue of power.

Under the Mughals, regional centralisation was already pre-cooked in the late-seventeenth-century process of zamindarisation. The new regional rulers of the eighteenth century, many of them having a zamindari background themselves, either suppressed or cooperated with their own local gentry in order to keep the imperial authorities or some other outsider at arm's length. Finally, both zamindarisation and regional centralisation were stimulated in the late eighteenth and early nineteenth centuries by the political and military expansion of the East India Company. To a certain extent, the new targets of the EIC came very close to the zamindar's dream of creating a well-demarcated, fully-settled homeland based on the close control of agricultural resources and, crucial in the context of this book, supported by a locally-recruited, peasant-based infantry army. The result was the transformation of the open, fluid inner frontiers of past empires into the pacified, cultivated fields surrounded by the closed and rigid outer boundaries of the colonial state. In due course, the zamindar's dream ended in the reality of the neatly defined space of the nation-state that cannot tolerate self-ruling bands of warriors, nomads and other *mawashis* undermining its lately achieved monopoly in administrating justice and using violence. All this would have been hardly conceivable, though, without the shifting military balance between cavalry and infantry.

Infantry revolution and colonial conquest

As stressed in Chapter 4, pre-Mughal India had been fully part of the military revolution involving the more effective use of the warhorse. The potential of this military breakthrough fully materialised in the most successful of Indian frontier empires: the Mughal Empire. In its mentality, organisation and weaponry the Mughal military was based on cavalry. Cavalry forces, supported by other locomotive means, such as elephants, dromedaries and oxen, sustained the *perpetuum mobile* of the imperial court. In the sixteenth and seventeenth centuries, infantry troops, whether equipped with the latest gunpowder weaponry or not, could hardly make an impression against the sheer size and mobility of Mughal cavalry armies consisting of light mounted archers and heavy shock-troopers protected by bullet- and arrow-proof armour. From the Mughal point of view, it could hardly have been foreseen that such infantry innovators as Maurice of Nassau and Gustavus Adolphus, whom they would have regarded as just two other examples of the primitive, rather pathetic, local zamindars they knew so well, would be succeeded, more than a century later, by the seemingly invincible peasant-soldier war machine of the British. So what made the difference?

What appears crucial in answering the question is the awareness that Europe, situated beyond what we have termed the Arid Zone, had somehow missed the full impact of the horse-warrior revolution. Because most of Europe lacked a nomadic population of its own, European wars were always predominantly fought using footsoldiers. Hence, military innovation focused on the tactics and weaponry of infantry, which gradually arrived at a stage where it could successfully beat off the charge of a few mounted knights. This was achieved mainly through the combined use of pikes and muskets in well-organised and drilled squares. It was only in this context that the military revolution involving gunpowder weaponry made sense. Combined with increasing levels of standardisation, the seventeenth-century innovations of the bayonet, the flintlock and prefab paper cartridges, almost invisibly tilted the military balance in favour of European infantry. Also in artillery, the seventeenth century saw increasing standardisation of ball, ball-weight and firing procedure, which produced much lighter, more accurate field pieces that could keep up with marching infantry.

Nonetheless, until the eighteenth century, European-drilled infantry remained the laughing stock of the Mughal rulers. Standardisation in weaponry, drill and uniform hardly appealed to the independent mindset of the Mughal horse-trooper. As witnessed in the case of the early Marathas, every ambitious new power on the sub-continent knew that they could only be successful if they were prepared to emulate the whole Mughal apparatus of horse-based honours, organisation, weaponry and tactics. This does not mean that modern gunpowder weaponry was not used very early in India. As observed in Chapter 5, matchlocks and cannon did play a prominent role in most Indian battles after Panipat, but their tactical use was always part of the function of the predominant cavalry arm or, also, merely in defence of fortification. It was mainly during the Anglo-French confrontations of the mid-eighteenth century that Indian powers began to realise the superiority of European-trained and -equipped infantry in pitched battles. Hence, from this time onward we see Indian rulers eagerly adopting European technology and fighting methods, hiring European experts or even whole regiments of infantry which, because of Anglo-French confrontation were in ready supply. All this undermined the prevalent cavalry system inherited from the Mughals.[3]

But apart from the purely military logic, instigated by the long-term developments in Western Europe, there were also other, indigenous considerations that stimulated the growing Indian preference for infantry. Even before the onset of the infantry revolution, the late-seventeenth-century process of zamindarisation of the Mughal military tended to increase the importance of locally raised peasant soldiers on foot as these were much cheaper and more pliable than the fully equipped cavalry units associated with the imperial tradition of the Mughals. With the decreasing radius of action of the Mughal emperor and his mansabdars, cavalry began to lose a great deal of its attraction as a military instrument. At this stage, though, the central organisation of the Mughal Empire was already waning, making room for the new regional polities of Jats, Rohillas and Marathas, or the increasingly autonomous provinces of Awadh, Bengal, Hyderabad and Arcot. Like the Mughal Empire before, these new ruling dynasties, in many ways strapping zamindars themselves, had to come to terms with the subordinate but also increasingly powerful gentry in their own realms. Obviously, in this struggle between regional and local powers, the former attempted to make their armed forces as independent as possible from the local zamindari levies. To achieve this, one option would have been to bring in foreign cavalry and distribute the revenue rights in jagirs among its main military leaders. Indeed, this had been the prevalent solution under the Mughal dispensation. More attractive, though, was the option to hire a mercenary, infantry army from abroad and pay it in ready cash. This had the gratifying side effect that it cut through the old link between army and local society, the latter always sustaining the former with money and manpower. Hence, apart from the military factor, the process of regional centralisation also explains the growing popularity of infantry armies during the eighteenth century, more and more of which were regular EIC regiments from Calcutta, Madras and Bombay. Since the sepoys of these regiments served for longer periods in relatively isolated barracks, they became more detached from their village background. Hence, the new battalions became closed worlds of their own, consisting of ever more rigidified castes and ethnic groups. All this was a clear break with the past when both mansabdari and zamindari recruitment had been accessible to all groups with military potential, and which had produced the eclecticism of the early Mughal war-band and, later, of the imperial camp. As a result, the relatively open and highly competitive military labour market under the Mughals changed into the more rigidified and institutionalised 'garrison state' under the British.[4]

As also witnessed in the European case, the garrison state produced its own logic of events. As armies became more professional and more detached from society, the purely military pattern of thinking began to prevail over other considerations. It engendered, for example, the phase of rapid British expansion between 1760 and 1830. One of the central war aims of the British was to monopolise power, at least in their own territories. This was at right angles to the fluid politics of the Mughal *ancien régime* that had aimed at sharing men and resources, and at having one's 'finger in every man's dish'.[5] Generally speaking, Mughal policy was usually aimed not at destroying but at incorporating the enemy, preferably by means of endless rounds of negotiations. But the Indian conception of honour did not coincide with that of eighteenth-century English gentlemen. The latter usually mistook Indian flexibility for devious duplicity and collaboration. As expressed in the words of Arthur Wellesley, the later Duke of Wellington, the British attitude was that of one who 'would sacrifice Gwalior, or every frontier of India, ten times over, in order to preserve our credit for scrupulous good faith'.[6] For the calculating Indian rulers of the day this mentality must have been sheer madness. It was the unsporting attitude of a party that suddenly and unilaterally changed the rules of the ongoing game. While Indian politics lost a great deal of its earlier openness and flexibility, war also lost much of its earlier playfulness and, instead, became deadly earnest. In the end, it was not the absentmindedness claimed by some colonial historians, but exactly this well-chosen earnestness of the British commanders, which, scrupulously or not, delivered them not only Gwalior but also each and every frontier of the Indian sub-continent.

APPENDIX

The Mughal dynasty 1526–1712

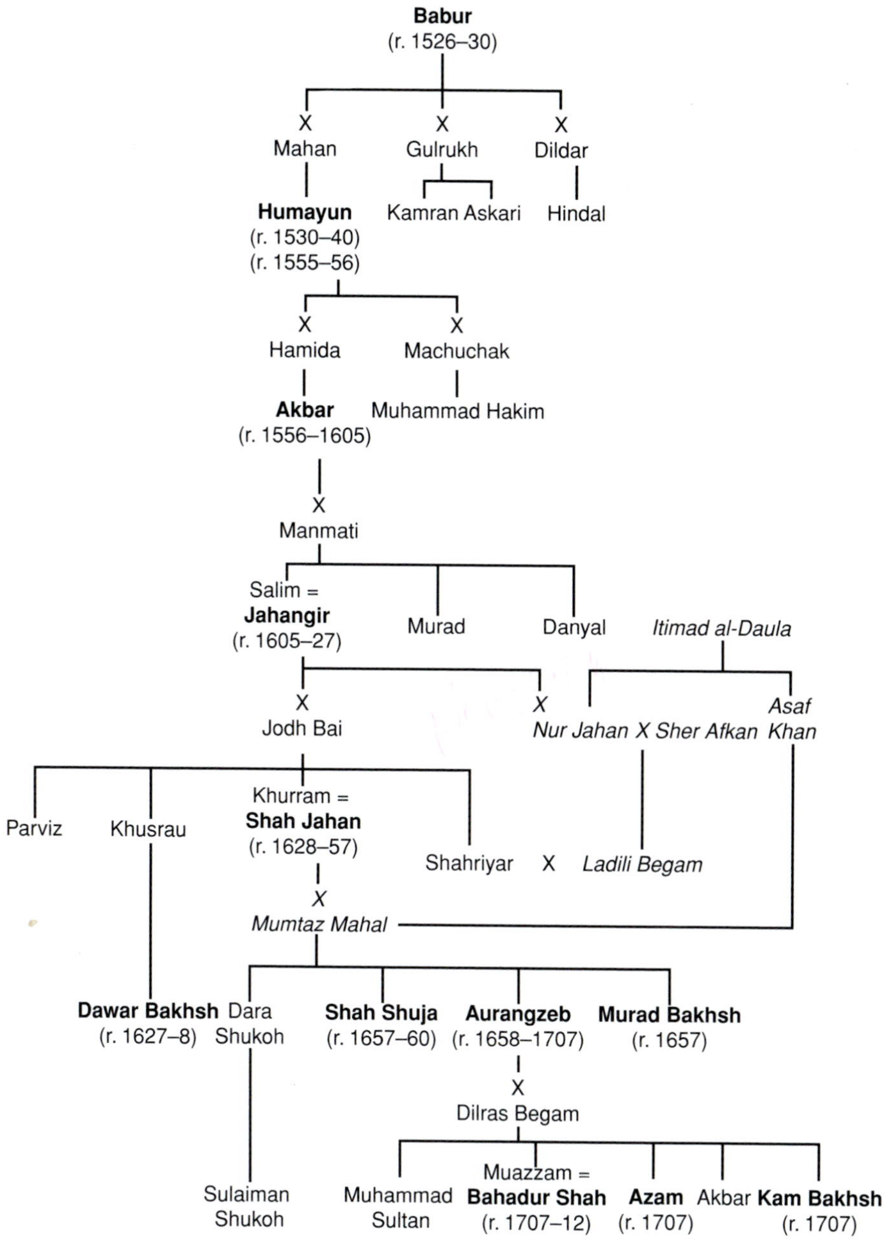

Notes

Introduction

1 P. Horn, *Das Heer- und Kriegswesen des Grossmoghuls* (Leiden, 1894); W. Irvine, *The Army of the Indian Moghals* (London, 1903).

2 For the various contributions of the scholars mentioned, see the bibliography. For a more extensive discussion on the medieval military historiography of South Asia, see the Introduction to J. Gommans and D.H.A. Kolff (eds), *Warfare and Weaponry in South Asia 1000–1800* (Delhi, 2001).

3 J. Huizinga, *Homo Ludens: Proeve eener Bepaling van het Spel-element der Cultuur* (Haarlem, 1938). The work has many later editions and has been translated into English.

4 *Md*, p. 9.

Chapter One

1 My thinking about the frontier was mainly inspired by the reading of O. Lattimore, *Studies in Frontier History: Collected Papers 1928–1958* (Paris and The Hague, 1962); E. Whiting Fox, *History in Geographic Perspective: The Other France* (New York, 1971); and C.R. Whittaker, *Frontiers of the Roman Empire: A Social and Economic Study* (Baltimore and London, 1997).

2 *GI,* IV, p. 313.

3 For an elaboration on this theme, see J. Gommans, 'The silent frontier of South Asia, *c.* 1100–1800 AD', *Journal of World History* , 9 (1998), pp. 1–23; and J. Gommans, 'Burma at the frontier of South, East and Southeast Asia: A geographic perspective', in J. Gommans and J. Leider (eds), *The Maritime Frontier of Burma: Exploring Political, Cultural and Commercial Interaction in the Indian Ocean World, 1200–1800* (Amsterdam and Leiden, 2002), pp. 1–9.

4 For the meaning of the Roman limes, see (apart from Whittaker, *Frontiers of the Roman Empire*) B. Isaac, *The Limits of Empire: The Roman Army in the East* (Oxford, 1993), pp. 408–18.

5 Although their meaning has been adjusted, both the terms 'saddle state' and 'perennial nuclear zones' derive from O.H.K. Spate and A.T.A. Learmonth, *India and Pakistan: A General and Regional Geography* (New Delhi, 1984), pp. 173–89.

6 Most of the geographical data in this chapter are gathered from Spate and Learmonth, *India and Pakistan*; and F. Durand-Dastès, *La Géographie de l'Inde* (Paris, 1965).

7 Mihir Shah *et al.* (eds), *India's Drylands: Tribal Societies and Development Through Environment Regeneration* (Delhi, 1998), pp. 104–39.

8 D.H.A. Kolff, Naukar, *Rajput and Sepoy: The Ethnohistory of the Military Labour Market in Hindustan, 1450–1850* (Cambridge, 1990), pp. 1–31.
9 J.C. Heesterman, 'Warrior, peasant and brahmin', *Modern Asian Studies*, 29 (1995), pp. 637–54; and B. Stein, 'Mahanavami: Medieval and modern kingly ritual in south India', in L. Bardwell (ed.), *Essays on Gupta Culture* (Delhi, 1983), pp. 67–90.
10 S. Gordon, 'Zones of military entrepreneurship in India, 1500–1700', in S. Gordon, *Marathas, Marauders, and State Formation in Eighteenth-century India* (Delhi, 1994), pp. 182–209.
11 F. Zimmermann, *The Jungle and the Aroma of Meats: An Ecological Theme in Hindu Medicine* (Berkeley and Los Angeles, 1982), pp. 1–95. For similar accounts, see also the various regional descriptions in *AA*.
12 C.A. Bayly, *Empire and Information: Intelligence Gathering and Social Communication in India, 1780–1870* (Cambridge, 1996), pp. 303–4.
13 The information on pastoralism is gathered from a whole range of published and unpublished sources, the latter mainly from *EIC* records, but very informative is R.O. Whyte, *Land, Livestock and Human Nutrition in India* (London, 1968). For other material, see Gommans, 'Silent frontier'; on horse breeding, see Gommans *The Rise of the Indo-Afghan Empire, c.1710–1780* (Leiden, 1995), pp. 68–104.
14 I. Habib, *The Agrarian System of Mughal India* (Delhi, 1999, rev. ed.), pp. 169, 170, 223.
15 See J. Gommans, 'The Eurasian frontier after the first millennium AD: Reflections along the fringe of time and space', *The Medieval History Journal*, 1 (1998), pp. 125–45.
16 J.C. Heesterman, 'Two types of spatial boundaries', in E. Cohen *et al.* (eds), *Comparative Social Dynamics* (Boulder and London, 1985), pp. 59–72.
17 B.M. Law, *Historical Geography of Ancient India* (Paris, 1954), pp. 1–60. Cf. Zimmermann, *Jungle*, pp. 30, 47.
18 J. Deloche, *La Circulation en Inde Avant la Révolution des Transports, I: La Voie de Terre* (Paris, 1980), pp. 91–4.
19 *MJ*, p. 100 [Persian text, p. 206].
20 S.N. Bhattacharya, *A History of Mughal North-east Frontier Policy* (Calcutta, 1929), p. 395; R.C. Foltz, *Mughal India and Central Asia* (Karachi, 1998), pp. 127–51.
21 *MJ*, p. 64 [Persian text, p. 169]. Alvi translates it differently as 'country (India) and Iran'.
22 For the most recent surveys, see S. Gole, *Indian Maps and Plans: From Earliest Times to the Advent of European Surveys* (Delhi, 1989); and J.E. Schwartzberg, 'South Asian cartography', in J.B. Harley and D. Woodward (eds), *History of Cartography, II, 1: Cartography in the Traditional Islamic and South Asian Societies* (Chicago and London, 1992), pp. 388–494, 504–10.
23 The term *mawas* has a whole range of connotations that all refer to the unsettled world of the jungle (Habib, *Agrarian System*, p. 379, as responding to J.C. Heesterman, *The Inner Conflict of Tradition: Essays in Indian Ritual, Kingship and Society* (Chicago, 1985), p. 243, n. 40. See also A.K.S. Lambton, *Landlord and Peasant in Persia* (London and New York, 1991), pp. 4 n. 2, 84, 94, 104, 123.
24 For the most recent revisionist interpretation of this source, see M. Alam and S. Subrahmanyam, 'L'État moghol et sa fiscalité, xvie–xviiie siècles', *Annales* (1994), pp. 189–217.
25 *AA*, II, p. 129 [Persian text, I, p. 387].
26 I. Habib, *An Atlas of the Mughal Empire: Political and Economic Maps with Detailed Notes, Bibliography and Index* (Delhi, 1986), pp. x–xi.

27 For an excellent historical survey of Mughal expansion, see J.F.
New Cambridge History of India, I, 5: The Mughal Empire (Cam
28 *AA*, II, p. 406 [Persian text, I, p. 590]. Cf. J. Arlinghaus, 'T
tion of Afghan tribal society: Tribal expansion, Mughal ir
the Roshaniyya insurrection, 1450–1600' (unpublished Ph.D
University, 1988), pp. 50–76.
29 *BN*, p. 172.
30 The *Khizana-i Amira* by Ghulam Ali Khan Bilgrami Azad in
Rao, *Eighteenth Century Deccan* (Bombay, 1963), p. 242.
31 *BN*, p. 170.
32 *BN*, p. 186.
33 *BN*, pp. 169–71; cf. *BN(B)*, p. 199.
34 Gommans, *Indo-Afghan Empire*, pp. 79–80. See also, Lieut. Irwin, 'Memoir on the climate, soil, produce and husbandry of Afghanistan and the neighbouring countries', *Journal of the Asiatic Society of Bengal*, 8 (1839), p. 888.
35 Cf. *MU*, I, p. 621 [Persian text, I, p. 567].
36 Gommans, 'Silent frontier', pp. 17–23; Arlinghaus, 'Transformation of Afghan tribal society', pp. 61–2.
37 *AN*, III, p. 402 [Persian text, III, p. 276].
38 For a more detailed analysis of the interaction between coast and interior in Mughal India, see J.C. Heesterman, 'Littoral et intérieur de l'Inde', in L. Blussé, H.L. Wesseling and G.D. Winius (eds), *History and Underdevelopment: Essays on Underdevelopment and European Expansion in Asia and Africa* (Leiden, 1980), pp. 87–92.
39 *MU*, II, p. 752 [Persian text, I, p. 655]. The partial withdrawal of this arrangement by Akbar's wazir Shah Mansur Shirazi caused the revolt of these nobles in 1579–80.
40 *MU*, I, p. 649 [Persian text, I, p. 652].
41 Spate and Learmonth, *India and Pakistan*, p. 575.
42 J. Deloche, *La Circulation en Inde Avant la Révolution des Transports, II: La Voie d'Eau* (Paris 1980), pp. 162–3.
43 The best analysis of these historical developments is given by R.M. Eaton, *The Rise of Islam and the Bengal Frontier, 1204–1760* (Berkeley, 1993), pp. 137–59, 194–207.
44 *MU*, I, p. 780 [Persian text, I, p. 751].
45 *WM*, p. 232.
46 J. Malcolm, *A Memoir of Central India Including Malwa and Adjoining Provinces* (London, 1824), I, pp. 8–15.
47 *TJ*, p. 414.
48 M.S. Mate and T.V. Pathy (eds), *Daulatabad (A Report on the Archaeological Investigations)* (Pune and Aurangabad, 1992), p. 46.
49 See especially G.D. Sontheimer, *Biroba, Mhaskoba und Khandoba: Ursprung, Geschichte und Umwelt von Pastoralen Gottheiten in Maharashtra* (Wiesbaden, 1976), pp. 148–62; and Ajay Dandekar, 'Landscapes in conflict: Flocks, hero-stones, and cult in early medieval Maharashtra', *Studies in History*, 7 (1991), pp. 301–24.
50 G. Michell and R. Eaton (eds), *Firuzabad: Palace City of the Deccan* (Oxford, 1992), p. 13.
51 For the various connections between the Konkan ports and the Deccan, see R.J. Barendse, *The Arabian Seas 1640–1700* (Leiden, 1998), pp. 10–60.
52 Cited in Sontheimer, *Biroba*, p. 161.
53 The geographical data on the Deccan and south India derive mainly from the historical survey of K.A. Nilakanta Sastri, *A History of South India from Prehistoric Times to the Fall of Vijayanagara*, (Delhi, 1975), pp. 34–48.

54 S. Subrahmanyam, *The Political Economy of Commerce: Southern India 1500–1650*, (Cambridge, 1990), p. 89.
55 This could equally mean waste or wilderness. I am grateful to Sanjay Subrahmanyam for providing me with the exact wording in the Persian text.
56 From the eighteenth-century chronicle *Tuzak-i Walahjahi* of the Munshi Burhan Khan Handi, cited by S. Subrahmanyam, 'Reflections on state-making and history-making in south India', *Journal of the Economic and Social History of the Orient*, 41 (1998), p. 397.
57 *TD*, II, p. 180.
58 For the northern horse trade in Tirupati, see *BL, OIOC*: Madras Military and Secret Proceedings: P/251/69: 'Brg. Gen. J. Smith to Brd, 6–5–1771', ff. 307–10; P/251/71: 'Letter Captain Tonyn, 1–6–1772', ff. 434–5; P/251/72: 'Letter Captain Tonyn, 14–7–1772', ff. 623–5; 2–11–1772, f. 880; P/253/33: 'Letter Montgomery, 4–10–1794', ff. 4109–10. See also the commercial report by Charles Malet, 8–8–1788, in *BL, OIOC*: Eur.F.149/5, ff. 397–8. For the developments of this trade in the early nineteenth century, see *Bl, OIOC*: Board of Control: F/4/517/12379, 'Political Consultations, 18–7–1815', ff. 5–12; 'Political Consultations, 29–6–1816', ff. 53–4.
59 Subrahmanyam, *Political Economy*, p. 88.
60 B. Stein, *Thomas Munro: The Origins of the Colonial State and his Vision of Empire* (Delhi, 1989), pp. 99, 119–20; R.W. Littlewood, *Livestock of Southern India* (Madras, 1936).
61 *MU*, II, p. 21 [Persian text, III, p. 400]. This is corroborated in R.V. Russell, *The Tribes and Castes of the Central Provinces of India*, II (London, 1916), pp. 168–70. Here the Banjaras are linked, however, to Asaf Khan's campaign against Ahmadnagar.
62 J. Sarkar, *History of Aurangzeb* (Calcutta, 1925–52), IV, pp. 244–52; V, pp. 138–44.
63 *AA*, II, p. 207 [Persian text, I, p. 456]. See also *MU*, I, p. 38 [Persian text, I, pp. 80–1].
64 *SJN*, pp. 154–66; *MU*, I, pp. 615, 757 [resp. Persian text, I, pp. 590–1; II, p. 218].
65 *SJN*, pp. 507–32.
66 From the *Fathiya-i Ibriyah* by Shihab al-Din Talish, cited by Bhattacharya, *Mughal North-east Frontier*, p. 18.
67 L. Petech, 'The Tibetan–Ladakhi–Moghul war of 1681–83', *Indian Historical Quarterly*, 23 (1947).

Chapter Two

1 Most inspiring for this study are C. Kafadar, *Between Two Worlds: The Construction of the Ottoman State* (Berkeley, 1995); and R.P. Lindner, *Nomads and Ottomans in Medieval Anatolia* (Bloomington, 1983).
2 Kafadar, *Between Two Worlds*, p. 56.
3 S.P. Blake, 'The patrimonial-bureaucratic empire of the Mughals', *Journal of Asian Studies*, 39 (1979), pp. 77–94.
4 J. Sarkar, *Mughal Administration*, (Calcutta, 1963), pp. 7–8.
5 See, e.g., *MJ*, p. 63 [Persian text, p. 168].
6 *AA*, I, pp. 1–10 [Persian text, I, pp. 1–7]; Cf. M. Weber, *Economy and Society* (Berkeley, 1978), II, pp. 1028–30; and Blake, *Shahjahanabad: The Sovereign City in Mughal India, 1639–1739* (Cambridge, 1991), pp. 17–25.
7 It is what S.F. Dale calls steppe humanism; see his 'Steppe humanism: The autobiographical writings of Zahir al-Din Muhammad Babur, 1483–1530', *International Journal of Middle Eastern Studies*, 22 (1990), pp. 37–58.

8 Kolff, Naukar, *Rajput and Sepoy*, p. 20.
9 Mainly based on the writings of A.R. Khan, especially his 'Gradation of nobility under Babur', *Islamic Culture* (1986), pp. 79–88.
10 Kolff, Naukar, *Rajput and Sepoy*.
11 *BN*, p. 294. Cf. p. 302.
12 *WM*, pp. 75, 87, 118, 136, 160–1, 199.
13 Cf. *BN*, p. 235.
14 See, e.g., R.M. Eaton, *Sufis of Bijapur 1300–1700: Social Roles of Sufis in Medieval India* (Princeton, 1978), pp. 19–39; and S. Bayly, *Saints, Goddesses and Kings: Muslims and Christians in South Indian Society 1700–1900*, (Cambridge, 1989), pp. 187–216.
15 S. Digby, 'The Naqshbandis in the Deccan in the late seventeenth and early eighteenth century AD: Baba Palangposh, Baba Musafir and their adherents', in M. Gaborieau *et al.* (eds), *Naqshbandis: Cheminements et Situation Actuelle d'un Ordre Mystique Musulman* (Istanbul and Paris, 1990), pp. 167–207.
16 *TSS*, pp. 249, 769. See also the life of one Ghazi Khan in *MU*, I, pp. 649–50 [Persian text, III, pp. 323–4].
17 *TSS*, pp. 378, 608.
18 S. Digby, 'Dreams and reminiscences of Dattu Sarvani, a sixteenth century Indo-Afghan soldier', *The Indian Economic and Social History Review*, 2 (1965), pp. 52–80; 3 (1965), pp. 178–94.
19 Gommans, *Indo-Afghan Empire*. The trust placed on Afghan descent is also repeatedly reported for the pre-Mughal Afghan dynasties.
20 *BN*, pp. 373–4. Earlier he had already given up the uttering of obscene poetry; see *BN*, p. 312.
21 *BN*, p. 387.
22 Obviously, the main elements of mawas culture are not much different from the way Turko-Mongolian tradition has been described. See, e.g., the excellent contributions by the late Joseph Fletcher: 'Turco-Mongolian monarchic tradition in the Ottoman Empire', *Harvard Ukrainian Studies*, 3–4 (1979–80), pp. 236–51; and 'The Mongols: Ecological and social perspectives', *Harvard Journal of Asiatic Studies*, 46 (1986), pp. 11–50.
23 H.W. Bodewitz, 'Hindu *ahimsa* and its roots', in J.E.M. Houben and K.R. van Kooij (eds), *Violence Denied: Violence, Non-violence and the Rationalization of Violence in South Asian Cultural History* (Leiden, 1999), p. 19.
24 During the last few years the literature on this subject has become vast, but for a critical survey see B. Chattopadhyaya, *Representing the Other? Sanskrit Sources and the Muslims* (Delhi, 1998).
25 Kolff, Naukar, *Rajput and Sepoy*.
26 There are various articles on the armed ascetic, as may be gathered from the most recent contribution by W.R. Pinch, 'Who was Himmat Bahadur? Gosains, Rajputs and the British in Bundelkhand, ca. 1800', *The Indian Economic and Social History Review*, 35 (1998), pp. 293–35.
27 *AN*, II, pp. 422–3 [Persian text, II, pp. 286–7].
28 See, e.g., *TD*, p. 32.
29 W.H. McLeod, *Who is a Sikh? The Problem of Sikh Identity* (Oxford, 1989), pp. 23–42.
30 Cited in D.N. Lorenzen, 'Warrior ascetics in Indian history', *Journal of the American Oriental Society*, 98 (1978), pp. 61–75.
31 W.R. Pinch, *Peasants and Monks in British India* (Berkeley, 1996), p. 50; and D. Gold, 'The Dadu-Panth: A religious order in its Rajasthan context', in K. Schomer *et al.* (eds), *The idea of Rajasthan: Explorations in Regional Identity, II: Institutions* (Delhi, 1994), pp. 242–64.

32 Eaton, *Sufis of Bijapur*, pp. 9–13.
33 See the various writings of G.D. Sontheimer, but in particular his *Biroba*. See also various contributions in A. Hiltebeitel (ed.), *Criminal Gods and Demon Devotees* (New York, 1989).
34 Pinch, 'Himmat Bahadur', p. 304.
35 For these manuals, see A. Ahmad, 'The British Museum Mirzanama and the seventeenth century mirza in India', *Iran*, 13 (1975), pp. 99–110; and M. Hidayat Husain, 'The Mirza Namah (The Book of the Perfect Gentlemen) of Mirza Kamran with an English translation', *Journal of the Asiatic Society of Bengal*, 9 (1913), pp. 1–13. These have also been extensively used in R. O'Hanlon, 'Manliness and imperial service in Mughal north India', *Journal of the Economic and Social History of the Orient*, 42 (1999), pp. 47–93.
36 Ahmad, 'British Museum Mirzanama', pp. 100–6. Interestingly, the learning of science was not part of the picture. This appears also in the account of the Irani Danishmand Khan, d. 1670 (*MU*, I, p. 448 [Persian text, II, p. 32]).
37 Ahmad, 'British Museum Mirzanama', p. 101.
38 Hidayat Husain, 'Mirza Namah', p. 5.
39 Ahmad, 'British Museum Mirzanama', p. 105.
40 *MU*, I, p. 354 [Persian text, I, p. 232].
41 See, e.g., the attitude of the Hindu amir Bhimsen in *TD*, pp. 31, 95.
42 See B.N.S. Yadava, *Society and Culture in Northern India in the Twelfth Century* (Allahabad, 1973), pp. 201–33. See also S. Pollock, 'Ramayana and political imagination in India', *The Journal of Asian Studies*, 53 (1993), pp. 261–97.
43 Kolff, Naukar, *Rajput and Sepoy*, pp. 72–3.
44 The information on the Rajputs is mainly taken from N. Ziegler's two excellent contributions: 'Some notes on Rajput loyalties during the Mughal period', in J.F. Richards (ed.), *Kingship and Authority in South Asia* (Madison, Wisconsin, 1978), pp. 215–52; and 'Evolution of the Rathor state of Marvar: Horses, structural change and warfare', in K. Schomer *et al.* (eds), The *Idea of Rajasthan: Explorations in Regional Identity, II: Institutions* (Delhi, 1994), pp. 192–217.
45 See, e.g., the zamindar of Baniyanchung Husain Khan, the Afghan chief Usman Khan Karrani, the Chishti governor of Bengal Qasim Khan, and the Persian noble and Mughal commander Mirza Nathan (*BG*, I, pp. 140, 191, 440; II, 594–5).
46 H. Scharfe, *The State in Indian Tradition* (Leiden, 1989), pp. 175–9; See also Yadava, *Society and Culture*.
47 J. Keegan, *A History of Warfare* (London, 1993), p. 390.
48 Cited in Ziegler, 'Evolution of the Rathor state', p. 207.
49 Wollebrandt Geleynssen de Jongh, *De Remonstrantie van W. Geleynssen de Jongh*, ed. W. Caland (The Hague, 1929), pp. 69, 89.
50 Ziegler, 'Evolution of the Rathor State', p. 207; See also similar reports by P[ieter] v[an] d[en] B[roeck], *Curieuse Beschrijving van de Gelegentheid, Zeden, Godsdienst en Ommegang van Verscheyden Oost-Indische Gewesten en Machtige Landschappen, etc. van Golconda en Pegu*, (Rotterdam, 1677), p. 57; and Geleynssen de Jongh, *Remonstrantie*, pp. 88–9.
51 *AAl*, p. 48. See also *AAl*, p. 105.
52 A. Wink, *Al-Hind: The Making of the Indo-Islamic World, II: The Slave Kings and the Islamic Conquest, 11th–13th Centuries* (Leiden, 1997), pp. 170–82.
53 Ziegler, 'Some notes', pp. 231–40.
54 Iranis, especially, kept an open eye on the courtly ritual, although they often preferred Persian to Mughal models and, thus, offended the Indian courtiers. See, e.g., *MU*, I, p. 300 [Persian text, I, p. 223].

55 For Ibn Khaldun, see *Md*.
56 For the prominence of these terms, see, e.g., *MJ*, p. 83 [Persian text, pp. 188–9]. For the meaning of *mahabba* in Islamic religion and philosophy, see the article by M. Arkoun, 'Ishk', *EI*, IV, pp. 118–19.
57 In the case of the ruler's love, *gratia*. The Arabic and Persian *mahabbat* may be used for the love of the ruler for his servants and vice versa. For the medieval European context of these concepts, see G. Althof, *Spielregeln der Politik im Mittelalter: Kommunikation in Frieden und Fehde* (Darmstadt, 1997).
58 This partly builds on the illuminating synthesis in D.E. Streusand's *The Formation of the Mughal Empire* (Delhi, 1989); although Streusand does not directly refer to the frontier, he sees a more or less similar dichotomy between Indian and Central Asian traditions.
59 On the importance of these wet-nurses, see *AN*, I, pp. 130–1 [Persian text, I, p. 44].
60 *MU*, I, p. 319 [Persian text, I, p. 675].
61 Most probably, she was merely his 'dry-nurse' since Adham Khan was of a different age to Akbar.
62 See also the report of Aurangzeb's foster-brother Khan Jahan Bahadur Zafar Jang Kokaltash in *MU*, I, pp. 789–91 [Persian text, I, pp. 808–13].
63 *MU*, I, pp. 319–34 [Persian text, I, pp. 675–93]. See also, e.g., *TD*, p. 202.
64 *MU*, II, p. 160 [Persian text, II, p. 535].
65 *MU*, I, pp. 409–11 [Persian text, II, p. 113].
66 On khanazadagi, see Streusand, *Formation*, pp. 146–8 and J.F. Richards, 'Norms of comportment among imperial Mughal officers', in B.D. Metcalf (ed.), *Moral Conduct and Authority: The Place of Adab in South Asian Islam* (Berkeley, 1984), pp. 255–89.
67 This anecdote is given by M.N. Pearson (ed.) in his introduction to the volume on F.W. Buckler: *Legitimacy and Symbols: The South Asian Writings of F.W. Buckler* (Ann Arbor, 1985), p. 29.
68 *MU*, I, p. 391 [Persian text, I, p. 735].
69 *MU*, II, p. 775 [Persian text, II, p. 607].
70 Derived from B. Lewis, *The Political Language of Islam* (Chicago, 1988), pp. 12–13.
71 *MU*, I, p. 796 [Persian text, I, p. 718]; Cf. *TD*, p. 256; and Manucci's tears during his separation from Dara Shukoh in Niccolao Manucci, *Storia do Mogor*, trans. W. Irvine (Delhi, 1981), I, pp. 303–4.
72 See Buckler's short but brilliant article in Pearson (ed.), *Legitimacy and Symbols*, pp. 176–87. The most recent contribution is S. Gordon, 'Robes of honour: A "transactional" kingly ceremony', *The Indian Economic and Social History Review*, 33 (1996), pp. 225–42. For the variety of *khilats*, see *MI*, pp. 161–2.
73 *MU*, I, pp. 585–6 [Persian text, II, pp. 859–61], which is slightly different from the description in *AA*, I, pp. 166–8 [Persian text, I, pp. 156–7].
74 See, e.g., *MU*, I, pp. 42, 740 [resp. Persian text II, p. 561; I, p. 616].
75 *SJN*, pp. 396–400.
76 S. Gordon, *The New Cambridge History of India, II, 4: The Marathas 1600–1818* (Cambridge, 1993), pp. 77–9. For the initial conditions agreed to by Jai Singh, see *HA*, pp. 74–5, 126.
77 For the importance of 'love' in sufism, see in particular A. Schimmel, *Mystical Dimensions of Islam* (Chapel Hill, 1975), pp. 130–43.
78 J.F. Richards, 'The formulation of imperial authority under Akbar and Jahangir', in Richards (ed.), *Kingship and Authority*, pp. 267–71.
79 As in the case of Mirza Nathan, see Richards, 'Formulation', p. 270. See also the jargon of service as used by Jai Singh in *HA*, pp. 59, 104.

80 *AA*, I, pp. 263–4. For the trusted positions of some of these chelas, see *MU*, I, pp. 380–1, 611 [resp. Persian text, I, pp. 427–9; I, pp. 605–11].
81 For the Middle Eastern context, see M. Chamberlain, *Knowledge and Social Practice in Medieval Damascus, 1190–1350* (Cambridge, 1994), pp. 113–16.
82 *MJ*, p. 81 [Persian text, p. 186]. Cf. *MU*, II, p. 243 [Persian text, III, p. 695].
83 *MJ*, p. 83 [Persian text, pp. 188–9]. Cf. *MU*, I, p. 218 [Persian text, I, p. 747].
84 *MJ*, pp. 85–6 [Persian text, pp. 191–2]. See also *TD*, p. 223. The importance of money is perhaps also reflected in stories about amirs practising alchemy (*muhauwisi*), see, e.g., *MU*, II, pp. 245, 341 [resp. Persian text, III, p. 698; III, pp. 788–9]. Primarily, though, alchemy aims at spiritual advantages.
85 *MU*, II, p. 547 [Persian text, III, p. 58].
86 Manucci, *Storia*, II, p. 436. See also Khafi Khan on Aurangzeb's public affection for Murad Bakhsh (*ML*, p. 31).
87 *MJ*, p. 72 [Persian text, p. 177].
88 *MJ*, p. 72 [Persian text, p. 178].
89 See, e.g., *TD*, pp. 58, 151, 176.
90 *MJ*, p. 73 [Persian text, pp. 178–9].
91 *MU*, II, p. 361 [Persian text, III, p. 223].
92 *MJ*, p. 76 [Persian text, p. 181].
93 *MJ*, p. 68 [Persian text, p. 173].
94 *MJ*, p. 76 [Persian text, p. 181]. See also similar remarks in *MU*, I, pp. 652, 685 [resp. Persian text, I, p. 587; I, p. 268]; by Azad (Madhava Rao, *Eighteenth Century*, p. 243); by Geleynssen de Jongh (*Remonstrantie*, p. 17); and by Pelsaert (Francisco Pelsaert, *De Geschriften van Francisco Pelsaert over Mughal Indië, 1627: Kroniek en Remonstrantie*, eds D.H.A. Kolff and H.W. van Santen (The Hague, 1979), p. 305).
95 See e.g. *MU*, I, p. 790 [Persian text, I, p. 811].
96 *MU*, II, p. 755 [Persian text, I, p. 658].
97 See N. Elias, *Uber den Prozeß der Zivilisation: Soziogenetische und Psychogenetische Untersuchungen*, 2 vols (Frankfurt am Main, 1991). See also the English translation of another work: *The Court Society*, trans. E. Jepcott (Oxford, 1983).
98 This is articulated by Muzaffar Alam in his recent writings: 'State building under the Mughals: Religion, culture and politics', *Cahier d'Asie Centrale*, 3–4 (1997), pp. 105–29; and 'The pursuit of Persian: Language in Mughal politics', *Modern Asian Studies*, 32 (1998), pp. 317–49.

Chapter Three

1 The term 'military labour market' derives from Kolff, Naukar, *Rajput and Sepoy*.
2 Fletcher, 'Turco-Mongolian monarchic tradition', p. 243.
3 *AA*, I. p. 170 [Persian text, I, p. 158].
4 Manucci, *Storia*, II, p. 353.
5 This follows the two classical studies on the subject of the Mughal nobility: Satish Chandra, *Parties and Politics at the Mughal Court, 1707–1740* (Aligarh, 1959); and M. Athar Ali, *The Mughal Nobility under Aurangzeb* (Delhi, 1997, rev. ed.). See also the latter's *The Apparatus of Empire: Awards of Ranks, Offices and Titles to the Mughal Nobility (1574–1658)* (Delhi, 1985).
6 See, e.g., John Fryer, *A New Account of East India and Persia Being Nine Years' Travels, 1672–1681,* ed. W. Crooke (London, 1909), I, p. 342. See also S. Inayat Ali Zaidi, 'Ordinary Khachawaha troopers serving the Mughul Empire: Composition and structure of the contingents of the Kachawaha nobles', *Studies in History*, 2 (1980), pp. 57–68.

7 For such an approach, see the recent study of Afzal Husain, *Nobility under Akbar and Jahangir: A Study of Family Groups* (Delhi, 1999).
8 Kolff, Naukar, *Rajput and Sepoy,* p. 20.
9 *AAl*, pp. 47–8; see also p. 88.
10 See, e.g., *AAl,* pp. 104–5.
11 For a recent study of Iranis in Mughal service, see A. Dadvar, *Iranians in Mughal Politics and Society 1606–1658* (New Delhi, 1999). For the Iranian impact all over the Indian Ocean, see S. Subrahmanyam's two studies: 'Iranians abroad: Intra-Asian elite migration and early modern state formation', *Journal of Asian Studies,* 51 (1992), pp. 340–63; and ' "Persianization" and "Mercantilism": two themes in Bay of Bengal history, 1400–1700', in O. Prakash and D. Lombard, *Commerce and Culture in the Bay of Bengal, 1500–1800* (Delhi, 1999), pp. 47–87; and J.J.L. Gommans, 'Trade and civilization around the Bay of Bengal, *c.*1650–1800', *Itinerario,* 19 (1995), pp. 82–109.
12 For the details of these Central Asian revolts, see Richards, *Mughal Empire,* pp. 17–19 and, in particular, Streusand, *Formation,* pp. 94–102. For Babur's relations with his Central Asian relatives, see M.E. Subtelny, 'Babur's rival relations: A study of kinship and conflict in 15th–16th century Central Asia', *Der Islam,* 17 (1980), pp. 101–18.
13 *TSS*, pp. 377–84.
14 *MU,* I, pp. 125–6 [Persian text, II, pp. 619–20]; see also *MU,* I, pp. 491, 797; II, pp. 166, 392 [resp. Persian text, II, p. 56; I, p. 720; III, pp. 375–6; III, p. 821].
15 Gommans, *Indo-Afghan Empire,* pp. 160–80. For a survey of Afghan participation in the Mughal Empire, see R. Joshi, *The Afghan Nobility and the Mughals (1526–1707)* (Delhi, 1985).
16 Athar Ali, *Mughal Nobility*, pp. 1–37.
17 For the Chishtis, see Husain, *Nobility*, 116–27; for the Shattaris, see *MU*, I, 85–93 [Persian text, II, pp. 573–83].
18 *MU,* II, p. 732 [Persian text, II, p. 590]. Of course, foreign nobles could also rise as a result of their sufi connections, such as the family of Abdulla Khan Firoz Jang, descendants of Khwaja Ubaidulla Nasir al-din Ahrar, a well-known mystic of the Naqshbandi order.
19 Respectively: *MU*, I, pp. 113–17 [Persian text, I, pp. 120–5]; *MU*, II, p. 595 [Persian text, II, p. 242]. For the incorporation of Raushaniyya soldiers, see also the contemporary account of Monserrate, *The Commentary of Father Monserrate, S.J. on his Journey to the Court of Akbar*, trans. J.S. Hoyland, ed. S.N. Banerjee (Oxford, 1922), p. 141.
20 See, e.g., C. Asher, 'Mughal sub-imperial patronage: The architecture of Raja Man Singh' in B. Stoler Miller (ed.), *The Powers of Art: Patronage in Indian Culture* (Delhi, 1992), pp. 183–202.
21 Husain, *Nobility*, p. 93.
22 Kolff, Naukar, *Rajput and Sepoy.*
23 The fortified temples refer to southern India (*TD*, p. 193).
24 *MU,* I, p. 342 [Persian text, I, pp. 418–19]. See also the depiction of the Sarnami sect at Narnaul, not far from Agra, in *ML*, p. 256 [Persian text, II, p. 252].
25 This section is based on *AA*, II, pp. 129–420 [Persian text, I, pp. 386ff.] and on the interpretation of the figures in Shireen Moosvi, *The Economy of the Mughal Empire c. 1595: A Statistical Study* (Delhi, 1987), pp. 174–91.
26 Cf. Moosvi, *Economy*, p. 183. See also her revealing map on p. 181.
27 Gordon, 'Zones of military entrepreneurship', pp. 182–209.
28 *ML*, p. 516 [Persian text, II, p. 525].

29 *ML*, pp. 515–28 [Persian text, II, pp. 525–39]; *TD*, pp. 125, 246–52. For a recent study on the Berads and the other tribal communities of the Deccan, see S. Guha, *Environment and Ethnicity in India, 1200–1991* (Cambridge, 1999).

30 Muslim bigotry on the part of Aurangzeb plays an important role in the interpretation of Mughal decline by Jadunath Sarkar, especially in his *History of Aurangzeb*. Much later, Richards pointed out that the imperial crisis in the Deccan was the result of deliberate decisions by the Mughal government to restrict the bestowal of jagirs (J.F. Richards, 'The imperial crisis in the Deccan', *Journal of Asian Studies*, 35 (1976), pp. 237–56).

31 This is the interpretation of the Aligarh historians following the main study on the subject by Athar Ali, *Mughal Nobility*. For his criticism on Richards, see the introduction, p. xxi.

32 On Mir Jumla as a 'portfolio capitalist', see Subrahmanyam, *Political Economy*, pp. 322–7.

33 V[an] d[en] B[roeck], *Curieuse Beschrijving*, pp. 69–72.

34 Sarkar, *History of Aurangzeb*, II, p. 233. The main study on Mir Jumla is by Jagdish Narain Sarkar, *The Life of Mir Jumla* (Calcutta, 1951).

35 The rise of the Afghan principalities in southern India is in need of further study, but see Subrahmanyam, 'Reflections on state-making', pp. 382–416.

36 Athar Ali, *Mughal Nobility*, pp. 29–30.

37 A. Wink, *Land and Sovereignty in India: Agrarian Society and Politics under Eighteenth-century Maratha Svarajya* (Cambridge, 1986).

38 The classic study on the role of the zamindars is S. Nurul Hasan, 'Zamindars under the Mughals' in R.E. Frykenberg (ed.), *Land Control and Social Structure in Indian History* (Madison, 1969), pp. 17–31. To see the seventeenth-century zamindari risings as peasant revolts, see the equally classic interpretation by Habib, *Agrarian System*.

39 See, e.g., *TD*, pp. 142–3, 230. See also Athar Ali, *Mughal Nobility*, pp. 169–70.

40 H. Inalcik, 'Military and fiscal transformation in the Ottoman Empire, 1600–1700', *Archivum Ottomanicum*, 6 (1980), pp. 283–313.

41 *AA*, I, p. 247 [Persian text, I, p. 178].

42 For the organisation of the nomadic band, see the recent contribution by P.B. Golden, ' "I will give the people unto thee": The Chinggisid conquests and their aftermath in the Turkic world', *Journal of the Royal Asiatic Society*, 10 (2000), pp. 21–41.

43 For Ottoman organisation, see R. Murphy, *Ottoman Warfare 1500–1700* (London, 1999), pp. 35–49.

44 For the organisation of the Safavid army, see *TM*; L. Lockhart, 'The Persian army in the Safavi period', *Der Islam*, 34 (1959), pp. 89–98; K. Röhrborn, 'Regierung und Verwaltung Irans unter den Safawiden', in B. Spuler (ed.) *Handbuch der Orientalistik: Erste Abteilung: Der Nahe und der Mittlere Osten, Bd 6, Abschnitt 5: Regierung und Verwaltung des Vorderen Orients in Islamischer Zeit, Teil 1* (Leiden, 1979), pp. 34–40; and the contribution under 'Army III. Safavid' by M. Haneda in *EIr*.

45 For their reputation as archers, see *MI*, p. 11.

46 For the ahadis, see *AA*, I, pp. 259–60 [Persian text, I, p. 187]. Some of these ahadis became great amirs, such as the well-known Mahabat Khan who staged a coup against Jahangir.

47 For the various retainers on foot, see *AA*, I, pp. 261–5 [Persian text, I, pp. 188–90]. Remarkably, the animal and artillery departments are not arranged under the army (*sipa*) but under the household (*manzil*) departments. See also S.P. Blake, 'The patrimonial-bureaucratic empire of the Mughals', *Journal of Asian Studies*, 39 (1979), pp. 77–94.

48 The eighteenth-century Bangash Nawabs of Farrukhabad, however, trained chelas as infantry musketeers (W. Irvine, 'The Bangash Nawabs of Farrukhabad', *Journal of the Asiatic Society of Bengal* 47 (1878), pp. 340–1).
49 Irvine, *Army*, pp. 43–4.
50 Gommans and Kolff (eds), *Warfare and Weaponry*, pp. 13–25.
51 Although the following interpretation of the mansabdari system is my own, it emerged from comparing the following detailed studies on the subject: W.H. Moreland, 'Ranks (mansab) in the Mughal service', *Journal of the Royal Asiatic Society* (1936), pp. 641–65; Abdul Aziz, *The Mansabdari System and the Mughal Army* (Lahore, 1945); I. Habib, 'The mansab system, 1595–1637', *Proceedings of the Indian History Congress* (1967), pp. 221–42; S. Moosvi, 'Evolution of the mansab-system under Akbar', *Journal of the Royal Asiatic Society*, 2 (1981), pp. 173–85; I. Habib, 'Mansab salary scale under Jahangir and Shahjahan', *Islamic Culture*, 59 (1985), pp. 203–28; and Athar Ali, *Mughal Nobility*, pp. 38–74.
52 *AN*, III, p. 95 [Persian text, III, p. 68].
53 See the introduction by M. Naseer-ud-Din Khan (ed.) in *Selected Documents of Shah Shah Jahan's Reign* (Hyderabad, 1950), p. x.
54 *MT*, II, p. 193 [Persian text, II, p. 190].
55 Manucci, *Storia*, II, pp. 353–4; see also *TD*, p. 233.
56 Moosvi, *Economy*.
57 Habib, *Agrarian System*, pp. 327.
58 *MU*, I, p. 447 [Persian text, II, p. 30]; Shah Jahan granted him a mansab of 1,000/100. Cf. Manucci, *Storia*, II, p. 354. See also the comments by Lala Mansaram in connection with the military recruitment by Nizam al-Mulk (Madhava Rao, *Eighteenth Century*, p. 86).
59 *HA*, pp. 78–9.
60 *HA*, p. 118. See also p. 89; and *TD*, pp. 48, 51.
61 See, e.g., *MU*, I, p. 219 [Persian text, I, p. 294]; *HA*, p. 92.
62 François Bernier, *Travels in the Mogul Empire* AD *1656–1668*, trans. A. Constable (London, 1934), pp. 211–12. See also Sir Thomas Roe, *The Embassy of Sir Thomas Roe to India*, ed. W. Forster (London, 1926), p. 89.
63 Abdul Aziz, *Mansabdari System*, pp. 144–5. Probably, those with a rank of 500 zat or more were considered as amirs, although it seems that the criterion later increased to 1,000 zat or more.
64 *MU*, II, p. 86 [Persian text, I, p. 622].
65 *AN*, III, pp. 95, 166 [resp. Persian text, III, pp. 68–9, 117]. See also Husain, *Nobility*, p. 184.
66 *AA*, I, p. 265 [Persian text, I, pp. 190–1].
67 *MT*, II, pp. 193–4 [Persian text, II, pp. 190–1].
68 See e.g. Pelsaert, *Geschriften*, p. 305.
69 *MU*, I, p. 652 [Persian text, I, p. 587].
70 *MU*, I, p. 685 [Persian text, I, p. 268].
71 *TD*, p. 58.
72 Abdul Aziz, *Mansabdari System*, p. 171.
73 *MU*, I, p. 641 [Persian text, I, p. 600].
74 *MU*, II, p. 154 [Persian text, III, pp. 213–14].
75 *MJ*, p. 90 [Persian text, p. 196].
76 Most forcefully argued in Habib, *Agrarian System*, pp. 364–406.
77 *TD*, p. 19.
78 Bayly, *Empire and Information*.
79 *AAl*, p. 49.
80 *MJ*, pp. 64, 76 [resp. Persian text, pp. 169, 181]. See also *AN*, III, p. 167 [Persian text, III, p. 118].

81 *AAl*, pp. 56, 116; *HA*, p. 117.
82 *ML*, p. 409 [Persian text, II, p. 410]; see also pp. 377–8 [Persian text, II, pp. 378–9].
83 *MU*, II, pp. 996–7 [Persian text, III, pp. 660–2]; *AAl*, p. 118.
84 Manucci, *Storia*, II, p. 15.
85 William Hawkins, 'Capt. William Hawkins his relations of the occurrents which happened in the time of his residence in India', in Samuel Purchas (ed.), *Hakluytus Posthumus, or Purchas his Pilgrims* (Glasgow, 1905–7), III, p. 12.
86 Jean-Baptiste Tavernier, *Travels in India*, trans. V. Ball, ed. W. Crooke (Delhi, 1977), I, p. 233.
87 *ARA*, *VOC* 1328, Letter Herbert de Jager to VOC headquarters in Batavia, 15 October 1677, ff. 659–69.
88 Sarkar, *Aurangzeb*, IV, pp.144–5.
89 Pelsaert, *Geschriften*, p. 232. See also Manuel Godinho, *Intrepid Itinerant: Manuel Godinho and his Journey from India to Portugal in 1663*, trans. V. Lobo; trans. and ed. J. Correia-Afonso (Bombay, 1990), p. 67.
90 Johann Albrecht von Mandelslo, *Schreiben von seiner ostindischen Reise* (Schleswig, 1645), p. 16.
91 *MT*, II, p. 243 [Persian text, II, p. 236].
92 Johan van Twist, 'Generale beschrijvinge van Indiën', in Isaac Commelin (ed.), *Begin en de Voortgangh van de Vereenighde Nederlandsche Geoctroyeerde Oost-Indische Compagnie* (Amsterdam, 1646), II, pp. 24–5. Cf. Hawkins, 'Relations', p. 35.
93 *MU*, I, pp. 678–9 [Persian text, II, pp. 813–14].
94 *SN*, p. 351.
95 The Ottoman and Safavid salaries are derived from Murphy, *Ottoman Warfare* and *TM,* and converted according to the exchange rates given in W. Hinz, *Islamische Währungen Umgerechnet in Gold* (Wiesbaden, 1991), which also shows the relative stability of the rupee. Of course, these comparisons are extremely rough as they provide no information on the internal purchasing power of the salaries.
96 Mandelslo, *Schreiben*, p. 14; For Ketelaar's comparison, see the unpublished MA thesis of Marianne Welten, 'De hofreis van Ketelaar naar het Perzische hof' (Leiden University, 1988), pp. 21–2. See also Roe, *Embassy*, p. 90; and Jean Chardin as cited in S.F. Dale, *Indian Merchants and Eurasian Trade, 1600–1750* (Cambridge, 1994), p. 16. An interesting eighteenth-century comment on Indian wealth is by the Irani traveller Abd al-Karim, cited in M. Alam and S. Subrahmanyam (eds), 'Empiricism of the heart: Close encounters in an eighteenth-century Indo-Persian text', *Studies in History*, 15 (1999), p. 284.
97 Manucci, *Storia*, II, pp. 353–4.
98 See, e.g., Engelbert Kaempfer, *Am Hofe des Persischen Großkönigs 1684–1685* (Tübingen and Basel, 1977), p. 97.
99 Sebastião Manrique, *Travels of Fray Sebastian Manrique, 1629–1643*, trans. C.E. Luard and H. Hosten (Oxford, 1926–7), I, pp. 266–7.
100 Madhava Rao, *Eighteenth Century*, p. 242.
101 R.P. Matthee, 'Politics and trade in late Safavid Iran: Commercial crisis and government reaction under Shah Solayman (1666–1694)' (unpublished Ph.D. thesis, University of California, Los Angeles, 1991), pp. 105–6.

Chapter Four

1 Cited in V. Berinstain, *Mughal India: Splendour of the Peacock Throne*, trans. P.G. Bahn (London, 1998), p. 138.
2 *TSS*, p. 652.

3 *AAl*, p. 53.
4 *AAl*, p. 95.
5 According to the *Ma'asir-i Nizami* by Lala Mansaram in Madhava Rao, *Eighteenth Century*, p. 62.
6 Heesterman, 'Warrior, peasant and brahmin', p. 642. Interestingly, Bilgrami Azad claims that the Muslim conquerors from Iran and Turan 'followed the tradition of Ashwamedh performed by Yudhisthir' (Madhava Rao, *Eighteenth Century*, p. 241).
7 M. Gronke, 'The Persian court between palace and tent: From Timur to Abbas I', in L. Golombek and M. Subtelny (eds), *Timurid Art and Culture: Iran and Central Asia in the Fifteenth Century* (Leiden, 1992), p. 20.
8 *TA*, pp. 61–2.
9 *AN*, II, p. 140; III, pp. 298, 1119 [resp. Persian text, II, p. 93; III, pp. 212, 748].
10 *AN*, III, pp. 74–8 [Persian text, III, pp. 51–6]. Cf. *MT*, II, p. 169 [Persian text, II, pp. 166–7] and *TA*, p. 208, which give, respectively, 400 and nearly 500 karohs.
11 *AN*, II, p. 95 [Persian text, II, p. 63].
12 Blake is referring to the period 1556–1739 (Blake, *Shahjahanabad*, p. 97).
13 C. Melville, 'The itineraries of Sultan Öljeitü, 1304–16', *Iran*, 28 (1990), p. 67. For more details, see C. Melville, 'From Qars to Qandahar: The itineraries of Shah 'Abbas I (995–1038/1587–1629)', in J. Calmard (ed.), *Études Safavides* (Paris and Teheran, 1993), pp. 195–225.
14 *AN*, III, p. 1140 [Persian text, III, p. 762].
15 *AN*, III, pp. 817, 839, 943 [resp. Persian text, III, pp. 537, 552, 616].
16 *AN*, III, p. 943 [Persian text, III, p. 616].
17 The more so because all imperial campaigns to the east started between May and October, the time for the sowing and harvesting of the kharif crops.
18 Bernier, *Travels*, p. 375. For the conflict between marching and tilling, see e.g. *WM*, p. 144; *TJ*, I, pp. 163, 182; *TA*, 127; *MU*, I, p. 342 [Persian text, I, p. 418].
19 Monserrate, *Commentary*, p. 80. See also Arlinghaus, 'Transformation', p.61.
20 J. Aubin, 'Réseau pastoral et réseau caravanier. Les grands routes du Khurasan a l'époque Mongole', *Le Monde Iranien et l'Islam*, 1 (1971), pp. 105–131.
21 See, e.g., H.C. Peyer, 'Das Reisekönigtum des Mittelalters', *Vierteljahrschrift für Sozial- und Wirtschaftgeschichte*, 51 (1964), pp. 1–21.
22 *TJ*, I, p. 101; II, p. 233.
23 Monserrate, *Commentary*, pp. 79–80; Bernier, *Travels*, p. 380; John Ovington, 'A voyage to Suratt in the year 1689', in J.P. Guha (ed.), *India in the Seventeenth Century* (New Delhi, 1984), p. 84.
24 Bernier, *Travels*, pp. 380–1; Edward Terry, 'A relation of a voyage to the eastern India', in Samual Purchas (ed.), *Hakluytus Posthumus, or Purchas his Pilgrims* (Glasgow, 1905–7), IX, p. 20.
25 Tavernier, *Travels*, I, p. 311. See also the eighteenth-century comparison between bread-based and rice-based armies made by Maistre de la Tour (Maistre de la Tour in G. Deleury (ed.), *Indes Florissantes: Anthologie des Voyageurs Français (1750–1820)* (Paris, 1991), p. 573).
26 *AA*, I, p. 17 [Persian text, I, p. 13].
27 Manucci, *Storia*, II, p. 354.
28 See, e.g., the statement of Jai Singh in *HA*, p. 93.
29 Abdul Aziz, *The Imperial Treasury of the Indian Mughuls* (Lahore, 1942), p. 30.
30 Nizam al-Mulk according to Lala Mansaram in Madhava Rao, *Eighteenth Century*, p. 65.
31 Manucci, *Storia*, II, pp. 62–4.
32 Mandelslo, *Schreiben*, p. 16; Monserrate, *Commentary*, p. 123.

33 For Abul Fazl's description of the system, see *AN*, III, p. 1139 [Persian text, III, p. 762].

34 See, e.g., the study by J.F. Richards on Khandesh, 'Official revenues and money flows in a Mughal province', in J.F. Richards, *The Imperial Monetary System of Mughal India* (Delhi, 1987), pp. 193–232.

35 Cf. M. van Creveld, *Supplying War: Logistics from Wallenstein to Patton* (Cambridge, 1977), pp. 1–39. See also the remarks by John Lynn in 'The history of logistics and supplying war' in J.A. Lynn (ed.), *Feeding Mars: Logistics in Western Warfare from the Middle Ages to the Present* (Boulder, San Francisco and Oxford, 1993), p. 18.

36 *MU*, II, pp. 511–14 [Persian text, III, pp. 62–6]; Monserrate, *Commentary*, p. 80.

37 *AN*, III, pp. 709, 735 [resp. Persian text, III, pp. 470–1, 487].

38 *AN*, III, pp. 817, 828, 835 [resp. Persian text, III, pp. 537, 543, 550].

39 *AN*, III, p. 1010 [Persian text, III, p. 658].

40 *TD*, p. 180. See also the various examples in Chetan Singh, 'Forests, pastoralists and agrarian society in Mughal India', in D. Arnold and R. Guha (eds), *Nature, Culture, Imperialism: Essays on the Environmental History of South Asia* (Delhi, 1995), pp. 21–48.

41 Ovington, 'Voyage', p. 83.

42 Bernier, *Travels*, p. 246; see also p. 220.

43 Monserrate, *Commentary*, p. 79.

44 Bernier, *Travels*, pp. 380–1.

45 Giovanni Francesco Gemelli Careri, 'The voyages of Thévenot and Careri', in J.P. Guha (ed.), *India in the Seventeenth Century* (New Delhi, 1984), p. 263. Bernier appears to be more realistic when he speaks of two-and-a-half leagues (*c.* six miles).

46 This comes fairly near to the annual distances covered by Shah Abbas (Melville, 'From Qars to Qandahar', p. 220).

47 Melville, 'From Qars to Qandahar', pp. 195–225. The calculated average, however, is merely 14 km for each day the Shah was actually moving (p. 221, footnote 89). The Mughals were also much slower than the movements of the relatively small entourage of the medieval kings of Western Europe.

48 Irvine, *Army*, p. 216.

49 *AN*, II, p. 528 [Persian text, II, p. 363].

50 *MU*, II, p. 543 [Persian text, III, p. 95].

51 C.A. Bayly, *Empire and Information*, p. 44.

52 *TD*, p. 233.

53 *AN*, II, pp. 122, 341, 517 [resp. Persian text, II, pp. 80, 221, 357].

54 *AN*, II, p. 442 [Persian text, II, p. 301]. See also *AN*, II, pp. 75–6; III, p. 1146 [resp. Persian text, II, pp. 47–50; III, p. 767]; *TA*, p. 271 and Monserrate, *Commentary*, pp. 74–5.

55 *MT*, II, p. 93 [Persian text, II, p. 92]; Horn, *Heer- und Kriegswesen*, p. 69.

56 According to Irvine, this kind of hunting was given up after the middle of Alamgir's (II?) reign (Irvine, *Army*, p. 189).

57 *AN*, II, pp. 251–3; III, pp. 307, 310, 915 [resp. Persian text, II, pp. 163–5; III, pp. 218, 220, 600].

58 *AN*, III, p. 345 [Persian text, III, p. 241]. For a similar description, see *AA*, I, p. 292 [Persian text, I, p. 204].

59 See, e.g., *QN*, pp. 83–4. Cf. Ahmad, 'British Museum Mirzanama', pp. 105–6. Jahangir, who was more or less addicted to hunting, promised on his fiftieth anniversary that he would give up injuring living things with his own hand (*TJ*, II, pp. 35–6).

60 Cf. Bernier, *Travels*, pp. 374–80; Tavernier, *Travels*, I, p. 312.

61 Most of the information on Indian horse breeding and trade in this chapter derives from Gommans, *Indo-Afghan Empire*, pp. 68–101.
62 A. Hyland, *Equus: The Horse in the Roman World* (London, 1990), p. 87; H. Hayes, *A Guide to Training and Horse Management in India* (Calcutta, 1878), p. 29.
63 Spate and Learmonth, *India and Pakistan*, p. 254.
64 Jean de Thévenot, 'The voyages of Thévenot and Careri', in J.P. Guha (ed.), *India in the Seventeenth Century* (New Delhi, 1984), p. 76; Tavernier, *Travels*, I, p. 226.
65 A. Hyland, *The Warhorse 1250–1600* (Stroud, 1998), p. 162.
66 J. Masson Smith Jr, 'Mongol society and military in the Middle East: Antecedents and adaptations', in Y. Lev (ed.), *War and Society in the Eastern Mediterranean, 7th–15th Centuries* (Leiden, 1997), pp. 249–66; 'Nomads on ponies vs. slaves on horses', *Journal of the American Oriental Society*, 118 (1998), pp. 54–62.
67 Hyland, *Equus*, p. 26.
68 *AA*, I, p. 142 [Persian text, I, pp. 141–2]. Three *bigha* would be about 1.8 acres, whereas the area needed for one free-grazing horse for one year would be about 120 acres (D. Sinor, 'Horse and pasture in Inner Asian history', *Oriens Extremus*, 19 (1972), pp. 181–2.
69 See, e.g., the rather positive remarks by Edward Terry (Terry, 'Relation', p. 25).
70 *AA*, I, pp. 140–50, 224–5, 243–6 [resp. Persian text, I, pp. 140–6, 162, 176–8]. Partly, higher allowances for better breeds were reflecting better diets, e.g. foreign breeds getting both more, and greener, fodder.
71 Pelsaert, *Geschriften*, pp. 120–1; Hawkins, 'Relations', pp. 33–4.
72 *AA*, I, p. 243–5 [Persian text, I, pp. 176–8]; *AA*, I, p. 141 [Persian text, I, pp. 140–1].
73 R.A. Alavi, 'New light on Mughal cavalry', in *Medieval India, a Miscellany*, 2 (1972), pp. 70–97.
74 Modave, *Voyage en Inde du Comte de Modave 1773–1776 (Nouveaux Mémoires sur l'État Actuel du Bengale et de l'Indoustan)*, ed. J. Deloche (Paris, 1971), p. 328.
75 See Sewell's translation of the accounts of Domingos Paes and Fernão Nunes, who were both horse-dealers (R. Sewell, *A Forgotten Empire (Vijayanagara): A Contribution to the History of India* (New Delhi, 1995), pp. 209, 307, 361, 381).
76 Sewell, *Forgotten Empire*, p. 126.
77 *ARA*, *VOC* 1061, Leonard Wolff, 'Remonstrantie van de gelegentheyt van Ballaguatta' (1605), ff. 185a–b.
78 Subrahmanyam, *Political Economy*, pp. 78–9.
79 Pietro della Valle, *The Travels of Pietro della Valle in India*, trans. G. Havers, ed. E. Grey (New Delhi, 1991), II, pp. 249, 334.
80 Fryer, *New account*, II, p. 58. See also *ML*, p. 224 [Persian text, II, p. 222].
81 Manucci, *Storia*, II, p. 366; Bernier, *Travels*, p. 203.
82 Modave speaks of 45–50,000 imported horses from Persia and Turkistan (*Voyage en Inde*, p. 328).
83 *BN*, p. 170.
84 Moosvi, *Economy*, pp. 376–9; Moosvi's figures are based on average prices of foreign (mainly Turkish) breeds that range from 44.5 muhrs (*c.* 400 rupees) for courtly horses, to 10 muhrs (*c.* 90 rupees) for zamindari horses. During the eighteenth century, average prices of foreign breeds were never under 400 rupees, probably due to ongoing or even increasing levels of demand and a breaking-up of the supply lines with Central Asia. Demand diminished significantly only at the end of the century. In South India, prices appear to have been about one-and-a-half to two times higher than in the north, ranging from 150 to 700 rupees – the Portuguese *pardao* roughly taken as equal to *c.* 0.625 *pagoda*, rounded up as *c.* 2 rupees (Sewell, *Forgotten Empire*, pp. 361, 381).

85 *AA*, I, p. 225 [Persian text, I, p. 162]. Abul Fazl adds, 'whenever a horse is given away as a present, the horse is calculated fifty per cent higher, and the recipient has to pay ten dams upon every muhur of the value of the horse'. (*AA*, I, p. 150 [Persian text, I, p. 146]).
86 Manucci, *Storia*, II, p. 366.
87 *WM*, p. 1, footnote 1.
88 *TN*, I. p. 557, *in casu* Muhammad b. Bakhtiar; *GI*, IV, pp. 13–4, *in casu* Sultan Hushang of Malwa.
89 *AAl*, p. 100.
90 Streusand, *Formation*, pp. 53–6.
91 Information on the composite bow derives from extensive literature produced by Latham, Patterson and McEwan between 1966 and 1979: W.F. Patterson's 'The archers of Islam', *Journal of the Economic and Social History of the Orient*, 9 (1966), pp. 69–87, and 'Archery in Moghul India', *The Islamic Quarterly*, 16 (1973), pp. 81–95; J.D. Latham's, 'Some technical aspects of archery in the Islamic miniature', *The Islamic Quarterly*, 12 (1968), pp. 226–34, and 'The archers of the Middle East: The Turco-Iranian background', *Iran*, 8 (1970), pp. 97–103; J.D. Latham and W.F. Paterson, *Saracen Archery: An English Version and Exposition of a Mameluke Work on Archery (ca. AD 1368)* (London, 1970); E. McEwan, 'Persian archery texts: Chapter eleven of Fakhr-i Mudabbir's *Adab al-harb* (Early Thirteenth Century), *The Islamic Quarterly*, 18 (1974), pp. 76–99; see also the shorter contributions of Latham and Patterson, and McEwan in R. Elgood (ed.), *Islamic Arms and Armour* (London, 1979).
92 J. Sarkar, *Military History of India* (Delhi, 1970), p. 156.
93 *BN*, p. 351.
94 Fryer, *New Account*, I, p. 342. See also the remark by Monserrate (*Commentary*, p. 85).
95 Hyland, *Warhorse*, pp. 170–1.
96 Manucci, *Storia*, II, pp. 115–16.
97 For a detailed description of Mughal armour, see Irvine, *Army*, pp. 62–72 and H. Russell Robinson, *Oriental Armour* (London, 1967), pp. 89–124.
98 *AA*, I, pp. 115–16 [Persian text, I, p. 118]; *SJN*, p. 441; *MU*, I, p. 559 [Persian text, III, p. 11]; Geleynssen de Jongh, *Remonstrantie*, p. 49.
99 Fryer, *New Account*, I, p. 336.
100 Geleynssen de Jongh, *Remonstrantie*, p. 50.
101 Monserrate, *Commentary*, p. 79. See also G.L. Coeurdoux, S.J., *L'Inde Philosophique entre Bossuet et Voltaire, I: Moeurs et Coutumes des Indiens (1777)*, ed. S. Murr (Paris, 1987), p. 183.
102 See, e.g., *TB*, p. 479; Duarte Barbosa, *The Book of Duarte Barbosa*, trans. and ed. M.L. Dames (London, 1918–21), I, pp. 180–1.
103 See the contributions by A. Soltani Gordfaramarzi, F. Viré, G. Douillet and D. Ayalon, under respectively 'Asp', in *EIr*; 'Faras' and 'Furusiyya' in *EI*.
104 *TSA*, pp. 51–3. This work is based on Hashimi's *Faras-nama* written in Gujarat in 1520. See also *FN*. For an extensive list, see C.A. Storey, *Persian Literature* (Leiden, 1977), II, 3, pp. 394–402.
105 Monserrate, *Commentary*, p. 86. For basic information on the Indian elephant, see the surveys under 'elephant' in G. Watt, *Dictionary of the Economic Products of India* (London, 1908), and E.G. Balfour, *The Cyclopaedia of India and of Eastern and Southern Asia* (London, 1885). See also R. Delort, *Les Éléphants, Piliers du Monde* (Paris, 1990).
106 See, e.g., the remark in *MU*, I, p. 82 [Persian text, II, p. 765].
107 Monserrate, *Commentary*, p.86.
108 Moosvi, *Economy*, p. 236.

109 Tavernier, *Travels*, I, p. 224. Hawkins tells us that the royal elephants ate as much as ten rupees every day in sugar, butter, grain and sugarcane ('Relations', p. 35).
110 *SJN*, pp. 201–4.
111 Tavernier, *Travels,* II, p. 206.
112 *AA*, I, pp. 124–5 [Persian text, I, p. 128]; Cf. *TJ*, I, p. 140.
113 J.H. van Linschoten, *Itinerario: Voyage ofte Schipvaert van J.H. van Linschoten naar Oost ofte Portugaels Indiën, 1579–1592*, eds. H. Kern and H. Terpstra (The Hague, 1955–7), I, p. 62; II, p. 56; Thévenot, 'Voyages', p. 77; Tavernier, *Travels*, I, p. 221; Bernier, *Travels*, p. 277.
114 P. van Dam, *Beschryvinge van de Oostindische Compagnie*, ed. F.W. Stapel (The Hague, 1932), II, 2, p. 405.
115 *Generale Missiven van Gouverneurs-Generaal en Raden aan Heren XVII der VOC*, eds W. Ph. Coolhaas, J. van Goor and J.E. Schooneveld-Oosterling (The Hague, 1960–97), VI, pp. 233, 253.
116 *AA*, I, pp. 295–6 [Persian text, I, p. 206]; *TJ*, II, pp. 4–5.
117 Hawkins, 'Relations', p. 36.
118 Moosvi, *Economy*, p. 237.
119 Digby estimates about one quarter of these to be actual war-elephants (Digby, *Warhorse and Elephant in the Delhi Sultanate* (Karachi, 1971), pp. 58–9.
120 Tavernier,*Travels*, I, p. 224.
121 Monserrate, *Commentary*, p. 85.
122 F. Edgerton, *The Elephant-lore of the Hindus: The Elephant-sport (Matanga-lila) of Nilakantha* (Delhi, 1985), p. 35.
123 Apart from Horn, *Heer- und Kriegswesen*, pp. 51–6, see Irvine, *Army*, pp. 175–81; Sarkar, *Military History*, pp. 163–8, and J.J.L. Gommans, 'Indian warfare and Afghan innovation during the eighteenth century', *Studies in History*, 11 (1995), p. 266–7. The latter three refer mainly to the eighteenth century.
124 Wink, *Al-Hind*, II, p. 95–110.
125 *AN*, II, p. 59; III, p. 176 [resp. Persian text, II, p. 36; III, p. 123]; *MT*, II, p. 7 [Persian text, II, p. 14]. See also the earlier Portuguese reports as mentioned in D.F. Lach, *Asia in the Making of Europe* (Chicago and London, 1994–8), I, 1, p. 399.
126 See, e.g., *AN*, III, p. 537 [Persian text, III, p. 365]. For rare examples of an elephant charges in Shah Jahan's reign, see *SJN*, pp. 108, 386.
127 Cf. P. Mason, *Matter of Honour: An Account of the Indian Army, its Officers and Men* (London, 1974), p. 44.
128 Khafi Khan, however, gives one instance in which a battle (near Golkonda) was won because horses threw off the riders in command following an encounter with an elephant (*ML*, p. 302 [Persian text, II, p. 298]).
129 For both these arguments, see Wink, *Al-Hind*, II, pp. 105–9.
130 W.E. Kaegi Jr, 'The contribution of archery to the Turkish conquest of Anatolia', *Speculum*, 39 (1964), pp. 96–108.
131 C.E. Bosworth, *The Ghaznavids: Their Empire in Afghanistan and Eastern Iran 994–1040* (Edinburgh, 1963), pp. 115–16.
132 Wink, *Al-Hind*, II, p. 99.
133 *AN*, II, p. 59 [Persian text, II, p. 36].
134 P. du Jarric, S.J., *Akbar and the Jesuits: An Account of the Jesuit Missions to the Court of Akbar by Father Pierre du Jarric, S.J.* trans. C.H. Payne (London, 1926), p. 7.
135 *AA*, I, p. 124 [Persian text, I, pp. 127–8]. This builds, however, on much earlier statements of Barani and Masudi (Wink, *Al-Hind*, II, p. 99). See also *SJN*, p. 100.

136 Geleynssen de Jongh, *Remonstrantie*, p. 51 (his *kokouanen* in Dutch are probably *kahak-banha* in Persian); Wouter Schouten, *Oost-Indische Voyagie* (Amsterdam, 1676), III, p. 90.
137 E.g. *SJN*, pp. 29, 59.
138 See the later French comments by Perrin, Dubois and Desvaulx in G. Deleury (ed.), *Indes Florissantes: Anthologie des Voyageurs Français (1750–1820)* (Paris, 1991), pp. 506–7, 551–4.
139 *SJN*, p. 123.
140 See also the reputed speed of Akbar's officer Nizam al-Din Ahmad's camel-corps (*MU*, II, p. 396 [Persian text, I, p. 662]).
141 R.W. Bulliet, *The Camel and the Wheel* (New York, 1990), pp. 141–75.
142 *AA*, I, p. 151 [Persian text, I, pp. 146–7].
143 Gommans, 'Indian warfare', pp. 275–7; Gommans, 'Silent frontier', pp. 10–12; I. Kölher-Rollefson, 'The one-humped camel in Asia: Origin, utilization and mechanism of dispersal', in D.R. Harris (ed.), *The Origins and Spread of Agriculture and Pastoralism in Eurasia* (London, 1996), pp. 288–9.
144 S. Westphal-Hellbusch and H. Westphal, *Zur Geschichte und Kultur der Jat* (Berlin, 1968), pp. 144–5.
145 S. Westphal-Hellbusch and H. Westphal, *Hinduistischer Viehzüchter im Nordwestlichen Indien, II: Die Bharwad und die Charan* (Berlin, 1976), pp. 103–23; H. Tambs-Lyche, *Power, Profit and Poetry: Traditional Society in Kathiawar, Western India* (Delhi, 1997).
146 *AA*, I, pp. 155–6 [Persian text, I, pp. 149–50].
147 Bernier, *Travels*, p. 217. See also Tavernier, *Travels*, II, p. 211.
148 Gommans, 'Indian warfare', pp. 276–7.
149 Tavernier, *Travels*, I, p. 33.
150 Tavernier, *Travels*, I, p. 36; Thévenot, 'Voyages', p. 88.
151 Pieter van den Broecke, *Pieter van den Broecke in Azië*, ed. W. Ph. Coolhaas (The Hague, 1962), I, p. 151.
152 Gommans, 'Silent frontier', pp. 10–13.

Chapter Five

1 J. Black, *War and the World: Military Power and the Fate of Continents 1450–2000* (New Haven and London, 1998), pp. 10–11.
2 M. Roberts, *The Military Revolution 1560–1660* (Belfast, 1956). See also J. Black, *A Military Revolution? Military Change and European Society* (London, 1991).
3 G. Parker, *The Military Revolution: Military Innovation and the Rise of the West 1500–1800* (Cambridge, 1988), p. 136. Parker made an exception for the Far East.
4 M.G.S. Hodgson, *The Venture of Islam, III: The Gunpowder Empires and Modern Times* (Chicago, 1974); W.H. McNeil, *The Pursuit of Power: Technology, Armed Forces and Society since AD 1000* (Chicago, 1982); Interview with William H. McNeill, *The Historian*, 53 (1990), pp. 1–16.
5 D. Ayalon, *Gunpowder and Firearms in the Mamluk Kingdom: A Challenge to Medieval Society* (London, 1956).
6 Inalcik, 'Military and fiscal transformation'.
7 B. Stein, 'State formation and economy reconsidered', *Modern Asian Studies*, 19 (1985), pp. 387–413. Apart from gunpowder, Stein also mentions the state's need to purchase warhorses.
8 Streusand, *Formation*, pp. 63–9.
9 Streusand, *Formation*, p. 69.

10 Cited in V. Narayana Rao, D. Shulman and S. Subrahmanyam, *Symbols of Substance: Court and State in Nayaka Period Tamilnadu* (Delhi, 1992), pp. 92–3.
11 *Md*, pp. 264–5.
12 J.R. Hale, 'To fortify or not to fortify? Machiavelli's contribution to a Renaissance debate', in H.C. Davis *et al.* (eds), *Essays in Honour of John Humphreys Whitfield* (London, 1975), pp. 99–119.
13 *TSS,* p. 761. Sarwani adds another road going from Lahore to Multan. Cf. *MT,* I, pp. 472–3 [Persian text, I, pp. 363–4]. Bada'uni mentions only the northern and southern route, replacing Burhanpur with Mandu (*MT*, I, p. 472).
14 *TSS*, p. 768.
15 *Ap*, pp. 219–20.
16 *TSS*, p. 764.
17 *KA*, II, pp. 56, 61; Cf. *KA*, III, p. 244.
18 *TSS*, pp. 538, 763.
19 *AN,* III, pp. 520–1 [Persian text, III, p. 355]. *Barzakh* also translates as 'interval' or, more appropriate in this case, 'a connecting link'.
20 *BN*, p. 334
21 Manucci, *Storia*, II, p. 418–19.
22 Scharfe, *State in Indian Tradition*, p. 201.
23 *Ap*, p. 222.
24 Six years later the outer walls were still under construction when the Marathas raided the city again. A detailed eighteenth-century map of Surat, showing the citadel and the two outer rings surrounding the city, is provided by Gole, *Indian Maps*, pp. 164–5.
25 This was part of their 'iconoclastic' policies in the hills of Bundelkhand and Garhwal. See, e.g., *SJN*, p. 289.
26 See, e.g., *TSS*, 258–1, 265; and the astute comments by Modave, *Voyage en Inde*, pp. 145–6.
27 Manucci, *Storia*, II, p. 419.
28 Narayana Rao, *et al.*, *Symbols of Substance*, pp. 82–112; 226–36. The laudatory assessment of south Indian forts in the early-seventeenth-century accounts of de Coutre and da Costa contrasts sharply with the negative evaluation in the late-seventeenth-century account of Manucci (Manucci, *Storia*, III, p. 461). For the importance of forts in Maratha landlordism, see S. Gordon, 'Forts and social control in the Marathi state', *Modern Asian Studies*, 13, 1 (1979), pp.1–17.
29 F.X. Wendel, *Les Mémoires de Wendel sur les Jats, les Pathan et les Sikh*, ed. J. Deloche (Paris, 1979), p. 9 (my translation).
30 See e.g. P. Jackson, *The Delhi Sultanate: A Political and Military History* (Cambridge, 1999), pp. 197–200.
31 The best recent survey is provided by P.E. Chevedden, Zvi Schiller, S.R. Gilbert and D.J. Kagay, 'The traction trebuchet: A triumph of four civilizations', *Viator,* 31 (2000), pp. 433–86. For the trebuchet in China, see J. Needham and R.D.S. Yates, *Science and Civilisation in China, V: Chemistry and Chemical Technology, Part 4: Military Technology: Missiles and Sieges* (Cambridge, 1994), pp. 203–40; for the Middle East, see D.R. Hill, 'Trebuchets', *Viator,* 4 (1973), pp. 99–115; and under the heading 'hisar', in *EI*; for India, see several references in *KF*, pp. 39, 40, 48, 53, 62, 65–8, 89 and *TFS*, pp. 165, 172, 174–5, 191, 202, 231.
32 *SJN*, 119.
33 *KF*, p. 65.
34 'Hisar', in *EI.*

35 Iqtidar Alam Khan, 'Coming of gunpowder to Islamic world and North India: Spotlight on the role of the Mongols', *Journal of Asian History*, 30, 1 (1996), pp. 27–45. For a survey of the available siege weaponry during the Delhi sultanate, see Ali Athar, 'Siege craft techniques of the Delhi sultans during 13th & 14th century', *Proceedings of the Indian History Conference* (1990), pp. 217–26.

36 Information on Indian forts has been gathered from various studies on specific forts. Of a more general nature are: S. Toy, *The Strongholds of India* (London, 1957) and its review by J. Burton-Page, 'A study of fortification in the Indian sub-continent from the thirteenth to the eighteenth century AD', *Bulletin of the School of Oriental and African Studies,* 23.3 (1960), pp. 508–22. Also of more general interest is P.V. Begde, *Forts and Palaces of India* (New Delhi, 1982). Paving the way for southern India is Jean Deloche, 'Études sur les fortifications de l'Inde, I: Les fortifications de l'Inde ancienne', *Bulletin de l'École française d'Extrême-Orient,* 79 (1992), pp. 89–131; and 'Études sur les fortifications de l'Inde, II: Les monts fortifiés du Maisur méridional (1re partie)', *Bulletin de l'École Française d'Extrême-Orient,* 81 (1994), pp. 219–66.

37 See, e.g., H. Kennedy, *Crusader Castles* (Cambridge, 1994), pp. 180–5.

38 R. Hillenbrand, 'Turco-Iranian elements in the medieval architecture of Pakistan: The case of the Tomb of Rukn-i Alam at Multan', *Muqarnas*, 9 (1991), pp. 148–74. A. Welch, 'Architectural patronage and the past: The Tughluq sultans of India', *Muqarnas,* 10 (1993), pp. 311–21.

39 M. Shokoohy and N. Shokoohy, 'Tughluqabad, the earliest surviving town of the Delhi sultanate', *Bulletin of the School of Oriental and African Studies*, 57, 3 (1994), pp. 516–50. See also by the same authors the fine study on Hisar: *Hisar-i Firuza: Sultanate and Early Mughal Architecture in the District of Hisar, India* (London, 1988).

40 Mate and Pathy, *Daulatabad*, p. 54.

41 On the Deccani forts we have the detailed studies of H. Cousens, *Bijapur and its Architectural Remains* (Bombay, 1916); H. Goetz, 'Purandhar, its monuments and their history', *Annals of the Bhandarkar Oriental Institute,* 30 (1949), pp. 215–37; G. Yazdani, *Bidar, its History and Monuments* (Oxford, 1974); Michell and Eaton, *Firuzabad*; Mate and Pathy, *Daulatabad.* For a more general survey, see M.S. Mate, 'Islamic architecture of the Deccan', *Bulletin of the Deccan College Research Institute,* 22 (1961–2), pp. 79–87 and, most recently, G. Michell and M. Zebrowski, *The New Cambridge History of India, I, 7: Architecture and Art of the Deccan Sultanate* (Cambridge, 1999), pp. 23–63.

42 *GI*, II, p. 303. Cf. Iqtidar Alam Khan, 'Origin and development of gunpowder technology in India: A.D. 1250–1500', *Indian Historical Review*, 4.1 (1977), pp. 26–7. This would be about thirty years after its first use in Europe in 1439 (C. Duffy, *Siege Warfare. The Fortress in the Early Modern World 1494–1660* (London, 1979), p.11).

43 *GI*, IV, pp. 56, 71. Since Firishta is a later source one should be careful with these references. For Gwalior, see Misra's account based on the equally late Tarikh-i Da'udi (B.D. Misra, *Forts and Fortresses of Gwalior and its Hinterland* (Delhi, 1993), p. 151).

44 *HA*, 58; *SJN*, 418, 433, 436.

45 *SJN*, p. 114. The technical terms in Persian have been checked with *PN* (I, p. 529).

46 Besides, Chitor was also taken by a Gujarati army in 1535, while Ranthambor's siege record is even less impressive, being taken as early as 1226 by Iltutmish and in 1254 by Balban.

47 *SJN*, pp. 47–8 (Daulatabad); 60–1 (Parenda); 70 (Kandahar); 79–80 (Bijapur). See also similar problems in Afghanistan (pp. 394–400; 491–3) and Garhwal (p. 153).

48 P.K. Datta, 'Impact of fire-arms on fort architecture in India in the Mughal period', *Bulletin of the Victoria Memorial*, 8 (1974), pp. 35–40.

49 R. Matthee, 'Unwalled cities and restless nomads: Firearms and artillery in Safavid Iran', in C. Melville (ed.), *Safavid Persia: The History and Politics of an Islamic Society* (London and New York, 1996), pp. 389–416.

50 Iqtidar Alam Khan: 'Origin and development', pp. 20–9; 'Early use of cannon and musket in India: AD 1442–1526', *Journal of Economic and Social History of the Orient*, 24 (1981), pp. 146–64; 'The nature of handguns in Mughal India: 16th and 17th centuries', *Proceedings of the Indian History Congress* (1992), pp. 378–389; 'Firearms in Central Asia and Iran during the fifteenth century and the origins and nature of firearms brought by Babur', *Proceedings of the Indian History Congress* (1995), pp. 435–46; 'Coming of gunpowder', pp. 27–45; 'The role of the Mongols in the introduction of gunpowder and firearms in South Asia', in B.J. Buchanan, *Gunpowder: The History of an International Technology* (Bath, 1996), pp. 33–45; 'The Indian response to firearms (1300–1750) (Presidential Address)', *Proceedings of the Indian History Congress* (1997), pp. 1–39; 'Nature of gunpowder artillery in India during the sixteenth century – a reappraisal of the impact of European gunpowder', *Journal of the Royal Asiatic Society*, 9 (1999), pp. 27–34.

51 For an elaboration of this distinction, see J. Needham *et al.*, *Science and Civilisation in China, V: Chemistry and Chemical Technology, Part 7: Military Technology: The gunpowder epic* (Cambridge, 1986), pp. 8–10.

52 Iqtidar Alam Khan is right to stress that the references to fifteenth-century firearms in the late-sixteenth-century and early-seventeenth-century sources, such as the *Tabaqat-i Akbari, Burhan-i Ma'asir, Tarikh-i Firishta* and *Mir'at-i Sikandari*, cannot be accepted at face value. However, his evidence for identifying *kaman-i rad* (literally, thunder-bow) with a true gun is equally inconclusive, since the context in which the term occurs in fifteenth-century texts is somewhat contradictory to say the least (Iqtidar Alam Khan, 'Early use', pp. 163–4; and 'Firearms in Central Asia', pp. 437–8), and could equally well refer to some kind of crossbow shooting fire-arrows (*tir-i atish*), a view supported by Iqtidar Alam Khan in 1977 ('Origin', p. 27). The conclusive evidence for Iqtidar Alam Khan is provided by Mir Khwand's *Rauzat al-Safa* in which a *rekhtagar* is mentioned. Following an eighteenth-century (!) lexicographer, Alam defines the term as 'one who melts brass, glass and similar other materials and pours it into moulds to make vessels or wares' (Iqtidar Alam Khan, 'Firearms in Central Asia', p. 438). Given the rapid change of the meaning of words connected with weaponry, it is strange to use an eighteenth-century definition for a fifteenth-century text, the more so since it is hard to conceive how a gun could have fired a stone of 1,200 kg, which would be twice the size of the largest-calibre stone-throwing gun still extant, the Punbart von Steyr, with a bore of some 80 cm intended to throw a stone shot weighing 697 kg (B.S. Hall, *Weapons and Warfare in Renaissance Europe: Gunpowder, Technology, and Tactics* (Baltimore and London, 1997), p. 59). In this case, the weight of the stone would suggest a counterweight trebuchet. Obviously, some kind of metallurgy could also be involved in making the huge iron fire-arrows (similar to the all-iron crossbow bolt with fins, about two metres long, and probably designed to carry a fire cartridge) that were discovered in the thirteenth- and fourteenth-century fortress of Vladimir in eastern Russia but possibly had a Mongol origin (D. Nicolle, *Medieval Warfare Source Book, II: Christian Europe and its Neighbours* (London, 1996), p. 121). Again, *kaman-i rad* could be a true gun, but it could equally mean a machine to throw or launch incendiary arrows or grenades like the Chinese *huo pao* or the *kaman-i gaw* (literally, ox-bow) as mentioned by Juvaini (Cf. Iqtidar Alam Khan, 'Firearms in Central Asia', p. 38).

53 See, e.g., the references by Firishta who claims that it was introduced in the Deccan by the Bahmanis (*GI*, II, 192–3), and by Babur who mentions the reputation of the Bengalis in this regard (*BN(B)*, p. 672; Cf. *BN*, 437). See also Iqtidar Alam Khan, 'Origin and development', pp. 24–7.

54 For grenades and rockets in the Chinese context, see Needham, *Gunpowder Epic*, pp. 161–92, 509–525. For rocketry in India, see P.K. Datta, 'Use of "rockets" in warfare in Moghul India', *Bulletin of the Victoria Memorial Hall*, 1 (1967), pp. 47–56. For its introduction into Europe, see F.H. Winter, *The Golden Age of Rocketry* (Washington and London, 1990).

55 Cited in R. Daehnhardt, *The Bewitched Gun: The Introduction of the Firearm in the Far East by the Portuguese* (Lisbon, 1994), p.37.

56 Barbosa, *The Book of Duarte Barbosa*, pp. 175–7.

57 Varthema mentions artillery in Chaul (Ludovico de Varthema, *The Travels of Ludovico di Varthema*, trans. J. Winter Jones and ed. G.P. Badger (London, 1928), p. 47) and, somewhat later, Pires even mentions 'much artillery' in Gujarat (Tomé Pires, *The Suma Oriental of Tomé Pires, an Account of the East . . . Written in 1512–1515*, ed. and trans. A. Cortesão (London, 1944), I, p. 33.

58 Apart from the anachronistic references in some of the Indo-Persian sources, there is the early-fifteenth-century account of Nicolò Conti mentioning the use of bombardas (R. Elgood, *Firearms of the Islamic World in the Tareq Rajab Museum, Kuwait* (London and New York, 1995), p. 132), as well as the pictorial evidence, provided via S. Digby and P.K. Datta by Iqtidar Alam Khan, the first showing a cannon in a painting prepared during the reign of Sikandar Lodi (1489–1517), the second showing handguns in a picture ascribed to the fifteenth century (Iqtidar Alam Khan: 'Early use of cannon', p. 159; 'Nature of handguns', p. 380).

59 *BN*, p. 270.

60 *BN(B)*, pp. 473–4. Beveridge uses the original terminology, whereas Thackston gives the wrong translation (*BN*, p. 326). See article under 'Barud' by R.M. Savory in *EI*, I, p. 1066 and under 'Firearms' by R. Mathee in *EIr*, p. 623. For the battle of Jam (1528), where the Safavids confronted the Uzbeks, we find the same tactics and ordnance as used during Babur's battle of Panipat a few years earlier. Following the contemporary Persian chronicle *Ahsan al-Tawarikh,* we find Tahmasp stationing in front of his army the wagons containing *zarbzan* and *tup-i firangi*. For an analysis of the references in the *Baburnama*, see Iqtidar Alam Khan, 'Firearms in Central Asia', pp. 438–444, in particular endnotes 10 and 11.

61 See the article under 'Barud' by V.J. Parry in *EI*, I, p. 1063.

62 *TR*, p. 474. Obviously, eight pairs would not be able to move a 47.5-pounder, which would need at least 40–50 bullocks (Cf. Irvine, *Army*, p. 115).

63 *TR*, p. 480.

64 Iqtidar Alam Khan, 'Nature of gunpowder', p. 31. This would come close to Abul Fazl's *narnal*, which could be carried by a single man (*AA*, I, p. 119 [Persian text, I, p. 125]). See, however, the pictorial evidence presented by Datta indicating a much heavier, but relatively light mortar (P.K. Datta, 'Cannon in India during the Mughal days', *Bulletin of the Victoria Memorial Hall*, 3–4 (1969–70), p. 39 (figure 19).

65 M. Lowery, 'The rise and fall of Bahadur Shah: A translation from the *Lendas da India* of Gaspar Correia', *Portuguese Studies*, 6 (1990), p. 40.

66 *AN*, I, p. 302 [Persian text, I, p. 131]; *GI*, II, pp. 48, 76.

67 Like Babur at Panipat by one Mustafa Rumi, Bahadur Shah at Mandasor was advised by one Rumi Khan (Khudawand), who later deserted the Gujarati sultan for the Mughals. For the Indian demand for Rumi gunners, see also the travels of Sidi Ali Reis in India during the 1550s (*MM*, pp. 24ff.).

68 The Gujaratis captured many cannon from the Portuguese after their failed attempt to take Diu in 1531 (*GI*, IV, p. 74).

69 In his latest contribution Iqtidar Alam Khan suggests that, during the fifteenth century, European armies preferred wrought-iron guns over those cast in bronze, not only because wrought-iron was comparatively cheaper but also owing to the general impression that cast-bronze mortars were far less reliable ('Nature of gunpowder', pp. 29–30). Here, he refers to Cipolla who suggests, however, exactly the opposite: 'during the course of the fifteenth century preference was given to cast bronze guns. Wrought-iron guns continued to be made but were rightly considered poor artillery' (C.M. Cipolla, *Guns, Sails, and Empires. Technological Innovation and the Early Phases of European Expansion, 1400–1700* (New York, 1965), p. 29). Hall supports the fifteenth-century trend towards bronze ordnance by stating that 'forging gradually came to be used only for the medium and smaller pieces. Single-piece cast bronze guns must have been safer than forged guns, for the single-piece casting could better contain the forces generated by larger powder charges' (Hall, *Weapons*, p. 93). This again suggests that the early Mughal artillery was very much in line with the then-current European state of the gunfounder's art.

70 *MS*, pp. 369 [Persian text, p. 290].

71 Hall, *Weapons*, pp. 92–4. At this time, even the navy preferred copper guns (J. Glete, *Warfare at Sea 1500–1650: Maritime Conflicts and the Transformation of Europe* (London, 2000), p. 23.

72 Sarkar, *Military History*, p. 55.

73 Robert Orme, *The History of the Military Transactions of the British Nation in Indostan,* 2 vols (London, 1763) and *Historical Fragments of the Mogul Empire* (London, 1805). Orme's work is still very influential in Jagadish Narayan Sarkar's *The Art of War in Medieval India* (Delhi, 1984). Irvine's work is, of course, his *The Army of the Indian Moghuls*. For Bruce Lenman, see his 'The weapons of war in the 18th century', *Journal of the Society for Army Historical Research*, 46 (1968), pp. 33–43; and his 'The transition to European military ascendancy in India, 1600–1800' in J.A. Lynn (ed.), *Tools of War: Instruments, Ideas and Institutions of Warfare, 1445–1871* (Champaign, 1989), pp. 100–30. Unfortunately, in my earlier publications on the subject I also was too eager to adopt what seemed to be the common view.

74 *ARA*, *VOC* 1360, de Jager (and van Heusden) to Hartsinck, 12 February 1680, f. 1509v; François Martin, *Mémoires de François Martin, Fondateur de Pondichéry (1665–1694)* (Paris, 1934), III, p. 343. Modave and Cossigny in Deleury (ed.), *Indes Florissantes*, pp. 471–3. See, however, the more positive view of Terry ('Relation', p. 36).

75 J.W. Hoover, 'Indian saltpetre and world gunpowder production: The East India trade and the military revolution 1600–1865' (Paper for the conference on the new military history of South Asia, Wolfson College, Cambridge, 15–17 July 1997), p. 24.

76 Hall, *Weapons*, pp. 67–87; B.S. Hall, 'The corning of gunpowder and the development of firearms in the Renaissance', in B.J. Buchanan (ed.), *Gunpowder: The History of an International Technology* (Bath, 1996), pp. 87–121.

77 Om Prakash, *The Dutch East India Company and the Economy of Bengal, 1630–1720* (Princeton, 1985), pp. 58–60.

78 Based on the often contradictory information in Prakash, *Dutch East India Company*, p. 59; E.M. Jacobs, *Koopman in Azië: De Handel van de Verenigde Oost-Indische Compagnie tijdens de 18de Eeuw* (Zutphen, 2000), pp. 96–100; 'Saltpetre' in Watt, *Dictionary*; Hoover, 'Indian saltpetre', pp. 12–14; and M.A.G. de Jong, 'De salpeterhandel van de EIC en VOC 1700–1760' (unpublished MA thesis, Leiden University, 1995), pp. 8–11.

79 W.H. Moreland, *From Akbar to Aurangzeb: A Study in Indian Economic History* (Delhi, 1994), pp. 120–3; Prakash, *Dutch East India Company*, pp. 112–13.
80 Cossigny in Deleury, *Indes Florissantes*, p. 471.
81 D.F. Harding, *Smallarms of the East India Company 1600–1856, Vol. III: Ammunition and Performance* (London, 1999), p. 21. For the European process, see Hall, 'Corning', pp. 104–5.
82 Harding, *Smallarms*, pp. 44, 53, 64, 65.
83 Personal communication by J. Lenselink, 8 January 2001.
84 Harding, *Smallarms*, p. 64.
85 Harding, *Smallarms*, pp. 99, 377–8.
86 J.N. Sarkar, 'Saltpetre industry in India (in the 17th century)', *The Indian Historical Quarterly*, 14 (1938), pp. 680–91; J.N. Sarkar, 'Transport of saltpetre in India in the seventeenth century', *Journal of the Bihar and Orissa Research Society*, 25 (1939), pp. 34–51. Aurangzeb, first as governor of Gujarat then as emperor, prohibited the sale of saltpetre to the English and the Christians in 1646 and 1689 respectively.
87 Prakash, *Dutch East India Company*, p. 59.
88 De Jong, 'Salpeterhandel', pp. 46–52, 69–76.
89 Manucci, *Storia*, I, pp. 150–1. Terry, 'Relation', p. 36. Iqtidar Alam Khan claims without any further reference that these cannon were pre-Mughal ('Nature of gunpowder', p. 29).
90 Roe, *Embassy*, p. 68.
91 Thévenot, 'Voyages', p. 75. For the current practice under Babur, see *BN*, p. 362. See Irfan Habib's remarks in his 'Technology and barriers to social change in Mughal India', *Indian Historical Review*, 5 (1978–9), pp. 166–7; 'The technology and economy of Mughal India', *Indian Economic and Social History Review*, 17 (1980), pp. 16–21; 'Changes in technology in medieval India', *Studies in History*, 2 (1980), pp. 36–7. Habib's insights are more or less repeated in Iqbal G. Khan's 'Metallurgy in medieval India – the case of the iron cannon', *Proceedings of the Indian History Congress* (1984), pp. 464–71; and his 'Metallurgy in medieval India 16th to 18th centuries', in Aniruddha Roy and S.K. Bagchi (eds), *Technology in Ancient and Medieval India* (Delhi, 1986), pp. 71–91. Cf. A.J. Qaisar, *Indian Response to European technology and culture (AD 1497–1707)* (Delhi, 1982).
92 W.K.V. Gale, 'Ferrous metals', in I. McNeil (ed.), *An Encyclopaedia of the History of Technology* (London, 1990), pp. 146–160; R.F. Tylecote, *A History of Metallurgy* (London, 1992), pp. 75–95.
93 'Iron' in Watt, *Dictionary*, p. 504.
94 G. Juleff, 'An ancient wind-powered iron smelting technology in Sri Lanka', *Letters to Nature*, 379 (1996), pp. 60–63.
95 See, e.g., *MS*, 178.
96 A. Williams, 'Ottoman military technology: The metallurgy of Turkish armour', in Lev (ed.), *War and society in the Eastern Mediterranean, 7th–15th Centuries* (Leiden, 1997), pp. 367–71. See also his, *The Metallurgy of Muslim Armour* (*Seminar on Early Islamic Science, Monograph No. 3*) (Manchester, 1978). The most recent research suggests that Damascus steel could only be produced from ores that were contaminated by vanadium. See the report in *NRC Handelsblad* (11 September 1999, p. 53) which refers to the work of J.D. Verhoeven and A.H. Pendray (see, e.g., their and E.D. Gibson's 'Wootz Damascus steel blades', *Materials Characterization*, 37 (1996), pp. 9–22.
97 Probably, the Indian armies also continued to rely on stone shot, whereas the European armies shifted to iron shot as early as the sixteenth century. The French used cartridges and grapeshot as early as the 1670s. See, e.g., the

account of Abbé Carré about the fighting between the French and the army of Golkonda at São Tomé (Abbé Carré, *The Travels of the Abbé Carré in India and the Near East 1672 to 1674*, trans. Lady Fawcett and C. Fawcett (Delhi, 1990), II, pp. 442, 475, 498, 501).

98 Cipolla, *Guns, Sails*, p. 65.

99 W.H. Moreland, 'The ships of the Arabian Sea about A.D. 1500', *Journal of the Royal Asiatic Society* (1939), pp. 182–91.

100 *AA*, I, pp. 120–1 [Persian text, I, p. 125].

101 Based on Harding, *Smallarms*, p. 377; and Z. Zygulsky, 'Oriental and Levantine firearms', in C. Blaire (ed.), *Pollard's History of Firearms* (New York, 1973), p. 451. See also the remarks of Habib in his 'Technology and economy', p. 18. A beautifully illustrated recent survey of Indian smallarms is provided by Elgood, *Firearms*, pp. 129–87.

102 *AA*, I, p. 120 [Persian text, I, p. 125] (Cf. Irvine, *Army*, p. 103).

103 See, e.g., the exercise of Khan Zaman's infantry unit (*MU*, I, pp. 805–6 [Persian text, I, p. 888]).

104 See, e.g., the exercise of Skinner's Horse.

105 Tavernier, *Travels*, I, p. 127. See also the positive account by Bernier in his *Travels*, p. 254.

106 As cited by Habib in his 'Technology and economy', p. 17. It is not clear whether Manrique refers to the technical meaning of an arquebus, i.e. a light gun, or to long smallarms in general.

107 According to Elgood, introduced by the Portuguese as early as 1536 (*Firearms*, p. 134).

108 Daehnhardt, *Bewitched Gun*, pp. 49–60.

109 *AA*, I, p. 120 [Persian text, I, p. 125]. See also the remarks of Irfan Habib in which he rectifies his earlier view that this must be a wheel-lock ('Changes in technology', p. 36, footnote 121).

110 Harding, *Smallarms*, p. 205; See also under 'Flint' in Watt, *Dictionary*, p. 404.

111 *AA*, I, p. 119 [Persian text, I, p. 124].

112 For south India, see the contributions of Sanjay Subrahmanyam: 'The *Kagemusha* effect. The Portuguese, firearms and the state in early modern south India', *Moyen Orient et Océan Indien*, 4 (1987), pp. 97–123; 'Warfare and state finance in Wodeyar Mysore, 1724–25: A missionary perspective', *Indian Economic and Social History Review*, 26 (1989), pp. 203–33; and together with Narayana Rao and Shulman, 'The art of war under the Nayakas' in their *Symbols of Substance*, pp. 220–42.

113 See the various references in C. Oman, *The Art of War in the Sixteenth Century* (London, 1937), pp. 607–771. For the battle of Jam, see Matthee, 'Unwalled cities', p. 623. For Mughal India, see the next chapter.

114 *AN*, I, p. 302 [Persian text, I, p. 131]; *MS*, p. 284 [Persian text, p. 308]. See also the supposedly superior firepower of the Gujaratis at the battle of Mahmudabad in 1535 (*MS*, pp. 393 [Persian text, pp. 318–19]).

115 See, however, the comments by van den B[roek] (probably inspired by Mir Jumla), which may suggest a much earlier onset of change (*Curieuse Beschrijving*, p. 38).

116 Sarkar, *Military History*, p. 55. See also the drawings in Datta, 'Cannon in India'.

117 For the use of swivel-guns on the back of dromedaries and elephants, see Chapter 4.

118 In the Indo-Persian sources also mentioned with the adjective *-i rizah* (small), *-i jambishi* (movable); *-i jinsi* (miscellaneous). Sometimes, cannon on wheels is referred to as simply cart or carriage, i.e. *arada* or *rakala*.

119 Bernier, *Travels*, p. 218, 352. See also the similar account in Careri, 'Voyages', p. 295.

120 This appears to be the general message behind the somewhat confusing and exaggerated remarks in Richard Bell's account ('The travels of Richard Bell (and John Cambell) in the East Indies, Persia, and Palestine', *The Indian Antiquary*, 35 (1906), pp. 203–5. See also the views of Manuel Godinho (*Intrepid Itinerant*, p. 71) and the Abbé Carré (*Travels*, II, pp. 442, 455), which appear to represent the common European opinion (and prejudice) at that time (*c.* 1660).

121 Bernier, *Travels*, p. 217.

122 Hall, *Weapons*, p. 214.

123 See R. Muir, *Tactics and the Experience of Battle in the Age of Napoleon* (New Haven and London, 1998), p. 76.

124 Geleynssen de Jongh, *Remonstrantie*, p. 50 (my translation). See also similar remarks by Schouten, *Oost-Indische Voyagie,* III, p. 90; and van Twist, 'Generale beschrijvinge', p. 28.

125 Manucci, *Storia*, II, p. 115.

126 Manucci, *Storia*, III, pp. 377–8.

127 Carré, *Travels*, II, p. 500. See also similar remarks by the Abbé on pp. 454, 463, 621. Apart from employing pistols, grenades, petards and bayonets, 'to which these orientals were not accustomed' (p. 481), the French continued to rely on matchlocks (p. 442). In all these clashes, the numbers of the Golkonda army were much fewer than Carré wants them to be (p. 448).

128 Bernier, *Travels*, p. 217.

129 Based on Glete, *Warfare at Sea*, pp. 17–40. Here Glete gives an excellent summary of the earlier historiography dominated by scholars such as Cipolla, Guilmartin and Parker. See also the survey of P. Padfield, *Tide of Empires: Decisive Naval Campaigns in the Rise of the West, I: 1481–1654* (London, 1979), pp. 42–74.

130 The main exception being the defeat of the Portuguese by the combined Mamluk–Gujarati fleet at Chaul in 1507 (M. Longworth Dames, 'The Portuguese and Turks in the Indian Ocean in the sixteenth century', *Journal of the Royal Asiatic Society* (1921), pp. 1–28).

131 Although the nomenclature of Indian ships is complicated by different regional traditions of shipbuilding, the, at times, sloppy transliterations and translations of Persian texts makes it even more difficult to recognise certain models. In general, however, Indian warshipping closely followed the Mediterranean tradition: the European *galley* corresponding to the Ottoman *qadirgha*, the Indo-Persian *jaliya* and the Marathi *galbat*; the European *galleass* corresponding to the Ottoman *mavna* or the larger *bastarda*, the Indo-Persian *ghurab*, and the Marathi *gurab* or the larger *pal*. (Compare Glete, *Warfare at Sea*, pp. 17–40; S. Soucek, 'Certain types of ships in Ottoman-Turkish terminology', *Turcica*, 7 (1975), pp. 233–49; A.J. Qaisar, 'Shipbuilding in the Mughal Empire during the seventeenth century', *The Indian Economic and Social History Review*, 5, 2 (1968), pp. 149–170; B.K. Apte, *A History of the Maratha Navy and Merchantships* (Bombay, 1973), pp. 119–40.)

132 See, e.g., the Portuguese ships mentioned by Georg Christoph Fernberger in his *Reisetagebuch (1588–1593) Sinai, Babylon, Indien, Heiliges Land, Osteuropa*, translated into German by R. Burger and R. Wallisch (Frankfurt am Main, 1999); and also, for the later period, della Valle, *Travels*, I, p. 387. For the most recent studies on Indian and Indo-Portuguese shipbuilding, see R.J. Barendse, 'Shipbuilding in seventeenth-century western India', *Itinerario*, 19, 3 (1995), pp. 175–196; and K.S Mathew, *Ship-building and Navigation in the Indian Ocean Region* AD *1400–1800* (Delhi, 1997).

133 Glete, *Warfare at Sea*, pp. 76–93, 165–86. See also A. Deshpande, 'Limitations of military technology: Naval warfare on the west coast, 1650–1800', *Economic and Political Weekly* (25 April 1992), pp. 900–2. Still useful for the early period is Moreland, 'Ships of the Arabian Sea'.

134 Perhaps, the stereo-typical Hindu taboo against sea voyages may also be related to the positive trade balance of the sub-continent. Although the textual evidence appears to support a growing taboo from the early medieval period onwards (see L. Gopal, 'Indian shipping in early mediaeval period', in V.L. Chandra (ed.) *India's Contribution to World Thought and Culture* (Madras, 1970), pp. 108–22), numerous Hindu merchants and traders crossed the Indian Ocean without any feelings of guilt or embarrassment. Similarly, the laissez-faire attitude of the Mughals does not mean that Mughal *mansabdars* were not involved in overseas trade and shipping. In fact, the study of Om Prakash shows the contrary (*Dutch East India Company*). Like the emperors, the Mughal mansabdars played their continental cards to secure their overseas interests.

135 In a rather brief discussion of the Mughal admiralty, Abul Fazl focuses on peaceful transport, making a special case for Turkey, Zanzibar and Europe where ships are used as excellent means of conquest (*AA*, I, 289 [Persian text, I, p. 202]). See also Manucci's account of Mughal weakness at sea (*Storia*, II, p. 42) and Khafi Khan disqualifying European land forces (*ML*, pp. 401 [Persian text, pp. 402–3])

136 S. Digby, 'Beyond the ocean: Perceptions of overseas in Indo-Persian sources of the Mughal period', *Studies in History*, 15, 2 (1999), pp. 249–50.

137 *ML*, pp. 401–2 [Persian text, p. 403].

138 Unfortunately, there is no modern study on the Sidis. Somewhat better studied are their eighteenth-century rivals, the so-called Angrias based in Kolaba and Vijayadurg, but their history is beyond the focus of the present study. For the possibilities offered by the Dutch archival material, see H.C.M. van de Wetering, 'De VOC en de kapers van Angria. Een expeditie naar de westkust van India in 1739', *Tijdschrift voor Zeegeschiedenis*, 10, 2 (1991), pp. 117–130.

139 See, e.g., the remarks of Mirza Nathan (*BG*, I, pp. 43, 148).

140 According to Abul Fazl's statistics, Bengal is the only province which supports not only foot-soldiers, horses and elephants, but also guns and boats (*AA*, II, p. 141 [Persian text, I, p. 393]).

141 *ML*, p. 191 [Persian text, p. 188].

142 R.D. Mookerji, *Indian Shipping: A History of the Sea-borne Trade and Maritime Activity of the Indians from the Earliest Times* (London, 1912), pp. 147–78; A.C. Roy, *A History of Mughal Navy and Naval Warfares* (Calcutta, 1972), pp. 52–71.

143 The ratio between *ghurabs*, *jalyas* (note that all translations give *jalba* instead of *jaliya*) and *kosas* was about 1:5:8. According to the *Fathiya-i Ibriya* of Shihab al-Din Talish (trans. J. Sarkar, *Studies in Aurangzeb's Reign* (Calcutta, 1933), p. 188) the Luso-Arakanese fleet in Chittagong consisted of 100 *jaliyas*. The remainder of the Chittagong fleet captured by the Mughals in 1666 consisted of 9 *ghurabs*, 67 *jalbas* and only 12 *kosas*, which number makes plausible the (*c*.) 200 galleys mentioned by Tavernier, as his galleys would probably include the *ghurabs* and the *jaliyas*. (*Travels*, I, pp. 105–6). The Mughal fleet in 1666 consisted of 21 *ghurabs*, 96 *jalyas* and 157 *kosas*. Cf. the fleet of Mir Jumla to Assam in the 1660s, which numbered 10 *ghurabs*, 48 *jalyas* and 159 *kosas*. Obviously, the Assamese waters required a relatively large number of the smaller *kosas*, although the ratio of about 1:5 between *ghurabs* and *jalyas* was maintained.

144 Sarkar, *Studies in Aurangzeb's Reign*, p. 180

145 This is in agreement with Roy's reading of the main Persian accounts (Roy, *Mughal Navy*, pp. 71–134).

146 For the Chittagong campaign, see the translated extracts of the *Fathiya-i Ibriya* in Sarkar, *Studies in Aurangzeb's Reign,* pp. 165–213. For the earlier road-building activities, see also *BG*, I, pp. 52, 61–2, 99, 107–9. According to Abul Fazl such an embanked road or *al* (from Sanskrit *ali*) had given Beng*al* its proper name (*AA*, II, p. 132 [Persian text, I, p. 388]).

Chapter Six

1 Mainly based on the contemporary account of Mirza Nathan (*BG*, I, 1–223) and the summary of events given in J. Sarkar (ed.) *The History of Bengal: Muslim Period 1200–1757* (Patna, 1973), pp. 234–88.

2 H. Blochmann, 'Contributions to the geography and history of Bengal (Muhammadan period), Part I', *Journal of the Asiatic Society of Bengal*, 42 (1873), p. 216.

3 H. Hosten, 'Jesuit letters from Bengal, Arakan and Burma (1599–1600)', *Bengal: Past and Present*, 30 (1925), p. 64.

4 *MU*, I, p. 693 [Persian text, I, p. 120]. On the Chishtis, see also Husain, *Nobility*, pp. 116–27, and E.B. Findly, *Nur Jahan: Empress of Mughal India* (New York and Oxford, 1993), pp. 187–91.

5 For example, Mirza Nathan himself became a personal *murid* of Jahangir after the latter was informed that he had cured the Mirza from an illness after appearing to him in a dream (*BG*, I, pp. 17, 74). See also Richards, 'Formulation', pp. 270–77.

6 *BG*, I, p. 97.

7 Many districts in Bengal have the Persian word *bazu*, literally 'arm' or 'wing', in their names, again indicating a network pattern of roads or rivers branching off.

8 *BG*, I, pp. 12–3. They also received jagirs in and around Midnapur in Orissa, again very much to be conquered, as appears from the zamindari 'revolt' in the area in 1611–12 (*BG*, I, p. 139).

9 *BG*, I, pp. 27–8.

10 *BG*, I, p. 57 (see also Sarkar (ed.), *History of Bengal*, p. 201). Ghoraghat was one of the first Muslim outposts in Bengal. During the reign of Muhammad Bakhtyar, in the early thirteenth century, it was already the main eastern frontier district under Ali Mardan Khilji. Later it became an important Muslim settlement mainly of Afghans and Qaqshal Turks. The area was also closely associated with the late-fifteenth-century saint Shah Isma'il Ghazi (G. Damont, 'Notes on Shah Isma'il Ghazi', *Journal of the Asiatic Society of Bengal* (1874), p. 215). It had also been a monsoon station of Raja Man Singh in 1596.

11 *BG*, I, pp. 34–5.

12 *BG*, I, pp, 28, 56.

13 *BG*, I, pp. 48–9.

14 *BG*, I, pp. 62, 66.

15 *BG*, I, pp. 64, 68, 82, 83.

16 *BG*, I, pp. 107–9.

17 *BG*, I, pp. 111–17.

18 *BG*, I, pp. 150–4.

19 It is possible that Jahangir's decision was prompted by Nur Jahan and her family who were ill disposed towards the Chishtis. See Husain, *Nobility*, pp. 120–1, and Findly, *Nur Jahan*, p. 211.

20 *BG*, I, pp. 173–90. See also *TJ*, I, pp. 208–15. For an Afghan perspective in which Usman's brother Khwaja Wali is accused of being secretly in league with Islam Khan, see B. Dorn, *History of the Afghans* (London, 1965), II, pp. 115–18.
21 Sarkar (ed.), *History of Bengal*, pp. 283–4.
22 Eaton, *Rise of Islam*, p. 151.
23 Mainly based on *PN*, II, pp. 449–709; *SJN*, pp. 329–403; and A. Burton, *The Bukharans: A Dynastic, Diplomatic and Commercial History 1550–1702* (Richmond, Surrey, 1997), pp. 213–64. Apart from the main Mughal ones, the latter uses various Russian and Central Asian sources.
24 Foltz, *Mughal India*, pp. 127–47.
25 By using the term Uzbek I am following current usage, although it is somewhat misleading as it actually refers to the non-Chingizid members of those Turko-Mongol tribal groupings who performed military and administrative functions but were not agnatic descendants of Chinggis Khan. Hence, it would be more proper to speak of the Tuqay-Timurid dynasty, after one of Chinggis Khan's grandsons Toqay-Timur (R.D. McChesney, *Waqf in Central Asia. Four Hundred Years in the History of a Muslim Shrine, 1480–1889* (Princeton, 1991), pp. 49–50).
26 *PN*, II, pp. 462–3.
27 *PN*, II, pp. 510–36.
28 *MU*, I, pp. 186–94 [Persian text, II, pp. 795–807].
29 Dadvar, *Iranians*, pp. 114–16.
30 *MU*, I, pp. 340–8 [Persian text, I, pp. 415–24].
31 *MU*, II, pp. 541–4 [Persian text, III, pp. 92–5].
32 *MU*, II, pp. 625–30 [Persian text, II, pp. 270–6].
33 *MU*, I, pp. 295–9 [Persian text, I, pp. 167–72].
34 *MU*, II, pp. 767–70 [Persian text, II, pp. 670–6].
35 *MU*, II, pp. 637–44 [Persian text, II, pp. 441–9].
36 Richards, *Mughal Empire*, p. 133.
37 *SJN*, pp. 336, 339–40.
38 *PN*, II, pp. 527–40, 549–54, as summarised in *SJN*, pp. 345–51.
39 Burton, *Bukharans*, pp. 238–9.
40 *SJN*, p. 351.
41 It is certainly possible that the coming birth of a child played an important role in Murad Bakhsh's eagerness to go home. On 12 August 1646 his son Sultan Muhammad Yar was born.
42 *PN*, II, pp. 614–24; *SJN*, 359–62, 366–70.
43 Burton, *Bukharans*, p. 246.
44 See, e.g., *SJN*, p. 441.
45 *SJN*, p. 391. For the various battles fought by Aurangzeb around Balkh, see *PN*, II, pp. 665–702, as summarised in *SJN*, pp. 382–92.
46 Burton, *Bukharans*, p. 250.
47 Actually, to soothe the Mughals he had sent his grandson Muhammad Qasim – the son of Khusrau who had already submitted to the Mughals at an earlier stage – to the Mughal camp instead (*SJN*, p. 399).
48 Usually, the Uzbek campaigns south of the Amu Darya waited for the spring, when there would be sufficient grazing for the horses (Burton, *Bukharans*, p. 255).
49 Burton, *Bukharans*, p. 254.
50 Gommans, *Indo-Afghan Empire*, pp. 45–66.
51 Mainly based on the primary accounts of *TD*, pp. 171–216 and Martin, *Mémoires*, III, pp. 125–310; as well as the detailed secondary accounts of: Rao

Bahadur and C.S. Srinivasachari, *A History of Gingee and its Rulers* (Annamalainagar, 1943), pp. 286–351; Sarkar, *Aurangzeb*, V, pp. 50–109; G.T. Kulkarni, *The Mughal–Maratha Relations: Twenty-five Fateful Years (1682–1707)* (Pune, 1983), pp. 89–188.

52 Richards, *Mughal Empire*, pp. 223–4.

53 *TD*, p. 223.

54 H. Heras, 'The city of Jinji at the end of the sixteenth century', *Indian Antiquary*, 54 (1925), pp. 41–3; Philippus Baldaeus, *Nauwkeurige Beschryvinge van Malabar en Choromandel* (Amsterdam, 1672), p. 157–8.

55 Richards, *Mughal Empire*, pp. 229–30; Subrahmanyam, 'Reflections' pp. 393–4.

56 The description of Gingee fort is mainly based on Toy, *Strongholds of India*, pp. 11–15; G. Michell, 'Courtly architecture at Gingee under the Nayakas', *South Asian Studies*, 7 (1991), pp. 143–60; G. Michell, *The New Cambridge History of India, I, 6: Architecture and Art of Southern India* (Cambridge, 1995), pp. 124–5; S. Subrahmanyam, 'Friday's child: Or how Tej Singh became Tecinkurajan', *The Indian Economic and Social History Review*, 36, 1 (1999), pp. 76–80. See also the published, contemporary sources under note 54. The latest contribution is by J. Deloche, *Senji (Gingi): Ville Fortifiée du Pays Tamoul* (Paris and Pondichéry, 2000).

57 *ARA*, *VOC* 1486, 'Report of the Company's Brahmin Kistnaja about his activities concerning the Mughal commander-in-chief (Sept.–Oct. 1690)', ff. 336–7; The Dutch report compares well with that of Martin (*Mémoires*, III, pp. 125–7).

58 In 1694, Shahaji of Tanjavur was compelled to promise an annual tribute of 3,000,000 rupees to the Mughal government (Sarkar, *Aurangzeb*, V, p. 81)

59 In Baldaeus' account (*c.* 1660) Gingee itself was equipped with only a few pieces of cannon, which were made of broad bars of iron held together with iron hoops and fired *stone* balls (Baldaeus, *Nauwkeurige Beschryvinge*, pp. 157–8).

60 See Martin, *Mémoires*, III, pp. 285–8. According to another rumour, Zulfiqar Khan had a secret understanding with Muhammad Azam Shah, an elder son of Aurangzeb who did not want his brother Kam Bakhsh to attract the emperor's favourable attention (*MN*, p. 161).

61 *TD*, p. 208. Bhimsen specifically refers to Shaista Khan when fighting Shivaji, but the argument remains valid afterwards. See also Manucci, *Storia*, II, p. 296.

62 *TD*, p. 207. Although the latter citation refers to a specific situation, it is used by Bhimsen to illustrate common practice.

63 Gordon, *Marathas*, pp. 98–9.

64 Martin, *Mémoires*, III, p. 271; translation adopted from L. Varadarajan, *India in the Seventeenth Century (Social, Economic and Political): Memoirs of François Martin (1670–1694)* (Delhi, 1985), II, 2, pp. 1472–3.

65 See, e.g., the defeats of Ali Mardan Khan at Conjeveram in 1692 and Qasim Khan at Dodderi in 1695.

66 *MU*, I, pp. 536, 796 [resp. Persian text, III, p. 9; I, p. 718].

67 Manucci, *Storia*, III, p. 480.

68 See the interesting notes by Bhimsen on the infantry tactics at the Malabar Coast (*TD*, p. 196).

Conclusion and epilogue

1 Translated from Rock Edict XIII as cited by A.L. Basham, *The Wonder that was India: A Survey of the Culture of the Indian Sub-continent Before the Coming of the Muslims* (London, 1954), p. 54. For the Sanskrit terminology, I have

used U. Schneider, *Die Großen Felsen-edikte Asokas: Kritische Ausgabe, Übersetzung und Analyse der Texte* (Wiesbaden, 1978), pp. 118–19. For an illuminating analysis of these edicts, see G. Fussman, 'Central and provincial administration in ancient India: The problem of the Mauryan Empire', *The Indian Historical Review*, 14 (1987–9), pp. 43–72.

2 The term 'regional centralisation' derives from M. Alam and S. Subrahmanyam, *The Mughal State 1526–1750* (Delhi, 1998), pp. 46–55.

3 The eighteenth-century developments deserve a separate book or even library. This summary of the technological aspects is primarily based on the contributions by Pemble, Cooper and Wagle, Gordon, and Lafont (J. Pemble, 'Resources and techniques in the second Maratha war', *The Historical Journal*, 19 (1976), pp. 375–404; R.G.S. Cooper and N.K. Wagle, 'Maratha artillery: From Dabhoi to Assaye', *Journal of the Ordnance Society*, 7 (1995), pp. 58–78; S. Gordon, 'The limited adoption of European-style military forces by eighteenth century rulers in India', *The Indian Economic and Social History Review*, 35 (1998), pp. 229–45; J.-M. Lafont, 'Observations on the French military presence in the Indian states 1750–1849', in K.S. Mathew and S. Jelaseela Stephen (eds), *Indo-French Relations* (Delhi, 1999), pp. 199–234; J-M. Lafont, 'Benoît de Boigne in Hindustan: His impact on the Doab, 1784–1795', in J-M. Lafont, *Indika: Essays in Indo-French Relations 1630–1976* (Delhi, 2000), pp. 177–204). In particular Cooper marginalises the technological influence of Europe, whereas Gordon and Lafont stress the European impact on weaponry, organisation and tactics.

4 For the garrison state, see D.M. Peers, *Between Mars and Mammon: Colonial Armies and the Garrison State in India 1819–35* (London, 1995). Cf. S. Alavi, *Sepoys and the Company: Traditions and Transition in Northern India 1770–1830* (Delhi, 1995).

5 Kolff, D.H.A., 'The end of an *ancien régime*: Colonial war in India, 1798–1818', in J.A. de Moor and H.L. Wesseling (eds), *Imperialism and War: Essays on Colonial Wars in Asia and Africa* (Leiden, 1989), pp. 45–6.

6 Cited by M. Glover in *Wellington as Military Commander* (London, 2001), p. 234.

Bibliography

Abbas Khan Sarwani, *Tarikh-i-Ser Sahi*, trans. B.P. Ambashthya (Patna, 1974).

Abdul Aziz, *The Imperial Treasury of the Indian Mughuls* (Lahore, 1942).

Abdul Aziz, *The Mansabdari System and the Mughal Army* (Lahore, 1945).

Abdul Hamid Lahauri, *Padshahnama*, eds Maulawis Kabir al-Din Ahmad and Abdul Rahim, 2 vols (Calcutta, 1866–72).

Abdulla Khan, *Tarjumah-i Salawtar-i Asban: Die Pferdeheilkunde des Abdullah Khan Emir am Hofe des Großmoguls*, trans. S. Oloff, from the English version by J. Earles (Munich, 1981).

Abul Fazl Allami, *The A-in-i Akbari*, trans. H. Blochmann and H.S. Jarrett, 2nd rev. ed. D.C. Phillott and J. Sarkar, 3 vols (New Delhi, reprint, 1989; first published 1927–49). Persian text ed. H. Blochmann, 2 vols (Calcutta, 1872–7).

Abul Fazl Allami, *The Akbarnama of Abul Fazl*, trans. H. Beveridge, 3 vols (Delhi, reprint, 1989–93; first published 1902–21). Persian text ed. Maulawi Abdul Rahim, 3 vols (Calcutta, 1875–86).

Ahmad, A., 'The British Museum Mirzanama and the seventeenth century mirza in India', *Iran*, 13 (1975).

Alam, M., 'State building under the Mughals: Religion, culture and politics', *Cahier d'Asie Centrale*, 3–4 (1997).

Alam, M., 'The pursuit of Persian: Language in Mughal politics', *Modern Asian Studies*, 32 (1998).

Alam, M. and S. Subrahmanyam, 'L'État moghol et sa fiscalité, xvie–xviiie siècles', *Annales* (1994).

Alam, M. and S. Subrahmanyam (eds), *The Mughal State 1526–1750* (Delhi, 1998).

Alam, M. and S. Subrahmanyam, 'Empiricism of the heart: Close encounters in an eighteenth-century Indo-Persian text', *Studies in History*, 15 (1999).

Alavi, R.A., 'New light on Mughal cavalry', in *Medieval India, a Miscellany*, 2 (1972).

Alavi, S., *Sepoys and the Company: Traditions and Transition in Northern India 1770–1830* (Delhi, 1995).

Ali Athar, 'Siege craft techniques of the Delhi sultans during 13th & 14th century', *Proceedings of the Indian History Conference* (1990).

Althof, G., *Spielregeln der Politik im Mittelalter: Kommunikation in Frieden und Fehde* (Darmstadt, 1997).

Amir Khusrau, *The Campaigns of Ala'ud-din Khilji Being the Khaza'inul Futuh (Treasures of Victory) of Hazrat Amir Khusrau of Delhi*, trans. M. Habib (Madras, 1931).

(Amir Muhammad Sami Ganj Ali Khan) *Tadhkirat al-Muluk: A Manual of Safavid Administration*, trans. and ed. V. Minorsky (Cambridge, 1980).

Apte, B.K., *A History of the Maratha Navy and Merchantships* (Bombay, 1973).
Archer, M. and T. Falk, *The Passionate Quest: The Fraser Brothers in India* (London: 1989).
Arlinghaus, J., 'The transformation of Afghan tribal society: Tribal expansion, Mughal imperialism and the Roshaniyya insurrection, 1450–1600' (Unpublished Ph.D. thesis, Duke University, 1988).
Asher, C., 'Mughal sub-imperial patronage: The architecture of Raja Man Singh' in B. Stoler Miller (ed.), *The Powers of Art: Patronage in Indian Culture* (Delhi, 1992).
Athar Ali, M., *The Apparatus of Empire: Awards of Ranks, Offices and Titles to the Mughal Nobility (1574–1658)* (Delhi, 1985).
Athar Ali, M., *The Mughal Nobility under Aurangzeb* (Delhi, 1997, rev. ed.).
Aubin, J., 'Réseau pastoral et réseau caravanier. Les grands routes du Khurasan a l'époque Mongole', *Le Monde Iranien et l'Islam*, 1 (1971).
Ayalon, D., *Gunpowder and Firearms in the Mamluk Kingdom: A Challenge to Medieval Society* (London, 1956).
(Baba Shah Musafir), *Sufis and Soldiers in Awrangzeb's Deccan: Malfuzat-i Naqshbandiyya*, trans. S. Digby (Oxford, 2001).
Babur, *Babur-Nama*, trans. by A.S. Beveridge (Delhi, reprint, 1989; first published 1921).
Babur, *The Baburnama: Memoirs of Babur, Prince and Emperor*, trans. W.M. Thackston (New York and Oxford, 1996).
Bada'uni, *Muntakhabu-t-Tawarikh*, trans. G.S.A. Ranking, W.H. Low and W. Haig, 3 vols (Delhi, reprint 1986; first published 1898–1924). Persian text ed. Maulawi Ahmad Ali, 3 vols (Calcutta, 1868–9).
Baldaeus, Ph., *Nauwkeurige Beschryvinge van Malabar en Choromandel* (Amsterdam, 1672).
Balfour, E.G., *The Cyclopaedia of India and of Eastern and Southern Asia* (London, 1885).
Barani, 'Tarikh-i Firoz Shahi', trans. H. Elliot, in H.M. Elliot and J. Dowson, *The History of India as Told by its Own Historians, III* (Delhi, reprint, 1990; first published 1867–77).
Barbosa, D., *The Book of Duarte Barbosa*, trans. and ed. M.L. Dames, 2 vols (London: 1918–21).
Barendse, R.J., 'Shipbuilding in seventeenth-century western India', *Itinerario*, 19 (1995).
Barendse, R.J., *The Arabian Seas 1640–1700* (Leiden, 1998).
Basham, A.L., *The Wonder that was India: A Survey of the Culture of the Indian Sub-continent Before the Coming of the Muslims* (London, 1954).
Bayly, C.A., *Empire and Information: Intelligence Gathering and Social Communication in India, 1780–1870* (Cambridge, 1996).
Bayly, S., *Saints, Goddesses and Kings: Muslims and Christians in South Indian Society 1700–1900* (Cambridge, 1989).
Begde, P.V., *Forts and Palaces of India* (New Delhi, 1982).
Bell, R., 'The travels of Richard Bell (and John Cambell) in the East Indies, Persia, and Palestine', *The Indian Antiquary*, 35 (1906).
Berinstain,V., *Mughal India: Splendour of the Peacock Throne* (London, 1998).
Bernier, F., *Travels in the Mogul Empire* AD *1656–1668*, trans. A. Constable (London, 1934).
Bhattacharya, S.N., *A History of Mughal North-east Frontier Policy* (Calcutta, 1929).
Bhimsen, *Sir Jadunath Sarkar Birth Centenary Commemoration Volume: English Translation of Tarikh-i-Dilkasha*, trans. J. Sarkar and V.G. Khobrekar (Bombay, 1972).

Black, J., *A Military Revolution? Military Change and European Society* (London, 1991).

Black, J., *War and the World: Military Power and the Fate of Continents 1450–2000* (New Haven and London, 1998).

Blake, S.P., 'The patrimonial-bureaucratic empire of the Mughals', *Journal of Asian Studies*, 39 (1979).

Blake, S.P., *Shahjahanabad: The Sovereign City in Mughal India, 1639–1739* (Cambridge, 1991).

Blochmann, H., 'Contributions to the geography and history of Bengal (Muhammadan period), Part I', *Journal of the Asiatic Society of Bengal*, 42 (1873).

Bodewitz, H.W., 'Hindu *ahimsa* and its roots', in J.E.M. Houben and K.R. van Kooij (eds), *Violence Denied: Violence, Non-violence and the Rationalization of Violence in South Asian Cultural History* (Leiden, 1999).

Bosworth, C.E., *The Ghaznavids: Their Empire in Afghanistan and Eastern Iran 994–1040* (Edinburgh, 1963).

Broecke, P. van den, *Pieter van den Broecke in Azië*, ed. W. Ph. Coolhaas, 3 vols (The Hague, 1962).

B[roeck], P[ieter] v[an] d[en], *Curieuse Beschrijving van de Gelegentheid, Zeden, Godsdienst en Ommegang van Verscheyden Oost-Indische Gewesten en Machtige Landschappen, etc. van Golconda en Pegu*, (Rotterdam, 1677).

Bulliet, R.W., *The Camel and the Wheel* (New York, 1990).

Burton, A., *The Bukharans. A Dynastic, Diplomatic and Commercial History 1550–1702* (Richmond, Surrey, 1997).

Burton-Page, J., 'A study of fortification in the Indian sub-continent from the thirteenth to the eighteenth century AD', *Bulletin of the School of Oriental and African Studies*, 23 (1960).

Careri, G.F.G., 'The voyages of Thévenot and Careri', in J.P. Guha (ed.), *India in the Seventeenth Century* (New Delhi, 1984).

Carré, Abbé, *The Travels of the Abbé Carré in India and the Near East 1672 to 1674*, trans. Lady Fawcett and C. Fawcett, 3 vols (Delhi, 1990).

Chamberlain, M., *Knowledge and Social Practice in Medieval Damascus, 1190–1350* (Cambridge, 1994).

Chattopadhyaya, B., *Representing the Other? Sanskrit Sources and the Muslims* (Delhi, 1998).

Chetan Singh, 'Forests, pastoralists and agrarian society in Mughal India', in D. Arnold and R. Guha (eds), *Nature, Culture, Imperialism: Essays on the Environmental History of South Asia* (Delhi, 1995).

Chevedden, P.E., Zvi Schiller, S.R. Gilbert and D.J. Kagay, 'The traction trebuchet: A triumph of four civilizations', *Viator*, 31 (2000).

Cipolla, C.M., *Guns, Sails, and Empires. Technological Innovation and the Early Phases of European Expansion, 1400–1700* (New York, 1965).

Cleveland Beach, M. and E. Koch, *King of the World: The Padshahnama, an Imperial Mughal Manuscript from the Royal Library, Windsor Castle* (London, 1997).

Coeurdoux, G.L. S.J., *L'Inde Philosophique entre Bossuet et Voltaire, I: Moeurs et Coutumes des Indiens (1777)*, ed. S. Murr (Paris, 1987).

Cooper, R.G.S. and N.K. Wagle, 'Maratha artillery: From Dabhoi to Assaye', *Journal of the Ordnance Society*, 7 (1995).

Cousens, H., *Bijapur and its Architectural Remains* (Bombay, 1916).

Creveld, M. van, *Supplying War: Logistics from Wallenstein to Patton* (Cambridge, 1977).

Dadvar, A., *Iranians in Mughal Politics and Society 1606–1658* (New Delhi, 1999).

Daehnhardt, R., *The Bewitched Gun: The Introduction of the Firearm in the Far East by the Portuguese* (Lisbon, 1994).

Dale, S.F., 'Steppe humanism: The autobiographical writings of Zahir al-Din Muhammad Babur, 1483–1530', *International Journal of Middle Eastern Studies*, 22 (1990).

Dale, S.F., *Indian Merchants and Eurasian Trade, 1600–1750* (Cambridge, 1994).

Dam, P. van, *Beschryvinge van de Oostindische Compagnie*, eds. F.W. Stapel and C.W.Th. van Boetzelaer, 4 vols, 7 parts (The Hague, 1927–54).

Damont, G., 'Notes on Shah Isma'il Ghazi', *Journal of the Asiatic Society of Bengal* (1874).

Dandekar, A., 'Landscapes in conflict: Flocks, hero-stones, and cult in early medieval Maharashtra', *Studies in History*, 7 (1991).

Datta, P.K., 'Use of "rockets" in warfare in Moghul India', *Bulletin of the Victoria Memorial Hall*, 1 (1967).

Datta, P.K., 'Cannon in India during the Mughal days', *Bulletin of the Victoria Memorial Hall*, 3–4 (1969–70).

Datta, P.K., 'Impact of fire-arms on fort architecture in India in the Mughal period', *Bulletin of the Victoria Memorial*, 8 (1974).

Deleury, G. (ed.), *Indes Florissantes: Anthologie des Voyageurs Français (1750–1820)* (Paris, 1991).

Deloche, J., *La Circulation en Inde Avant la Révolution des Transports*, 2 vols (Paris, 1980).

Deloche, J., 'Études sur les fortifications de l'Inde, I: Les fortifications de l'Inde ancienne', *Bulletin de l'École Française d'Extrême-Orient*, 79 (1992).

Deloche, J., 'Études sur les fortifications de l'Inde, II: Les monts fortifiés du Maisur méridional (1re partie)', *Bulletin de l'École Française d'Extrême-Orient*, 81 (1994).

Deloche, J., *Senji (Gingi): Ville Fortifiée du Pays Tamoul* (Paris and Pondichéry, 2000).

Delort, R., *Les Eléphants, Piliers du Monde* (Paris, 1990).

Deshpande, A., 'Limitations of military technology: Naval warfare on the west coast, 1650–1800', *Economic and Political Weekly* (25 April 1992).

Digby, S., 'Dreams and reminiscences of Dattu Sarvani, a sixteenth century Indo-Afghan soldier', *The Indian Economic and Social History Review*, 2–3 (1965).

Digby, S., *Warhorse and Elephant in the Delhi Sultanate* (Karachi, 1971).

Digby, S., 'The Naqshbandis in the Deccan in the late seventeenth and early eighteenth century AD: Baba Palangposh, Baba Musafir and their adherents', in M. Gaborieau *et al.* (eds), *Naqshbandis: Cheminements et Situation Actuelle d'un Ordre Mystique Musulman* (Istanbul and Paris, 1990).

Digby, S., 'Beyond the ocean: Perceptions of overseas in Indo-Persian sources of the Mughal period', *Studies in History*, 15, 2 (1999).

Dorn, B., *History of the Afghans*, 2 vols (London, 1965).

Duffy, C., *Siege Warfare: The Fortress in the Early Modern World 1494–1660* (London, 1979).

Durand-Dastès, F., *La Géographie de l'Inde*, (Paris, 1965).

Eaton, R.M., *Sufis of Bijapur 1300–1700: Social Roles of Sufis in Medieval India* (Princeton, 1978).

Eaton, R.M., *The Rise of Islam and the Bengal Frontier, 1204–1760* (Berkeley,1993).

Edgerton, F., *The Elephant-lore of the Hindus: The Elephant-sport (Matanga-lila) of Nilakantha* (Delhi, 1985).

Elgood, R. (ed.), *Islamic Arms and Armour* (London, 1979).

Elgood, R., *Firearms of the Islamic World in the Tareq Rajab Museum, Kuwait* (London and New York, 1995).

Elias, N., *The Court Society*, trans. E. Jepcott (Oxford, 1983).

Elias, N., *Über den Prozeß der Zivilisation: Soziogenetische und Psychogenetische Untersuchungen*, 2 vols (Frankfurt am Main, 1991).

Encyclopaedia Iranica (London and New York, 1985-).

Encyclopaedia of Islam (Leiden, 1954–).

Encyclopaedic Dictionary of Medieval India: Mirat-ul-Istilah, trans. T. Ahmad (Delhi, 1993).

Fernberger, G.C., *Reisetagebuch (1588–1593) Sinai, Babylon, Indien, Heiliges Land, Osteuropa*, trans. and ed. R. Burger and R. Wallisch (Frankfurt am Main, 1999).

Findly, E.B., *Nur Jahan: Empress of Mughal India* (New York and Oxford, 1993).

Firishta, *History of the Rise of the Mahomedan Power in India* [*Gulshan-i Ibrahimi*], trans. J. Briggs, 4 vols (Delhi, reprint, 1981; first published in 1829).

Fletcher, J., 'Turco-Mongolian monarchic tradition in the Ottoman Empire', *Harvard Ukrainian Studies*, 3–4 (1979–80).

Fletcher, J., 'The Mongols: Ecological and social perspectives', *Harvard Journal of Asiatic Studies*, 46 (1986).

Foltz, R.C., *Mughal India and Central Asia* (Karachi, 1998).

Fryer, J., *A New Account of East India and Persia Being Nine Years' Travels, 1672–1681*, ed. W. Crooke, 3 vols (London, 1909).

Fussman, G., 'Central and provincial administration in ancient India: The problem of the Mauryan Empire', *The Indian Historical Review*, 14 (1987–9).

Gahlin, S., *The Courts of India: Indian Miniatures from the Collection of the Fondation Custodia, Paris* (Zwolle, 1991).

Gale, W.K.V., 'Ferrous metals', in I. McNeil (ed.), *An Encyclopaedia of the History of Technology* (London, 1990).

Geleynssen de Jongh, W., *De Remonstrantie van W. Geleynssen de Jongh*, ed. W. Caland (The Hague, 1929).

Generale Missiven van Gouverneurs-Generaal en Raden aan Heren XVII der VOC, eds W. Ph. Coolhaas, J. van Goor and J.E. Schooneveld-Oosterling, 10 vols (The Hague, 1960–97).

Glete, J., *Warfare at Sea 1500–1650: Maritime Conflicts and the Transformation of Europe* (London, 2000).

Glover, M., *Wellington as Military Commander* (London, 2001).

Godinho, M., *Intrepid Itinerant: Manuel Godinho and his Journey from India to Portugal in 1663*, trans. V. Lobo; trans. and ed. J. Correia-Afonso (Bombay, 1990).

Goetz, H., 'Purandhar, its monuments and their history', *Annals of the Bhandarkar Oriental Institute*, 30 (1949).

Gold, D., 'The Dadu-Panth: A religious order in its Rajasthan context', in K. Schomer *et al.* (eds), *The Idea of Rajasthan: Explorations in Regional Identity, II: Institutions* (Delhi, 1994).

Golden, P.B., ' "I will give the people unto thee": The Chinggisid conquests and their aftermath in the Turkic world', *Journal of the Royal Asiatic Society*, 10 (2000).

Gole, S., *Indian Maps and Plans: From Earliest Times to the Advent of European Surveys* (Delhi, 1989).

Gommans, J.J.L., *The Rise of the Indo-Afghan Empire, c.1710–1780* (Leiden, 1995).

Gommans, J.J.L., 'Indian warfare and Afghan innovation during the eighteenth century', *Studies in History*, 11 (1995).

Gommans, J.J.L., 'Trade and Civilization around the Bay of Bengal, *c.* 1650–1800', *Itinerario*, 19 (1995).

Gommans, J.J.L. 'The silent frontier of South Asia, *c.* 1100–1800 AD', *Journal of World History*, 9 (1998).

Gommans, J.J.L., 'The Eurasian frontier after the first millennium AD: Reflections along the fringe of time and space', *The Medieval History Journal*, 1 (1998).

Gommans, J.J.L., 'Burma at the frontier of South, East and Southeast Asia: A geographic perspective', in J. Gommans and J. Leider (eds), *The Maritime Frontier of Burma: Exploring Political, Cultural and Commercial Interaction in the Indian Ocean World, 1200–1800* (Amsterdam and Leiden, 2002).

Gommans, J.J.L. and D.H.A. Kolff (eds), *Warfare and Weaponry in South Asia 1000–1800* (Delhi, 2000).

Gopal, L., 'Indian shipping in early mediaeval period', in V.L. Chandra (ed.), *India's Contribution to World Thought and Culture* (Madras, 1970).

Gordon, S., 'Forts and social control in the Marathi state', *Modern Asian Studies*, 13 (1979).

Gordon, S., *The New Cambridge History of India, II, 4: The Marathas 1600–1818* (Cambridge, 1993).

Gordon, S., 'Zones of military entrepreneurship in India, 1500–1700', in S. Gordon, *Marathas, Marauders, and State Formation in Eighteenth-century India* (Delhi, 1994).

Gordon, S., 'Robes of honour: A "transactional" kingly ceremony', *The Indian Economic and Social History Review*, 33 (1996).

Gordon, S., 'The limited adoption of European-style military forces by eighteenth century rulers in India', *The Indian Economic and Social History Review*, 35 (1998).

Gronke, M., 'The Persian court between palace and tent: From Timur to Abbas I', in L. Golombek and M. Subtelny (eds), *Timurid Art and Culture: Iran and Central Asia in the Fifteenth Century* (Leiden, 1992).

Guha, S., *Environment and Ethnicity in India, 1200–1991* (Cambridge, 1999).

Habib, I., 'The mansab system, 1595–1637', *Proceedings of the Indian History Congress* (1967).

Habib, I., 'Technology and barriers to social change in Mughal India', *Indian Historical Review*, 5 (1978–9).

Habib, I., 'The technology and economy of Mughal India', *Indian Economic and Social History Review*, 17 (1980).

Habib, I., 'Changes in technology in medieval India', *Studies in History*, 2 (1980).

Habib, I., 'Mansab salary scale under Jahangir and Shahjahan', *Islamic Culture*, 59 (1985).

Habib, I., *An Atlas of the Mughal Empire: Political and Economic Maps with Detailed Notes, Bibliography and Index* (Delhi, 1986).

Habib, I., *The Agrarian System of Mughal India* (Delhi, 1999, rev. ed.).

Hale, J.R., 'To fortify or not to fortify? Machiavelli's contribution to a Renaissance debate', in H.C. Davis *et al.* (eds), *Essays in Honour of John Humphreys Whitfield* (London, 1975).

Hall, B.S., 'The corning of gunpowder and the development of firearms in the Renaissance', in B.J. Buchanan (ed.), *Gunpowder: The History of an International Technology* (Bath, 1996).

Hall, B.S., *Weapons and Warfare in Renaissance Europe: Gunpowder, Technology, and Tactics* (Baltimore and London, 1997).

Hamid al-Din Khan Bahadur, *Anecdotes of Aurangzib* [*Ahkam-i Alamgiri*], trans. J. Sarkar (Calcutta, 4th edition, 1963).

Harding, D.F., *Smallarms of the East India Company 1600–1856, III: Ammunition and Performance* (London, 1999).

Harley, J.B. and D. Woodward (eds), *The History of Cartography II, 1: Cartography in the Traditional Islamic and South Asian Societies* (Chicago, 1992).

Hawkins, W., 'Capt. William Hawkins his relations of the occurrents which happened in the time of his residence in India', in Samuel Purchas (ed.), *Hakluytus Posthumus, or Purchas his Pilgrims*, III (Glasgow, 1905–7).

Hayes, H., *A Guide to Training and Horse Management in India* (Calcutta, 1878).

Heesterman, J.C., 'Littoral et intérieur de l'Inde', in L. Blussé, H.L. Wesseling and G.D. Winius, (eds), *History and Underdevelopment: Essays on Underdevelopment and European Expansion in Asia and Africa* (Leiden, 1980).

Heesterman, J.C., *The Inner Conflict of Tradition: Essays in Indian Ritual, Kingship and Society* (Chicago, 1985).

Heesterman, J.C., 'Two types of spatial boundaries', in E. Cohen *et al.* (eds), *Comparative Social Dynamics* (Boulder and London ,1985).

Heesterman, J.C., 'Warrior, peasant and brahmin', *Modern Asian Studies*, 29 (1995).

Heras, H., 'The city of Jinji at the end of the sixteenth century', *Indian Antiquary*, 54 (1925).

Hidayat Husain, M., 'The Mirza Namah (The Book of the Perfect Gentlemen) of Mirza Kamran with an English translation', *Journal of the Asiatic Society of Bengal*, 9 (1913).

Hill, D.R., 'Trebuchets', *Viator*, 4 (1973).

Hillenbrand, R., 'Turco-Iranian elements in the medieval architecture of Pakistan: The case of the tomb of Rukn-i Alam at Multan', *Muqarnas*, 9 (1991).

Hiltebeitel, A. (ed.), *Criminal Gods and Demon Devotees* (New York, 1989).

Hinz, W., *Islamische Währungen Umgerechnet in Gold* (Wiesbaden, 1991).

Hodgson, M.G.S., *The Venture of Islam, III: The Gunpowder Empires and Modern Times* (Chicago, 1974).

Hoover, J.W., 'Indian saltpetre and world gunpowder production: The East India trade and the military revolution 1600–1865' (Paper for the conference on the new military history of South Asia, Wolfson College, Cambridge, 15–17 July 1997).

Horn, P., *Das Heer- und Kriegswesen des Grossmoghuls* (Leiden, 1894).

Hosten, H., 'Jesuit letters from Bengal, Arakan and Burma (1599–1600)', *Bengal: Past and Present*, 30 (1925).

Huizinga, J., *Homo Ludens: Proeve eener Bepaling van het Spel-element der Cultuur* (Haarlem, 1938).

Husain, A., *Nobility under Akbar and Jahangir: A Study of Family Groups* (Delhi, 1999).

Hyland, A., *Equus: The Horse in the Roman World* (London, 1990).

Hyland, A., *The Warhorse 1250–1600* (Stroud, 1998).

Ibn Battuta, *The Travels of Ibn Battuta* AD *1325–1354*, trans. H.A.R. Gibb and C.F. Beckingham, 4 vols (Cambridge and London, 1958–94).

Ibn Khaldun, *The Muqaddimah: An Introduction to History*, trans. F. Rosenthal and N.J. Dawood (London, 1987).

Inalcik, H., 'Military and fiscal transformation in the Ottoman Empire, 1600–1700', *Archivum Ottomanicum*, 6 (1980).

Inayat Ali Zaidi, S., 'Ordinary Khachawaha troopers serving the Mughul Empire: Composition and structure of the contingents of the Kachawaha nobles', *Studies in History*, 2 (1980).

Inayat Khan, *The Shah Jahan Nama of Inayat Khan*, trans. W.E. Begley and Z.A. Desai (Delhi, 1990).

Iqtidar Alam Khan, 'Origin and development of gunpowder technology in India: AD 1250–1500', *Indian Historical Review*, 4 (1977).

Iqtidar Alam Khan, 'Early use of cannon and musket in India: AD 1442–1526', *Journal of Economic and Social History of the Orient*, 24 (1981).

Iqtidar Alam Khan, 'The nature of handguns in Mughal India: 16th and 17th centuries', *Proceedings of the Indian History Congress* (1992).

Iqtidar Alam Khan, 'Firearms in Central Asia and Iran during the fifteenth century and the origins and nature of firearms brought by Babur', *Proceedings of the Indian History Congress* (1995).

Iqtidar Alam Khan, 'The role of the Mongols in the introduction of gunpowder and firearms in South Asia', in B.J. Buchanan (ed.), *Gunpowder: The History of an International Technology* (Bath, 1996).

Iqtidar Alam Khan, 'Coming of gunpowder to Islamic world and North India: Spotlight on the role of the Mongols', *Journal of Asian History*, 30 (1996).

Iqtidar Alam Khan, 'The Indian response to firearms (1300–1750) (Presidential Address)', *Proceedings of the Indian History Congress* (1997).

Iqtidar Alam Khan, 'Nature of gunpowder artillery in India during the sixteenth century – a reappraisal of the impact of European gunpowder', *Journal of the Royal Asiatic Society*, 9 (1999).

Irvine, W., 'The Bangash Nawabs of Farrukhabad', *Journal of the Asiatic Society of Bengal* 47 (1878).

Irvine, W., *The Army of the Indian Moghuls* (London, 1903).

Irwin, Lieut., 'Memoir on the climate, soil, produce and husbandry of Afghanistan and the neighbouring countries', *Journal of the Asiatic Society of Bengal*, 8 (1839).

Isaac, B., *The Limits of Empire. The Roman Army in the East* (Oxford, 1993).

Jackson, P., *The Delhi Sultanate: A Political and Military History* (Cambridge, 1999).

Jacobs, E.M., *Koopman in Azië: De Handel van de Verenigde Oost-Indische Compagnie tijdens de 18de Eeuw* (Zutphen, 2000).

Jahangir, *The Tuzuk-i-Jahangiri or Memoirs of Jahangir*, trans. A. Rogers and H. Beveridge (Delhi, reprint, 1978; first published 1909–14).

Jarric, P. du, S.J., *Akbar and the Jesuits: An Account of the Jesuit Missions to the Court of Akbar by Father Pierre du Jarric, S.J.* trans. C.H. Payne (London, 1926).

Jong, M.A.G. de, 'De salpeterhandel van de EIC en VOC 1700–1760' (unpublished MA thesis, Leiden University, 1995).

Joshi, R., *The Afghan Nobility and the Mughals (1526–1707)* (Delhi, 1985).

Juleff, G., 'An ancient wind-powered iron smelting technology in Sri Lanka', *Letters to Nature*, 379 (1996).

Kaegi Jr, W.E., 'The contribution of archery to the Turkish conquest of Anatolia', *Speculum*, 39 (1964).

Kaempfer, E., *Am Hofe des Persischen Großkönigs 1684–1685* (Tübingen and Basel, 1977).

Kafadar, C., *Between Two Worlds: The Construction of the Ottoman State* (Berkeley, 1995).

Kai Ka'us Ibn Iskandar, *The Mirror for Princes, the Qabus Nama by Kai Ka'us Ibn Iskandar Prince of Gurgan*, trans. R. Levy (London, 1951).

Kautiliya, *The Kautiliya Arthasastra: A Critical Edition with a Glossary*, ed. and trans. R.P. Kangle, 3 vols (Delhi, 1988; first published 1960).

Keegan, J., *A History of Warfare* (London ,1993).

Kennedy, H., *Crusader Castles* (Cambridge, 1994).

Khafi Khan, *Khafi Khan's History of Alamgir* [*Muntakhab al-Lubab*], part. trans. S. Moinul Haq (Karachi, 1975). Persian text ed. Kabir al-Din Ahmad and T.W. Haig, 3 vols (Calcutta, 1869–1925).

Khan, A.R., 'Gradation of nobility under Babur', *Islamic Culture*, 1986.

Khan, I.G., 'Metallurgy in medieval India – the case of the iron cannon', *Proceedings of the Indian History Congress* (1984).

Khan, I.G., 'Metallurgy in medieval India 16th to 18th centuries', in Aniruddha Roy and S.K. Bagchi (eds), *Technology in Ancient and Medieval India* (Delhi, 1986).

Kolff, D.H.A., 'The end of an *ancien régime*: Colonial war in India, 1798–1818', in J.A. de Moor and H.L. Wesseling (eds), *Imperialism and War: Essays on Colonial Wars in Asia and Africa* (Leiden, 1989).

Kolff, D.H.A., Naukar, *Rajput and Sepoy. The Ethnohistory of the Military Labour Market in Hindustan, 1450–1850* (Cambridge, 1990).

Kölher-Rollefson, I., 'The one-humped camel in Asia: Origin, utilization and mechanism of dispersal', in D.R. Harris (ed.), *The Origins and Spread of Agriculture and Pastoralism in Eurasia* (London, 1996).

Kulkarni, G.T., *The Mughal–Maratha Relations: Twenty-five Fateful Years (1682–1707)* (Pune, 1983).
Lach, D.F. (and E.J. van Kley), *Asia in the Making of Europe*, 3 vols, 9 parts (Chicago and London, 1994–8).
Lafont, J.-M., 'Observations on the French military presence in the Indian states 1750–1849', in K.S. Mathew and S. Jelaseela Stephen (eds), *Indo-French Relations* (Delhi, 1999).
Lafont, J.-M., 'Benoît de Boigne in Hindustan: His impact on the Doab, 1784–1795', in J.-M. Lafont, *Indika: Essays in Indo-French Relations 1630–1976* (Delhi, 2000).
Lambton, A.K.S., *Landlord and Peasant in Persia* (London and New York, 1991).
Latham, J.D., 'Some technical aspects of archery in the Islamic miniature', *The Islamic Quarterly*, 12 (1968).
Latham, J.D., 'The archers of the Middle East: The Turco-Iranian background', *Iran*, 8 (1970).
Latham, J.D. and W.F. Paterson, *Saracen Archery: An English Version and Exposition of a Mameluke Work on Archery (ca. AD 1368)* (London, 1970).
Lattimore, O., *Studies in Frontier History: Collected Papers 1928–1958* (Paris and The Hague, 1962)
Law, B.M., *Historical Geography of Ancient India* (Paris, 1954).
Lenman, B., 'The weapons of war in the 18th century', *Journal of the Society for Army Historical Research*, 46 (1968).
Lenman, B., 'The transition to European military ascendancy in India, 1600–1800' in J.A. Lynn (ed.), *Tools of War: Instruments, Ideas and Institutions of Warfare, 1445–1871* (Champaign, 1989).
Lewis, B., *The Political Language of Islam* (Chicago, 1988).
Lindner, R.P., *Nomads and Ottomans in Medieval Anatolia* (Bloomington, 1983).
Linschoten, J.H. van, *Itinerario: Voyage ofte Schipvaert van J.H. van Linschoten naar Oost ofte Portugaels Indiën, 1579–1592*, eds. H. Kern and H. Terpstra, 3 vols (The Hague, 1955–7).
Littlewood, R.W., *Livestock of Southern India* (Madras, 1936).
Lockhart, L., 'The Persian army in the Safavi period', *Der Islam*, 34 (1959).
Longworth Dames, M., 'The Portuguese and Turks in the Indian Ocean in the sixteenth century', *Journal of the Royal Asiatic Society* (1921).
Lorenzen, D.N., 'Warrior ascetics in Indian history', *Journal of the American Oriental Society*, 98 (1978).
Lowery, M., 'The rise and fall of Bahadur Shah: A translation from the *Lendas da India* of Gaspar Correia', *Portuguese Studies*, 6 (1990).
Lynn, J., 'The history of logistics and supplying war' in J.A. Lynn (ed.), *Feeding Mars: Logistics in Western Warfare from the Middle Ages to the Present* (Boulder, San Francisco and Oxford, 1993).
Madhava Rao, P.S., *Eighteenth Century Deccan* (Bombay, 1963).
Malcolm, J., *A Memoir of Central India Including Malwa and Adjoining Provinces*, 2 vols (London, 1824).
Mandelslo, J.A. von, *Schreiben von seiner Ostindischen Reise* (Schleswig, 1645).
Manrique, S., *Travels of Fray Sebastian Manrique, 1629–1643*, trans. C.E. Luard and H. Hosten (Oxford, 1926–7).
Manucci, N., *Storia do Mogor*, trans. W. Irvine, 4 vols (Delhi, 1981).
Martin, F., *Mémoires de François Martin, Fondateur de Pondichéry (1665–1694)*, 3 vols (Paris, 1934); trans. L. Varadarajan, *India in the Seventeenth Century (Social, Economic and Political): Memoirs of François Martin (1670–1694)*, 3 vols (Delhi, 1985).
Mason, P., *Matter of Honour: An Account of the Indian Army, its Officers and Men* (London, 1974).

Masson Smith Jr, J., 'Mongol society and military in the Middle East: Antecedents and adaptations', in Y. Lev (ed.), *War and Society in the Eastern Mediterranean, 7th–15th Centuries* (Leiden, 1997).

Masson Smith Jr, J., 'Nomads on ponies vs. slaves on horses', *Journal of the American Oriental Society*, 118 (1998).

Mate, M.S., 'Islamic architecture of the Deccan', *Bulletin of the Deccan College Research Institute*, 22 (1961–2).

Mate, M.S. and T.V. Pathy (eds), *Daulatabad (A Report on the Archaeological Investigations)* (Pune and Aurangabad, 1992).

Mathew, K.S., *Ship-building and Navigation in the Indian Ocean Region* AD *1400–1800* (Delhi, 1997).

Matthee, R.P., 'Politics and trade in late Safavid Iran: Commercial crisis and government reaction under Shah Solayman (1666–1694)' (unpublished Ph.D. thesis, University of California, Los Angeles, 1991).

Matthee, R.P., 'Unwalled cities and restless nomads: Firearms and artillery in Safavid Iran', in C. Melville (ed.), *Safavid Persia: The History and Politics of an Islamic Society* (London and New York, 1996).

McChesney, R.D., *Waqf in Central Asia. Four Hundred Years in the History of a Muslim Shrine, 1480–1889* (Princeton, 1991).

McEwan, E., 'Persian archery texts: Chapter eleven of Fakhr-i Mudabbir's *Adab al-harb* (Early Thirteenth Century)', *The Islamic Quarterly*, 18 (1974).

McLeod, W.H., *Who is a Sikh? The Problem of Sikh Identity* (Oxford, 1989).

McNeil, W.H., *The Pursuit of Power: Technology, Armed Forces and Society since* AD *1000* (Chicago, 1982).

McNeil, W.H., Interview, *The Historian*, 53 (1990).

Melville, C., 'The itineraries of Sultan Öljeitü, 1304–16', *Iran*, 28 (1990).

Melville, C., 'From Qars to Qandahar: The itineraries of Shah 'Abbas I (995–1038/1587–1629)', in J. Calmard (ed.), *Études Safavides* (Paris and Teheran, 1993).

Michell, G., 'Courtly architecture at Gingee under the Nayakas', *South Asian Studies*, 7 (1991).

Michell, G., *The New Cambridge History of India, I, 6: Architecture and Art of Southern India* (Cambridge, 1995).

Michell, G. and R. Eaton (eds), *Firuzabad: Palace City of the Deccan* (Oxford, 1992).

Michell, G. and M. Zebrowski, *The New Cambridge History of India, I, 7: Architecture and Art of the Deccan Sultanate* (Cambridge, 1999).

Mihir Shah, Debashis Benerji, P.S. Vijayshankar, Pramathesh Ambasta (eds), *India's Drylands: Tribal Societies and Development Through Environment Regeneration* (Delhi, 1998).

Minhaj al-Din, *Tabakat-i Nasiri: A General History of the Muhammadan Dynasties of Asia, Including Hindustan*, trans. H.G. Raverty, 2 vols (New Delhi reprint, 1970; first published Calcutta, 1881).

Mirza Muhammad Haidar Dughlat, *The Tarikh-i-Rashidi*, trans. E. Denison Ross (Delhi, reprint, 1986; first published 1895).

Mirza Nathan, *Baharistan-i-Ghaybi. A History of the Mughal Wars in Assam, Cooch Behar, Bengal, Bihar and Orissa During the Reigns of Jahangir and Shah Jahan by Mirza Nathan*, trans. M.I. Borah, 2 vols (Gauhati, 1936).

Misra, B.D., *Forts and Fortresses of Gwalior and its Hinterland* (Delhi, 1993).

Modave, *Voyage en Inde du Comte de Modave 1773–1776 (Nouveaux Mémoires sur l'État Actuel du Bengale et de l'Indoustan)*, ed. J. Deloche (Paris, 1971).

Monserrate, *The Commentary of Father Monserrate, S.J. on his Journey to the Court of Akbar*, trans. J.S. Hoyland, ed. S.N. Banerjee (Oxford, 1922).

Mookerji, R.D., *Indian Shipping: A History of the Sea-borne Trade and Maritime Activity of the Indians from the Earliest Times* (London, 1912).

Moosvi, S., 'Evolution of the mansab-system under Akbar', *Journal of the Royal Asiatic Society*, 2 (1981).

Moosvi, S., *The Economy of the Mughal Empire c. 1595: A Statistical Study* (Delhi, 1987).

Moreland, W.H., 'Ranks (mansab) in the Mughal service', *Journal of the Royal Asiatic Society* (1936).

Moreland, W.H., 'The ships of the Arabian Sea about AD 1500', *Journal of the Royal Asiatic Society* (1939).

Moreland, W.H., *From Akbar to Aurangzeb: A Study in Indian Economic History* (Delhi, 1994).

Muhammad Arif Qandhari, *Tarikh-i-Akbari*, trans. Tasneem Ahmad (Delhi, 1993).

Muhammad Baqir Najm-i Sani, *Advice on the Art of Governance: Mau'izah-i Jahangiri of Muhammad Baqir Najm-i Sani: An Indo-Islamic Mirror for Princes*, ed. and trans. S.S. Alvi (Albany, NY, 1989).

Muir, R., *Tactics and the Experience of Battle in the Age of Napoleon* (New Haven and London, 1998).

Munshi Udairaj alias Taliyar Khan, *The Military Despatches of a Seventeenth Century Indian General [Haft Anjuman]*, trans. J.N. Sarkar (Calcutta, 1969).

Murphy, R., *Ottoman Warfare 1500–1700* (London, 1999).

Narayana Rao, V., D. Shulman and S. Subrahmanyam, *Symbols of Substance: Court and State in Nayaka Period Tamilnadu* (Delhi, 1992).

Naseer-ud-Din Khan, M. (ed.), *Selected Documents of Shah Shah Jahan's Reign* (Hyderabad, 1950).

Nawab Samsam al-Daula Shah Nawaz Khan and his son Abdul Hayy, *The Maathir-ul-umara*, trans. H. Beveridge and Baini Prashad, 2 vols in 4 parts (Delhi, reprint, 1979; first published 1911–64). Persian text eds Maulawi Abdul Rahim and Mirza Ashraf Ali, 3 vols (Calcutta, 1888–91).

Needham, J. and R.D.S. Yates, *Science and Civilisation in China, V: Chemistry and Chemical Technology, Part 4: Military Technology: Missiles and Sieges* (Cambridge, 1994).

Needham, J. *Science and Civilisation in China, V: Chemistry and Chemical Technology, Part 7: Military Technology: The Gunpowder Epic* (Cambridge, 1986).

Nicolle, D., *Medieval Warfare Source Book, II: Christian Europe and its Neighbours* (London, 1996).

Nilakanta Sastri, K.A., *A History of South India from Prehistoric Times to the Fall of Vijayanagara*, (Delhi, 1975).

Nurul Hasan, S., 'Zamindars under the Mughals' in R.E. Frykenberg (ed.), *Land Control and Social Structure in Indian History* (Madison, Wisconsin, 1969).

O'Hanlon, R., 'Manliness and imperial service in Mughal north India', *Journal of the Economic and Social History of the Orient*, 42 (1999).

Oman, C., *The Art of War in the Sixteenth Century* (London, 1937).

Orme, R., *The History of the Military Transactions of the British Nation in Indostan*, 2 vols (London, 1763).

Orme, R., *Historical Fragments of the Mogul Empire* (London, 1805).

Ovington, J., 'A voyage to Suratt in the year 1689', in J.P. Guha (ed.), *India in the Seventeenth Century* (New Delhi, 1984).

Padfield, P., *Tide of Empires: Decisive Naval Campaigns in the Rise of the West, I: 1481–1654* (London, 1979).

Parker, G., *The Military Revolution: Military Innovation and the Rise of the West 1500–1800* (Cambridge, 1988).

Patterson, W.F., 'The archers of Islam', *Journal of the Economic and Social History of the Orient*, 9 (1966).

Patterson, W.F., 'Archery in Moghul India', *The Islamic Quarterly*, 16 (1973).

Pearson, M.N. (ed.), *Legitimacy and Symbols: The South Asian Writings of F.W. Buckler* (Ann Arbor, 1985).

Peers, D.M., *Between Mars and Mammon: Colonial Armies and the Garrison State in India 1819–35* (London, 1995).

Pelsaert, F., *De Geschriften van Francisco Pelsaert over Mughal Indië, 1627: Kroniek en Remonstrantie*, eds D.H.A. Kolff and H.W. van Santen (The Hague, 1979).

Pemble, J., 'Resources and techniques in the second Maratha war', *The Historical Journal*, 19 (1976).

Petech, L., 'The Tibetan–Ladakhi–Moghul war of 1681–83', *Indian Historical Quarterly*, 23 (1947).

Peyer, H.C., 'Das Reisekönigtum des Mittelalters', *Vierteljahrschrift für Sozial- und Wirtschaftgeschichte*, 51 (1964).

Pinch, W.R., *Peasants and Monks in British India* (Berkeley, 1996).

Pinch, W.R., 'Who was Himmat Bahadur? Gosains, Rajputs and the British in Bundelkhand, ca. 1800', *The Indian Economic and Social History Review*, 35 (1998).

Pires, T., *The Suma Oriental of Tomé Pires, an Account of the East . . . written in 1512–1515*, ed. and trans. A. Cortesão, 2 vols (London, 1944).

Pollock, S., 'Ramayana and political imagination in India', *The Journal of Asian Studies*, 53 (1993).

Prakash, O., *The Dutch East India Company and the Economy of Bengal, 1630–1720* (Princeton, 1985).

Qaisar, A.J., 'Shipbuilding in the Mughal Empire during the seventeenth century', *The Indian Economic and Social History Review*, 5 (1968).

Qaisar, A.J., *Indian Response to European Technology and Culture (AD 1497–1707)* (Delhi, 1982).

Ramachandrapant Amatya, 'The Ajnapatra or Royal Edict', trans. S.V. Puntambekar, *Journal of Indian History*, 1–2 (1928).

Rao Bahadur and C.S. Srinivasachari, *A History of Gingee and its Rulers* (Annamalainagar, 1943).

Richards, J.F., 'The imperial crisis in the Deccan', *Journal of Asian Studies*, 35 (1976).

Richards, J.F., 'The formulation of imperial authority under Akbar and Jahangir', in J.F. Richards (ed.), *Kingship and Authority in South Asia* (Madison, Wisconsin, 1978).

Richards, J.F., 'Norms of comportment among imperial Mughal officers', in B.D. Metcalf (ed.), *Moral Conduct and Authority: The Place of Adab in South Asian Islam* (Berkeley, 1984).

Richards, J.F., 'Official revenues and money flows in a Mughal province', in J.F. Richards, *The Imperial Monetary System of Mughal India* (Delhi, 1987).

Richards, J.F., *The New Cambridge History of India, I, 5: The Mughal Empire* (Cambridge, 1993).

Roberts, M., *The Military Revolution 1560–1660* (Belfast, 1956).

Roe, T., *The Embassy of Sir Thomas Roe to India*, ed. W. Forster (London, 1926).

Röhrborn, K., 'Regierung und Verwaltung Irans unter den Safawiden', in B. Spuler (ed.) *Handbuch der Orientalistik: Erste Abteilung: Der Nahe und der Mittlere Osten, Bd 6, Abschnitt 5: Regierung und Verwaltung des Vorderen Orients in Islamischer Zeit, Teil 1* (Leiden, 1979).

Roy, A.C., *A History of Mughal Navy and Naval Warfare* (Calcutta, 1972).

Ruka'at-i-Alamgiri or Letters of Aurangzebe, trans. J.H. Bilimoria (London and Bombay, 1908).

Russell Robinson, H., *Oriental Armour* (London, 1967).

Russell, R.V., *The Tribes and Castes of the Central Provinces of India*, II (London, 1916).

Sa'adat Yar Khan Rangin, *Faras-nama*, trans. D.C. Phillott (London, 1911).
Saqi Musta'id Khan, *Maasir-i-Alamgiri: A History of the Emperor Aurangzib-Alamgir*, trans. J. Sarkar (Delhi, reprint, 1986; first published 1947).
Sarkar, J., *Studies in Aurangzeb's Reign* (Calcutta, 1933).
Sarkar, J., *History of Aurangzeb*, 5 vols (Calcutta, 1925–52).
Sarkar, J., *Mughal Administration*, (Calcutta, 1963).
Sarkar, J., *Military History of India* (Delhi, 1970)
Sarkar, J. (ed.), *The History of Bengal: Muslim Period 1200–1757* (Patna, 1973).
Sarkar, J.N., 'Saltpetre industry in India (in the 17th century)', *The Indian Historical Quarterly*, 14 (1938).
Sarkar, J.N., 'Transport of saltpetre in India in the seventeenth century', *Journal of the Bihar and Orissa Research Society*, 25 (1939).
Sarkar, J.N., *The Life of Mir Jumla* (Calcutta, 1951).
Sarkar, J.N., *The Art of War in Medieval India* (Delhi, 1984).
Satish Chandra, *Parties and Politics at the Mughal Court, 1707–1740* (Aligarh, 1959).
Scharfe, H., *The State in Indian Tradition* (Leiden, 1989).
Schimmel, A., *Mystical Dimensions of Islam* (Chapel Hill, 1975).
Schneider,U., *Die Großen Felsen-edikte Asokas: Kritische Ausgabe, Übersetzung und Analyse der Texte* (Wiesbaden, 1978).
Schouten, W., *Oost-Indische Voyagie,* 3 vols (Amsterdam, 1676).
Schwartzberg, J.E., 'South Asian cartography', in J.B. Harley and D. Woodward (eds), *History of Cartography, II, 1: Cartography in the Traditional Islamic and South Asian Societies* (Chicago and London, 1992).
Sewell, R., *A Forgotten Empire (Vijayanagara): A Contribution to the History of India* (New Delhi, 1995).
Shaikh Rizqulla Mushtaqi, *Waqi'at-e-Mushtaqui*, trans. I.H. Siddiqui (Delhi, 1993).
Shokoohy, M. and N. Shokoohy, *Hisar-i Firuza: Sultanate and Early Mughal Architecture in the District of Hisar, India* (London, 1988).
Shokoohy, M. and N. Shokoohy, 'Tughluqabad, the earliest surviving town of the Delhi sultanate', *Bulletin of the School of Oriental and African Studies*, 57 (1994).
Sidi Ali Reis, *The Travels and Adventures of the Turkish Admiral Sidi Ali Reis [Mir'at al-Mamalik]*, trans. A. Vambery (London, 1899).
Sikandar b. Muhammad Manjhu, *The Local Muhammadan Dynasties: Gujarat* [*Mir'at-i Sikandiri*], part. trans. E.C. Bayley and Nagendra Singh (Delhi, reprint, 1970; first published 1886). Persian text eds S.C. Misra and M.L. Rahman (Baroda, 1961).
Sinor, D., 'Horse and pasture in Inner Asian history', *Oriens Extremus*, 19 (1972).
Sontheimer, G.D., *Biroba, Mhaskoba und Khandoba: Ursprung, Geschichte und Umwelt von Pastoralen Gottheiten in Maharashtra* (Wiesbaden, 1976).
Soucek, S., 'Certain types of ships in Ottoman-Turkish terminology', *Turcica*, 7 (1975).
Spate, O.H.K. and A.T.A. Learmonth, *India and Pakistan: A General and Regional Geography* (New Delhi, 1984).
Stein, B., 'Mahanavami: Medieval and modern kingly ritual in south India', in L. Bardwell (ed.), *Essays on Gupta Culture* (Delhi, 1983).
Stein, B., 'State formation and economy reconsidered', *Modern Asian Studies*, 19 (1985).
Stein, B., *Thomas Munro: The Origins of the Colonial State and his Vision of Empire*, (Delhi, 1989).
Storey, C.A., *Persian Literature: A Bio-bibliographic Survey*, 3 vols (in progress) (London, 1927–84). (Leiden, 1977).
Streusand, D.E., *The Formation of the Mughal Empire* (Delhi, 1989).

Subrahmanyam, S., 'The *Kagemusha* effect. The Portuguese, firearms and the state in early modern south India', *Moyen Orient et Océan Indien*, 4 (1987).

Subrahmanyam, S., 'Warfare and state finance in Wodeyar Mysore, 1724–25: A missionary perspective', *Indian Economic and Social History Review*, 26 (1989).

Subrahmanyam, S., *The Political Economy of Commerce: Southern India 1500–1650*, (Cambridge, 1990).

Subrahmanyam, S., 'Iranians abroad: Intra-Asian elite migration and early modern state formation', *Journal of Asian Studies*, 51 (1992).

Subrahmanyam, S., 'Reflections on state-making and history-making in south India', *Journal of the Economic and Social History of the Orient*, 41 (1998).

Subrahmanyam, S., ' "Persianization" and "Mercantilism": two themes in Bay of Bengal history, 1400–1700', in O. Prakash and D. Lombard, *Commerce and Culture in the Bay of Bengal, 1500–1800* (Delhi, 1999).

Subrahmanyam, S., 'Friday's child: Or how Tej Singh became Tecinkurajan', *The Indian Economic and Social History Review*, 36, 1 (1999).

Subtelny, M.E., 'Babur's rival relations: A study of kinship and conflict in 15th–16th century Central Asia', *Der Islam*, 17 (1980).

Tambs-Lyche, H., *Power, Profit and Poetry: Traditional Society in Kathiawar, Western India* (Delhi, 1997).

Tavernier, J.-B., *Travels in India*, trans. V. Ball, ed. W. Crooke, 2 vols (Delhi, 1977).

Terry, E., 'A relation of a voyage to the eastern India', in Samual Purchas (ed.), *Hakluytus Posthumus, or Purchas his Pilgrims*, IX (Glasgow, 1905–7).

Thévenot, J. de, 'The voyages of Thévenot and Careri', in J.P. Guha (ed.), *India in the Seventeenth Century* (New Delhi, 1984).

Toy, S., *The Strongholds of India* (London, 1957).

Twist, J. van, 'Generale beschrijvinge van Indiën', in Isaac Commelin (ed.), *Begin en de Voortgangh van de Vereenighde Nederlandsche Geoctroyeerde Oost-Indische Compagnie*, Vol. 2 (Amsterdam, 1646).

Tylecote, R.F., *A History of Metallurgy* (London, 1992).

Valle, P. della, *The Travels of Pietro della Valle in India*, trans. G. Havers, ed. E. Grey, 2 vols (New Delhi, 1991).

Varadarajan, L., *India in the Seventeenth Century (Social, Economic and Political): Memoirs of François Martin (1670–1694)*, 3 vols (Delhi, 1985).

Varthema, L. de, *The Travels of Ludovico di Varthema*, trans. J. Winter Jones and ed. G.P. Badger (London, 1928).

Verhoeven, J.D., A.H. Pendray and E.D. Gibson, 'Wootz Damascus steel blades', *Materials Characterization*, 37 (1996).

Watt, G., *Dictionary of the Economic Products of India* (London, 1908).

Weber, M., *Economy and Society* (2 vols) (Berkeley, 1978).

Welch, A., 'Architectural patronage and the past: The Tughluq sultans of India', *Muqarnas*, 10 (1993).

Welten, M., 'De hofreis van Ketelaar naar het Perzische hof' (unpublished MA thesis, Leiden University, 1988).

Wendel, F.X., *Les Mémoires de Wendel sur les Jats, les Pathan et les Sikh*, ed. J. Deloche (Paris, 1979).

Westphal-Hellbusch, S. and H. Westphal, *Zur Geschichte und Kultur der Jat* (Berlin, 1968).

Westphal-Hellbusch, S. and H. Westphal, *Hinduistischer Viehzüchter im Nordwestlichen Indien, II: Die Bharwad und die Charan* (Berlin, 1976).

Wetering, H.C.M. van de, 'De VOC en de kapers van Angria. Een expeditie naar de westkust van India in 1739', *Tijdschrift voor Zeegeschiedenis*, 10 (1991).

Whiting Fox, E., *History in Geographic Perspective: The Other France* (New York, 1971).
Whittaker, C.R., *Frontiers of the Roman Empire: A Social and Economic Study* (Baltimore and London, 1997).
Whyte, R.O., *Land, Livestock and Human Nutrition in India* (London, 1968).
Williams, A., *The Metallurgy of Muslim Armour (Seminar on Early Islamic Science, Monograph No. 3)* (Manchester, 1978).
Williams, A., 'Ottoman military technology: The metallurgy of Turkish armour', in Y. Lev (ed.) *War and Society in the Eastern Mediterranean, 7th–15th Centuries* (Leiden, 1997).
Wink, A., *Land and Sovereignty in India: Agrarian Society and Politics under Eighteenth-century Maratha Svarajya* (Cambridge, 1986).
Wink, A., *Al-Hind: The Making of the Indo-Islamic World, II: The Slave Kings and the Islamic Conquest, 11th–13th Centuries* (Leiden, 1997).
Winter, F.H., *The Golden Age of Rocketry* (Washington and London, 1990).
Yadava, B.N.S., *Society and Culture in Northern India in the Twelfth Century* (Allahabad, 1973).
Yazdani, G., *Bidar, its History and Monuments* (Oxford, 1974).
Ziegler, N., 'Some notes on Rajput loyalties during the Mughal period', in J.F. Richards (ed.), *Kingship and Authority in South Asia* (Madison, Wisconsin, 1978).
Ziegler, N., 'Evolution of the Rathor state of Marvar: Horses, structural change and warfare', in K. Schomer *et al.* (eds), *The Idea of Rajasthan: Explorations in Regional Identity, II: Institutions* (Delhi, 1994).
Zimmermann, F., *The Jungle and the Aroma of Meats: An Ecological Theme in Hindu Medicine* (Berkeley and Los Angeles, 1982).
Zygulsky, Z., 'Oriental and Levantine firearms', in C. Blaire (ed.), *Pollard's History of Firearms* (New York, 1973).

Index